# THE GLOBAL AGENDA

## ISSUES AND PERSPECTIVES

S0-AAC-724

# THE GLOBAL AGENDA

## ISSUES AND PERSPECTIVES

THIRD EDITION

## Charles W. Kegley, Jr.
University of South Carolina

## Eugene R. Wittkopf
Louisiana State University

**McGRAW-HILL, INC.**

New York   St. Louis   San Francisco   Auckland   Bogotá   Caracas
Lisbon   London   Madrid   Mexico   Milan   Montreal   New Delhi
Paris   San Juan   Singapore   Sydney   Tokyo   Toronto

This book was set in Times Roman by The Clarinda Company.
The editors were Bertrand W. Lummus and Fred H. Burns;
the production supervisor was Louise Karam.
The cover was designed by Albert M. Cetta.
R. R. Donnelley & Sons Company was printer and binder.

**THE GLOBAL AGENDA**

Issues and Perspectives

1 2 3 4 5 6 7 8 9 0 DOC DOC 9 0 9 8 7 6 5 4 3 2 1

ISBN 0-07-033707-1

# ABOUT THE AUTHORS

CHARLES W. KEGLEY, JR., is Pearce Professor of International Relations at the University of South Carolina. He has also held appointments at Georgetown University, the University of Texas, and Rutgers University. He has recently edited *The Long Postwar Peace: Contending Explanations and Projections* and *After the Cold War: Questioning the Morality of Nuclear Deterrence,* and has published articles in *Ethics and International Affairs, International Interactions, International Organization, International Studies Quarterly,* the *Journal of Peace Research,* the *Journal of Politics,* and elsewhere.

EUGENE R. WITTKOPF is professor of political science at Louisiana State University. He has also held appointments at the University of Florida and the University of North Carolina at Chapel Hill. He is author of *Faces of Internationalism: Public Opinion and American Foreign Policy* (1990) and has contributed articles on international politics and foreign policy to a number of books and journals, including the *American Political Science Review, International Organization, International Studies Quarterly, Journal of Politics, Polity, Social Science Quarterly,* and the *Washington Quarterly,* among others.

Together Professors Kegley and Wittkopf have published *Perspectives on American Foreign Policy: Selected Readings* (1983), *The Domestic Sources of American Foreign Policy: Insights and Evidence* (1988), *The Nuclear Reader: Strategy, Weapons, War* (2d ed., 1989), *World Politics: Trend and Transformation* (3d. ed., 1989), *American Foreign Policy: Pattern and Process* (4th ed., 1991), and *The Future of American Foreign Policy* (1992).

v

For Lisa and Suzanne
CWK

For Barbara, Debra, and Jonathan
ERW

# CONTENTS

# PREFACE

*There is no scientific antidote [to the atomic bomb], only education. You've got to change the way people think. I am not interested in disarmament talks between nations. . . . What I want to do is to disarm the mind. After that, everything else will automatically follow. The ultimate weapon for such mental disarmament is international education.*

—Albert Einstein

Change and constancy seem to describe most accurately the nature of contemporary international politics. Dramatic new developments during recent years have combined with less rapidly unfolding but no less important trends to produce new issues, cleavages, and a new international climate. Simultaneously, traditional controversies continue to color relations among nations. Hence the study of contemporary international politics must give attention to the factors that produce change and also to those that promote changelessness in relations among political actors on the global stage.

Because change is endemic to international politics, it is understandable that the new issues that now crowd the global agenda challenge the analytical perspectives long used by scholars and policymakers to understand world politics, as recorded in the first and second editions of this book. Thus our purpose in preparing a third edition is to bring the coverage up to date by presenting current, informed commentary on the dominant issues in contemporary international politics and the analytical perspectives that have been devised to understand them. But the overarching goals that motivated the first two editions remain: to make available to students what we, as editors, believe to be the best introductions to the contemporary issues that animate contemporary world politics and, also, to introduce the major analytical perspectives and organizing concepts that have been fashioned to make these issues comprehensible.

*The Global Agenda: Issues and Perspectives* categorizes readings into four "baskets" that build on the distinction between "high politics" (peace and security issues) and "low politics" (nonsecurity welfare issues). The criteria that guided the selection of particular articles within each part and the rationale that underlies the organization of the book are made explicit in our introductions to each part, which are designed to help students connect individual readings to common themes.

The organization of the book is intended to capture the diversity of global issues and patterns of interaction that presently dominate the attention of world political actors and precipitate policy responses. Its thematic organization allows treatment of the breadth of global issues and of the analytical perspectives that give them meaning, ranging from classic theoretical formulations to the newer analytic focuses and concepts that have arisen to account for recent developments in world affairs. In preparing the volume in this manner, we have proceeded from the assumption that there is need for educational materials treating description and theoretical exposition in a balanced manner and exposing a variety of normative interpretations without advocating any particular one. It seems to us that, to a greater or lesser degree, coverage of these important elements comprising both the theory and evidence of international politics as a social science is missing in most standard texts (by design and necessity) and that a supplementary anthology is the logical place for them.

Several people have contributed to the development of this book as it has gone through various iterations. We chose not to list them individually at the risk of slighting someone, but our gratitude to all remains, especially to Bert Lummus and Fred Burns at McGraw-Hill for their continuing enthusiasm for this project.

*Charles W. Kegley, Jr.*

*Eugene R. Wittkopf*

# THE GLOBAL AGENDA

## ISSUES AND PERSPECTIVES

PART **ONE**

# ARMS AND INFLUENCE

The contemporary international political system began to acquire its present shape and definition more than three centuries ago with the emergence of a state system in Europe following the highly destructive Thirty Years War. As the Westphalian treaties brought that war to an end and political, economic, and social intercourse grew among the states of Europe, new legal norms were embraced in an effort to regulate interstate behavior. The doctrine of state sovereignty, according to which no legal authority is higher than the state, emerged supreme. Thus the emergent international system was based on the right of states to control without interference from others their internal affairs, and to manage their relations with other states, with which they collaborated or competed as they saw fit. Foremost in this system was the belief, reinforced by law, that the state possessed the right, indeed, the obligation, to take whatever measures it deemed necessary to ensure its preservation.

Although the international system and patterns of interaction among its political actors have changed profoundly since the 1648 Peace of Westphalia gave birth to the state system, contemporary world politics remains significantly colored by its legacy. World politics continues to be conducted in an atmosphere of anarchy. As in the past, the system remains fragmented and decentralized, with no higher authority above nation-states, which, as the principal actors in world politics, remain free to behave toward one another largely as they choose.

This is not meant to imply either that states exercise their freedoms with abandon or that they are unconstrained in the choices they make. The political,

1

legal, moral, and circumstantial constraints on states' freedom of choice are formidable. Moreover, states' national interests are served best when they act in a manner that does not threaten the stability of their relations with others or of the global system that protects their autonomy. Hence, the international system, as the British political scientist Hedley Bull reminds us, may be an anarchical society, but it is one of "ordered anarchy" nonetheless.

The world has grown increasingly complex and interdependent as contact, communication, and exchange have increased among the actors in the state system and as the number of nation-states and other nonstate international actors has grown since the conclusion of World War II in 1945. Expanded interaction among countless international and transnational actors reflects the enlarged range of possible mutually beneficial exchanges between and among states. But just as opportunities for cooperation have expanded, so have the possible sources of disagreement. That we live in an age of conflict is a cliché that contains elements of truth, for differences of opinion and efforts to resolve disputes to one's advantage, often at the expense of others, are part of any long-term relationship. Thus, as the world has grown smaller, the mutual dependence of transnational political actors on one another has grown and the number of potential rivalries, antagonisms, and disagreements has increased correspondingly. Friction and tension therefore appear to be endemic to the relations of nations; the image of world politics conveyed in newspaper headlines does not suggest that a shrinking world has become a more peaceful one. Instead, even as the Cold War wanes, competition and conflict persist, as demonstrated by Iraq's brutal invasion of Kuwait in August 1990 and the international community's subsequent military response to it.

Given the persistent characteristics of contemporary world politics, the number of *issues* that at any one time are in dispute among nation-states and other global actors appears to have increased greatly. The multitude of contentions renders the *global agenda* —the list of issues that force their way into consideration and command that they be addressed, peacefully or not—more crowded and complex. Because the responses that are made to the issues on the global agenda shape our lives both today and into the future, it is appropriate that we direct attention to those matters that animate world politics and stimulate the attention and activities of national decision makers. At the same time, as different state and nonstate actors view global political issues from often widely varying vantage points, it is appropriate that we remain sensitive to the various perceptual lenses through which the items on the global agenda are viewed. Accordingly, *The Global Agenda: Issues and Perspectives* seeks to focus on the range of issues that dominates world politics and also on the multitude of analytical and interpretive perspectives from which those issues are viewed.

The issues and perspectives discussed in *The Global Agenda* are grouped into four broad, somewhat overlapping, but analytically distinct issue areas: (1) arms and influence, (2) discord and collaboration, (3) politics and markets, and

(4) ecology and politics. Broadly speaking, the first two issue areas deal with states' security interests, often referred to as matters of *high politics.* The latter two, again broadly speaking, deal with the nonsecurity issues, often referred to as matters of *low politics,* that increasingly have come to occupy, if not dominate, the attention of actors on the world stage. In all four issue areas, we seek to convey not only the range of issues now facing those responsible for political choices but also the many vantage points from which they are typically viewed.

We begin in Part One with consideration of a series of issues appropriately subsumed under the collective rubric *Arms and Influence.* As the term "high politics" suggests, the issues and perspectives treated here focus on the prospects for peace and security in a world of competitive nation-states armed with increasingly lethal weapons with which to inflict violence and destruction.

## ARMS AND INFLUENCE

It is often argued that states strive for power, security, and domination in a global environment punctuated by the threat of violence and death. This viewpoint flows naturally from the characteristics of the international political system, which continues to be marked by the absence of central institutions empowered to manage and resolve conflict. Hence, preoccupation with preparations for defense to promote national security becomes understandable, for the fear persists that one adversary might use force against another to realize its goals or to vent its frustrations. In such an environment, arms are widely perceived useful not only to enhance security but also as a means to realize and extend one's influence. Hence, nations frequently see their interests best served by a search for power, by whatever means. Understandably, therefore, *power* and *influence* remain perhaps the core concepts in the study of world politics.

Appropriately, our first essay, "Power, Capability, and Influence in International Politics," by K. J. Holsti, provides a thoughtful discussion of the meaning of power, capability, and influence as these concepts relate to the foreign policy behavior of states in contemporary world politics. The essay provides insights important not only for evaluating the subsequent essays in this book but also for evaluating the use to which these necessary but ambiguous terms are often put in other interpretations of global issues. For almost invariably such discussions make reference, implicitly or explicitly, to the interrelationships among power, capability, and influence.

If the purpose of statecraft is the pursuit of political power, then a critical question is: What are the most appropriate means through which states might rise to a position of prominence in the international hierarchy? In "Force or Trade: The Costs and Benefits of Two Paths to Global Influence," Richard Rosecrance outlines rival approaches to the realization of that goal. The first encompasses the conventional path: the acquisition of military might as a way to position and power. The United States and the Soviet Union exhibited steadfast dedication to this tradition throughout the Cold War, as did other participants in the post–World War II struggle for arms and influence. In contrast, other states—in Europe, Latin America, and Asia—have chosen a second path by emulating the Japanese model; this approach emphasizes the search for global power through trade expansion instead of territorial control and force. Rosecrance concludes that global leadership is destined to pass to what he calls "the new trading states"; he contends that those who remain wedded to the pursuit of power through territorial control and military spending are destined to experience an erosion of their power and influence. States have a clear choice and must weigh the trade-off between economic and military power, Rosecrance argues, for prosperity through economic power cannot be achieved simultaneously with excessive military spending. His conclusion, that trade instead of arms provides the most viable path to both prosperity and peace, finds a prominent place on the global agenda because it poses a dilemma no policymaker can ignore, especially now that the Cold War competition between the United States and the Soviet Union has receded and the economic battleground arguably has become the primary locus in the struggle for power and influence. At issue is how security is to be realized and welfare assured.

Rosecrance's thesis is, of course, open to theoretical and empirical challenge. In our third selection, "The Future of Military Power: The Continuing Utility of Force," Eliot A. Cohen takes exception to the view that military force no longer plays a decisive role in world politics now that the Cold War has thawed and liberal democratic institutions have begun to spread to Eastern Europe and elsewhere. Contrary to Rosecrance's argument, Cohen maintains that the usability and usefulness of military force have not diminished and that, even in the era of thermonuclear weapons and the abrupt (but reversible?) end of superpower animosity, the threat and actual use of military force retain many of their traditional functions and advantages. Cohen argues that whereas preparation for war is costly and the use of force risky, they are often necessary nonetheless; accordingly, he questions the view that "methods of commerce are displacing military methods." Moreover, he questions the validity of three popular theories of the use of force: that "the horrific quality of modern military technology, the spread of democracy, and the rise of transnational issues and actors" giving rise to conditions of interdependence will inhibit recourse to war and give birth to a new age of lasting peace. Cohen maintains that none of these arguments is persuasive, and that the trends and conditions that make them plausible are unlikely to endure. None warrants the conclusion that military power is obsolete. Instead, "war, and potential war, will remain a feature of international politics." Hence, Cohen concludes that the ends of military power remain many and that military force continues to occupy a central place in international politics.

Cohen's thesis is compelling. However, the picture and prescriptions it presents must be weighed against the long-term implications of one of the most profound achievements in post–World War II international politics: in the period since World War II the great powers have experienced the longest period of uninterrupted peace since the advent of the territorial state system in 1648. The face of war and international politics *have* been transformed. Whether weapons produced this outcome—or whether this long postwar peace occurred despite these weapons—thus deserves consideration.

In "The Obsolescence of Major War," John Mueller explores the policy and moral implications of this accomplishment, in which war has passed from a noble institution to one in which it is now widely regarded as illegal, immoral, and counterproductive. The steps to this global awakening are traced in an account that sees the contribution of nuclear weapons as essentially irrelevant to the preservation of the long postwar peace. While recognizing that "war in the developed world . . . has not become impossible" and war in the Third World remains frequent and increasingly lethal, Mueller nonetheless sees hope for the future in the fact that "peoples and leaders in the developed world—where war was once endemic—have increasingly found war to be disgusting, ridiculous, and unwise." The charter of UNESCO insists that "war begins in the minds of men." If that is the case, Mueller responds, then "it can end there." Such an outcome would indeed alter the way the world has conventionally thought about arms, influence, and peace. In such a world (Professor Cohen's assessment notwithstanding), the utility of force would certainly command far less respect than in the past.

The applicability of military force to the resolution of political problems is challenged most provocatively by the destructiveness of modern weapons, of which nuclear weapons are doubtless the most lethal. For that reason, the prevention of a nuclear World War III is an issue of explosive global interest. *The Fate of the Earth,* as Jonathan Schell's popular book published in 1982 on the subject is titled, is at stake.

Since the atomic age began in 1945, considerable effort has been devoted to devising ways of avoiding resort to nuclear weapons. *Deterrence*—preventing a potential adversary from doing something it might otherwise do, such as launching a military attack—has dominated strategic thinking about nuclear weapons since their creation. The failure of deterrence, particularly in a war between the United States and the Soviet Union, could, of course, ignite a global conflagration culminating in the destruction of human civilization, which means that the entire world has a stake in the operation of a successful deterrent strategy.

Many people place great faith in nuclear weapons as instruments able to keep peace. Indeed, the most popular theory of the general war avoidance since 1945 is the claim that nuclear weapons have made system-wide war obsolete. But others endorse John Mueller's thesis that nuclear weapons are "essentially irrelevant" in the prevention of major war. As Mueller argues at length in his well-known book *Retreat from Doomsday,* the growing aversion to war in general, in conjunction with the inhibiting fear of another major *conventional* war, in particular, explain the obsolescence of war among the advanced industrial societies of the developed world. As noted, however, others disagree with this argument; they offer an opposing interpretation that treats nuclear weapons as categorically different from conventional weapons and far more potent in deterring another worldwide war.

Kenneth N. Waltz, a neo-realist, is one of them. In "Nuclear Myths and Political Realities," Waltz argues that nuclear weapons have had a pacifying impact on the course of world affairs since World War II, and that in the absence of nuclear weapons the post–World War II world might have been far less stable. Thus Waltz responds to Mueller by reminding us that, because nuclear weapons threaten all parties to a conflict with enormous and rapid destruction, their political effects are qualitatively different from conventional weapons, with the result that the stability of the postwar world cannot be attributed to conventional deterrence. Waltz warns, however, that scholars and policymakers have not understood the true strategic implications of nuclear weapons and the reasons why they dominate strategy, with the result that the advantages of nuclear weapons have not been properly appreciated. Thus Waltz advances the controversial conclusion that nuclear weapons have been "a tremendous force for peace" which "afford nations who possess them the possibility of security at reasonable cost."

The debate about the role of weapons in keeping peace (and making war) illustrates the importance of the theoretical perspective the observer takes toward these controversies. Because arms both threaten and protect, there exists a congeries of rival hypotheses about the causes of armed conflict and of peace in the nuclear age. In "The Causes of War: Contending Theories," Jack S. Levy summarizes many of the leading ideas. He notes that the outbreak of war derives from factors internal to individual states and many external to them, both of which combine to influence its occurrence. His primary focus, however, is on "systemic" factors, that is, attributes of the international system writ large. Levy examines three major "structural" explanations for the continuing outbreak of war: (1) international anarchy and the security dilemma it creates, (2) theories of international equilibrium such as the balance of power and the questionable operation of a successful balance under the emerging conditions of multipolarity, and (3) "power transition" theories and their most important variant, "long cycle" theories. His review suggests that, because war clearly has multiple potential causes, its control is difficult and depends on a varied combination of tangible and intangible factors. Arms, therefore, may be necessary instruments of modern warfare, but the reasons for the call to arms—and the means to their control—must be located elsewhere, since arming and engaging in violence typically derive from many deep-seated underlying factors.

The problems of international security and the inadequacy of control measures are compounded further by the strong probability that the number of states possessing nuclear weapons will soon increase beyond the small club that presently possesses them. Controlling *nuclear proliferation* is a major arms control issue. But, as Lewis A. Dunn warns in "Four Decades of Nuclear Nonpro-liferation: Lessons for the 1990s," the proliferation issue is complex. Many states have powerful incentives to join the nuclear club and are actively pursuing development of nuclear capabilities. Dunn inventories the problems and prospects confronting the world community on this global issue and finds the obstacles to the further expansion of the number of nuclear states insufficient. Surveying initiatives to contain the spread of nuclear weapons capabilities over four decades, he finds a "mixed" record of "wins," "losses," and "draws." Whereas important steps have been taken to reduce the incentives that could lead to the acquisition of nuclear weapons and to increase the technological and institutional obstacles to acquisition, proliferation continues. Paradoxically, the process of proliferation is accelerated by the major powers who, while protesting it, either inadvertently or clandestinely contribute to the problem and its dangers. Thus nuclear proliferation remains a prominent issue on the global agenda.

National leaders have dreamed since the dawn of the nuclear age of a solution to the nuclear dilemma and the threat it poses. Fortunately, the superpowers have managed to avoid the nuclear precipice. Their ability to prevent nuclear war has required the successful management of the many crises that have punc-tuated their relationships during the past several decades. Many of these crises have involved Third World countries that have themselves frequently faced crises. Indeed, crisis has become so prevalent a feature of world politics that some theorists see it as a substitute for war, which is why, perhaps, ours is often characterized as an "age of crisis."

What paths and policies most facilitate the successful management of crisis is not entirely clear, however. Richard Ned Lebow examines the nature of interna-tional crises and their resolution in "Is Crisis Management Always Possible?" Tying his definition of a crisis to the incipience of war, Lebow provides an insightful discussion of the causes, evolution, and outcomes of crises, and exposes the risks associated with the reassuring but unwarranted belief that cri-sis management can resolve conflicts on the brink of war in future international crises.

A dramatic increase in the capacity to destroy is among the inevitable conse-quences of nations' efforts to enhance their influence through the purchase or production of increasingly sophisticated armaments. Many political analysts see the prospects for peace dramatically reduced by these efforts. Michael T. Klare is among them. In "The Arms Trade with the Third World: Changing Patterns in the 1990s," he reaches the pessimistic prediction that the prevailing policies and practices of both suppliers and purchasers militate against imposition of mean-ingful controls. In fact, he warns that the arms trade is likely to expand rather than decline now that the Cold War has ended. Why? Because "in an ironic twist of fate, the forthcoming Soviet and American arms reductions in Europe will produce massive supplies of surplus weapons which are likely to be funneled into the arms inventories of emerging Third World powers." This sobering conclusion derives from Klare's analysis of the shifting patterns of suppliers and buyers. These trends suggest that nations' appetite for arms has not been satisfied, and that the instruments of war will be readily available to Third World powers ("regional hegemons") in the 1990s.

As noted, many observers contend that the use of force has declined as a viable instrument of foreign policy because of the increasing destructiveness of modern weapons, whose use would be so devastating as to threaten the interests and security of both the attacker and the attacked. The proponents of this thesis point to the rise of new forms of violence—often referred to as "low-intensity conflict"—as evidence supporting this interpretation; they allege that such conflict waged without large inventories of weapons permits the continued exercise of power through force by the weak on the world stage. Their argument has proved persuasive to many, who focus their attention on perhaps the most conspicuous and threatening form of "low-intensity conflict": international terrorism. In "Reflections on Terrorism," Walter Laqueur offers a timely and illuminating discussion of the nature of international terrorism and the prospects for its control. Because different actors view the issue of international terrorism differently, and, in fact, bring contending perspectives to its definition, Laqueur is pessimistic about the possibility of bringing this terrifying force under control. But he contends that efforts to grapple with it must begin with a sober account of its meanings and purposes and, in destroying much of the myth and cant that surround the emotional discussion of international terrorism, he provides a basis for making this phenomenon understandable.

Finally, we conclude Part One of *The Global Agenda* with an assessment of the changing nature of power and influence in light of the turbulent transformations in world politics that have occurred in recent years. In "The Changing Nature of World Power," Joseph S. Nye, Jr. provides us with the tools with which to assess how the relationships among arms, influence, and world leadership are likely to change as the last decade of the twentieth century unfolds. He provides a broad survey as well as critique of current thinking and theorizing about the changing sources of power, the balance of power, and hegemony in modern history. By comparing rival models (for example, realist interpretations of hegemonic transitions, the neo-Marxist view of hegemony, and the long cycle theory of world leadership), he also provides a theoretical foundation with which to predict the future of American power and evaluate the risks of world war as we approach the twenty-first century.

The issues discussed in the eleven essays in Part One inevitably focus attention on only some of the many issues relating to the role of arms and influence in a world of interdependent and often competitive states, but they do offer insight into the complexities of the issues of high politics with which national decision makers must grapple. Part Two, in which we shift attention to the nature of discord and collaboration in world politics, adds further insight into the politics of peace and security.

# 1

# POWER, CAPABILITY, AND INFLUENCE IN INTERNATIONAL POLITICS

### K. J. Holsti

**In this essay K. J. Holsti clarifies the meaning of three concepts crucial to the conduct of international politics—power, capability, and influence—and examines the complexities of each as it relates to states' efforts to realize their foreign policy objectives. Holsti is professor of political science at the University of British Columbia. His publications include *Why Nations Realign* (1982) and *The Dividing Discipline: Hegemony and Diversity in International Theory* (1987).**

. . . [A foreign policy] act is basically a form of communication intended to change or sustain the behavior of those upon whom the acting government is dependent for achieving its own goals. It can also be viewed as a "signal" sent by one actor to influence the receiver's image of the sender.[1] In international politics, acts and signals take many different forms. The promise of granting foreign aid is an act, as are propaganda appeals, displays of military strength, wielding a veto in the Security Council, walking out of a conference, organizing a conference, issuing a warning in a diplomatic note, sending arms and money to a liberation movement, instituting a boycott on the goods of another state, or declaring war. These types of acts and signals, and the circumstances in which

Reprinted from K. J. Holsti, *International Politics: A Framework for Analysis*, 4th ed., pp. 144–159. © 1983. Used by permission of Prentice-Hall, Inc. Some footnotes have been deleted.

[1]A comprehensive treatment of how governments "signal" each other is in Robert Jervis, *The Logic of Images in International Relations* (Princeton, N.J.: Princeton University Press, 1970).

**9**

they are likely to succeed, will be discussed. . . . Our organizing principle will be the amount of threat involved in the various techniques of influence. Diplomatic persuasion seemingly involves the least amount of threat; economic pressures, subversion, intervention, and various forms of warfare involve increasingly great amounts of threat and punishment. To help understand what all these types of action or techniques of influence have in common, however, we will discuss in a more abstract manner the behavior governments show when they turn toward each other to establish orientations, fulfill roles, or achieve and defend objectives.

The international political process commences when any state—let us say state A—seeks through various acts or signals to change or sustain the behavior (for instance, the acts, images, and policies) of other states. Power can thus be defined as the general capacity of a state to control the behavior of others. This definition can be illustrated as follows, where the solid line represents various acts:

A seeks to influence B because it has established certain objectives that cannot be achieved (it is perceived) unless B (and perhaps many other states as well) does X. If this is the basis of all international political processes, the capacity to control behavior can be viewed in several different ways:

**1** Influence (an aspect of power) is essentially a *means* to an end. Some governments or statesmen may seek influence for its own sake, but for most it is instrumental, just like money. They use it primarily for achieving or defending other goals, which may include prestige, territory, souls, raw materials, security, or alliances.

**2** State A, in its acts toward state B, uses or mobilizes certain *resources.* A resource is any physical or mental object or quality available as an instrument of inducement to persuade, reward, threaten, or punish. The concept of resource may be illustrated in the following example. Suppose an unarmed robber walks into a bank and asks the clerk to give up money. The clerk observes clearly that the robber has no weapon and refuses to comply with the order. The robber has sought to influence the behavior of the clerk, but has failed. The next time, however, the robber walks in armed with a pistol and threatens to shoot if the clerk does not give up the money. This time, the clerk complies. In this instance, the robber has mobilized certain resources or capabilities (the gun) and succeeds in influencing the clerk to comply. But other less tangible resources may be involved as well. The appearance of the person, particularly facial expression, may convey determination, threat, or weakness, all of which may subtly influence the behavior of the clerk. In international politics, the diplomatic gestures and words accompanying actions may be as important as the acts themselves. A government that places troops on alert but insists that it is doing so for domestic reasons will have an impact abroad quite different from the government that organizes a similar alert but accompanies it with threats to go to war. "Signals" or diplomatic "body language" may be as important as dramatic actions such as alerts and mobilizations.

**3** The act of influencing B obviously involves a *relationship* between A and B, although, as will be seen later, the relationship may not even involve overt communication. If the relationship covers any period of time, we can also say that it is a *process.*

**4** If A can get B to do something, but B cannot get A to do a similar thing, then we can say that A has more power than B regarding that particular issue. Power, therefore, can also be viewed as a *quantity,* but as a quantity it is only meaningful when compared to the power of others. Power is therefore relative.

To summarize, power may be viewed from several aspects: It is a means; it is based on resources; it is a relationship and a process; and it can be measured, at least crudely.

We can break down the concept of power into three distinct analytic elements: power comprises (1) the *acts* (process, relationship) of influencing other states; (2) the *resources* used to make the wielding of influence successful; and (3) the *responses* to the acts. The three elements must be kept distinct. Since this definition may seem too abstract, we can define the concept in the more operational terms of policy makers. In formulating policy and the strategy to achieve certain goals, they would explicitly or implicitly ask the five following questions:

**1** Given our goals, what do we wish B to do or not to do? (X)

**2** How shall we get B to do or not to do X? (implies a relationship and process)

**3** What resources are at our disposal so that we can induce B to do or not to do X?

**4** What is B's probable response to our attempts to influence its behavior?

**5** What are the *costs* of taking actions 1, 2, or 3—as opposed to other alternatives?

Before discussing the problem of resources and responses, we have to fill out our model of the influence act to account for the many patterns of behavior that may be involved in an international relationship. First, the exercise of influence implies more than merely A's ability to *change* the behavior of B. Influence may also be seen when A attempts to get B to *continue* a course of action or policy that is useful to, or in the interests of, A.[2] The exercise of influence does not always cease, therefore, after B does X. It is often a continuing process of reinforcing B's behavior.

Second, it is almost impossible to find a situation where B does not also have some influence over A. Our model has suggested that influence is exercised only in one direction, by A over B. In reality, influence is multilateral. State A, for example, would seldom seek a particular goal unless it has been influenced in a particular direction by the actions of other states in the system. At a minimum, there is the problem of feedback in any relationship: If B complies with A's wishes and does X, that behavior may subsequently prompt A to change its own behavior, perhaps in the interest of B. The phenomenon of feedback may be illustrated as follows:

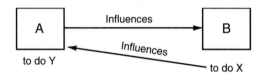

Third, there is the type of relationship that includes "anticipated reaction."[3] This is the situation where B, anticipating rewards or punishments from A, changes his behavior, perhaps even before A makes any "signals" about possible action. Deterrence theory clearly assumes that B—the potential aggressor against A—will not attack (where it might, were there no deterrent), knowing that an unacceptable level of punishment would surely result. A similar situation, but in reverse, is also common in international politics. This is where A might wish B to do X, but does not try to influence B for fear that B will do Y instead, which is an unfavorable response from A's point of view. In a hypothetical situation, the government of India might wish to obtain arms from the United States to build up its own defenses, but does not request such arms because it fears that the United States would insist on certain conditions for the sale of arms that might compromise India's nonalignment. This anticipated reaction may also be multilateral, where A wishes B to do X, but will not try to get B to do it because it fears that C, a third state, will do Y, which is unfavorable to A's interests. India wants to purchase American arms, but does not seek to influence the United States to sell them for fear that Pakistan (C) will then build up its own armaments and thus accelerate the arms race between the two coun-

---

[2]J. David Singer, "Inter-Nation Influence: A Formal Model," *American Political Science Review,* 57 (1963), 420–30. State A might also wish state B to do W, Y, and Z, which may be incompatible with the achievement of X.

[3]Herbert A. Simon, "Notes on the Observation and Measurement of Political Power," *Journal of Politics,* 15 (1953), 500–16. For further analysis, see David A. Baldwin, "Inter-Nation Influence Revisited," *Journal of Conflict Resolution,* 15 (December 1971), 478–79.

tries. In this situation, Pakistan (C) has influence over the actions of the Indian government even though it has not deliberately sought to influence India on this particular matter or even communicated its position in any way. The Indian government has simply perceived that there is a relatively high probability that if it seeks to influence the United States, Pakistan will react in a manner contrary to India's interests.

Fourth, power and influence may be measured by scholars, but what is important in international politics is the *perceptions* of influence and capabilities held by policy makers and the way they interpret another government's signals. The reason that governments invest millions of dollars for gathering intelligence is to develop a reasonably accurate picture of other states' capabilities and intentions. Where there is a great discrepancy between perceptions and reality, the results to a country's foreign policy may be disastrous. To take our example of the bank robber again, suppose that the person held a harmless toy pistol and threatened the clerk. The clerk perceived the gun to be real and deduced the robber's intention to use it. As a result, the clerk complied with the demand. In this case, the robber's influence was far greater than the "objective" character of the robber's capabilities and intentions; and distorted perception by the clerk led to an act which was unfavorable to the bank.

Finally, as our original model suggests, A may try to influence B *not to do* X. Sometimes this is called negative power, or deterrence, where A acts in a manner to *prevent* a certain action it deems undesirable to its interests. This is a typical relationship in international politics. By signing the Munich treaty, the British and French governments hoped to prevent Germany from invading Czechoslovakia; Israeli attacks on PLO facilities in Lebanon are designed to demonstrate that PLO guerrilla operations against Israel will be met by vast punishments, the costs of which to the PLO would far outweigh the gains of the terrorist acts. Such a cost-benefit analysis, the Israelis hope, would deter the PLO from undertaking further operations. The reader should keep in mind the distinction between compellence and deterrence.

## RESOURCES

The second element of the concept of power consists of those resources that are mobilized in support of the acts taken to influence state B's behavior. It is difficult to assess the general capacity of a state to control the actions and policies of others unless we also have some knowledge of the capabilities involved.[4] Nevertheless, it should be acknowledged that social scientists do not understand all the reasons why some actors—whether people, groups, governments, or states—wield influence successfully, while others do not.

---

[4]We might assess influence for historical situations solely on the basis of whether A got B to do X, without our having knowledge of either A's or B's capabilities.

It is clear that, in political relationships, not everyone possesses equal influence. In domestic politics, it is possible to construct a lengthy list of capabilities and attributes that seemingly permit some to wield influence over large numbers of people and important public decisions. Robert Dahl lists such tangibles as money, wealth, information, time, political allies, official position, and control over jobs, and such intangibles as personality and leadership qualities.[5] But not everyone who possesses these capabilities can command the obedience of other people. What is crucial in relating resources to influence, according to Dahl, is that one *mobilize them for one's political purposes* and possess the skill to mobilize them. One who uses wealth, time, information, friends, and personality for political purposes will probably be able to influence others on public issues. A person, on the other hand, who possesses the same capabilities but uses them to invent a new mousetrap is not apt to be important in politics. The same propositions also hold true in international politics. The amount of influence a state wields over others can be related to the capabilities *mobilized* in support of *specific* foreign-policy objectives. To put this proposition in another way, we can argue that resources do not determine the uses to which they will be put. Nuclear power can be used to provide electricity or to deter and perhaps destroy other nations. The use of resources depends less on their quality and quantity than on the external objectives a government formulates for itself.

The *variety* of foreign-policy instruments available to a nation for influencing others is partly a function of the quantity and quality of capabilities. What a government seeks to do—the type of objectives it formulates—and how it attempts to do it will depend at least partially on the resources it finds available. A country such as Thailand, which possesses relatively few resources, cannot, even if it would desire, construct intercontinental ballistic missiles with which to intimidate others, establish a worldwide propaganda network, or dispense several billion dollars annually for foreign aid to try to influence other countries. We can conclude, therefore, that how states *use* their resources depends on their external objectives, but the choice of objectives and the instruments to achieve those objectives are limited or influenced by the quality and quantity of available resources.

## THE MEASUREMENT OF RESOURCES

For many years, students of international politics have made meticulous comparisons of the potential capabilities of various nations, assuming that a nation was powerful, or capable of achieving its objectives, to the extent that it possessed certain "elements of power." Comparative data relating to production of iron ore, coal, and hydroelectricity, economic growth rates, educational levels, population growth rates, military resources, transportation systems, and sources of

[5]Robert A. Dahl, *Who Governs?* (New Haven, Conn.: Yale University Press, 1961).

raw materials are presented as indicators of a nation's power. Few have acknowledged that these comparisons do not measure a state's power or influence but only its potential capacity to wage war. Other resources, such as diplomatic or propaganda skills, are seldom measured; but surely they are as important as war-making potential. Measurements and assessments are not particularly useful anyway unless they are related to specific foreign-policy issues. Capability is always the capability to do something; its assessment is most meaningful when carried on within a framework of certain foreign-policy objectives.

The deduction of actual influence from the quantity and quality of potential and mobilized capabilities may, in some cases, give an approximation of reality, but historically there have been too many discrepancies between the basis of power and the amount of influence to warrant adopting this practice as a useful approach to international relations. One could have assumed, for example, on the basis of a comparative study of technological and educational levels and general standards of living in the 1920s and 1930s that the United States would have been one of the most influential states in international politics. A careful comparison of certain resources, called the "great essentials,"[6] revealed the United States to be in an enviable position. In the period 1925 to 1930, it was the only major country in the world that produced from its own resources adequate supplies of food, power, iron, machinery, chemicals, coal, iron ore, and petroleum. If actual diplomatic influence had been deduced from the quantities of "great essentials" possessed by the major nations, the following ranking of states would have resulted: (1) United States, (2) Germany, (3) Great Britain, (4) France, (5) Russia, (6) Italy, (7) Japan. However, the diplomatic history of the world from 1925 to 1930 would suggest that there was little correlation between the resources of these countries and their *actual influence.* If we measure influence by the impact these states made on the system and by the responses they could invoke when they sought to change the behavior of other states, we would find for this period quite a different ranking, such as the following: (1) France, (2) Great Britain, (3) Italy, (4) Germany, (5) Russia, (6) Japan, (7) United States.

Indeed, many contemporary international relationships reveal how often the "strong" states do not achieve their objectives—or at least have to settle for poor substitutes—even when attempting to influence the behavior of "weak" states. How, for instance, did Marshal Tito's Yugoslavia effectively resist all sorts of pressures and threats by the powerful Soviet Union after it was expelled from the Communist bloc? Why, despite its overwhelming superiority in capabilities, was the United States unable in the 1960s to achieve its major objectives against a weak Cuba and North Vietnam? How have "small" states gained trading privi-

---

[6]Frank H. Simonds and Brooks Emeny, *The Great Powers in World Politics* (New York: American Book, 1939).

leges and all sorts of diplomatic concessions from those nations with great economic wealth and military power? The ability of state A to change the behavior of state B is, we would assume, enhanced if it possesses physical resources to use in the influence act; but B is by no means defenseless or vulnerable to diplomatic, economic, or military pressures because it fails to own a large modern army, raw materials, and money for foreign aid. The successful exercise of influence is also dependent upon such factors as personality, perceptions, friendships, and traditions, and, not being easy to measure, these factors have a way of rendering power calculations and equations difficult. . . .

## VARIABLES AFFECTING THE EXERCISE OF INFLUENCE

One reason that gross quantities of resources cannot be equated with effective influence relates to the distinction between a state's overall capabilities and the *relevance* of resources to a particular diplomatic situation. A nuclear force, for example, is often thought to increase the diplomatic influence of those who possess it. No doubt nuclear weaponry is an important element in a state's general prestige abroad and may be an effective deterrent against a strategic attack on its homeland or "core" interests. Yet the most important aspect of a nuclear capability—or any military capability—is not its possession, but its relevance and the ability to signal one's determination to use it. Other governments must know that the capability is not of mere symbolic significance. The government of North Vietnam possessed a particular advantage over the United States (hence, influence) because it knew that in almost no circumstances would the American government use strategic nuclear weapons against its country. It therefore effectively broke through the significance of the American nuclear capability as far as the Vietnam War was concerned. A resource is useless unless it is both mobilized in support of foreign-policy objectives and made credible. Likewise, nuclear weapons would be irrelevant in negotiations on cultural exchanges, just as the Arab countries' vast oil resources could not be effectively mobilized to influence the outcome of international negotiations on satellite communications. Influence is always specific to a particular issue, and resources must be relevant to that issue.

A second variable that determines the success or failure of acts of influence is the extent to which there are *needs* between the two countries in any influence relationship. In general, a country that needs something from another is vulnerable to its acts of influence. This is the primary reason that states that are "weak" in many capabilities can nevertheless obtain concessions from "strong" countries. Consider the case of France and Germany and some of the "weak" states in the Middle East. Both European countries are highly dependent upon Arab lands for oil supplies. They have an important need, which only the Arab countries can satisfy at a reasonable cost. On the other hand, the Middle Eastern countries that control these oil resources may not be so dependent upon Germany and

France, particularly if they can sell their oil easily elsewhere. Because, in this situation, needs are not equal on both sides, the independent states (in terms of needs) can make demands (or resist demands made against them) on the dependent great powers and obtain important concessions. The German and French governments know that if they do not make these concessions or if they press their own demands too hard, the Arab states can threaten to cut off oil supplies. Their dependence thus makes them vulnerable to the demands and influence acts of what would otherwise be considered "weak" states. To the Arab states, oil is much more important as a capability than military forces—at least in their relations with major powers. In the form of a general hypothesis, we can suggest that, regardless of the quantity, quality, and credibility of a state's capabilities, the more state B needs, or is dependent upon, state A, the more likely that state A's acts—threats, promises, rewards, or punishments—will succeed in changing or sustaining B's behavior.

A third variable that has assumed increasing importance in the past several decades, and one that can be considered an important resource, is level of technical expertise. An increasing number of issues on the international and foreign-policy agendas are highly technical in nature: law of the sea, satellite broadcasting, international monetary matters, and the like. Many of these issues are discussed in international fora, where leadership often depends more on knowledge of the technical issues than on other types of resources. Those governments which come armed with technical studies, have a full command of the nature of the problem, and are prepared to put forth realistic solutions are more likely to wield influence than are governments which have only rudimentary knowledge of the problem and no scientific studies to back their national positions. A number of recent case studies have demonstrated conclusively that the outcomes of negotiations on technical questions cannot be predicted from the gross power of the participants and that knowledge, among other factors, accounts for more than raw capabilities.[7]

Understanding the dynamics of power relationships at the international level would be relatively easy if resource relevance, credibility, need, and knowledge were the only variables involved. Unfortunately, political actions do not always conform to simple hypotheses, because human characteristics of pride, stubbornness, prestige, and friendship enter into all acts of influence as well. A government may be highly dependent upon some other state and still resist its demands; it may be willing to suffer all sorts of privations, and even physical destruction and loss of independence, simply for the sake of pride. The government of North Vietnam was willing to accept a very high level of destruction of

---

[7]See, for example, the case studies in Robert O. Keohane and Joseph S. Nye, *Power and Interdependence: World Politics in Transition* (Boston: Little, Brown and Company, 1977). See also David Baldwin's strong emphasis on the relevance of resources to particular situations in "Power Analysis and World Politics," *World Politics,* 31 (January 1979), 161–94.

lives and productive facilities by American bombers rather than make diplomatic or military concessions to the United States.

Additional variables affecting the exercise of influence can be observed in the situation where two small states of approximately equal capabilities make similar demands upon a "major" power and neither of the small states is dependent upon the large—or vice versa. Which will achieve its objectives? Will both exercise influence equally? Hypothetically, suppose that the ambassadors of Norway and Albania go to the British Foreign Office on the same day and ask the British government to lower tariffs on bicycles, a product that the two countries would like to export to England. Assume that the quality and price of the bicycles are approximately the same and that the British government does not wish to allow too many imports for fear of damaging the domestic bicycle industry. Assume further that both the Norwegian and Albanian ambassadors offer roughly equal concessions if the British will lower their tariffs on bicycles. Both claim they will lower their own tariffs on English automobiles. Which ambassador is most likely to succeed—that is, to achieve his government's objectives? Chances are that the British government would favor the request of the Norwegian ambassador and turn down the representation by the diplomat from Tirana. The explanation of this decision can probably not be found in the resources of either of the small countries (both offered approximately equal rewards) or in need, since in this hypothetical situation Britain needs neither of the small countries' automobile markets. Norway would get the favorable decision because British policy makers are more *responsive* to Norwegian interests than to those of Albania. Albania represents a Communist state whose government normally displays through its diplomacy and propaganda strong hostility toward England.

After relevant resources, need, and knowledge, the fourth variable that determines the effectiveness of acts of influence is thus the ephemeral quality of responsiveness.[8] Responsiveness can be seen as a disposition to receive another's requests with sympathy, even to the point where a government is willing to sacrifice some of its own values and interests in order to fulfill those requests; responsiveness is the willingness to be influenced. In one study, it was shown that members of the State Department in the United States may take considerable pains to promote the requests and interests of other governments among their superiors and in other government agencies, provided that the requesting government feels that the issue is important or that the need must be fulfilled.[9] In

[8]The concept of responsiveness is introduced by Karl W. Deutsch et al., *Political Community and the North Atlantic Area* (Princeton, N.J.: Princeton University Press, 1957); developed by Dean G. Pruitt, "National Power and International Responsiveness" *Background,* 7 (1964), 165–78. See also Dean G. Pruitt, "Definition of the Situation as a Determinant of International Action," in *International Behavior: A Social-Psychological Analysis,* ed. Herbert C. Kelman (New York: Holt, Rinehart & Winston, 1965), pp. 393–432.

[9]Pruitt, "National Power," 175–76.

our hypothetical case, if the quality of responsiveness is present in the case of the Norwegian request, members of the British Foreign Office would probably work for the Norwegians and try to persuade other government agencies concerned with trade and commerce to agree to a lowering of the tariff on bicycles. In the British reaction to the Albanian request, it is not likely that the government would display much responsiveness. Suspicion, traditional animosities, lack of trust, and years of unfavorable diplomatic experience would probably prevent the development of much British sympathy for Albania's needs or interests. . . . When the other variables, such as resources or need, are held constant or made equal, the degree of responsiveness will determine the success or failure of acts taken to influence other states' behavior.

If effective influence cannot be deduced solely from the quantity and quality of physical capabilities, how do we proceed to measure influence? If we want to assess a situation that has already occurred, the easiest way to measure influence is to study the *responses* of those in the influence relationship.[10] If A can get B to do X, but C cannot get B to do the same thing, then in that particular issue, A has more influence. If B does X despite the protestations of A, then we can assume that A, in this circumstance, did not enjoy much influence over B. It is meaningless to argue that the Soviet Union is more powerful than the United States unless we cite how, for what purposes, and in relation to whom the Soviet Union and the United States are exerting influence. . . .

## HOW INFLUENCE IS EXERCISED

Social scientists have noted several fundamental techniques that individuals and groups use to influence each other. In a political system that contains no one legitimate center of authority that can command the members of the group or society, bargaining has to be used among the sovereign entities to achieve or defend their objectives. Recalling that A seeks one of three courses of conduct from B (B to do X in the future, B not to do X in the future, or B to continue doing X), it may use six different tactics, involving acts of:

1. **PERSUASION.** By persuasion we mean simply initiating or discussing a proposal with another and eliciting a favorable response without explicitly holding out the possibility of rewards or punishments. We cannot assume that the exercise of influence is always *against* the wishes of others and that there are only two possible outcomes of the act, one favoring A, the other favoring B. For example, state A asks B to support it at a coming international conference on the control of narcotics. State B might not originally have any particular interest in the conference or its outcome; but it decides, on the basis of A's initiative, that something positive might be gained, not only by supporting A's proposals, but

---

[10]Robert A. Dahl, "The Concept of Power," *Behavioral Science,* 2 (1957), 201–15.

also by attending the conference. In this case, B might also expect to gain some type of reward in the future, although not necessarily from A. Persuasion would also include protests and denials that do not involve obvious threats.

**2. THE OFFER OF REWARDS.** This is the situation where A promises to do something favorable to B if B complies with the wishes of A. Rewards may be of almost any type in international relations. To gain the diplomatic support of B at the narcotics conference, A may offer to increase foreign-aid payments, lower tariffs on goods imported from B, support B at a later conference on communications facilities, or promise to remove a previous punishment. The last tactic is used often by negotiators. After having created an unfavorable situation, they promise to remove it in return for some concessions by their opponents.

**3. THE GRANTING OF REWARDS.** In some instances, the credibility of a government is not very high, and state B, before complying with A's wishes, may insist that A actually give the reward in advance. Frequently, in armistice negotiations neither side will unilaterally take steps to demilitarize an area or demobilize troops until the other shows evidence of complying with the agreements. One of the clichés of cold-war diplomacy holds that deeds, not words, are required for the granting of rewards and concessions.

**4. THE THREAT OF PUNISHMENT.** Threats of punishment may be further subdivided into two types: (a) positive threats, where, for example, state A threatens to increase tariffs, institute a boycott or embargo against trade with B, or use force; and (b) threats of deprivation, where A threatens to withdraw foreign aid or in other ways withhold rewards or other advantages that it already grants to B.

**5. THE INFLICTION OF NONVIOLENT PUNISHMENT.** In this situation, threats are carried out in the hope of altering B's behavior, which, in most cases, could not be altered by other means. The problem with this tactic is that it often results in reciprocal measures by the other side, thus inflicting damage on both, and not necessarily bringing about a desired state of affairs. If, for example, A threatens to increase its military capabilities if B does X and then proceeds to implement the threat, it is not often that B will comply with A's wishes, because it, too, can increase its military capabilities. In this type of situation, both sides indulge in the application of punishments that may escalate into more serious forms unless the conflict is resolved. Typical acts of nonviolent punishment include breaking diplomatic relations, raising tariffs, instituting boycotts and embargoes, holding hostages, organizing blockades, closing frontiers, or walking out of a diplomatic conference.

**6. FORCE.** In previous eras, when governments did not possess the variety of foreign-policy instruments available today, they frequently had to rely upon the use of force in the bargaining process. Force and violence were not only the most efficient tactics, but in many cases the only means possible for influencing. Today, the situation is different. As technological levels rise and dependencies develop, other means of inducement become available and can serve as substitutes for force.

## PATTERNS OF INFLUENCE IN THE
## INTERNATIONAL SYSTEM

Most governments at some time use all their techniques for influencing others, but probably over 90 percent of all relations between states are based on simple persuasion and deal with relatively unimportant technical matters. Since such interactions seldom make the headlines, we often assume that most relations between states involve the making or carrying out of threats. But whether a government is communicating with another over an unimportant technical matter or over a subject of great consequence, it is likely to use a particular type of tactic in its attempts to influence, depending on the past tradition of friendship or hostility between those two governments and the amount of compatibility between their objectives and interests. Allies, for example, seldom threaten each other with force or even make blatant threats of punishment, but governments that disagree over a wide range of policy objectives and hold attitudes of suspicion and hostility toward each other are more likely to resort to threats and imposition of punishments. The methods of exerting influence between Great Britain and the United States are, typically, persuasion and rewards, whereas the methods of exerting influence between the Soviet Union and the United States in the early post–World War II era were typically threatening and inflicting punishments of various types. . . .

To summarize this analysis of power, we can suggest that power is an integral part of all political relationships; but in international politics we are interested primarily in one process: how one state influences the behavior of another in its own interests. The act of influencing becomes a central focus for the study of international politics, and it is from this act that we can best deduce a definition of power. If we observe the act of influencing, we can see that power is a process, a relationship, a means to an end, and even a quantity. Moreover, we can make an analytical distinction among the act of influencing, the basis, or resources, upon which the act relies, and the response to the act. Resources are an important determinant of how successful the wielding of influence will be, but they are by no means the only determinant. The nature of a country's foreign-policy objectives, the skill with which a state mobilizes its capabilities for foreign-policy purposes, its needs, responsiveness, costs, and commitments are equally important. Acts of influencing may take many forms, the most important of which are the offer and granting of rewards, the threat and imposition of punishments, and the application of force. The choice of means used to induce will depend, in turn, upon the general nature of relations between any two given governments, the degree of involvement between them, and the extent of their mutual responsiveness. . . .

# 2

# FORCE OR TRADE: THE COSTS AND BENEFITS OF TWO PATHS TO GLOBAL INFLUENCE

### Richard Rosecrance

Throughout history, states have pursued power through the acquisition of military capabilities and the use of force. This convention, argues Richard Rosecrance, has been challenged by post–World War II developments in the global arena. "The trading state"—the nation that expands its resources through economic development and foreign trade—has demonstrated the advantages of economic approaches to world power and global influence. Trade, it is argued, has replaced territorial expansion and military might as the vehicle for prosperity and preeminence on the world stage. Rosecrance is professor of political science and associate director of the Center for International Strategic Affairs at the University of California at Los Angeles. Among his many books and articles are his pioneering *Action and Reaction in World Politics* (1963) and *America's Economic Resurgence* (1990).

The notion of the state as a sovereign unit, dependent in the final analysis only on itself, has largely captured intellectual fashion. But today, no state can aspire to the degree of independence that such concepts have entailed. Even the United States and the USSR are dependent on other nations, and most of all on each other, for their continued existence. The theory of international exchange and trade gives a basis for mutual cooperation and mutual benefit, and it applies to

Reprinted from Richard Rosecrance, *The Rise of the Trading State: Commerce and Conquest in the Modern World*. Copyright © 1986 by Richard Rosecrance. Used by permission of Basic Books, a division of HarperCollins Publishers. Footnotes have been deleted.

the essence of what states do day by day. When noticed, trading is dismissed as "low politics," pejoratively contrasting it with the "high politics" of sovereignty, national interest, power, and military force. However, it is possible for relationships among states to be entirely transformed or even reversed by the low politics of trade. Through trade Japan has become the third industrial nation in the world, and it will soon become the second nation, surpassing the Soviet Union. It may in time exceed the United States of America. [Since this was written, Japan has surpassed the Soviet Union to become the second largest industrial power.—Eds.]

Many have misunderstood the differences between Japan and America, believing that Japan is simply a youthful, smaller edition of the United States, a still not fully developed major power with political and economic interests that have yet to be defined on a world stage. Sooner or later, many feel, Japan too will become a world power with commensurate political and military interests. This is a misconception of the Japanese role in world affairs and a mistaken assimilation of a trading state to the military-political realm. Even if, at some distant future time, Japan increased her defense expenditure to 2 percent of gross national product, she would not follow the United States and Soviet strategy in international politics or try to become the world's leading naval or military power. As a trading state it would not be in her interest to dominate the world, control the sea lanes to the Persian Gulf, or guarantee military access to markets in Europe or the western hemisphere. She depends upon open trading and commercial routes to produce entry for her goods. It is not the American model that Japan will ultimately follow. Rather, it is the Japanese model that America may ultimately follow.

It is thus important to consider how states advance themselves and to bring the trading strategy into a regular and durable place in the theory of international politics. . . .

## THE WORLDS OF INTERNATIONAL RELATIONS: THE MILITARY-POLITICAL WORLD, THE TRADING WORLD

The choice between territorial and trading means to national advancement has always lain before states. Most often, however, nations have selected a point between extremes though nearer the territorial end. In the early years of the modern period in the sixteenth and seventeenth centuries, that point was close to the territorial and military pole; at mid-nineteenth century it briefly moved toward the trading pole. In World Wars I and II the military and territorial orientation was chosen once again. Only after 1945 did a group of trading nations emerge in world politics. Over time this group has grown and its success, at least in economic terms, has been greater than that of either the United States or the Soviet Union. . . .

## The Military-Political World

In a military-political world nations are ranged in terms of power and territory from the greatest to the weakest. States in such a world are homogeneous in form; that is, they do not have differentiated objectives or perform a variety of functions. They all seek the same territorial objectives and each, at least among the major powers, strives to be the leading power in the system. None of the contenders wishes to depend upon any other for any vital function, from the provision of defense to economic resources. . . .

The military-political world involves a continual recourse to war because the units within it compete for primacy. None is content to accept the hegemony of one of their number if it can be prevented; each is afraid that the dominance of one power will undermine its domestic autonomy and perhaps its very existence. Hence the balance of power becomes a means of resistance to threatened hegemony. The means of constructing a balance ultimately involves a resort to force to discipline an ambitious pretender. Warfare may be stabilizing if it succeeds in restraining challenge, but it cannot be acceptable if the destruction it causes more than outweighs the evil it seeks to prevent. In addition, since every state in a political-military order seeks to be self-sufficient, each strives to grow larger in order to achieve full independence. This drive itself is a cause of war.

## The Trading World

In contrast, the trading world is not composed of states ranked in order of their power and territory, all seeking preponderance. Instead, it is composed of nations differentiated in terms of function. Each may seek to improve its position, but because nations supply different services and products, in defense as well as economics, they come to depend upon each other. While some will be stronger than others, their functions give them a kind of equality of status. They may specialize in terms of particular defense functions: conventional or nuclear forces. They may offer raw materials or primary products to the international trading system as opposed to manufactured goods. Within the category of manufacturers, there may be intra-industry specialization in terms of technology. Certain industrial countries may concentrate, like Switzerland and Italy, on producing goods of very high quality and craftsmanship. Others, like Korea or Taiwan, may produce shoes, watches, textiles, steel, or ships on an efficient low-cost basis. Trading states will also normally form alliances as a precaution against sudden intrusion by military-political nations.

While trading states try to improve their position and their own domestic allocation of resources, they do so within a context of accepted interdependence. They recognize that the attempt to provide every service and fulfill every function of statehood on an independent and autonomous basis is extremely inefficient, and they prefer a situation which provides for specialization and division of labor among nations. One nation's attempt to improve its own access to products and resources, therefore, does not conflict with another state's attempt to do the same. The incentive to wage war is absent in such a system for war disrupts trade and the interdependence on which trade is based. Trading states recognize that they can do better through internal economic development sustained by a worldwide market for their goods and services than by trying to conquer and assimilate large tracts of land. . . .

In international society where government does not exist, nations will have power conflicts unless they can work out a system of interdependence to satisfy their needs. Only the reciprocal exchange and division of labor represented by the trading world can prevent conflict in such an anarchic environment. Industrial and population growth strengthen interdependence and make it harder to achieve national objectives autonomously. When technology was rudimentary and population sparse, states had little contact with one another and did not generally get in each other's way. With the commercial and industrial revolutions, however, they were brought into closer proximity. As the Industrial Revolution demanded energy resources—great quantities of food, coal, iron, water power, and petroleum—the number of states which could be fully independent declined. Those which sought complete autonomy and even autarchy had to conquer the lands which contained the materials they needed. The military-political and territorial system, then, required more war. Only a shift in direction toward an interdependent trading system, giving up autonomy in return for greater access to world resources and markets, could produce greater cooperation among nations.

The trading system does not require large, self-sufficient units. As the national objective is exchange and trade with other states, trading countries do not need large territories and populations. Like Singapore and Hong Kong, they may be small countries, little more than cities, which manufacture the raw materials of other nations into finished commodities, gaining a high return in foreign trade. . . .

The creation of the International Monetary Fund at Bretton Woods in 1944 was a giant step toward a trading system of international relations. The new regime called for an open world economy with low tariffs and strictly limited depreciation of currencies. Tariff hikes and competitive devaluation of currencies were to be restricted by the General Agreement on Tariffs and Trade (GATT) and by the Fund. Unlike the situation after World War I, nations were to be persuaded not to institute controls by offering them liquid funds to float over any period of imbalance in international payments. They would then have a grace period to get their economies in order, after which they could repay the loans.

The plethora of small nations created after the war by the decolonization process in Africa, Asia, the Middle East, and Oceania were generally not large or strong enough to rely on domestic resources, industry, agriculture, and markets for all their needs. Unless they could trade, they could not live. This meant that the markets of the major Western and industrial economies had to take their exports and they in return would need manufacturing exports from the developed countries. The open international economy was critical to their growth and stability. This is not to say that there were no other factors which supported the independence of new nations in the post–World War II period. Military factors and superpower rivalries made the reconquest of colonial areas very costly; ethnic and cultural differences limited the success of attempts to subdue one country or another. But political and military viability were not enough. Small states could not continue to exist as independent entities unless they could earn an economic livelihood. To some degree economic assistance from developed nations or from multilateral agencies met this need. If tariffs and restrictions had inhibited the trade of new nations, however, they would not have been able to function as independent units.

But the open economy of the trading world did not benefit only small nations. The growth of world trade, which increased faster than gross national product until 1980, attracted larger states as well. As the cost of using force increased and its benefits declined, other means of gaining national welfare had to be found. The Federal Republic of Germany, following Hanseatic precedents, became more dependent on international trade than the old united Germany had been. The United Kingdom, France, Italy, Norway, Switzerland, Germany, Belgium, Holland, and Denmark had imports and exports which equalled 30 percent or more of their gross national product, nearly three times the proportion attained in the United States. Japan's huge economy was fueled by foreign trade, which amounted to 20 percent of her GNP total.

The role of Japan and Germany in the trading world is exceedingly interesting because it represents a reversal of past policies in both the nineteenth century and the 1930s. It is correct to say that the two countries experimented with foreign trade because they had been disabused of military expansion by World War II. For a time they were incapable of fighting war on a major scale; their endorsement of the trading system was merely an adoption of the remaining policy alternative. But the endorsement did not change even when the economic strength of the two nations might have sustained a much more nationalistic and militaristic policy. Given the choice between military expansion to achieve self-sufficiency (a choice made more difficult by modern conventional and nuclear weapons in the hands of other powers) and the procurement of necessary markets and raw materials through international commerce, Japan and Germany chose the latter. . . .

The increasing prevalence of the trading option since 1945 raises peaceful possibilities that were neglected during the late nineteenth century and the 1930s. It seems safe to say that an international system composed of more than 160 states cannot continue to exist unless trade remains the primary vocation of most of its members. Were military and territorial orientations to dominate the scene, the trend to greater numbers of smaller states would be reversed, and larger states would conquer small and weak nations. . . .

The basic effect of World War II was to create much higher world interdependence as the average size of countries declined. The reversal of past trends toward a consolidation of states created instead a multitude of states that could not depend on themselves alone. They needed ties with other nations to prosper and remain viable as small entities. The trading system, as a result, was visible in defense relations as well as international commerce. Nations that could not stand on their own sought alliances or assistance from other powers, and they offered special defense contributions in fighting contingents, regional experience, or particular types of defense hardware. Dutch electronics, French aircraft, German guns and tanks, and British ships all made their independent contribution to an alliance in which no single power might be able to meet its defense needs on a self-sufficient basis. Israel developed a powerful and efficient small arms industry, as well as a great fund of experience combating terrorism. Israeli intelligence added considerably to the information available from Western sources, partly because of its understanding of Soviet weapons systems accumulated in several Arab-Israeli wars. . . .

At least among the developed and liberal countries, interdependent ties since 1945 have come to be accepted as a fundamental and unchangeable feature of the situation. This recognition dawned gradually, and the United States may perhaps have been the last to acknowledge it, which was not surprising. The most powerful economy is ready to make fewer adjustments, and America tried initially to pursue its domestic economic policies without taking into account the effect on others, on itself, and on the international financial system as a whole. Presidents Kennedy and Lyndon B. Johnson tried to detach American domestic growth strategies from the deteriorating United States balance of payments, but they left a legacy of needed economic change to their successors. Finally, in the 1980s two American administrations accepted lower United States growth in order to control inflation and began to focus on the international impact of  United States policies. The delay in fashioning a strategy of adjustment to international economic realities almost certainly made it more difficult. Smaller countries actively sought to find a niche in the structure of international comparative advantage and in the demand for their goods. Larger countries with large internal markets postponed that reckoning as long as they could. By the 1980s, however, such change could no longer be avoided, and United States leaders embarked upon new industrial and tax policies designed to increase economic growth and enable America to compete more effectively abroad. . . .

## FORCE OR TRADE: THE COSTS AND BENEFITS

The growing preference of states for a trading strategy in international relations stems not only from the benefits of commerce; it reflects the difficulties represented by the continuing stalemate in the military-political world. Since 1945 a few nations have borne the crushing weight of military expenditure, while others have gained a relative advantage by becoming military free-riders who primarily rely on the security provided by others. While the United States spent nearly 50 percent of its research and development budget on arms, Japan devoted 99 percent to civilian production. Meanwhile the Soviet Union's growth rate slowed from 6 to 4 to 2 percent per year and her industrial investment languished, as a result of the 12 to 14 percent of GNP per year which she spends on the military. Japan, with less than 1 percent of its GNP devoted to armaments, further enhanced its trillion dollar economy through trade and productivity gains. In the West, and particularly in the United States, large government deficits, caused in the most part by immense military spending of nearly $300 billion a year, generated high interest rates which slowed investment, hiked currency values, and limited American export competitiveness. All these expenditures raised the opportunity costs of a military-political and territorial system. . . .

The disadvantages of high military spending in sacrificing other economic opportunities, however, are not its only costs; direct costs are also involved. The industrialization of warfare, with concomitant acceleration in the expense of weapons, has imposed its own burdens. Until the mid-nineteenth century, the cost of uniforms and food for troops and horses was the main expense of war, and, as Russia showed, a populous power could be strong without a well-developed industry. But by World War I industrial strength had become a decisive factor in war, and it was production during the war that determined its outcome. It appeared that the machine age could produce weapons almost indefinitely, and the problem became finding soldiers who would fight. After the early battles of World War I, conscription brought in new recruits when needed, but these became less willing to sacrifice themselves as casualties mounted and the battle lines remained more or less fixed. New means of offensive war had to be found, or there would be a political resistance of great magnitude. The armored tank was then developed to protect men in the forward battle area. Increased protection, firepower, and maneuvering speed were heralded as substitutes for massed infantry attacks. But the new tanks, artillery, and airplanes that performed these functions became very expensive. In constant dollar terms, tanks went from less than $50,000 per unit in 1918 to more than $2,000,000 in 1980. Fighter planes that cost less than $100,000 in 1944 rose to at least $10,000,000 per copy forty years later. Paradoxically, as manpower became more expensive politically, the weapons that were to replace it became even more costly. This would not have been a major factor if weapons had lasted longer, but tanks and aircraft were subject to enormous rates of attrition on the battlefield. Ships became obsolescent and were rendered vulnerable to attack by surface missiles. In the end, all but the very strongest powers needed economic help to purchase armaments for long wars. Israel could not have continued to fight after two weeks in 1973 without shipments of arms from the United States. British rearmament would have ceased without Lend-Lease financial assistance from the United States in World War II, and the Soviet Union still has to acknowledge the enormous help it received from military equipment provided by Western powers. In wars after

1945, Vietnam, Israel, Egypt, Jordan, and Syria could not have fought without huge amounts of outside help.

Rapid innovation in weapons technology, producing AWACS (Airborne Warning and Control Systems), precision-guided munitions, and new forms of defense has made the battlefield a more hostile place for attacking tanks and planes. To survive, tanks must carry more armor and move faster, but this takes more fuel, which is expensive to transport. Enormous utilization rates in wartime require that large numbers of weapons and supplies be stockpiled beforehand. But powers hesitate to buy too many copies of any one weapon for fear that it will become outmoded. In modern war, there is no relatively fixed design, like the battleship *Dreadnought,* which could be bought, with minor improvements, by a decade of European naval ministers.

The conventional battlefield has become even more uncertain than its early-twentieth-century predecessor. Technology that might appear to give the advantage to a sudden offensive thrust—such as the tank and jet aircraft—could well be nullified by antitank and antiaircraft defenses. Defensive abilities to counter a tank attack by destroying second echelon forces, logistics, and supply bases behind the lines could transfer the initiative to a defender who might then be able to unleash a counteroffensive into enemy territory. Unlike the German Schlieffen Plan in 1914, which assumed that the surprise turning of the French left flank with a huge force would bring victory in six weeks, no contemporary commander can predict the outcome against a comparably equipped enemy force. Instead, uncertainties dominate the outcome.

The one outcome that is not uncertain is that the peacetime stockpiling of military hardware will become more expensive, rising at least 3–5 percent above inflation per year. This will progressively reduce the number of weapons that can be deployed and provide extra incentives for arms control. The economic costs of a military-political world are not its only defects; political costs are also rising. In Western states there has been a growing revulsion against fighting in overseas wars that are not quick and decisive. Ever since World War I and particularly since World War II, the political costs of military service have been increasing. Patriotism has been a fluctuating asset and one which declines with the length and indecisiveness of war. Political and international limits on conventional conflicts, dictating that they not violate nearby frontiers, have limited the scope, but probably increased the length of engagements. The results have typically been inconclusive, reflecting the political stamina of respective opponents. Often the same conflicts break out again and again. Futile wars have not inspired the loyalty of those who are forced to fight in them; only short, dynamic, and successful conflicts command approval and support.

The decline of military loyalty is also a product of political ineffectiveness and uncertainty. In an environment of growing interdependence, modern governments have been unable to fulfill the demands of their populations for economic welfare, security, and peace; domestic alienation has grown. Tax revolts have fed on governmental inefficiency and bureaucracy. If the government cannot provide for their needs with tax revenues, the people prefer to keep the money. In many countries, informed citizens resent military appropriations of billions per year, believing that such expenditures only feed the arms race as the opponent is forced to respond in kind. The security dilemma—where a defensive protection for one state means greater offensive power against another—suggests that more expenditure may actually mean less security. Western political support for arms reduction has grown greatly.

The pervasiveness of interdependence has another effect. As late as the 1930s, it was still possible for nations to calculate that they had a reasonable chance of seizing and holding by force territories containing needed raw materials and markets. In Japan's intervention in China in the 1930s she sought to conquer a vast market for her goods. This invasion was doomed to failure because she could never absorb China ethnically, politically, or militarily. But her move into Southeast Asia held some hope of success so long as the United States stayed out of the war. Hitler's drive into East Europe might have succeeded if he had not invaded the Soviet Union as well. In Rumania and Poland he sought the oil and coal that would enable Germany to ride out a long war with the Western powers. Except for the Soviet Union such ambitions are now beyond the reach of any major industrial nation. At present it is much easier to obtain needed access to raw materials and markets through trade than to try to control them territorially by force.

The defects of the military-political world do not stem only from its inherent weaknesses but also from the counterattractions of the trading world. However, despite its benefits, the trading strategy may not be elected by major and minor powers. Russia and to some degree the United States remain wedded to the older orientation. Borrowing precedents in the seventeenth and eighteenth centuries, Russia has westernized but has cut herself off from any significant dependence upon trade with European countries and the United States. . . .

In the past the military-political world was efficient. It was cheaper to seize another state's territory by force than to develop the sophisticated economic and trading apparatus needed to derive benefit from commercial exchange with it. Nomads and barbarians proved that lesser-developed nations could, by honing their military skills, defeat better-developed states and economies. Force made up the disadvantage and allowed peripheral nations to seize the benefits of Western economic systems. Rome gave way to the barbarian tribes on its borders. The trading world of the Mediterranean was interrupted once by Islam and again by the rise of the Ottoman Turks. Portugal's new naval skills allowed her to intercept Eastern Mediterranean trade at its source, and undercut the link between Venice and India. In their incursions into North Italy, France and Austria, the Hapsburgs hoped to seize the most developed and civilized region of Europe. Throughout history the excessive brightness of a civilization nearing sunset has tempted aggressors to seize what they could not emulate. In a similiar way Western civilization has afforded a constant temptation to the Russians.

In one of those reversals to which history is prone, however, the pathway of aggression is no longer smooth. Western or Eastern riches do not lie at the feet of any organized power with fleets or horsemen. At least since the seventeenth century, economic development and cultural advancement have been associated with military power, and, as the record of imperialism shows, the better-developed initially subdued the lesser-developed regions of world politics. In the later twentieth century, the balance has become more even: Western weapons and technology have confronted Eastern numbers and ideological zeal. Where both sides have access to modern weapons, staying power decides the outcome. The very arms race has itself complicated the seizure of new territory, for arms are now readily available in world markets, and defenders have as much access to them as aggressors. Both sides may spend more, but the result is still indecisive. The costs of the military-political world are not likely to decrease, and they may increase further. The trade-off between military-political and trading worlds will be more significant because the particular nations that might choose one can always choose the other. The great economic nations will have military choices. The great military nations will have trading choices.

Such decisions are also influenced by changes in domestic politics. As wars have become more difficult and costly to win, domestic support for such wars has declined. The size of the state may have peaked in 1914, but domestic cohesion and support for state policy continued to grow spasmodically until the 1930s, when it reached its coercive apogee with the National Socialist regime of Adolf Hitler. For a time it appeared that World War II might have provided a different lesson in the exemplary fighting of the "good war." But the campaigns afterward were neither so morally unambiguous nor decisive. The result was that citizens in democratic countries came to resent and oppose them. Wars had to be short and decisive like the Falklands or Grenada to gain approval. . . . Even the Soviet Union and the internal system of Communist repression have not solved the problem of popular laxity, indifference, and lack of support. Such trends do not increase the benefits or reduce the costs of the military-political system.

Since 1945 the world has been paralyzed between trading and territorial imperatives. One group of states has largely focused on trade, keeping their military expenditures limited; another group, particularly the superpowers and certain Middle Eastern states, has engaged in arms races, military interventions, and occasional war. If the balance starts to tip, the world could slide all the way to the military-political and territorial pole. Weak states in Africa, Southeast Asia, or the Middle East could then fall prey to successful military powers allied to one of the superpowers or to one of the two giants themselves. Successful aggression by one group of nations would call for counteraction by the other, and the globe could then be plunged into another period of massive conflict. The onset of a sudden world depression causing nations to clamp on trade restrictions could lead some to think in terms of military remedies to their economic problems. An intensification of the world debt and financial crisis could precipitate such an economic collapse and trigger, as it did in the 1930s, a resurgence of military expansion. But such an outcome is not foredestined. The very success of economic and trading nations might serve as a beacon to those who had traditionally pursued their great power callings through military rivalries, arms races, and nuclear crisis. In time it might even be possible to bring the superpowers to mitigate their rivalry in military-political terms and to express it through peaceful economic competition. The trading world would then have transformed international politics. Which strategy will be dominant cannot presently be predicted, but if history is any guide, indecision and ambivalence is unlikely to endure. After the 1870s the territorial system reasserted itself against the British trading system, as it did later in the 1930s. Unless critical great powers agree to contend their struggles in different terms, such a transformation is possible once again.

# 3

# THE FUTURE OF MILITARY POWER: THE CONTINUING UTILITY OF FORCE

Eliot A. Cohen

**This essay questions the proposition that military force has lost its utility in contemporary world politics. Challenging three core arguments about the diminishing importance of force in world politics, Eliot A. Cohen suggests why "war, and potential war, will remain a feature of international politics," and why, accordingly, military force will retain its importance in the post–Cold War era of destructive weapons and burgeoning democracies. This thesis is supported by examples drawn from the events and experiences since World War II, and especially in the 1980s and early 1990s. The author of many publications on military issues and American foreign policy, Cohen is professor of strategic studies at the Nitze School of Advanced International Studies, Johns Hopkins University. His most recent book, co-authored with John Gouch, is *Military Misfortunes: The Anatomy of Failure in War* (1990).**

What direction should . . . strategy take? Indeed, does it have a future at all, or has the end of the Cold War and the apparent triumph of liberal democracy and capitalism in Eastern Europe rendered it obsolete? If the need for strategy—defined as the preparation and use of military power for the ends of policy—does persist, how should [the West] prepare . . . to meet the challenges of the last decade of this century? . . .

The revolutions of 1989 have by no means ended, but surely enough has occurred to make it obvious that international politics has undergone an epochal

Used by permission of Eliot A. Cohen.

change. The Soviet empire has collapsed. The Kremlin has allowed its Eastern European glacis to crumble away even as the forces of dissent and hatred undermine the USSR itself. The multiple crises of the Soviet Union reinforce each other. Although by a combination of statecraft and luck the Soviet Union may survive, it is equally likely that it will fragment into a loose federation of independent republics or even collapse altogether.

For over forty years [Western] strategy and defense planning has focused on the Soviet threat. That threat is disintegrating, and Soviet military power is undergoing a long-term and irreversible reduction. If so, one must ask where [Western] defense planning should concentrate its attention henceforth, and how it should adapt to new challenges. Such a mammoth practical and conceptual task would be complex enough in any circumstances. It is made more difficult, however, by a variety of arguments to the effect that military force is no longer an important factor in world politics, that traditional considerations of *Machtpolitik* will lose or have lost their primacy; that force, in other words, is finished.

A lively debate has already occurred . . . on this latter point, focusing on Francis Fukuyama's audacious argument that history has come to, or is coming to, an end. Others have advanced similar arguments for the obsolescence of force. Even an analyst of such impeccably hawkish credentials as Edward Luttwak has put forth the proposition that the "methods of commerce are displacing military methods," and that the "decay of the military grammar of geopolitics" is a central fact of contemporary international politics.[1] On the whole, those who argue that military force is becoming less important appeared to be gaining the day, at least until the invasion of Kuwait by Iraq. This debate, however, transcends the jolt delivered by Saddam Hussein, and merits examination on its own terms. In the unlikely event of a peaceful solution in the Persian Gulf, it will reemerge; in the case of war, many will choose to see the Kuwaiti episode as a staggering error made by a dictator at odds with the deeper forces of his time.

There are three core arguments for the dwindling importance of force in international politics. First, it is maintained that the development of the techniques of warfare has made military power increasingly unappealing as a tool of international politics; or, more extreme, that modern weapons have made military power *unusable* for purposes of foreign policy. Nuclear weapons create the kind of stalemate that perversely but blessedly created the long peace of the

---

[1]Fukuyama's essay, "The End of History?" appeared in *The National Interest,* no. 16 (Summer 1989). Responses to it in that issue and the next, most notably Samuel P. Huntington, "No Exit: The Errors of Endism" in the Fall 1989 issue, cover some of the same ground that are dealt with here, but with a rather different focus. See also John Mueller, *Retreat From Doomsday: The Obsolescence of Major War* (New York: Basic Books, 1989). Fred C. Iklé, "The Ghost in the Pentagon," *The National Interest,* no. 19 (Spring 1990), also deals with some of the issues covered in this essay. Edward Luttwak's "From Geopolitics to Geo-Economics" appeared in *The National Interest,* no. 20 (Summer 1990).

Cold War; chemical weapons serve as the poor man's atomic bomb; conventional weaponry including such modern refinements as cluster bombs, fuel-air explosives, and multiple rocket launchers make even that form of conflict too difficult to control. Not man's virtue, but his diabolical ingenuity in creating engines of destruction, has brought peace. Or has it?

Nuclear weapons probably—one cannot be certain about events that did not happen—prevented an all-out U.S.-Soviet war. But nuclear weapons have most assuredly not prevented the launching of wars, some quite large, against nuclear-armed states. The North Koreans and Chinese in the Korean War, the Vietnamese Communists in the Indochina War, the Arabs in the Yom Kippur War, and the Argentines in the Falklands War did not let their opponents' nuclear weapons stop them from using a great deal of force to secure their political objectives. Vast disproportions in firepower attributable to nuclear weapons did not prevent the Vietnamese from fighting a bitter frontier war with China, Afghan mountaineers from harassing Soviet invaders, or Palestinian and Shiite terrorists from raiding Israeli border settlements. And the real or potential existence of nuclear weapons has come very close to *inducing* warfare, as indicated by Soviet feelers about preventive war against China in the Nixon administration and the Israeli raid on the Iraqi Osirak reactor. Nuclear weapons exercise certain kinds of inhibiting effects on conflict, but in other cases they may provoke it—would the United States, indeed *should* the United States stand idly by if Muammar Qaddafi were to acquire an atomic bomb?

In other cases, nuclear weapons clearly do not prevent warfare, although they may set certain limits to it. It would be a terrible mistake to think that the elaborate and arid logic of nuclear deterrence that operated between the superpowers will continue to hold elsewhere. The U.S.-Soviet confrontation took place between a stable, pacific, and contented democracy and a highly rational, cautious dictatorship that found nothing inherently shameful about retreating in the face of superior force. It was, in many ways, an ideal opposition, and one highly unlikely to be repeated.

Are chemical weapons the equivalent of nuclear weapons in their deterrent effects? One should not overdo the comparison, either in terms of destructiveness (bad weather can drastically reduce the impact of a chemical attack) or psychology. After Hiroshima and Nagasaki there was an altogether healthy taboo on the use of nuclear weapons, which we should attempt to preserve. Chemical weapons, in contrast, were used repeatedly during World War I and on many occasions since, including, it appears, in Southeast Asia. The Iraqi use of chemicals in the war with Iran was particularly chilling: chemical weapons were used openly and successfully (in both the tactical and strategic senses). No international sanctions followed their use. (Indeed, in that conflict the United States tilted toward the side that had used them.) Probably the day will come when the civilized nations will regret their failure to punish those who used such weapons. For we may be entering an age in which chemical weapons are used by more parties rather than fewer.

Has conventional conflict become so terrible that man cannot wage it? The view has been pressed so many times in the past—from Ivan Bloch's dire predictions before 1914 of the slaughter that would ensue, to the terrifying predictions of annihilation through aerial bombardment in the interwar period—that a certain skepticism is warranted. Some modern weapons—highly precise long-range cruise missiles for example—appear to make violence more controllable. And other modern weapons contribute to the persistence of war, because they give the underdog a fighting chance. The Soviets discovered this unpleasant fact in battles with Afghan tribesmen who, despite their poverty and rudimentary educations, managed to master the use of Stinger missiles in a few weeks. Certain kinds of conventional weapons are now much easier to acquire than ever before, since Chilean, Chinese, and South African suppliers, among many others, ask few embarrassing questions about the uses of their cluster bombs, ballistic missiles, and long-range artillery.

What is almost certain is that we are entering a period of technological change in warfare so dramatic that it justifies the Soviet description: "the revolution in military affairs," a term they have applied to the invention of nuclear weapons, and before that, the advent of the tank and airplane. It is a revolution brought about by a host of technologies, particularly those involving information processing. Although the Soviets have thought through some of its implications, neither they nor we can claim fully to understand it. What this means, however, is that war will take very different forms than it did in the past, not that it will cease to exist.

In the past, changes in technology and in politics drastically altered the destructiveness of war (compare the wars of religion in the seventeenth century with those of kings in the eighteenth and those of nations in the nineteenth). Similar changes may be expected in the future, but the essence of war—armed conflict between political entities—will not become impossible. In his *Memoirs: Fifty Years of Political Reflections,* Raymond Aron observes that "our century, in fact, presents simultaneously the most varied forms of combat, from the terrorist act to carpet bombing—war has never been so polymorphous, it has never been so omnipresent." The ambush in a Kashmiri village, the terrorist outrage in a London office building, the stone-throwing of masked youths in a West Bank village—these are battles in larger campaigns every bit as much as the set piece engagements of the battle for the Faw Peninsula in Iraq or the siege of Cuito Cuanavale in Angola.

The technological arguments for the obsolescence of war are thus either flimsy or partial. A more persuasive case is made by those who point to the spread of free enterprise and liberal democracy, and the death of communism. They rightly scoff at those who contend that in principle the United States and Canada, newly-united Germany, and France will be potential military opponents once the overarching fear of the USSR has vanished. Small-scale fighting may go on in obscure corners of the world, they argue, but the advanced, secure, and liberal democracies of North America, Europe, and Australia will never contemplate armed conflict with each other. As liberal regimes spread, so too will the zone of peace. Meanwhile, the overwhelming preponderance of military power residing in the free world, and its irrelevance to political and economic disputes within that world, will debase traditional strategy to only marginal importance.

But the argument for peace through democracy needs to be qualified in many ways. It was, after all, the democratization of conflict in the nineteenth century that restored a ferocity to warfare unknown since the seventeenth century; the bloodiest war in American history remains the one fought between two (by today's standards flawed) democracies—the Civil War. Concentration camps appeared during another conflict between two limited democracies, the Boer War. World War I was launched by two regimes—Wilhelmine Germany and Austria-Hungary—that had greater representation and more equitable legal systems than those of many important states today. And even when modern liberal democracies go to war they do not necessarily moderate the scope of the violence they apply; indeed, sensitivity to their own casualties sometimes leads to profligate uses of firepower or violent efforts to end wars quickly. Shaky democracies fight each other all the time. [In the spring of 1990] India and Pakistan came close, once again, to open warfare. We must remind ourselves just how peculiar the wealthy and secure democracies of the West are, how painful their evolution to stability and the horror of war with each other has been. Perhaps other countries will find short-cuts to those conditions, but it would be foolish to assume they will.

Moreover, although at the moment Western-style liberal democracy appears to be the most appealing form of government, we should not be complacent about its durability, especially where it is newly established. Will its global popularity withstand major economic setbacks, or even a prolonged failure to deliver the goods to developing nations eager to reach European, Japanese, and American standards of living? George Orwell observed in 1940:

> Nearly all Western thought since the last war, certainly all "progressive" thought, has assumed tacitly that human beings desire nothing beyond ease, security and avoidance of pain. . . . Hitler, because in his own joyless mind he feels it with exceptional strength, knows that human beings *don't* only want comfort, safety, short working-hours, hygiene, birth-control, and, in general, common sense; they also, at least intermittently, want struggle and self-sacrifice, not to mention drums, flags and loyalty parades. . . . Whereas socialism, and even capitalism in a more grudging way, have said to people "I offer you a good time," Hitler has said to them "I offer you struggle, danger and death," and as a result, a whole nation flings itself at his feet.[2]

---

[2]George Orwell, "Review of *Mein Kampf* by Adolf Hitler," in Sonia Orwell and Ian Angus, ed., *The Collected Essays, Journalism and Letters of George Orwell, Vol. II, My Country Right or Left, 1940–1943* (New York: Harcourt Brace Jovanovich, 1968), p. 14. Orwell noted that "Perhaps later on they will get sick of it and change their minds, as at the end of the last war. After a few years of slaughter and starvation 'greatest happiness of the greatest number' is a good slogan, but at this moment 'better an end with horror than a horror without end' is a winner."

Can we disregard this entirely as a relic of far off times? Saddam Hussein's seizure of Kuwait [in 1990] initially made him more popular at home, not less. The "end of history" argument, intriguing though it is, has many flaws. One may sum up one critique of it by noting how much of its plausibility hinges on one's view of Auschwitz. If one believes that the mad slaughter of the Holocaust was merely a horrible blip in man's general progress to consumerism, one may accept the argument. If, however, one sees in Hitler's war proof that anything is possible, that history is not linear, and that evil, including the evil that breeds civilization-shattering wars, is a permanent part of man's makeup, one cannot think that history is at an end or ending.

Liberal democracy gained victory in the Cold War by showing a persistence and a courage that many did not expect, and by delivering a prosperity that few could have imagined a half century ago. But the collapse of the Soviet empire owes as much, and perhaps more, to the fundamental hollowness and self-destructive nature of Marxism-Leninism. But other ideologies, as yet dimly fore-seen, may pose threats equivalent to those of communism in its heyday, as may organized religions. Secular Western intellectuals, themselves immune to reli-gious passion, may underestimate the power such beliefs exert not only on back-ward cobblers and peasant farmers, but on computer programmers, engineers, professors, and generals.

Furthermore, democracy may come under assault from wholly novel angles of attack. Are we certain, for instance, that the biological bases of liberal democ-racy, which assume equality and free will, will remain secure? If it becomes possible, as it well might, to breed men and women as easily as cattle are now bred, can we be quite certain that no one will exploit such awful possibilities for political purposes? "The present nature of man is tough and resilient. It casts up its sparks of genius in the darkest and most unexpected places." Thus wrote Churchill as he wondered about this very question in a prescient essay entitled "Fifty Years Hence" (in *Amid These Storms*). But suppose, he asked, a political elite could alter that nature in the laboratory? How will democra-cies adapt to the possibility that, despite Jefferson's famous dictum, some men may indeed be born with spurs on their feet, and others with saddles on their backs?

A third and final argument for the obsolescence of force comes from the rise of global economic interdependence, and the general (or rather purported) decline in the autonomy and importance of the nation-state. Here again, an awareness of history inclines one to skepticism: Norman Angell traced this kind of interdependence before World War I and proclaimed that it made war impos-sible. In the 1970s a band of academic theorists put forward the same arguments, which crumbled in the face of wars in the Middle East and Soviet-supported conflicts in Africa and Asia. Of course, the case should not be overstated: "geo-economics," as Edward Luttwak terms it, *is* of rising importance, and so too are such novel problems as those of environmental pollution.

But just as it would be foolish to ignore the emergence of new transnational forces and agencies on the one hand, and difficult global problems on the other, it would be wrong to succumb to the fallacy of interpreting all international developments as portents of global peace. Political entities fight wars; indeed, it is the political character of warfare that distinguishes it from the violence of organized crime. War can do quite well in the absence of nation-states: empires, city-states, confederations, and aspiring subnational groups have all used warfare to preserve or aggrandize themselves. And as the Crown Prince of Jordan . . . warned [in 1990], we may see greater conflict because of the attempt to break up nation-states. Certainly, the crack-up of empires is rarely peaceful, and we stand on the verge of the dissolution of the world's greatest continental empire, the Soviet Union. The fissiparous tendencies of modern ethnic strife—in the USSR, Yugoslavia, Ethiopia, South Asia, and Lebanon—carry an implicit threat of violence. International institutions such as the European Community may breed peace, although the rise of the EC is surely as much a consequence of peace as a cause of it. In any case, the EC is the exception, not the rule: other organizations such as ASEAN, the OAU, and the OAS have not had anything like the vigor of the European Community.

It is unlikely that new collective security arrangements—directed not against a potential enemy but against any and all potential aggressors—can replace the traditional forms of armament and alliances. The history of such pacts, and most notably of the League of Nations, is that they simply do not work. When the crunch comes, states either cannot agree on the definition of aggression, do not find it in their interests to oppose the aggressor, or simply do not have the stomach to use force. Collective security pacts therefore become marginal talking shops (which is all the Conference on Security and Cooperation in Europe, for example, can ever be) or they scare off potential members. If the U.S. Senate, for instance, thought that by ratifying a treaty it would commit the country to military intervention in a border war between Hungary and Romania, say, would it ever go along with such a notion?

All three arguments for an era of peace—the horrific quality of modern military technology, the spread of democracy, and the rise of transnational issues and actors—contain important truths. But neither separately nor together do they warrant a general conclusion that military power is becoming obsolete, or that war will not be used by states and other political groups. The causes of war remain as they were described by Thucydides, namely fear, ambition, and the desire for gain. It is only appropriate to celebrate the spread of freedom in and the waning of the threat from the East. But it would be well to temper our optimism with Alexander Hamilton's unsparing assessment of human affairs. In the *Federalist Papers* No. 6, he warned those who would believe in the "paradox of perpetual peace" that men are "ambitious, vindictive, and rapacious." "Momentary passions, and immediate interests," he argued, "have a more active and imperious control over human conduct than general or remote considerations of policy, utility, or justice." And democratic governments are not immune from such drives. They too are "subject to the impulses of rage, resentment, jealousy, avarice, and other irregular and violent propensities."

Senator Alan Simpson likes to tell a story of Senator Robert Dole's June 1990 trip to Iraq. Dole, who had been wounded in World War II, told the Iraqi dictator Saddam Hussein:

> "I've never spoken personally like this, but do you see this arm?" and he gestured with his withered right arm. "I have this daily reminder of the futility of war," he said. "That's why we're here." Even the Iraqi leader sat in stunned silence, Simpson said.[3]

Dole had expressed a profoundly untrue piety of contemporary politics. [At the time it was plausible to speculate that] Saddam's "stunned silence" reflected an awareness that Dole had, in fact, fought in the *least* futile war of the twentieth century. But [since then it became clear] that a victorious warlord who routinely (and on occasion, it is said, personally) executes political opponents would find it impossible to take seriously a senior statesman in the world's most powerful nation who thus dismissed the uses of force. And less than two months later, Saddam demonstrated his view of the utility of force (and opinion of American statesmanship) by one of the most blatant acts of aggression since the Munich crisis of 1938.

War, and potential war, will remain a feature of international politics. Its sources will be many and changing, from ethnic animosity to irredentism, from competition for power to religious fanaticism. Its stakes will include territory (including valuable off-shore properties), water rights, and control of populations. It will result from traditional kinds of animosities, but also from the second and third order consequences of developments that are intrinsically unforeseeable. Economic depression, for instance, need not breed violence directly, but it may, as in the 1930s, abet the development of new forms of tyranny, or increase the likelihood of the resort to violence by desperate countries.

The state system is undergoing its most dramatic changes since decolonization in the 1950s and 1960s. Entirely new states will probably break off the hulk of the Soviet empire, creating the potential for a civil war as widespread and disruptive as any the world has known. In other parts of the world—even in Canada—there is more splitting, and Balkanization characterizes world politics as much as unification. No one can foresee the consequences of this kind of fragmentation, but it is hard to believe that it will necessarily be peaceful. Just the reverse, in fact: border disputes, the flight of ethnic refugees, and desperate efforts to build or maintain large political aggregations do not look to have entirely peaceful consequences. Neither, for that matter, do such structural problems as massive demographic pressures in North Africa, or competition for water in the Middle East. . . .

[3]"Dole Puts Bitterness of '88 Race Aside to Carry Out Bush Agenda," *Washington Post,* June 11, 1990, p. A8.

# 4

# THE OBSOLESCENCE OF MAJOR WAR

### John Mueller

Observing the virtual absence of war between or among the great powers since World War II (alongside its continuation in the same period among the powerful and the weak in the Third World), John Mueller explores the various reasons why the probability of another major or general world war appears to have receded, and the consequences of the demise of the Cold War for this "imperfect" but prolonged postwar peace. A prolific writer on international affairs, Mueller has recently authored *Retreat from Doomsday* (1989). He is a professor of political science at the University of Rochester, where he serves as director of the Watson Center for the Study of International Peace and Cooperation.

In discussing the causes of international war, commentators have often found it useful to group theories into what they term levels of analysis. In his classic work, *Man, the State and War,* Kenneth N. Waltz organizes the theories according to whether the cause of war is found in the nature of man, in the nature of the state, or in the nature of the international state system. More recently Jack Levy, partly setting the issue of human nature to one side, organizes the theories

Used by permission of John Mueller. Some footnotes have been deleted, and others have been renumbered to appear in consecutive order.

41

according to whether they stress the systemic level, the nature of state and society, or the decisionmaking process.[1]

In various ways, these level-of-analysis approaches direct attention away from war itself and toward concerns which may influence the incidence of war. However, war should not be visualized as a sort of recurring outcome that is determined by other conditions, but rather as a phenomenon that has its own qualities and appeals. And over time these appeals can change. In this view, war is merely an idea, an institution, like dueling or slavery, that has been grafted onto human existence. Unlike breathing, eating, or sex, war is not something that is somehow required by the human condition, by the structure of international affairs, or by the forces of history.

Accordingly, war can shrivel up and disappear; and this may come about without any notable change or improvement on any of the level-of-analysis categories. Specifically, war can die out without changing human nature, without modifying the nature of the state or the nation-state, without changing the international system, without creating an effective world government or system of international law, and without improving the competence or moral capacity of political leaders. It can also go away without expanding international trade, interdependence, or communication; without fabricating an effective moral or practical equivalent; without enveloping the earth in democracy or prosperity; without devising ingenious agreements to restrict arms or the arms industry; without reducing the world's considerable store of hate, selfishness, nationalism, and racism; without increasing the amount of love, justice, harmony, cooperation, good will, or inner peace in the world; without establishing security communities; and without doing anything whatever about nuclear weapons.

Not only *can* such a development take place: it *has* been taking place for a century or more, at least within the developed world, once a cauldron of international and civil war. Conflicts of interest are inevitable and continue to persist within the developed world. But the notion that war should be used to resolve them has increasingly been discredited and abandoned there. War is apparently becoming obsolete, at least in the developed world: in an area where war was once often casually seen as beneficial, noble, and glorious, or at least as neces-

---

[1]Kenneth N. Waltz, *Man, the State and War* (New York: Columbia University Press, 1959); Jack S. Levy, "The Causes of War: A Review of Theories and Evidence," in Philip E. Tetlock, Jo L. Husbands, Robert Jervis, Paul C. Stern and Charles Tilly, eds., *Behavior, Society, and Nuclear War,* vol. 1 (New York: Oxford University Press, 1989), pp. 209–333. See also J. David Singer, "The Levels of Analysis Problem in International Relations," in Klaus Knorr and Sydney Verba, eds., *The International System* (Princeton, NJ: Princeton University Press, 1961), pp. 77–92; and James N. Rosenau, "Pretheories and Theories of Foreign Policy," in R. B. Farrell, ed., *Approaches to Comparative and International Politics* (Evanston, IL: Northwestern University Press, 1966), pp. 27–92.

sary or inevitable, the conviction has now become widespread that war would be intolerably costly, unwise, futile, and debased.[2]

Some of this may be suggested by the remarkable developments in the Cold War in the late 1980s. The dangers of a major war in the developed world clearly declined remarkably: yet this can hardly be attributed to an improvement in human nature, to the demise of the nation-state, to the rise of a world government, or to a notable improvement in the competence of political leaders.

## TWO ANALOGIES: DUELING AND SLAVERY

It may not be obvious that an accepted, time-honored institution which serves an urgent social purpose can become obsolescent and then die out because many people come to find it obnoxious. But the argument here is that something like that has indeed been happening to war in the developed world. To illustrate the dynamic, [consider] two analogies: the processes by which the once-perennial institutions of dueling and slavery have all but vanished from the face of the earth.

### Dueling

In some important respects, war in the developed world may be following the example of another violent method for settling disputes, dueling. Up until a century ago dueling was common practice in Europe and the USA among a certain class of young and youngish men who liked to classify themselves as gentlemen.[3] Men of the social set that once dueled still exist, they still get insulted, and they are still concerned about their self-respect and their standing among their peers. But they no longer duel. However, they do not avoid dueling today because they evaluate the option and reject it on cost-benefit grounds. Rather, the option never percolates into their consciousness as something that is available. That is, a form of violence famed and fabled for centuries has now sunk from thought as a viable, conscious possibility.

The Prussian strategist, Carl von Clausewitz, opens his famous 1832 book, *On War,* by observing that "War is nothing but a duel on a larger scale." If war, like dueling, comes to be viewed as a thoroughly undesirable, even ridiculous, policy, and if it can no longer promise gains, or if potential combatants come no

---

[2]For a further development of these arguments, see John Mueller, *Retreat from Doomsday: The Obsolescence of Major War* (New York: Basic Books, 1989).

[3]For other observations of the analogy between war and dueling, see Bernard Brodie, *War and Politics* (New York: Macmillan, 1973), p. 275; Norman Angell, *The Great Illusion* (London: Heinemann, 1914), pp. 202–203; G. P. Gooch, *History of Our Time, 1885–1911* (London: Williams & Norgate, 1911), p. 249; J. E. Cairnes, 'International Law', *Fortnightly Review,* vol. 2, 1 November 1865, p. 650 n.

longer to value the things it can gain for them, then war can fade away as a coherent possibility even if a truly viable substitute or "moral equivalent" for it were never formulated. Like dueling, it could become unfashionable and then obsolete.

## Slavery

From the dawn of prehistory until about 1788 slavery, like war, could be found just about everywhere in one form or another, and it flourished in every age. Around 1788, however, the anti-slavery forces began to argue that the institution was repulsive, immoral, and uncivilized: and this sentiment gradually picked up adherents. . . .

Thus the abolitionists were up against an institution that was viable, profitable, and expanding, and moreover one that had been uncritically accepted for thousands—perhaps millions—of years as a natural and inevitable part of human existence. To counter this powerful and time-honored institution, the abolitionists' principal weapon was a novel argument: it had recently occurred to them, they said, that slavery was no longer the way people ought to do things.

As it happened, this was an idea whose time had come. The abolition of slavery required legislative battles, international pressures, economic travail, and, in the United States, a cataclysmic war (but it did *not* require the fabrication of a functional equivalent or the formation of an effective supranational authority). Within a century slavery, and most similar institutions like serfdom, had been all but eradicated from the face of the globe. Slavery became controversial and then obsolete.

## War

Dueling and slavery no longer exist as effective institutions; they have largely faded from human experience except as something we read about in books. While their re-establishment is not impossible, they show after a century of neglect no signs of revival. Other once-popular, even once-admirable, institutions in the developed world have been, or are being, eliminated because at some point they began to seem repulsive, immoral, and uncivilized: bearbaiting, bareknuckle fighting, freak shows, casual torture, wanton cruelty to animals, burning heretics, flogging, vendetta, deforming corsetting, laughing at the insane, the death penalty for minor crimes, eunuchism, public cigarette smoking.

War may well be in the process of joining this list of recently-discovered sins and vices. War is not, of course, the same as dueling or slavery. Like war, dueling is an institution for settling disputes; but it was something of a social affectation and it usually involved only matters of "honor," not ones of physical gain. Like war, slavery was nearly universal and an apparently inevitable part of human existence, but it could be eliminated area by area: a country that abolished slavery did not have to worry about what other countries were doing, while a country that would like to abolish war must continue to be concerned about those that have kept it in their repertory.

On the other hand, war has against it not only substantial psychic costs, but also obvious and widespread physical ones. Dueling brought death and destruction but, at least in the first instance, only to a few people who had specifically volunteered to participate. And while slavery may have brought moral destruction, it generally was a considerable economic success.

In some respects then, the fact that war has outlived dueling and slavery is curious. But there are signs that, at least in the developed world, it too has begun to succumb to obsolescence.

## TRENDS AGAINST WAR BEFORE 1914

There were a number of trends away from war in the developed world before World War I. Two of these deserve special emphasis.

### The Hollandization Phenomenon

As early as 1800 a few once-warlike countries in Europe, like Holland, Switzerland, and Sweden, quietly began to drop out of the war system. While war was still generally accepted as a natural and inevitable phenomenon, these countries found solace (and prosperity) in policies that stressed peace. People who argue that war is inherent in nature and those who see war as a recurring, cyclic phenomenon need to supply an explanation for these countries. Switzerland, for example, has avoided all international war for nearly 200 years. If war is inherent in human nature or if war is some sort of cyclic inevitability, surely the Swiss ought to be roaring for a fight by now.

### The Rise of an Organized Peace Movement

While there have been individual war opponents throughout history, the existence of organized groups devoted to abolishing war from the human condition is quite new. The institution of war came under truly organized and concentrated attack only after 1815, and this peace movement did not develop real momentum until the end of the century. . . .

Peace advocates were a noisy gadfly minority by 1900, and they had established a sense of momentum. Their arguments were inescapable, but, for the most part they were rejected and derided by the majority which still held to the traditional view that war was noble, natural, thrilling, progressive, manly, redemptive, and beneficial. Up until 1914, as Michael Howard has observed, war "was almost universally considered an acceptable, perhaps an inevitable and for many people a desirable way of settling international differences."

## THE IMPACT OF WORLD WAR I

The holocaust of World War I turned peace advocates into a pronounced majority in the developed world and destroyed war romanticism. As Arnold Toynbee points out, this war marked the end of a "span of five thousand years during which war had been one of mankind's master institutions." Or, as Evan Luard observes, 'the First World War transformed traditional attitudes toward war. For the first time there was an almost universal sense that the deliberate launching of a war could now no longer be justified.'

World War I was, of course, horrible. But horror was not invented in 1914. History had already had its Carthages, its Jerichos, its wars of 30 years, of 100 years. Seen in historic context, in fact, World War I does not seem to have been all that unusual in its duration, destructiveness, grimness, political pointlessness, economic consequences, breadth, or intensity. However, it does seem to be unique in that it was the first major war to be preceded by substantial, organized anti-war agitation, and in that, for Europeans, it followed an unprecedentedly peaceful century during which Europeans had begun, perhaps unknowingly, to appreciate the virtues of peace.[4]

Obviously, this change of attitude was not enough to prevent the wars that have taken place since 1918. But the notion that the institution of war, particularly war in the developed world, was repulsive, uncivilized, immoral, and futile—voiced only by minorities before 1914—was an idea whose time had come. It is one that has permeated most of the developed world ever since.

## WORLD WAR II

It is possible that enough war spirit still lingered, particularly in Germany, for another war in Europe to be necessary to extinguish it there. But analysis of opinion in the interwar period suggests that war was viewed with about as much horror in Germany as any place on the continent. To a remarkable degree, major war returned to Europe only because of the astoundingly successful machinations of Adolf Hitler, virtually the last European who was willing to risk major war. As Gerhard Weinberg has put it: "Whether any other German leader would indeed have taken the plunge is surely doubtful, and the very warnings Hitler received from some of his generals can only have reinforced his belief in his personal role as the one man able, willing, and even eager to lead Germany and drag the world into war." That is, after World War I a war in Europe could only be brought about through the maniacally dedicated manipulations of an exceptionally lucky and spectacularly skilled entrepreneur; before World War I, any dimwit—e.g. Kaiser Wilhelm—could get into one.

---

[4]For a further development of this argument, see John Mueller, "Changing Attitudes Toward War: The Impact of World War I," *British Journal of Political Science,* forthcoming.

The war in Asia was, of course, developed out of the expansionary policies of distant Japan, a country which neither participated substantially in World War I nor learned its lessons. In World War II, Japan got the message most Europeans had received from World War I.

## THE COLD WAR, THE LONG PEACE, AND NUCLEAR WEAPONS

Since 1945 major war has been most likely to develop from the Cold War that has dominated postwar international history. The hostility of the era mostly derives from the Soviet Union's ideological—even romantic—affection for revolution and for revolutionary war. While this ideology is expansionistic in some respects, it has never visualized major war in the Hitler mode as a remotely sensible tactic.

East and West have never been close to major war, and it seems unlikely that nuclear weapons have been important determinants of this—insofar as a military deterrent has been necessary, the fear of escalation to a war like World War I or II supplies it. Even allowing considerably for stupidity, ineptness, miscalculation, and self-deception, a large war, nuclear or otherwise, has never been remotely in the interest of the essentially-contented, risk-averse, escalation-anticipating countries that have dominated world affairs since 1945. This is not to deny that nuclear war is appalling to contemplate and mind-concentratingly dramatic, particularly in the speed with which it could bring about massive destruction. Nor is it to deny that decisionmakers, both in times of crisis and in times of non-crisis, are well aware of how cataclysmic a nuclear war could be. It is simply to stress that the horror of repeating World War II is not all that much less impressive or dramatic, and that leaders essentially content with the status quo will strive to avoid anything that they feel could lead to either calamity. A jump from a fiftieth-floor window is probably quite a bit more horrible to contemplate than a jump from a fifth-floor one, but anyone who finds life even minimally satisfying is extremely unlikely to do either.[5]

In general the wars that have involved developed countries since World War II have been of two kinds, both of them declining in frequency and relevance. One of these concerns lingering colonial responsibilities and readjustments. Thus the Dutch got involved in (but did not start) a war in Indonesia, the French in Indochina and Algeria, the British in Malaya and the Falklands.

The other kind relates to the Cold War contest between East and West. The communists have generally sought to avoid major war, not so much because they necessarily find such wars to be immoral, repulsive, or uncivilized, but

---

[5]For a further development of this argument, see John Mueller, "The Essential Irrelevance of Nuclear Weapons: Stability in the Postwar World," *International Security*, vol. 13, no. 2, Fall 1988, pp. 55–79.

because they find them futile—dangerous, potentially counter-productive, wildly and absurdly adventurous. However, for decades after 1945 they retained a dutiful affection for what they came to call wars of national liberation—smaller wars around the world designed to further the progressive cause of world revolution. The West has seen this threat as visceral and as one that must be countered even at the cost of war if necessary. Wars fought in this context, such as those in Korea and Vietnam, have essentially been seen to be preventive—if communism is countered there, it will not have to be countered later, on more vital, closer turf.

The lesson learned (perhaps overlearned) from the Hitler experience is that aggressive threats must be dealt with by those who abhor war when the threats are still comparatively small and distant; to allow the aggressive force to succeed only brings nearer the day when a larger war must be fought. Thus some countries which abhor war have felt it necessary to wage them in order to prevent wider wars.

## CONSEQUENCES OF THE DEMISE OF THE COLD WAR

Because of economic crisis and persistent ideological failure, it now appears that the Cold War has ended as the Soviet Union, following the lead of its former ideological soulmate, China, abandons its quest for ideological expansion, questing instead after prosperity and a quiet, normal international situation. Unless some new form of conflict emerges, war participation by developed countries is likely to continue its decline.

As tensions lapse between the two sides in what used to be known as the Cold War, there is a natural tendency for the arms that backed that tension, and in a sense measured it, to atrophy. Both sides have begun what might be called a negative arms race. Formal arms negotiations will probably be only slow and pedantify this natural process, and might best be abandoned at this point. It may also be time to confederate the East–West alliances (rather than allowing them to fragment) with the combined organization serving to regulate the remarkable changes going on in Europe.[6]

The demise of the Cold War should also facilitate further expansion of international trade and interdependence. Trade and interdependence may not lead inexorably to peace, but peace does seem to lead to trade, interdependence, and economic growth—or, at any rate, it facilitates them. That is, peace ought to be seen not as a dependent but rather as an independent variable in such considerations. The 1992 economic unity of Europe and the building of a long-envisioned Channel tunnel are the consequences of peace, not its cause.

Left alone, enterprising business people will naturally explore the possibilities of investing in other countries or selling their products there. Averse to dis-

---

[6]On these two policy proposals, see John Mueller, "A New Concert of Europe," *Foreign Policy,* Winter 1989–90, pp. 3–16.

astrous surprises, they are more likely to invest if they are confident that peace will prevail. But for trade to flourish, governments must stay out of the way not only by eschewing war, but also by eschewing measures which unnaturally inhibit trade.

Furthermore, if nations no longer find it sensible to use force or the threat of force in their dealings with one another, it may be neither necessary nor particularly desirable to create an entrenched international government or police force (as opposed to ad hoc arrangements and devices designed to meet specific problems). Indeed, an effective international government could be detrimental to economic growth since, like domestic governments, it could be manipulated to reward the inefficient, coddle the incompetent, and plague the innovative.

## WAR IN THE THIRD WORLD

War has not, of course, become fully obsolete. While major war—war among developed countries—seems to be going out of style, war obviously continues to flourish elsewhere. The demise of the Cold War suggests that the United States and the Soviet Union, in particular, are likely to involve themselves less in these wars. Moreover, it is possible that the catastrophic Iran–Iraq war will sober people in the Third World about that kind of war. And it does seem that much of the romance has gone out of the concept of violent revolution as Third World countries increasingly turn to the drab, difficult, and unromantic task of economic development.

Thus it is possible that the developed world's aversion to war may eventually infect the rest of the world as well (international war, in fact, has been quite rare in Latin America for a century). But this development is not certain, nor is its pace predictable. As slavery continued to persist in Brazil even after it had been abolished elsewhere, the existence of war in some parts of the world does not refute the observation that it is vanishing, or has vanished, in other parts.

## IMPERFECT PEACE

War, even war within the developed world, has not become impossible—nor could it ever do so. When it has seemed necessary, even countries like the United States and Britain, which were among the first to become thoroughly disillusioned with war, have been able to fight wars and to use military force—often with high morale and substantial public support, at least at first. The ability to make war and the knowledge about how to do so can never be fully expunged—nor, for that matter, can the ability or knowledge to institute slavery, eunuchism, crucifixion, or human sacrifice. War is declining as an institution not because it has ceased to be possible or fascinating, but because peoples and leaders in the developed world—where war was once endemic—have increasingly found war to be disgusting, ridiculous, and unwise.

The view presented in this [chapter] is based upon the premise that, in some important respects, war is often taken too seriously. War, it seems, is merely an idea. It is not a trick of fate, a thunderbolt from hell, a natural calamity, or a desperate plot contrivance dreamed up by some sadistic puppeteer on high. If war begins in the minds of men, as the UNESCO charter insists, it can end there as well. Over the centuries, war opponents have been trying to bring this about by discrediting war as an idea; the argument here is that they have been substantially successful at doing so. The long peace since World War II is less a product of recent weaponry than the culmination of a substantial historical process. For the last two or three centuries, major war has gradually moved toward terminal disrepute because of its perceived repulsiveness and futility.

It could also be argued that, to a considerable degree, people have tended to take *peace* too seriously as well. Peace is merely what emerges when the institution of war is neglected. It does not mean that the world suddenly becomes immersed in those qualities with which the word "peace" is constantly being associated: love, justice, harmony, cooperation, brotherhood, good will. People still remain contentious and there still remain substantial conflicts of interest. The difference is only that they no longer resort to force to resolve their conflicts, any more than young men today resort to formal dueling to resolve their quarrels. A world at peace would not be perfect, but it would be notably better than the alternative.

# 5

# NUCLEAR MYTHS AND POLITICAL REALITIES

Kenneth N. Waltz

**In this essay, Kenneth N. Waltz theorizes about the role that nuclear weapons and the deterrence strategies and doctrines governing their use have played in preventing great-power conflicts from escalating to war. Contrasting the logic of conventional and nuclear weaponry and tracing the history of the doctrines the superpowers have constructed to govern their use, Waltz evaluates why the age of nuclear "overkill" may provide a better foundation for the prevention of war than that afforded by reliance on conventional weapons. Waltz is a professor in the department of political science at the University of California, Berkeley, and has served as president of the American Political Science Association. Author of *Man, the State and War* (1959) and *Theory of International Politics* (1979), he is well known for his writing on deterrence and international security affairs.**

Nuclear weapons have been given a bad name. . . . Uneasiness over nuclear weapons and the search for alternative means of security stem in large measure from widespread failure to understand the nature and requirements of deterrence. Not unexpectedly, the language of strategic discourse has deteriorated over the decades. This happens whenever discussion enters the political arena, where words take on meanings and colorations reflecting the preferences of their users.

From *The American Political Science Review* (September 1990); originally presented as the presidential address at the annual meeting of the American Political Science Association in Washington, D.C., 1988. Used by permission of Kenneth N. Waltz and the American Political Science Association.

Early in the nuclear era *deterrence* carried its dictionary definition, dissuading someone from an action by frightening that person with the consequences of the action. To deter an adversary from attacking one need have only a force that can survive a first strike and strike back hard enough to outweigh any gain the aggressor had hoped to realize. Deterrence in its pure form entails no ability to defend; a deterrent strategy promises not to fend off an aggressor but to damage or destroy things the aggressor holds dear. Both defense and deterrence are strategies that a status quo country may follow, hoping to dissuade a state from attacking. They are different strategies designed to accomplish a common end in different ways, using different weapons differently deployed. Wars can be prevented, as they can be caused, in various ways.

Deterrence antedates nuclear weapons, but in a conventional world deterrent threats are problematic. . . . Nuclear weapons purify deterrent strategies by removing elements of defense and war-fighting. Nuclear warheads eliminate the necessity of fighting and remove the possibility of defending, because only a small number of warheads need to reach their targets.

Ironically, as multiplication of missiles increased the ease with which destructive blows can be delivered, the distinction between deterrence and defense began to blur. Early in President Kennedy's administration, Secretary McNamara began to promote a strategy of Flexible Response, which was half-heartedly adopted by NATO in 1967. Flexible Response calls for the ability to meet threats at all levels from irregular warfare to conventional warfare to nuclear warfare. In the 1970s and 1980s more and more emphasis was placed on the need to fight and defend at all levels in order to "deter." The melding of defense, war-fighting, and deterrence overlooks a simple truth about nuclear weapons proclaimed in the title of a book edited by Bernard Brodie in 1946: Nuclear weapons are absolute. Nuclear weapons can carry out their deterrent task no matter what other countries do. If one nuclear power were able to destroy almost all of another's strategic warheads with practical certainty or defend against all but a few strategic warheads coming in, nuclear weapons would not be absolute. But because so much explosive power comes in such small packages, the invulnerability of a sufficient number of warheads is easy to achieve and the delivery of fairly large numbers of warheads impossible to thwart, both now and as far into the future as anyone can see. The absolute quality of nuclear weapons sharply sets a nuclear world off from a conventional one.

## WHAT DETERS?

Most discussions of deterrence are based on the belief that deterrence is difficult to achieve. In the Eisenhower years "massive retaliation" was the phrase popularly used to describe the response we would supposedly make to a Soviet Union attack. Deterrence must be difficult if the threat of massive retaliation is required to achieve it. As the Soviet Union's arsenal grew, MAD (mutual assured destruction) became the acronym of choice, thus preserving the notion that deterrence depends on being willing and able to destroy much, if not most, of a country.

That one must be able to destroy a country in order to deter it is an odd notion, though of distinguished lineage. During the 1950s emphasis was put on the *massive* in *massive retaliation.* Beginning in the 1960s the emphasis was put on the *assured destruction* in the doctrine of MAD. Thus viewed, deterrence becomes a monstrous policy, as innumerable critics have charged. One quotation can stand for many others. In a warning to NATO defense ministers that became famous, Henry Kissinger counseled the European allies not to keep "asking us to multiply strategic assurances that we cannot possibly mean or if we do mean, we should not want to execute because if we execute, we risk the destruction of civilization." . . . The notion that the failure of deterrence would lead to national suicide or to mutual annihilation betrays a misunderstanding of both political behavior and nuclear realities.

Introducing the Eisenhower administration's New Look policy in January of 1954, John Foster Dulles gave the impression that aggression anywhere would elicit heavy nuclear retaliation. Just three months later, he sensibly amended the policy. Nuclear deterrence, Dulles and many others quickly came to realize, works not against minor aggression at the periphery, but only against major aggression at the center, of international politics. Moreover, to deter major aggression, Dulles now said, "the probable hurt" need only "outbalance the probable gain." . . . Like Brodie before him, Dulles based deterrence on the principle of proportionality: "Let the punishment fit the crime."

What would we expect the United States to do if the Soviet Union launched a major conventional attack against vital U.S. interests—say, in Western Europe? Military actions have to be related to an objective. Because of the awesome power of nuclear weapons, the pressure to use them in ways that achieve the objective at hand while doing and suffering a minimum of destruction would be immense. It is preposterous to think that if a Soviet attack broke through NATO's defenses, the United States would strike thousands of Soviet military targets or hundreds of Soviet cities. Doing so would serve no purpose. Who would want to make a bad situation worse by launching wantonly destructive attacks on a country that can strike back with comparable force, or, for that matter, on a country that could not do so? In the event, we might strike a target or two—military or industrial—chosen to keep casualties low. If the Soviet Union had run the preposterous risk of attacking the center of Europe believing it could escape retaliation, we would thus show them that they were wrong while conveying the idea that more would follow if they persisted. Among countries with abundant nuclear weapons, none can gain an advantage by striking first. The purpose of demonstration shots is simply to remind everyone—should anyone forget—that catastrophe threatens. Some people purport to believe that if a few warheads go off, many will follow. This would seem to be the least likely of all the unlikely possibilities. That no country gains by destroying another's cities and then seeing a comparable number of its own destroyed in return is obvious to everyone.

Despite widespread beliefs to the contrary, deterrence does not depend on destroying cities. Deterrence depends on what one *can* do, not on what one *will* do. What deters is the fact that we can do as much damage to them as we choose, and they to us. The country suffering the retaliatory attack cannot limit the damage done to it; only the retaliator can do that.

With nuclear weapons, countries need threaten to use only a small amount of force. This is so because once the willingness to use a little force is shown, the adversary knows how easily more can be added. This is not true with conventional weapons. Therefore, it is often useful for a country to threaten to use great force if conflict should lead to war. The stance may be intended as a deterrent one, but the ability to carry the threat through is problematic. With conventional weapons, countries tend to emphasize the first phase of war. Striking hard to achieve a quick victory may decrease the cost of war. With nuclear weapons, political leaders worry not about what may happen in the first phase of fighting but about what may happen in the end. As Clausewitz wrote, if war should ever approach the absolute, it would become "imperative . . . not to take the first step without considering what may be the last. . . ."

Since war now approaches the absolute, it is hardly surprising that President Kennedy echoed Clausewitz's words during the Cuban Missile Crisis of 1962. "It isn't the first step that concerns me," he said, "but both sides escalating to the fourth and fifth step—and we don't go to the sixth because there is no one around to do so. . . ." In conventional crises, leaders may sensibly seek one advantage or another. They may bluff by threatening escalatory steps they are in fact unwilling to take. They may try one stratagem or another and run considerable risks. Since none of the parties to the struggle can predict what the outcome will be, they may have good reason to prolong crises, even crises entailing the risk of war. A conventional country enjoying military superiority is tempted to use it before other countries right the military balance. A nuclear country enjoying superiority is reluctant to use it because no one can promise the full success of a disarming first strike. As Henry Kissinger retrospectively said of the Cuban Missile Crisis, the Soviet Union had only "60–70 truly strategic weapons while we had something like 2,000 in missiles and bombs." But, he added, "with some proportion of Soviet delivery vehicles surviving, the Soviet Union could do horrendous damage to the United States." . . . In other words, we could not be sure that our two thousand weapons would destroy almost all of their sixty or seventy. Even with numbers immensely disproportionate, a small force strongly inhibits the use of a large one.

The catastrophe promised by nuclear war contrasts sharply with the extreme difficulty of predicting outcomes among conventional competitors. This makes one wonder about the claimed dependence of deterrence on perceptions and the alleged problem of credibility. In conventional competitions, the comparative qualities of troops, weaponry, strategies, and leaders are difficult to gauge. So complex is the fighting of wars with conventional weapons that their outcomes have been extremely difficult to predict. Wars start more easily because the uncertainties of their outcomes make it easier for the leaders of states to entertain illusions of victory at supportable cost. In contrast, contemplating war when the use of nuclear weapons is possible focuses one's attention not on the probability of victory but on the possibility of annihilation. Because catastrophic outcomes of nuclear exchanges are easy to imagine, leaders of states will shrink in horror from initiating them. With nuclear weapons, stability and peace rest on easy calculations of what one country can do to another. Anyone—political leader or man in the street—can see that catastrophe lurks if events spiral out of control and nuclear warheads begin to fly. The problem of the credibility of deterrence, a big worry in a conventional world, disappears in a nuclear one. . . .

## WHY NUCLEAR WEAPONS DOMINATE STRATEGY

Deterrence is easier to contrive than most strategists have believed. With conventional weapons, a number of strategies are available, strategies combining and deploying forces in different ways. Strategies may do more than weapons to determine the outcomes of wars. Nuclear weapons are different; they dominate strategies. As [Bernard Brodie] clearly saw, the effects of nuclear weapons derive not from any particular design for their employment in war but simply from their presence. . . . Indeed, in an important sense, nuclear weapons eliminate strategy. If one thinks of strategies as being designed for defending national objectives or for gaining them by military force and as implying a choice about how major wars will be fought, nuclear weapons make strategy obsolete. Nevertheless, the conviction that the only reliable deterrent force is one able to win a war or at least end up in a better position than the Soviet Union is widespread. . . .

NATO policy well illustrates the futility of trying to transcend deterrence by fashioning war-fighting strategies. The supposed difficulties of extending deterrence to cover major allies has led some to argue that we require nuclear superiority, that we need nuclear war-fighting capabilities, and that we must build up our conventional forces. Once the Soviet Union achieved nuclear parity, confidence in our extended deterrent declined in the West. One wonders whether it did in the East. Denis Healey once said that one chance in a hundred that a country will retaliate is enough to deter an adversary, although not enough to reassure an ally. Many have repeated his statement; but none, I believe, has added that reassuring allies is unnecessary militarily and unwise politically. Politically, allies who are unsure of one another's support have reason to work harder for the sake of their own security. Militarily, deterrence requires only that conventional forces be able to defend long enough to determine that an attack is a major one and not merely a foray. For this, a trip wire force as envisioned in the 1950s, with perhaps fifty thousand U.S. troops in Europe, would be sufficient. Beyond that, deterrence requires only that forces be invulnerable and that the area protected be of manifestly vital interest. West European countries can be counted on to maintain forces of trip wire capability.

Nuclear weapons strip conventional forces of most of their functions. Bernard Brodie pointed out that in "a total war" the army "might have no function at all." . . . Herman Kahn cited "the claim that in a thermonuclear war it is important to keep the sea lanes open" as an example of the "quaint ideas" still held by the military. . . . Conventional forces have only a narrow role in any confrontation between nuclear states over vital interests, since fighting beyond the trip wire level serves no useful purpose. Enlarging conventional capabilities does nothing to strengthen deterrence. Strategic stalemate does shift military competition to the tactical level. But one must add what is usually omitted: nuclear stalemate limits the use of conventional forces and reduces the extent of the gains one can seek without risking devastation. For decades U.S. policy has nevertheless aimed at raising the nuclear threshold in Europe. Stronger conventional forces would presumably enable NATO to sustain a longer war in Europe at higher levels of violence. At some moment in a major war, however, one side or the other—or perhaps both—would believe itself to be losing. The temptation to introduce nuclear weapons might then prove irresistible, and they would be fired in the chaos of defeat with little chance of limited and discriminant use. Early use would promise surer control and closer limitation of damage. In a nuclear world a conventional war-fighting strategy would appear to be the worst possible one, more dangerous than a strategy of relying on deterrence.

Attempts to gain escalation dominance, like efforts to raise the nuclear threshold, betray a failure to appreciate the strategic implications of nuclear weapons. Escalation dominance, so it is said, requires a "seamless web of capabilities" up and down "the escalation ladder." Earlier, it had been thought that the credibility of deterrence would be greater if some rungs of the escalation ladder were missing. The inability to fight at some levels would make the threat to use higher levels of force easy to credit. But again, since credibility is not a problem, this scarcely matters militarily. Filling in the missing rungs neither helps nor hurts. Escalation dominance is useful for countries contending with conventional weapons only. Dominance, however, is difficult to achieve in the absence of a decisive weapon. Among nuclear adversaries the question of dominance is pointless because one second-strike force cannot dominate another. Since strategic nuclear weapons will always prevail, the game of escalation dominance cannot be played. Everyone knows that anyone can quickly move to the top rung of the ladder. Because anyone can do so, all of the parties in a serious crisis have an overriding incentive to ask themselves one question: How can we get out of this mess without nuclear warheads exploding? Deescalation, not escalation, becomes the problem that the presence of nuclear weapons forces them to solve.

To gain escalation dominance, if that were imaginable, would require the ability to fight nuclear wars. War-fighting strategies imply that nuclear weapons are not absolute but relative, so that the country with more and better nuclear weapons could in some unspecified way prevail. No one, however, has shown how such a war could be fought. Indeed, Desmond Ball [in 1981] . . . argued that a nuclear war could not be sustained beyond the exchange of strategic warheads numbered not in the hundreds but in the tens. . . . After a small number of exchanges no one would know what was going on or be able to maintain control. Yet nuclear weapons save us from our folly: fanciful strategies are irrelevant because no one will run the appalling risk of testing them.

Deterrence has been faulted for its lack of credibility, its dependence on perceptions, its destructive implications, and its inability to cover interests abroad. The trouble with deterrence, however, lies elsewhere: The trouble with deterrence is that it can be implemented cheaply. The claim that we need a seamless web of capabilities in order to deter does serve one purpose: It keeps military budgets wondrously high. Efforts to fashion a defensive and war-fighting strategy for NATO are pointless because deterrence prevails and futile because strategy cannot transcend the military conditions that nuclear weapons create.

## NUCLEAR ARMS AND DISARMAMENT

The probability of major war among states having nuclear weapons approaches zero. But the "real war" may, as William James claimed, lie in the preparation for waging it. The logic of deterrence, if followed, circumscribes the causes of "real wars." . . . Nuclear weapons make it possible for a state to limit the size of its strategic forces as long as other states are unable to achieve disarming first-strike capabilities by improving their forces. . . .

Many who urge us to build ever more strategic weapons in effect admit the military irrelevance of additional forces when, as so often, they give political rather than military reasons for doing so: spending less, it is said, would signal weakness of will. Yet militarily, only one perception counts, namely, the perception that a country has second-strike forces. Nuclear weapons make it possible for states to escape the dynamics of arms racing; yet the United States and the Soviet Union have multiplied their weaponry far beyond the requirements of deterrence. Each has obsessively measured its strategic forces against the other's. The arms competition between them has arisen from failure to appreciate the implications of nuclear weapons for military strategy and, no doubt, from internal military and political pressures in both countries.

Many of the obstacles to arms reduction among conventional powers disappear or dwindle among nuclear nations. For the former, the careful comparison of the quantities and qualities of forces is important. Because this is not so with nuclear weapons, the problem of verifying agreements largely disappears. Provisions for verification may be necessary in order to persuade the Senate to ratify an agreement, but the possibility of noncompliance is not very worrisome. Agreements that reduce one category of conventional weapons may shift competition to other types of weapons and lead to increases in their numbers and capabilities. Because with nuclear weapons sufficiency is easily defined, there is no military reason for reductions in some weapons to result in increases in others. Conventionally, multiparty agreements are hard to arrive at because each party has to consider how shifting alignments may alter the balance of forces if agreements are reached to reduce them. In a world of second-strike nuclear forces, alliances have little effect on the strategic balance. The Soviet Union's failure to insist that British, French, and Chinese forces be counted in strategic arms negotiations may reflect its appreciation of this point. Finally, conventional powers have to compare weapons of uncertain effectiveness. Arms agreements are difficult to reach because their provisions may bear directly on the prospects for victory or defeat. Because in a nuclear world, peace is maintained by the presence of deterrent forces, strategic arms agreements do not have military, but economic and political, significance. They can benefit countries economically and help to improve their relations.

A minority of U.S. military analysts have understood the folly of maintaining more nuclear weapons than deterrence requires. In the Soviet Union, Mikhail Gorbachev and some others have put forth the notion of "reasonable sufficiency," defined as having a strategic force roughly equal to ours and able to inflict unacceptable damage in retaliation. [In 1989] Edward Warner [pointed] out that some civilian analysts have gone further, "suggesting that as long as the USSR had a secure second-strike capability that could inflict unacceptable damage, it would not have to be concerned about maintaining approximate numerical parity with U.S. strategic nuclear forces." . . . If leaders in both countries come to accept the minority view—and also realize that a deterrent force greatly reduces conventional requirements on central fronts—both countries can enjoy security at much lower cost.

## STRATEGIC DEFENSE

Strategic defenses would radically change the propositions advanced here. The Strategic Defense Initiative, in Reagan's vision, was to provide an area defense that would protect the entire population of the United States. Strategic defenses were to pose an absolute defense against what have been absolute weapons, thus rendering them obsolete. The consequences that would follow from mounting such a defense boggle the mind. That a perfect defense against nuclear weapons could be deployed and sustained is inconceivable.

First, nuclear weapons are small and light; they are easy to move, easy to hide, and easy to deliver in a variety of ways. Even an unimaginably perfect defense against ballistic missiles would fail to negate nuclear weapons. Such a defense would instead put a premium on the other side's ability to deliver nuclear weapons in different ways: firing missiles on depressed trajectories, carrying bombs in suitcases, placing nuclear warheads on freighters to be anchored in American harbors. Indeed, someone has suggested that the Soviet Union can always hide warheads in bales of marijuana, knowing we cannot keep them from crossing our borders. To have even modestly effective defenses we would, among other things, have to become a police state. We would have to go to extraordinary lengths to police our borders and exercise control within them. Presumably, the Soviet Union does these things better than we do. It is impossible to imagine that an area defense can be a success because there are so many ways to thwart it. In no way can we prevent the Soviet Union from exploding nuclear warheads on or in the United States if it is determined to do so.

Second, let us imagine for a moment that an airtight defense, however defined, is about to be deployed by one country or the other. The closer one country came to deploying such a defense, the harder the other would work to overcome it. When he was secretary of defense, Robert McNamara argued that the appropriate response to a Soviet defensive deployment would be to expand our deterrent force. More recently, Caspar Weinberger and Mikhail Gorbachev have made similar statements. Any country deploying a defense effective for a moment cannot expect it to remain so. The ease of delivering nuclear warheads and the destructiveness of small numbers of them make the durability of defenses highly suspect.

The logic of strategic defense is the logic of conventional weaponry. Conventional strategies pit weapons against weapons. That is exactly what a strategic defense would do, thereby recreating the temptations and instabilities that have plagued countries armed only with conventional weapons. If the United States and the Soviet Union deploy defensive systems, each will worry— no doubt excessively—about the balance of offensive and defensive capabilities. Each will fear that the other may score an offensive or defensive breakthrough. If one side should do so, it might be tempted to strike in order to exploit its temporary advantage. The dreaded specter of the hair trigger would reappear. Under such circumstances a defensive system would serve as the shield that makes the sword useful. An offensive-defensive race would introduce many uncertainties. A country enjoying a momentary defensive advantage would be tempted to strike in the forlorn hope that its defenses would be able to handle a ragged and reduced response to its first strike. Both countries would prepare to launch on warning while obsessively weighing the balance between offensive and defensive forces. . . . Strategic considerations should dominate technical ones. In a nuclear world defensive systems are predictably destabilizing. It would be folly to move from a condition of stable deterrence to one of unstable defense.

## CONCLUSION

Nuclear weapons dissuade states from going to war more surely than conventional weapons do. In a conventional world, states going to war can at once believe that they may win and that, should they lose, the price of defeat will be bearable. World Wars I and II called the latter belief into question before atomic bombs were ever dropped. If the United States and the Soviet Union were now armed only with conventional weapons, the lesson of those wars would be strongly remembered—especially by Russia, since she has suffered more in war than [the United States has]. If the atom had never been split, the United States and the Soviet Union would still have much to fear from each other. The stark opposition of countries of continental size armed with ever-more-destructive conventional weapons would strongly constrain them. Yet in a conventional world even forceful and tragic lessons have proved to be exceedingly difficult for states to learn. Recurrently in modern history one great power or another has looked as though it might become dangerously strong: Louis XIV's and Napolean's France, Wilhelm II's and Hitler's Germany. Each time, an opposing coalition formed, if belatedly, and turned the expansive state back. The lesson would seem to be clear: in international politics, success leads to failure. The excessive accumulation of power by one state or coalition of states elicits the opposition of others. . . .

How can we perpetuate peace without solving the problem of war? This is the question that states with nuclear weapons must constantly answer. Nuclear states continue to compete militarily. With each state tending to its security interests as best it can, war is constantly possible. Although the possibility of war remains, nuclear weapons have drastically reduced the probability of its being fought by the states that have them. Wars that might bring nuclear weapons into play have become extraordinarily hard to start. Over the centuries great powers have fought more wars, and lesser states have fought fewer: the frequency of war has correlated less closely with the attributes of states than with the international standing. Yet because of a profound change in military technology, waging war has more and more become the privilege of poor and weak states. Nuclear weapons have reversed the fates of strong and weak states. Never since the Treaty of Westphalia in 1648, which conventionally marks the beginning of modern history, have great powers enjoyed a longer period of peace than we have known since the Second World War. One can scarcely believe that the presence of nuclear weapons does not greatly help to explain this happy condition.

# 6

# THE CAUSES OF WAR: CONTENDING THEORIES

Jack S. Levy

In this essay Jack S. Levy examines several theories that trace the roots of war to underlying structural forces in the international system, which emphasizes the disagreements among theorists regarding the most important causes of war. Levy is professor of political science at Rutgers University and author of many publications assessing the causes of war, including *War in the Modern Great Power System, 1495–1975* (1983).

States have been fighting wars for millennia, and in spite of the enormous technological, economic, political, and cultural changes over the ages, there is little evidence that war will soon cease to exist as a regular pattern of behavior in world politics. Although many in the West were optimistic that the end of the Cold War between the United States and the Soviet Union would significantly reduce the likelihood of major wars in the world and provide a substantial "peace dividend," Iraq's invasion of Kuwait and the ensuing Gulf crisis abruptly shattered these illusions. Most of us would like to eliminate war or at least to control its destructive consequences, yet that requires first that we understand its causes. This question has become particularly urgent in an era in which an all-

This essay was written especially for the second edition of this book and revised for the third edition. The research was supported by the Stanford Center for International Security and Arms Control and by the Carnegie Corporation. The views expressed here do not necessarily represent those of the center or the foundation. Used by permission of Jack S. Levy.

out war between the most powerful states in the system could bring an end to modern civilization as we know it, where medium powers have themselves acquired substantial military capabilities, and where the specter of chemical warfare and nuclear proliferation to revisionist states has induced new fears among political leaders and peoples. Although philosophers, historians, social theorists, and others have been trying to understand why wars occur ever since Thucydides' account of the Peloponnesian War between Athens and Sparta nearly twenty-five centuries ago, no consensus has emerged regarding the answer to this vital question.[1]

Some scholars argue that the underlying causes of war can be found in the structure of power and alliances in the international system or in the way that structure changes over time.[2] Others trace the roots of war to political, economic, social, and psychological factors internal to the nation-state. Immanuel Kant and many liberal theorists argue that liberal democratic regimes are inherently peaceful whereas authoritarian regimes are more warlike.[3] Marxist-Leninists argue that war results primarily from the tendencies of capitalist states to expand in search of external markets, investment opportunities, and raw materials.[4] War has also been traced to attempts by political leaders to solve their internal political problems through the adoption of hostile foreign policies, on the assumption that external conflict will promote internal harmony.[5] Some theorists argue that war results from misperception, the effects of stress on crisis decision making, bureaucratic rigidities, and other flaws in the decision-making process which prevent the selection of those policies that are most likely to advance the national interest.[6] Others insist that decisions for war are based on very careful cost-benefit calculations incorporating interests, constraints, and uncertainties.[7]

Scholars disagree on other things besides the identity of the most important causes of war. Some argue that a single theory (usually their own) explains all wars. Others argue that each war is unique and has a unique set of causes, or that

[1]Thucydides, *History of the Peloponnesian War,* trans. by Rex Warner (New York: Penguin, 1954).

[2]The leading proponents of a "structural" theory of international politics include Hans Morgenthau, *Politics Among Nations,* 4th ed. (New York: Knopf, 1967); Kenneth N. Waltz, *Theory of International Politics* (Reading, Mass.: Addison-Wesley, 1979).

[3]Immanuel Kant, "Eternal Peace," in C. J. Friedrich, ed., *The Philosophy of Kant* (New York: Modern Library, 1949).

[4]V. I. Lenin, *Imperialism: The Highest Stage of Capitalism* (New York: International Publishers, 1939).

[5]Jack S. Levy, "The Diversionary Theory of War: A Critique." In Manus I. Midlarsky, ed., *Handbook of War Studies* (London: Unwin-Hyman, 1989), pp. 259–288.

[6]Robert Jervis, *Perception and Misperception in International Politics* (Princeton, N.J.: Princeton University Press, 1976); Richard Ned Lebow, *Between Peace and War* (Baltimore: Johns Hopkins, 1981), chaps. 5–7; Robert Jervis, Richard Ned Lebow, and Janis Gross Stein, *Psychology and Deterrence* (Baltimore: Johns Hopkins, 1985); Jack S. Levy, "Misperception and the Causes of War," *World Politics* 35 (October 1983): 76–99, and "Organizational Routines and the Causes of War," *International Studies Quarterly* 30 (June 1986): 193–222.

[7]Bruce Bueno de Mesquita, *The War Trap* (New Haven, Conn.: Yale University Press, 1981).

there are several different casual sequences leading to war and that these arise under different and often unpredictable circumstances. Some theorists say that because of the enormous changes from one historical era to the next in military technology and forms of social and political organization, the causes of war have changed over time. Others argue that patterns of international behavior in general and of war in particular have demonstrated a profound continuity over time, and that the causes of war in the nuclear era are no different from the causes of war in the age of Thucydides. These disagreements apply not only to the question of the causes of war in general but also to the question of the causes of particular wars. Historians are nearly as divided regarding the origins of individual wars as political scientists are regarding an explanation for the general phenomenon of war.

It will not be possible to examine all of the theories of the causes of war in this essay or to reach a definitive conclusion as to which is most consistent with the historical record.[8] Instead, we will restrict our attention to a few of the more important theories which focus on the underlying structural forces in the international system. These "systemic-level" theories assume that political leaders select those policies which best enable them to achieve their national interests, and that the primary determinants of war are the external constraints and opportunities affecting those foreign policy choices. This essay begins by examining international anarchy, or the absence of a centralized political authority in the world system, which is the most general structural characteristic of that system. It then turns to balance-of-power theory, one of the oldest theories of international relations. It ends with a consideration of power-transition theory and one of its important variations, long-cycle theory. One thing that should be noted about all of these structural systemic theories is that they are more concerned with the behavior of the strongest states in the international system (the great powers) and with the major wars between them than with the actions of other states.

## ANARCHY AND THE SECURITY DILEMMA

Whereas in domestic political systems there exists a government with the legitimate authority and the power to regulate the disputes between individual citizens within the state, there is no such institution to regulate disputes between individual states in the international system. In the absence of a higher authority, sovereign states are forced to rely on themselves to provide for their security and other interests, so that each state is the ultimate judge and ultimate protector of

[8]For more thorough discussions of the causes of war see Geoffrey Blainey, *The Causes of War* (New York: Free Press, 1973); Jack S. Levy, "The Causes of War: A Review of Theories and Evidence," in Philip E. Tetlock, Jo L. Husbands, Robert Jervis, Paul C. Stern, and Charles Tilly, eds., *Behavior, Society, and Nuclear War*, vol. 1 (New York: Oxford University Press, 1989), pp. 209–333.

its own interests. Force is the final arbiter of disputes, and in this sense wars occur because of the absence of anything to prevent them. States might usually prefer to settle their disputes peacefully; but since it is possible that any state might use force, all others must be prepared to use force or be willing to suffer the consequences of weakness. In such a high-threat environment, the maintenance of a minimal level of security tends to become the primary goal of states, one that must be satisfied before attention can be directed to other goals. The main means by which states provide for their security is the accumulation of military power and economic strength and the formation of alliances. The problem is that power and security tend to be relative rather than absolute. As Jean-Jacques Rousseau once argued,

> The state . . . always feels itself weak if there is another that is stronger. Its security and preservation demand that it make itself more powerful than its neighbors. It can increase, nourish and exercise its power only at their expense. . . . Because the grandeur of the state is purely relative it is forced to compare itself to that of the others. . . . It becomes small or great, weak or strong, according to whether its neighbor expands or contracts, becomes stronger or declines.[9]

Thus there is no natural limit to the pursuit of power and security, and therefore states, and particularly the leading states in the system, engage in a continuous effort to increase or at least maintain their power and influence relative to their rivals. This contributes to the processes leading to war by generating conflicting and sometimes mutually incompatible interests between states. Because a purely fortress defense is not viable, states attempt to maintain an extended defense through the control of territory, resources, strategic areas, and vital sea lanes beyond their own borders. The external defense requirements of two or more states may be in direct conflict, however, and this is particularly likely for contiguous states. The conflict is especially serious if the political authorities of one state believe that their external security requirements include the control over part of the territory within another state, as illustrated by the current Israeli occupation of the Syrian Golan Heights. A related problem is that states often try, if they can, to minimize threats to their security by attempting to influence or even control the internal political processes of other states, especially those on their borders. This often takes the form of attempting to assure the ideological compatibility of adjacent states, as illustrated by the Soviet Union in Eastern Europe during much of the post–World War II era. Intervention in the internal affairs of other states is a major source of conflict between great powers and secondary states, and since the latter have an incentive to secure protection through an alliance with another great power, these conflicts sometimes escalate to great power confrontations. Great powers' perceptions of their security inter-

---

[9]Quoted in Robert Gilpin, *U.S. Power and the Multinational Corporation* (New York: Basic Books, 1975), pp. 34–35.

ests tend to expand even further, however, to include the maintenance of a balance of power, which prevents any rival from achieving such a dominant position that it is able to interfere with one's own ability to maintain an extended defense beyond one's borders. These conflicts between the concrete strategic interests of rival states trying to provide for their own security in an anarchic state system have undoubtedly been one of the most important causes of war.

The relativity of security and the continuous pursuit of power would be mitigated if it were possible for statesmen to distinguish between the aggressive and defensive intentions of others and between offensive and defensive weapons systems. But most weapons can serve offensive as well as defensive functions, and most actions of other states are inherently ambiguous. Even if the political leadership of the adversary were fully trusted, there is no guarantee how long they would be in power or that they would necessarily be succeeded by others with equally benign intentions. Given this uncertainty, political leaders prefer to err on the side of safety and to engage in worst-case analysis. They recognize that false pessimism regarding the adversary's intentions might lead unnecessarily to a further escalation of tensions, but they fear that the consequences of a false optimism would be even worse. Thus even actions that are purely defensive in intent are often perceived as threatening by another state and lead it to take defensive countermeasures, which in turn are perceived as threatening by the first state, and so on. This action-reaction cycle or conflict spiral that often results from sincere attempts to increase one's security without threatening others may in fact decrease the security of oneself as well as one's adversaries. This classic "security dilemma" is extremely important, because it explains how states with primarily defensive motivations can be induced by the structure of the system to take actions that leave all states worse off than before.[10] Under certain conditions, the security dilemma can lead directly to war. If the nature of military technology is such as to give a major advantage to the state that strikes first in a crisis, states can be induced to initiate a preemptive attack even though both states would prefer to avoid war. The origins of World War I, for example, are often traced to the offensive war plans and rapid mobilization schedules that created strong incentives for both Germany and Russia to act preemptively.[11] Similarly, Israel was led by worst-case logic to act preemptively against Egypt in the 1967 war. Thus, while limited political objectives may decrease the likelihood of war, they do not guarantee that war will be avoided.

Although international anarchy and the security dilemma help explain the generally high level of conflict in the international system, they cannot explain the many extended periods of peace. More specific theories are needed to specify

---

[10]Robert Jervis, "Cooperation under the Security Dilemma," *World Politics* 30 (January 1978): 167–214.

[11]Steven E. Miller, ed., *Military Strategy and the Origins of the First World War* (Princeton, N.J.: Princeton University Press, 1985); Jack S. Levy, "Preferences, Constraints, and Choices in July 1914," *International Security* 15 (Winter 1990–91): 151–186.

the conditions under which the continuous struggle for power and security is most likely to trigger an irreconcilable conflict of vital interests or a conflict spiral, and the conditions under which these escalate to war. Let us now turn to a few of these theories.

## BALANCE-OF-POWER THEORY

For a variety of reasons, this is not a well-articulated theory but, instead, a weakly integrated collection of propositions regarding the behavior of the leading states in an anarchic international system and the conditions for stability in such a system. Although the key concepts are ambiguous and some of the propositions inconsistent, the "theory" has had a tremendous impact on the study of international relations for the last century. In spite of their disagreements on a number of specific issues, most balance-of-power theorists share a common set of general assumptions: that states define their interests primarily in terms of security, that they attempt to maximize their power, and that power is defined mainly in terms of military strength. The primary means by which states increase their power is through the formation of alliances, internal increases in their military capabilities and the economic foundations of military potential, and, if necessary, territorial compensations and the threat or use of military force for intervention or war. The balance-of-power system is said to function effectively or to be "stable" if no single state achieves a dominant position, if the independence of the great powers is assured, and if major wars are avoided, though there is some disagreement regarding the relative importance of these different criteria.[12]

One key proposition on which all balance-of-power theorists agree is that if any single state threatens to achieve a position of "hegemony" from which it could dominate over the other states in the system, a military coalition of nearly all the other great powers will form to block it and a general or "hegemonic war" will follow to restore equilibrium to the system. There are several historical cases that appear to fit this hypothesis, including the wars against Philip II of Spain in the late sixteenth century, wars involving Louis XIV of France in the late seventeenth century, the French Revolution and the Napoleonic wars a century later, and the two world wars with Germany in this century. Blocking coalitions are also likely to emerge if one state threatens to establish dominance over a regional system, as illustrated by the response to Saddam Hussein of Iraq in 1990.

This hypothesis regarding anti-hegemonic coalitions is an extension of the common balance-of-power hypothesis that a relatively equal distribution of military capabilities among the great powers is conducive to the avoidance of a major war, whereas the concentration of capabilities tends to be destabilizing. An

---

[12]Inis L. Claude, Jr., *Power and International Relations* (New York: Random House, 1962); Edward Vose Gulick, *Europe's Classical Balance of Power* (New York: Norton, 1955).

alternative to this "parity hypothesis" is the "power preponderance" hypothesis, which asserts that parity only tempts aggressors whereas preponderance reinforces deterrence and stability, as illustrated by the periods of peace enforced by ancient Rome and by nineteenth-century Britain. Whereas preponderance theorists argue that war is too risky for weaker states and unnecessary for the dominant state, balance-of-power theorists are more skeptical of the peaceful intentions of dominant states. They believe in the corrupting effects of power and in the tendency for a state's expansionist ambitions to increase along with its strength; therefore they fear the consequences of the absence of countervailing power.

The parity/preponderance question is related to the debate over whether multipolar systems, characterized by several leading great powers, are more stable than bipolar systems, characterized by only two leading powers. In the context of the apparent end of the Cold War, these conflicting hypotheses have generated an interesting debate about whether the current transformation of the international system from bipolarity to multipolarity will lead to an increase in the instability of the system.[13]

Balance-of-power theorists also emphasize the role of alliances, though they generally make a distinction between relatively permanent peacetime alliances and "ad hoc" alliances. Ad hoc alliances, which form in response to specific threats of aggression or to dangerous shifts in the distribution of power in the system, are necessary to maintain an equilibrium in the system and are considered to be stabilizing. Permanent alliances, on the other hand, are said to be destabilizing because they limit the "flexibility" of the system to respond to threats of aggression by reducing the number of coalitions that might form against a potential aggressor (since some states are already committed). Permanent alliances are particularly destabilizing if they become polarized, creating two rival alliance blocs. These tend to increase tensions, reduce possibilities for compromise because states must defend their allies' interests as well as their own, and increase both the probability of war and of its expansion into a general conflict involving all of the major states. World War I is considered a classic case of the destabilizing effects of a polarized alliance system.[14]

## POWER-TRANSITION THEORY

One critic of balance-of-power theory is A. F. K. Organski, who argues that the theory's focus on territory, armaments, and allies as the basis of power and secu-

---

[13]On the greater stability of multipolar systems, see Morgenthau, chap. 21; Claude, chaps. 2–3. On the stability of bipolarity, particularly when combined with nuclear weapons, see Waltz, chap. 8; John Lewis Gaddis, "The Long Peace," *International Security* 10 (Spring 1986):99–142; John J. Mearsheimer, "Back to the Future: Instability in Europe After the Cold War," *International Security* 15 (Summer 1990): 5–56.

[14]Balance-of-power theorists also suggest other conditions affecting international stability and peace, but those involving the distribution of power in the system and the pattern of alliances are the most important.

rity is too narrow. It ignores the importance of internal development in general and industrialization in particular as a source of the changing military power and potential of states. Organski's power-transition theory emphasizes that industrialization leads to uneven rates of economic growth and therefore to changing distributions of power in the international system, and that these changing power differentials between states have been the primary cause of war between the great powers for the last two centuries. Organski conceives of the international system as consisting of one dominant state at the top of the power hierarchy, a handful of rival great powers directly below, and a number of weaker states. As some great powers begin to grow in strength as a result of industrialization, they become increasingly dissatisfied with the existing international system and their own role in it and wish a share of the benefits and influence in the system commensurate with their newly acquired power. They also become an increasing military threat to the dominant state in the system. Organski argues that the likelihood of a major war is highest when the military power of a rising great power begins to approach that of the leading state in the system. The rising but still weaker challenger has an incentive to initiate a war in order to accelerate the power transition and secure the benefits to which it feels entitled by virtue of its military power. The underlying cause of World War I, in this view, was the rise of Germany and its challenge to the dominant position of Britain. It should be noted that in power-transition theory, in contrast to balance-of-power theory, alliances play very little role either as a factor affecting the distribution of power in the system or as a factor in the dynamic processes leading to major war.[15]

One curious element in power-transition theory is the fact that the rising challenger initiates a war against the dominant state while it is still militarily inferior, rather than waiting until the underlying trends in economic and military power thrust it into a stronger position. This has led some scholars to argue that the more likely mechanism by which power transitions lead to war is the initiation of a "preventive war" by the dominant state in a desperate attempt to block or retard the rise of the challenger before it is surpassed in strength. The declining leader has an incentive to fight a war now rather than risk a war under worsening circumstances later. Robert Gilpin suggests that preventive war is often perceived as the best option by a leading state in decline, and numerous historical cases have been interpreted as preventive wars. Many have argued that World War I was an attempt by Germany to secure its position before an increasingly powerful Russia had achieved a position of equality with Germany (which the latter expected to happen by 1917).[16]

---

[15]A. F. K. Organski, *World Politics*, 2nd ed. (New York: Knopf, 1968), chaps. 11–12; A. F. K. Organski and Jacek Kugler, *The War Ledger* (Chicago: University of Chicago Press, 1980), chap 1.

[16]The Israeli strike against the Iraqi nuclear reactor in 1981 was also basically preventive in motivation. Robert Gilpin, *War and Change in World Politics* (Cambridge, Eng.: Cambridge University Press, 1981), p. 191; Jack S. Levy, "Declining Power and the Preventive Motivation for War," *World Politics* 40 (October 1987): 82–107.

Regardless of who initiates the war, differential rates of growth and the power transition are important phenomena in international relations. It is not necessary, however, to restrict the scope of the theory to the modern industrial era, as Organski does. In fact, Thucydides argued with respect to the Peloponnesian War that "What made war inevitable was the growth of Athenian power and the fear which this caused in Sparta," suggesting that differential rates of growth, power transitions, and preventive war were important long before the industrial revolution. Gilpin has analyzed the general economic, social, and political dynamics contributing to hegemonic wars and transitions in any historical era, and Paul Kennedy has provided a detailed historical analysis of the rise and fall of great powers since 1500.[17] Rather than examine these studies in detail, however, we will look instead at "long-cycle theory." The theory is similar, but is supported with statistical evidence as well as historical analysis.

## LONG-CYCLE THEORY

Developed by George Modelski and William R. Thompson, long-cycle theory identifies regular cycles of world leadership and global war over the past five centuries of world politics. Whereas balance-of-power theory tends to focus (at least until 1945) on the European balance of power, the primacy of land-based military power, the anarchic nature of the system, and the effectiveness of the balancing mechanism in preventing the dominance of any single state, long-cycle theory emphasizes the global scope of the system and the dominance of a single state by virtue of its control over sea power (air power in the twentieth century) and world trade. The system is not truly anarchic, because the world power emerging from its victory in global war is able to use its strength to restructure the global political and economic systems in its own interests and to maintain order in the system. Ultimately, however, the costs of world leadership and the emergence of new rivals lead to a deconcentration of power and a global war to determine the successor to the position of world power. The cycle begins anew and, according to Modelski and Thompson, regularly repeats itself every hundred years. The two world wars, from this perspective, represent a continuous global war resulting from the decline of British world leadership, a deconcentration of power, and a failed bid by Germany to become the successor world power.[18]

If this theory is valid, we should expect a decline of American leadership, the rise of new rivals, and [conditions conducive to] the outbreak of another global

---

[17]Thucydides, p. 49; Gilpin (1981); Paul Kennedy, *The Rise and Fall of the Great Powers* (New York: Random House, 1987).

[18]George Modelski, "The Long Cycle of Global Politics and the Nation-State," *Comparative Studies in Society and History* 20 (April 1978): 214–35; William R. Thompson, *On Global War* (Columbia: University of South Carolina Press, 1988); Karen A. Rasler and William R. Thompson, *War and State Making: The Shaping of the Global Powers* (Boston: Unwin Hyman, 1989).

war early in the twenty-first century to determine the successor to the role of world power. There are numerous grounds on which to dispute the theory, however. Historically, its emphasis on a global war fought for the world leadership role in a global system based on sea power is less persuasive than the balance-of-power conception of hegemonic wars fought by a coalition of great powers against a bid for European hegemony by a land-based military power. Recall that the two world wars of this century and the other hegemonic wars listed earlier involved coalitions against the leading European land power, not the leading sea power. The emergence of the superpowers and the shift of power away from Europe may very well have broken this cycle of struggles for European hegemony. Although there may be a similar dynamic operating on the global level, that cannot be extrapolated directly from historical experience. In fact, it appears that one transition of global leadership, from Britain to the United States early in this century, was about to be accomplished peacefully, and the outbreak of World War I had more to do with the balance of power on the European continent than with the transition of global leadership from Britain to the United States. Moreover, the end of the Cold War and the reunification of Germany will have profound consequences for the international system as a whole, but these changes have (so far) been accomplished peacefully. Long-cycle theory, as well as other theories of hegemonic transitions, give too little emphasis to the possibility of peaceful power transitions.[19]

## CONCLUSIONS

This essay has examined only a very few of the numerous theories of the causes of war—those focusing on the most general forces in the international system that shape the security policies of states. These theories are biased toward the behavior of the great powers and toward major wars, and do little to explain wars between secondary states in the system or low-intensity conflicts, which are so pervasive today and which will probably be the most common form of warfare in the future. These theories differ along several important dimensions, including the importance of the international power structure, changes in that structure, the relative effects of parity versus preponderance, the importance of alliances, and the extent to which the system is managed by a dominant power or is totally anarchic. References to World War I have been included in order to illustrate the consequences of these theoretical differences for the interpretation of the causes of individual wars. Disagreements regarding the causes of war

---

[19]For a summary and critique of various theories of hegemonic transitions and their lists of hegemonic wars, as well as a view that emphasizes a Eurocentric balance-of-power orientation, see Jack S. Levy, "Theories of General War," *World Politics* 37 (April 1985): 344–74; also, Levy, "Long Cycles, Hegemonic Transitions, and the Long Peace," in Charles W. Kegley, Jr., ed., *The Long Postwar Peace* (New York: HarperCollins, 1991), pp. 147–176.

would be even greater were we to include factors internal to states that help determine more precisely how national interests are defined, how threats to those interests are identified, how tradeoffs between conflicting interests are resolved, how uncertainties regarding the intentions of other states and the consequences of various policies are handled, whether war is perceived as the best policy to advance the national interest given these constraints and uncertainties, the extent to which domestic and bureaucratic interests (as opposed to the national interest) are allowed to influence policy, and the extent to which policies are affected by pathologies in the decision-making process that lead to departures from a rational cost-benefit calculus based on a full use of available information. There is an enormous diversity of opinion regarding the political, economic, social, and psychological factors affecting each of these important considerations. These disagreements among scholars regarding the conditions and processes affecting the likelihood of war only complicate the dilemmas facing policymakers in their efforts to defend the interests of the state while at the same time minimizing the risks of war.

# 7

# FOUR DECADES OF NUCLEAR NONPROLIFERATION: LESSONS FOR THE 1990S

Lewis A. Dunn

**The spread of nuclear weapons has continued, despite various efforts to bring nuclear proliferation under control. This essay reviews three broad sets of initiatives to control the dispersion of nuclear weapons over forty years of the nuclear age, and inventories a balance sheet of "wins," "losses," and "draws" exhibited in this mixed record of success and failure, especially as seen from the perspective of the United States. Lewis A. Dunn served as assistant director of the U.S. Arms Control and Disarmament Agency and holds the position of assistant vice president and manager of the negotiations and planning division of Science Applications International Corporation. He has written on arms control issues in many journals and authored** *Controlling the Bomb* **(1982).**

For more than four decades, the United States has opposed the spread of nuclear weapons to other countries. This basic policy has rested on the belief that nuclear proliferation would result in new threats to . . . security, heighten global and regional instabilities, and quite possibly lead to the use of nuclear weapons. That assumption continues to guide U.S. policy today.

Over the years, . . . nuclear nonproliferation efforts have relied on three broad sets of specific actions [initiatives have been] taken in order to reduce the

From Aspen Strategy Group, *New Threats: Responding to the Proliferation of Nuclear, Chemical, and Delivery Capabilities in the Third World* (Lanham, Md.: University Press of America and Aspen Strategy Group, 1990). Used by permission of the Aspen Institute.

political incentives that could lead countries to acquire nuclear weapons; technical obstacles have been created in order to make acquisition more difficult; and international nonproliferation institutions have been established.

It is especially timely to reconsider the record of nuclear nonproliferation efforts over the course of the [1980s]. With open or unacknowledged nuclear proliferation throughout the world, . . . renewed attempts to head off a world of many nuclear weapon states [are required]. Equally, with policy attention focusing on the problems of chemical weapons and missile proliferation, examination of the nuclear nonproliferation experience could provide lessons for those two areas. . . .

## NUCLEAR NONPROLIFERATION WINS

There are five acknowledged nuclear weapon states: the United States (1945), the Soviet Union (1949), the United Kingdom (1952), France (1960), and China (1964). In addition, India detonated a nuclear explosive device in 1974, but claimed it was only for peaceful purposes; and Israel is believed publicly to have manufactured nuclear weapons. Top officials in both South Africa and Pakistan have stated publicly that their countries have "the capability" to make nuclear weapons should they desire to do so.

Today, proliferation is quite different from what many officials and observers in the late 1950s and early 1960s thought would be the case. Back then, it was feared widely that 15–20 states, if not more, would possess nuclear weapons by the mid-1970s. Behind the difference between past predictions and the current situation are a series of nuclear nonproliferation wins.

### Decisions by West European Countries Not to Acquire the Bomb

In thinking about steps to slow overt or unacknowledged nuclear proliferation, we rightly focus on today's so-called problem countries, such as Pakistan, India, North and South Korea, Taiwan, Israel, Iran, Iraq, Libya, Syria, and South Africa. Two decades ago, however, the list of problem countries was quite different. Rather than Third World countries, that list included the West European countries of France, West Germany, Italy, Switzerland, and Sweden. Japan also should be put in the category of early potential problem countries, even though there was considerably less serious discussion of nuclear weapons acquisition there. With the exception of France, all of these countries eventually chose not to acquire nuclear weapons.

The decision by West European countries and Japan to renounce nuclear weapons . . . was not a foregone conclusion: at differing times in the 1950s or 1960s, acquisition of nuclear weapons was an open question in virtually all of the above mentioned countries. . . . [Many] explanations [exist] for this nuclear nonproliferation win. . . .

### Third World Incentives and the Nuclear Nonproliferation Norm

The establishment and strengthening of the nuclear nonproliferation norm . . . has helped contain the spread of nuclear weapons to the Third World, while reinforcing the decisions of most Western countries to renounce nuclear weapons.

This norm encompasses several changes in thinking about nuclear weapons and nuclear proliferation. [Global] opinion increasingly has rejected the legitimacy of acquiring nuclear weapons. Equally important, a widespread belief has emerged that the spread of nuclear weapons could add to regional and global insecurity. Unlike the early 1960s, moreover, the current perception is that a world of dozens of nuclear weapon states is not the inevitable wave of the future. Similarly, the acquisition of nuclear weapons no longer is seen as a main route to international prestige and recognition. . . .

This norm probably has been most important in containing proliferation incentives in those Third World countries that are not today's problem countries, but that could have been driven to seek nuclear weapons by fear of their neighbors' long-term intentions, by prestige, or by the simple belief that sooner or later all important countries would have nuclear weapons. This group includes, for example, Indonesia, the Philippines, Singapore, Venezuela, Mexico, Chile, Egypt, Algeria, Nigeria, and Yugoslavia. At the same time, the norm of nuclear nonproliferation . . . also . . . undoubtedly partly explains . . . the decision not to move to open pursuit of a nuclear weapons capability in several problem countries, such as India and Pakistan. Finally, this norm has helped to prevent the reconsideration of earlier decisions by most Western countries to opt for nonnuclear status.

### The Nuclear Supply Regime

Beginning in the mid-1950s, U.S. policymakers also took the lead in establishing a set of international institutions, procedures, and agreements to regulate peaceful nuclear cooperation and the supply of nuclear materials, facilities, and technology to other countries, which became a nuclear supply and export control regime. This regime now consists of U.S. conditions for agreements on bilateral cooperation; International Atomic Energy Agency (IAEA) safeguards that monitor the peaceful uses of nuclear energy; the so-called Zangger trigger lists that specify the items that NPT nuclear suppliers can export under safeguards, which have become the basis for rejecting export requests from problem countries; and the London Nuclear Suppliers' Guidelines that extend controls to technology and include commitments to restraint in the transfer of sensitive reprocessing and enrichment equipment or technology. [In 1990] efforts [were] underway to extend the nuclear export control and supply regime to meet the challenges posed by the so-called dual-use exports, items with both nuclear and nonnuclear uses, and by new enrichment technologies. . . .

IAEA safeguards have been the principal means whereby recipients of peaceful nuclear equipment and materials could reassure both suppliers and their neighbors that such support was not misused for the manufacture of nuclear weapons. Although problems have arisen and challenges remain, IAEA safeguards on balance have done a credible job in providing that assurance. . . .

However, at another level, the limits of export controls and nuclear supplier restraint must be acknowledged frankly. Problem countries increasingly have developed sophisticated methods to circumvent controls. The implementation of regulations by some key U.S. allies may be half-hearted, while high-level U.S. officials sometimes have been reluctant to expend political capital on export control diplomacy. [It] has been clear since the Soviet detonation of an atomic bomb in 1949 that export controls, secrecy, and denial of technology alone cannot prevent the further spread of nuclear weapons.

### Winning Widespread Adherence to the NPT

. . . In adhering to the NPT, . . . nearly 140 countries have renounced the right to manufacture or acquire nuclear weapons. Although in a few cases this undertaking might be open to question, for virtually all others, adherence both significantly binds a country's future policy and provides reassurance to its neighbors. . . .

Nonetheless, the commitment of several countries to the Treaty increasingly has become open to question. The most notable cases include Iraq, Iran, and Libya in the Middle East, and North Korea in Asia. If these countries eventually were to acquire nuclear weapons, the NPT's credibility would be damaged. In addition, in 1995 the parties to the NPT are to decide by majority vote whether ". . . the Treaty shall continue in force indefinitely, or shall be extended for an additional fixed period or periods." The adherence of many small Third World countries with potentially little direct security interest in and, therefore, reason to support the NPT could prove a problem in mustering the required majority vote.

### Regularizing U.S.–Soviet Nonproliferation Discussions

Another example of successful institution-building is the pattern of regular bilateral discussions between the United States and the Soviet Union on nuclear nonproliferation that has been established. Begun sporadically in the late 1970s, these exchanges have taken place approximately every six months since 1983. . . .

These U.S.–Soviet exchanges have proved most useful for policy discussions regarding multilateral nuclear nonproliferation institutions, from how to handle challenges to Israel's right to participate in IAEA meetings to cooperative efforts to ensure success at the five-year review of the NPT in 1985. They also have helped to coordinate U.S.–Soviet efforts to buttress nuclear export controls, by upgrading the Zangger trigger lists to include additional items. Sufficient habits of cooperation were built up over time in order to make it possible to use these bilateral discussions for nonpolemical consideration of what steps either side might take to head off problem country nuclear weapon programs. In some instances, actions resulted. Nonetheless, the reluctance of both sides to use available influence with such countries—because of other political interests—as well as the limits of influence frequently stood out.

## NUCLEAR NONPROLIFERATION LOSSES

The record also contains a number of nuclear nonproliferation losses, suggesting the limits of what . . . nuclear nonproliferation policy can accomplish. . . .

### Additional Nuclear Weapon States: Could More Have Been Done?

The failure to prevent additional countries from acquiring nuclear weapons or a nuclear weapons capability is the most obvious nuclear nonproliferation loss. In addition to the five acknowledged nuclear weapon states, four other countries widely are assumed either to possess nuclear weapons capability or to be able to acquire it within the short-term. At the same time, the pattern of this additional proliferation activity has changed. Since China detonated a nuclear weapon in 1964, no other country openly has opted for nuclear weapons status. Instead, a new group of neither acknowledged nuclear weapon states nor questioned non-nuclear weapon states is emerging.

[The] record makes clear that if a country has strong incentives to acquire a nuclear weapons capability and a sufficiently broad industrial base, it will not be possible to prevent the country from eventually achieving that goal. This became evident at the start [and has remained applicable ever since, as the cases of the Soviet Union in 1949 and the entry of the other four nuclear weapons states illustrates; the continuing relevance of this principle is suggested by the nuclear development programs of South Africa, Pakistan, Iraq, and Israel, the author explains—eds.]

Taken together, these [activities] suggest that . . . [some] losses are unavoidable, regardless of what the United States and other like-minded countries attempt to do. Export controls can only slow a determined country. . . .

## The NPT Holdouts

That a group of countries has refused to sign the NPT . . . is another nuclear nonproliferation loss. Four of these NPT holdouts are high on all lists of problem countries: Pakistan, India, Israel, and South Africa. The other countries that appear to be further away from possession of a nuclear weapons capability include Argentina, Brazil, and Chile in Latin America, and Algeria in Africa. France and China, also holdouts, are nuclear weapon states. . . .

The reasons for nonadherence vary. For virtually all holdout countries, refusal to adhere is, in part, a means to keep open the option to make nuclear weapons. Rejection of adherence also is buttressed in some cases, such as India, Argentina, and Brazil, by arguments about the NPT's discriminatory character. These arguments emphasize that nuclear weapons states are not required to renounce their nuclear arsenals, nor do they have to accept IAEA safeguards on their peaceful nuclear activities. For China, nonadherence is a residue of earlier attitudes that stressed the benefits for communism of the proliferation of nuclear weapons. French nonadherence is tied up as much with Gallic pride and the logic of independence as with French criticism of the NPT's discriminatory elements. Some French NPT critics also claim to be concerned that adherence to the NPT would make it more difficult to continue the testing of nuclear weapons.

## Widespread Civilian Use of Plutonium

The growing prospect of the widespread commercial use of plutonium is a somewhat different nuclear nonproliferation loss. Although estimates vary, several tens of thousands of kilograms of separated plutonium could be circulating in international commerce by the year 2000. Most of this plutonium will be used as nuclear fuel in light-water reactors in Japan, France, Germany, Switzerland, and some other West European countries. With time, South Korea again could seek access to plutonium for use in its substantial civilian nuclear power program. . . .

The increased commercial use of plutonium and its frequent international shipment will place new strains on the ability of countries to ensure its adequate physical security. The risk of plutonium theft, whether by terrorists, extortionists, radical governments, or thieves could well be high. Problems with tracking and accounting for large shipments and stocks of plutonium—especially because some amount in use always will be unaccounted for—will open up the possibility of insider collusion in any such thefts.

## Failures of Nuclear Supplier Cooperation

. . . Two types of supply failure have occurred: specific export control breakdowns and broader inability among the major nuclear suppliers to agree to hold regular multilateral discussions of nonproliferation.

At one time or another, the export control system of virtually all nuclear suppliers has failed to block exports of concern to a problem country, despite good faith efforts by the supplier. Also, there have been instances in which the nuclear export control bureaucracy of a given country has not paid sufficient attention to potentially troublesome exports or to entreaties to stop particular exports of nonproliferation concern.

In addition, since 1977 it has not proved possible to convene a meeting of the entire London Nuclear Suppliers' Group, which brought together both East bloc and the major Western nuclear suppliers. France and Germany, in particular, have opposed that meeting on the grounds that it likely would antagonize Third World countries, and despite U.S. and Soviet counterarguments, neither country has been prepared to shift its position. The lack of regular meetings of all nuclear suppliers has made it harder to reach consensus on new supply initiatives, such as dealing with the problems posed by so-called dual-use exports with both nuclear and nonnuclear uses. . . .

## NUCLEAR NONPROLIFERATION DRAWS

Still other developments of the past decades fall into the category of nuclear nonproliferation draws. . . .

### Some Nuclear Weapons Program Shutdowns?

It is well known that in the mid-1970s both South Korea and Taiwan had active nuclear weapons programs, but under political pressure from the United States, both countries shut down such activities. Nonetheless, this termination must be considered only a nuclear nonproliferation draw, because under certain circumstances both programs could spring back to life. . . .

### The Treaty of Tlatelolco: An Almost Nuclear-Free Zone

Although the Treaty of Tlatelolco provides the legal framework to make Latin America a nuclear weapons–free zone, . . . Chile and Cuba have not signed, Argentina has not ratified, and despite having signed and ratified, Brazil has yet to wave it into force. As such, the Treaty of Tlatelolco remains as much a nuclear nonproliferation promise as reality. . . .

### Nonuse of Nuclear Weapons

[The] nonuse of nuclear weapons over the past four decades also has . . . contributed significantly to the emergence and widespread acceptance of the belief that nuclear weapons were not simply advanced conventional weapons. This oft-remarked nuclear taboo, in turn, has affected the calculations of some of the first generation problem countries regarding the benefits and need for nuclear weapons. . . .

More widespread nuclear weapons proliferation, however, could lead to a future use of nuclear weapons. Depending on the specifics, such use could either greatly strengthen the nuclear taboo and associated nonproliferation norm, or undermine it. For that reason and because it had little to do with nonproliferation per se, nonuse is considered a draw.

## SOME IMPLICATIONS FOR CHEMICAL WEAPONS AND MISSILE NONPROLIFERATION

[In the late 1980s] countries [began] to place greater emphasis on measures to control the spread of ballistic and cruise missiles and chemical weapons (CW). A Missile Technology Control Regime, with a list of sensitive items and guidelines for their control, has been concluded among the United States, the United Kingdom, France, Germany, Japan, Italy, and Canada. China and the Soviet Union remain outside, although the Soviets have indicated interest in creation of such a multilateral control regime. In turn, a group of Western countries, the so-called Australia Group, has compiled a list of key chemicals needed to make chemical weapons and steps have been taken by individual countries in order to control their export. Negotiations also are underway at the Geneva Conference on Disarmament . . . to ban the development, stockpiling, production, transfer, and use of chemical weapons. [The United States and the Soviet Union have also agreed] to reduce each country's CW stocks.

There is a series of lessons for missile and CW nonproliferation from the nuclear nonproliferation record. By way of conclusion, these lessons are sketched briefly, with some thoughts on the similarities and differences of nuclear weapons, chemical weapons, and missile nonproliferation.

First, a key to longer-term success likely will be the establishment of an international consensus or norm in favor of control. The norm of nuclear nonproliferation significantly influenced the calculations and decisions both of potential nuclear weapons states and of suppliers of nuclear technology, and provided the legitimacy for all other nonproliferation measures. No comparable norm now exists in the area of missiles. The Geneva Protocol norm against use of chemical weapons was undermined badly by repeated successful and unpunished Iraqi use of chemical weapons in [its war with Iran in the 1980s].

A second lesson is that export controls and technology denial can make it harder, more time consuming, and more complex for countries to develop advanced military capabilities. They can buy time for other measures to be implemented, but, with some exceptions, they alone cannot prevent proliferation and should not be called on to do so. The impact of export controls, moreover, is likely to be even weaker in the chemical weapons area. Legitimate civilian chemical activities are more widespread, the number of firms and countries involved greater, and the unique constraints of radioactivity to assist control are lacking. For missiles, export controls again seem most useful to slow the process and to buy time. Although access to guidance technologies could be a key bottleneck, this would apply only to countries seeking more sophisticated capabilities.

Third, . . . ensuring effective export controls will be a continuing political and not only technical struggle. Problem countries will continue to find new ways to circumvent their impact. More important, other supplier countries often will lack the will, mechanisms, or personnel to implement effective export regulations. A growing number of suppliers will compound the problem. Recent experience with both chemical weapons and missile export controls serves only to reinforce this point.

Fourth, the existence of a legally binding international obligation to enforce export controls can be especially helpful in obtaining the support of other countries to alleviate some of the above weaknesses. In the nuclear nonproliferation area, the NPT made it easier for governments to convince legislatures to place restrictions on trade. . . .

Fifth, the nuclear nonproliferation record also drives home the importance of influencing incentives to acquire advanced military technologies. Steadily growing skepticism about the utility of nuclear weapons . . . has been most critical in the nuclear field. By contrast, Iraq's recent successful uses of chemical weapons have sent the opposite signal. The problems of assistance to countries threatened with chemical weapons and sanctions against users have yet to be addressed. With regard to missile proliferation, it may be feasible to take measures via tactical missile defenses to negate directly the benefits for Third World countries of acquiring missiles. Absent that, perceptions of the utility of missiles also are likely to rise over time, again partly boosted by Iraq's use of missiles in the war of the cities as well as by . . . Afghan government use of Soviet SCUD missiles.

Sixth, four decades of nuclear nonproliferation clearly demonstrate that nonproliferation efforts in any area must be placed into a broader national, regional, and international political perspective. . . .

Finally, the nuclear nonproliferation record reflects both the benefits and the limits of U.S.–Soviet cooperation. Cooperation between the two countries was essential to put in place a strong nuclear supply regime, buttress the NPT, support the IAEA, and defuse at least some problem country hot spots. Still, U.S.–Soviet regional interests also have differed on occasion, restricting the possibility of common nonproliferation action. Similarly, limits even on their joint influence have been evident. These same strains can be expected in trying to put together a parallel approach to CW and missile nonproliferation.

## CONCLUSION

[The] record of four decades of nuclear nonproliferation . . . makes clear both the potential influence and the continuing limits of . . . efforts to prevent the further spread of nuclear weapons around the globe. Equally, the lessons of the record of the past decades need to be reflected in the new measures now rising to prominence in order to prevent the spread of chemical weapons and missiles. To do so could increase measurably the prospects for their success.

# 8

# IS CRISIS MANAGEMENT ALWAYS POSSIBLE?

### Richard Ned Lebow

**The characteristics of international crises and their susceptibility to successful management are evaluated by Richard Ned Lebow. His discussion demonstrates not only the important role that crises play in international affairs but also the critical relationship they bear to war and to peace and the magnitude of the challenges that must be met to prevent their escalation to war. Lebow is professor of government and director of the Peace Studies Program at Cornell University. He has written extensively on international security affairs and deterrence, and has published *Nuclear Crisis Management: A Dangerous Illusion* (1989).**

After the Cuban missile crisis had been resolved, President John F. Kennedy confessed that the odds of the Soviets going to war seemed to him at the time "somewhere between one out of three and even." Kennedy's judgment has remained a matter of controversy among scholars and members of the "Ex Com," the informal working group the President assembled to help him manage the crisis. Robert McNamara and McGeorge Bundy contend that it may have been a reasonably accurate estimate of the risks at the time. Dean Acheson and Paul Nitze, by contrast, argued that the President greatly exaggerated the prospect of war. Even if he did, Kennedy's judgment nevertheless reflects an

From Richard Ned Lebow, *Nuclear Crisis Management: A Dangerous Illusion.* Copyright 1987 by Cornell University. Used by permission of Cornell University Press. Some footnotes have been deleted and others have been renumbered to appear in consecutive order.

undisputed political reality: the Cuban missile crisis was, relatively speaking, the closest the superpowers had ever come to nuclear war. It was not an experience that any of the participants looked forward to repeating.

Whether by skill or by circumstance, or both, the superpowers have managed to avoid war-threatening confrontations since. There have been crises, to be sure, but none of them of the magnitude of Cuba. Even the 1973 Middle East crisis, the most serious superpower clash after 1962, was by all accounts a faint echo of its famous predecessor. The participants never seem to have doubted that it would be resolved by diplomacy.

But our good fortune cannot be taken for granted. . . . There is always the possibility that one of the superpowers, by design or miscalculation, will do something that the other is unwilling to tolerate. . . .

No one knows how such a crisis would occur, although many of us have a favorite scenario. Mine concerns weapons in space. The United States is committed to developing a space-based defense against ballistic missiles, something the Soviets strongly oppose. Moscow has already dropped hints that it is prepared to interfere with the deployment of such a weapons system. Suppose the United States, deeply committed to the project, disregards Soviet warnings and at some point begins to put important components of a missile defense system into space. To show their displeasure, the Soviets orbit space mines in the vicinity. The United States, in turn, sends up a shuttle mission to remove or disarm the threat. But the mines, having been salvage fused (set, that is, to go off if tampered with), explode and kill six astronauts. . . .

The point about this or any other scenario is not its inherent plausibility but the fact that such hypothetical situations are taken seriously by the U.S. foreign policy and defense establishments. Such possible futures form the basis of political-military simulations used for planning and training purposes. The prevalence of these simulations implicitly recognizes that a serious superpower confrontation remains a real if disturbing possibility. So it is important to inquire how such a confrontation could occur, how the superpowers would be likely to respond to it, what our chances are of emerging unscathed, and what, if anything, can be done to enhance them.

The Cuban missile crisis is an obvious starting point for an analysis of this kind. It is our best example of an acute superpower confrontation. However, Cuba is also misleading in important ways. Kennedy's success in avoiding war *and* getting the Russians to back down has encouraged the belief that this is a feasible objective in future confrontations. It has also led responsible political analysts to exaggerate the efficacy of military capability and demonstrations of resolve. In the decade following Cuba, American scholars legitimized both expectations. Political scientists enshrined the need for resolve at the core of widely accepted theories of deterrence and compellence, while decision-making theorists idealized Kennedy's handling of the crisis and held it out as proof that confrontations of this kind could be managed ably and successfully.

Even without these questions of interpretation there would be important structural differences between Cuba and any future superpower crisis of the same magnitude. These differences would make such a crisis very much more difficult to resolve. In 1962 the United States had overwhelming nuclear superiority and conventional superiority in the Caribbean, the arena of the confrontation. Cuba was all one-sided in terms of military escalation. The United States brought its nuclear and conventional forces up to a high level of readiness; the Strategic Air Command was put on Defense Condition II, the only time any component of U.S. forces has ever been ordered to go to this level of readiness. The Soviet Union, by contrast, refrained from any buildup, perhaps because of its disadvantage and the fear that a strategic alert on its part could trigger American preemption. But a future crisis will take place in an environment of strategic parity. The Soviets may be the ones to have the conventional advantage next time, depending on where the crisis occurs. If they do, they might not feel as constrained as in Cuba. A Soviet alert, conventional or nuclear, matching or matched by an American alert, would make any crisis more acute and correspondingly difficult to resolve. It would also make it more difficult to control.

Cuba took place in a much less sophisticated institutional environment. Many communication links were entirely ad hoc, the number of players was relatively small, and their roles were often undefined. Strategic weapons, mostly bombers, were slow and recallable. In the years since, the command and control systems of both superpowers have grown enormously in size and complexity. They have also become tightly coupled. Strategic weapons put more stress on these systems. They are capable of striking the adversary's political leadership and strategic forces in a matter of minutes instead of hours. They are also less tolerant of error, because missiles, unlike bombers, cannot be recalled. All of these developments mean less tolerance for the kinds of incidents and mishaps that plagued Kennedy's handling of Cuba. But there is reason to believe that the organizational complexity of the 1980s nevertheless makes mishaps more rather than less likely.

Today's strategic environment requires a significant shift in our ways of thinking about international crises. Leaders must show more profile and less courage. They must be less concerned with "winning" and more concerned with controlling crises, because the principal danger is no longer that the adversary will get his way but that one or both of the protagonists will set in motion a chain of events that will lead to an undesired and catastrophic war. But a conceptual shift of this kind has not occurred. Political leaders and their advisers still give every indication of believing that crisis management consists of controllable and reversible steps up a ladder of escalation, steps taken to moderate an adversary's behavior. . . .

This dangerous political orientation is complemented by an equally fruitless and counterproductive technical approach to the problems of crisis management. Crisis management in the United States bears a disturbing resemblance to the ancient art of alchemy. Alchemists of old sought to transmute base elements into gold by simple chemistry and magical incantation. They failed because their quest was based on a false premise; elements cannot be transmuted by chemical processes. The transmutation of metals requires alteration of their nuclear structure, something that has become technically feasible only in the last fifty years. Even today, it requires vast amounts of money and energy to produce even the tiniest amount of a heavy element.

Government officials, and many academic researchers, have embarked upon a similarly fruitless quest for the secret keys to nuclear crisis management. Convinced, as were the alchemists before them, that their goal is attainable, they search for the modern day equivalent of the philosopher's stone: the organizational structures and decision-making techniques that will transmute the dark specter of nuclear destruction into the glitter of national security. Once again, the task is hopeless. Good crisis management cannot be fabricated from communication nodes, computer software, and special action groups. It requires fundamental changes in the force structures, the doctrines, and the target sets that define contemporary nuclear strategy. Like transmutation, crisis stability is theoretically possible, but for the foreseeable future it lies beyond the power of political alchemists.

Nuclear crisis management may be an oxymoron, but this does not mean that the behavior of leaders is irrelevant to what happens in crises—only that a narrow focus on the techniques and technology of crisis management is unlikely to result in significantly improved performance. Good decision making is associated with certain underlying conditions. The most important of these are a relatively open decision-making environment, a consensus within the policy-making elite with regard to fundamental political values and institutional procedures, and freedom from the kinds of domestic political pressures which compel leaders to pursue risky foreign policies. Good decision making in crisis also demands that leaders have a working knowledge of the details of military planning and operations. None of these conditions can be created by fiat while a crisis is unfolding. If they exist at all, they are the product of extensive precrisis efforts that leaders initiate to educate themselves and to build an environment conducive to vigilant information processing and responsive policy implementation. All too often, success in this regard depends on fortuitous historical and political circumstances over which leaders have relatively little control.

A shift is also required, therefore, in the focus of contemporary research and planning for crisis management. Too often, such efforts are directed at improving only the external environment in which policy makers operate, by providing greater or more rapid access to key information and individuals. Even those efforts which focus on the actual process of decision making and implementation tend to limit their horizons to the course of the crisis itself. By doing so, however, they look only at the tip of the proverbial iceberg. How a political system performs in crisis is a function of personal, group, institutional, and cultural patterns and interactions that were established long before the onset of the crisis.

The most pressing task for those who study crisis management, therefore, is to delineate more clearly the precise nature of the links between performance and these underlying factors. Only then can really productive efforts be made to improve the quality of decision making.

We must also recognize that good decision making is not the same thing as successful decision making. The two are related but not synonymous; a host of other conditions also affect crisis outcomes. Among the most important are the degree of concern of leaders on both sides to avoid war, the latitude leaders have to explore a wide range of possible settlements, the time pressures they confront, the nature, gravity and compatibility of the issues at stake, and the level of military escalation and the threat of war associated with it. Any one of these conditions can compel leaders to settle for a less than favorable outcome or prevent resolution of the crisis altogether—whatever officials on both sides might desire.

Stress, organization complexity, and time pressure are likely to characterize any future superpower confrontation. They will certainly make good decision making essential—but at the same time, it will be less of a determinant of the outcome. The reason for this apparent contradiction lies in the particular strategic, political and psychological factors that would shape superpower interactions. Those factors will make it very difficult for leaders to resolve such a confrontation *regardless* of their skill and mutual commitments to avoid war.

This is not the first [analysis] to expound the dangers of superpower crises and some of the structural reasons for it. Most of these studies have emphasized the critical vulnerability of strategic command and control and the unsettling dilemma this creates for leaders.[1] This critical aspect of nuclear strategy has been until quite recently neglected. In 1981, Desmond Ball wrote the first work to describe the architecture of the U.S. strategic command, control, and communication ($C^3$) system and to demonstrate its extreme vulnerability to sabotage and nuclear attack. Since then Bruce Blair has documented the vulnerability of $C^3$ to Soviet attack from the early 1960s to the present day. Both authors wanted to influence strategic policy. By demonstrating the vulnerability of American $C^3$ to nuclear assault, Ball hoped to demonstrate the absurdity of controlled, protracted nuclear war, a capability deemed essential by current U.S. strategic doctrine. Blair had an even more far-reaching objective in mind: he sought to shift American attention away from its decades-old fixation on the possible vulnerability of its strategic forces to the greater and more significant vulnerability of the command and control of those forces. He thereby hoped to win support for extensive measures to enhance the survivability of $C^3$.

---

[1]John Steinbruner, "Nuclear Decapitation," *Foreign Policy* 45 (Winter 1981–82): 16–28; Desmond Ball, *Can Nuclear War Be Controlled?* Adelphi Paper no. 169 (London: International Institute of Strategic Studies, 1981); Paul Bracken, *The Command and Control of Nuclear Forces* (New Haven: Yale University Press, 1983); Bruce G. Blair, *Strategic Command and Control: Redefining the Nuclear Threat* (Washington, D.C.: Brookings, 1985).

John Steinbruner and Paul Bracken have been more concerned with the implications of $C^3$ vulnerability for war-prevention in crisis. . . . In 1981, Steinbruner drew attention to one of the policy dilemmas created by $C^3$ vulnerability, and in particular by the vulnerability of the political leadership to destruction at the outset of hostilities. If policy makers feared they might not be able to retaliate to nuclear attack, he argued, they would have a strong incentive to shoot first in circumstances where nuclear war appeared likely. Bracken highlighted another destabilizing aspect of contemporary command and control: the difficulty of controlling nuclear forces once alerted, and the risk of accidental war that such alerts accordingly entail. In his 1983 study he described the evolution and growing complexity of U.S. strategic $C^3$. Drawing upon insights from organization theory, Bracken warned that the American-Soviet strategic warning and response systems had a propensity to perform in crisis situations in unanticipated and possibly catastrophic ways.

These several works have based their analyses on an examination of the physical machinery and organizational structure of American command and control. They go on to describe strategic imperatives these give rise to and the ways in which such imperatives could hinder resolution of a crisis. Studies of this kind constitute an important first step toward understanding the causes of crisis instability. It would be wrong, however, to suppose that strategic problems can be entirely, or even best, understood in terms of engineering or organizational criteria. There is more to command and control than its technical aspects and more to crisis management than command and control. Like all strategic issues, crisis management has critically important political and psychological dimensions. To date, these remain largely unexplored.

At least some of the "strategic realities" responsible for crisis stability are as much political and conceptual as they are structural. The prince aptly opines in *Hamlet* that "There is nothing either good or bad, but thinking makes it so." This is to a marked degree true of nuclear strategy. Strategic force vulnerability is an obvious case in point. Minuteman vulnerability has not decreased one iota in recent years; presumably it has become worse as Soviet missiles have improved their accuracy. But the problem has receded in importance, to a large degree because of the successful effort of the Scowcroft Commission in 1983 to disparage its strategic significance.

An example more specific to the realm of crisis concerns the attractiveness of preemption in a confrontation in which war appears imminent. A thorough examination of the pros and cons of preemption reveals that there are no circumstances in which preemption is an advisable policy. Both the fear that retaliation would be impossible and the advantages that preemption, some allege, confers can be shown to be greatly exaggerated. Conversely, faulty and incomplete understanding of the problems of loss of control and miscalculated escalation has led strategists in and out of government to underestimate the threats these problems would pose to crisis resolution.

There are things that can be done to reduce crisis instability, and with it the likelihood of war. Better understanding of the dynamics of crisis could reduce the attractiveness of preemption and of the kinds of policies that court loss of control or miscalculated escalation. It could also sensitize policy makers to the need to prepare themselves and their subordinates to cope with the possibly debilitating stress that superpower nuclear crisis would generate. My primary goal is to encourage a conceptual shift in thinking about the nature of crisis and the appropriate means of coping with it.

The policy recommendations that grow out of my analysis are not offered as any kind of panacea. There are important structural causes of crisis instability that would be not the least bit affected if both superpowers were to adopt more enlightened approaches to crisis. The threat to peace by crisis instability can be overcome only by far-reaching changes in force structure, strategic doctrine, and targeting policy—the structural factors primarily responsible for the problem. . . .

## THE CAUSES OF WAR

No serious student of strategy believes that World War III will start as a gratuitous act of nuclear aggression. Only in paperback adventures does the leader of one of the superpowers wake up one morning, decide that the correlation of forces is highly favorable, and give the order to push the button. The incredible destruction that nuclear war would bring about, even to the side that struck first, is far too great to warrant its consideration as a rational act of policy. Leaders on both sides know this. So do their national security advisers and military establishments. They are all in accord that nuclear war would constitute the greatest disaster in the history of mankind.

Nor is a superpower nuclear war likely to come about as the result of an accident, an act of terrorism, or the efforts of a third party to start one. The prospect of an accidental launch when forces are on day-to-day alert is exceedingly remote. Nuclear terrorism is an even more unrealistic scenario. Despite the appeal the subject has for popular fiction writers, nuclear weapons and delivery systems are not easy objects to steal. Terrorists who overcame this basic hurdle would still have to find some way of arming the weapons in the absence of the necessary code. Even if they managed to do so, it is unclear how an act of nuclear terrorism would prompt one superpower to attack the other.

Nuclear war orchestrated by a third party also seems improbable, although the idea has from time to time aroused the concern of the superpowers. The usual scenario involves a nuclear attack on one superpower by another power that attempts to make the attack appear the work of the second superpower. The deception would be difficult to achieve, however, because the United States and the Soviet Union can track incoming reentry vehicles (RVs) and bombers and determine where they came from. A better possibility would be a submarine launched missile, but even that would be likely to have a telltale MIRV separation pattern. Moreover, a limited nuclear attack, regardless of what form it took, would be certain to arouse suspicions because it is the very last thing that either superpower expects the other to do.

If there is a World War III, it is most likely to be the result of either a miscalculation or an act of desperation in a crisis or conventional war. The paradigm of such a situation is 1914. World War I was brought about more by accident than by design; it was the largely unanticipated outcome of a series of amplifying miscalculations by Austria-Hungary, Germany, Russia, France, and Britain. It might have been prevented by a greater realization on the part of European leaders of the consequences of mobilization. At the same time, we would be wrong to suppose that the war was entirely attributable to poor leadership; more astute statesmen would also have found it difficult to control the cascading events of July 1914. The domestic political situation of several of the powers generated strong pressures in the direction of war while their elaborate military plans imposed severe constraints on the power and imagination of leaders.

Although there are important differences between 1914 and today, the origins of World War I hold significant lessons for hawks and doves alike. For hawks, the Great War offers insight into how and why an adversary can be tempted to exploit his perceived political-military advantages. The crisis began as an attempt by Austria-Hungary, backed by Germany, to use the assassination of Archduke Franz Ferdinand as a pretext for destroying Serbia. German and Austrian leaders expected that Russia, Serbia's principal backer, would stand aside rather than confront their combined military might. If Russia nevertheless entered the fray, they were convinced that France, Russia's ally, would remain neutral. The July crisis was therefore envisaged as the catalyst for a localized Balkan war.

In point of fact, Germany and Austria made a grievous miscalculation. Not only did Russia back Serbia to the hilt, but France proved steadfast in its support of Russia. Because of this, Austria's démarche triggered a European war. Germany, much to its horror, had to fight Britain as well as Russia and France, because of its ill-advised invasion of Belgium. For doves, 1914 accordingly sheds light on how attempts at coercion can have unforeseen and disastrous consequences.

Better understanding of the dynamics behind both brinkmanship and miscalculation would help us manage adversarial relationships and the conflicts they spawn in a more sophisticated and successful manner. One way to do this would be to explore the role of both phenomena in 1914 in an attempt to mine that case for more widely applicable lessons of conflict management. As I have previously done with regard to brinkmanship, I focus here on miscalculation and its causes.

The first causal sequence to war is *preemption.* It occurs when one of the protagonists in a crisis goes to war because its leaders believe that their adversary is on the verge of doing so. When hostilities appear unavoidable, preemption can be an attractive option if it is believed that striking first will confer a significant or even decisive advantage. It is entirely conceivable that mutual recognition of this asymmetry could prompt one or other of the protagonists to go to war even though both would prefer to keep the peace. Thomas Schelling has called this "the reciprocal fear of surprise attack." He reasons:

> If surprise carries an advantage, it is worthwhile to avert it by striking first. Fear that the other may be about to strike in the mistaken belief that we are about to strike gives us a motive for striking, and so justifies the other's motive. . . . It looks as though a modest temptation on each side to sneak in a first blow—a temptation too small by itself to motivate an attack—might become compounded through a process of interacting expectations, with additional motive for attack being produced by successive cycles of "He thinks we think he thinks we think . . . he thinks we think he'll attack; so he thinks we shall; so he will; so we must."[2]

Until quite recently, most of the literature conceived of crisis stability in terms essentially similar to Schelling's. Analyses of this kind for the most part ignored the possibility that war could break out in the absence of any deliberate decisions by leaders on either side to fight it. They failed to consider a second sequence to war, *loss of control.*

Loss of control can take a variety of forms and can have diverse causes. It can result from fragmented political authority, domestic pressures that leaders are powerless to resist, or an institutional malfunction or breakdown. It can also be the inadvertent and unanticipated outcome of military preparations taken to protect oneself in a crisis or to convey resolve to an adversary. As 1914 revealed, interacting organizational routines can lead to war in a quasi-mechanical manner. Luigi Albertini and A. J. P. Taylor, two of the eminent historians of that conflict, considered this to have been one of its most important proximate causes. Political leaders, they argued, in effect "made" decisions for war without realizing at the time that they were doing so.[3]

Contemporary organizational theorists argue that World War III could start in the same way. Paul Bracken warns that an amplifying feedback loop could develop between the warning and response systems of the superpowers as a result of any significant military preparations by either one of them. Suppose the United States went on strategic alert in order to demonstrate resolve in a crisis; "the Russians would monitor some of the changes taking place in American

---

[2]Early theoretical treatments of preemption include Thomas C. Schelling, *The Strategy of Conflict* (Cambridge, Mass.: Harvard University Press, 1960), 207–54, and *Arms and Influence* (New Haven: Yale University Press, 1966), 221–48; Glenn H. Snyder, *Deterrence and Defense* (Princeton, N.J.: Princeton University Press, 1961), 97–114. The quotation is from *Strategy of Conflict,* 207. . . .

[3]Luigi Albertini, *The Origins of the War of 1914,* 3 vols., trans. Isabella M. Massey (London: Oxford University Press, 1952), 2:253; A.J.P. Taylor, *The Struggle for the Mastery of Europe, 1848–1918* (New York: Oxford University Press, 1969), 444.

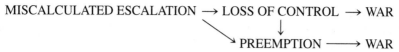

**FIGURE 1.**
Possible Paths to War in Crisis

monitoring operations and in reaction might speed their preparations for attack. America might respond in kind. What started as mere brinkmanship," Bracken fears, "might end in nuclear war."

A third sequence to war is *miscalculated escalation,* when one of the adversaries crosses the other's threshold to war in the false expectation that his action will be tolerated. The Russian mobilization is a classic example. In the opinion of most historians, it was the step that made war all but unavoidable. However, Russian political leaders mobilized in 1914 in the belief that mobilization would be a deterrent to war. The American decision to invade and occupy North Korea in 1950, Nasser's remilitarization of the Sinai in 1967, and Argentina's occupation of the Falklands in 1982 have also been described as instances of miscalculated escalation. In each of these confrontations, the initiator took action unlikely, he thought, to provoke a violent response. All three led to war. Little of a theoretical nature has been written about the phenomenon of miscalculated escalation, even though it is probably the most important cause of inadvertent war.

These three sequences to war are conceptually distinct. Any of them can be described separately but to demonstrate their practical effect, they must be analyzed in conjunction with another. The relevant analogy here is to epidemics, which also have multiple and interrelated causes. Among the most important of these are the presence of a pathogen, a mechanism for its spread among humans, and low human resistance because of the absence of antibodies or the debilitated state of the population. Sanitary conditions and the nature and rapidity of any institutional response will also influence the progress of the disease. It is the totality of these conditions which determines whether the disease becomes an epidemic.

So it is with crisis; the collective interaction of the three causal sequences, each with its own individual probability, determines whether war breaks out (see Figure 1). In 1914, for example, Russia's miscalculated escalation prompted Germany's decision to preempt. Loss of control, in turn, was a cause contributing both to Russia's miscalculated escalation and to Germany's preemption.

Efforts to minimize the risk of war in crisis are also interrelated. Preemption, loss of control, and miscalculated escalation have some distinctive but also some common causes. Civilian ignorance of war plans, to cite one example, can be shown to contribute to all three. Successful efforts to educate political leaders about the process of escalation and the details of military alerts would constitute an important step toward reducing the likelihood that some future superpower crisis will erupt into war. There are other measures that would have a similar ameliorating effect across the board.

Unfortunately, some of the most important ways of preventing particular sequences to war would also make other sequences more likely. This is true of many measures designed to cope with preemption or loss of control. We can reduce pressure to preempt in a crisis, for example, by reliance on a launch-on-warning (LOW) capability, predelegation of launch authority, or prepackaged targeting options to be executed automatically in response to a breakdown in the chain of command. But all three policies court loss of control; they increase the likelihood that war will start in circumstances in which a president or premier remains committed to keeping the peace.

Many measures designed to reduce the chances of loss of control entail similar trade-offs. The installation of Permissive Action Links—physical locks to prevent weapons aboard bombers and missiles from being armed in the absence of an Emergency Action Message from the National Command Authority—and the probable decision of any president to remain in Washington throughout a crisis, all make retaliation more difficult to carry out. Uncertainty about the nation's ability to respond to nuclear attack in turn generates pressure to preempt once war appears unavoidable.

Clearly, any comprehensive attempt to build greater crisis stability involves difficult trade-offs. Before decisions can be made, however, we must know more about the causes and mechanisms of each sequence to war, the relative danger that each would pose in a future crisis, and the likely impact upon all three sequences of any measure designed to reduce the chances that any one of them will lead to war.

# 9

# THE ARMS TRADE WITH THE THIRD WORLD: CHANGING PATTERNS IN THE 1990S

Michael T. Klare

International arms transfers comprise a significant component of the post–World War II international system, affecting considerably the distribution of military power and the prospects for regional and global security. In this essay Michael T. Klare reviews recent trends in the global arms trade, including the nature of the weapons available, the suppliers, and the recipients. He also assesses the consequences of the arms trade, which continues to accelerate. The failure to arrest the global trade in arms leads Klare to sobering conclusions about the future. Klare is associate professor at Hampshire College, where he directs the Five-College Program in Peace and World Security Studies. His recent books include *American Arms Supermarket* (1985), *Low-Intensity Warfare* (1988), and *Peace and World Order Studies* (1989).

In an ironic twist of fate, the forthcoming Soviet and American arms reductions in Europe will produce massive supplies of surplus weapons which are likely to be funneled into the arms inventories of emerging Third World powers. Already, the United States has promised 700 surplus M-60A1 tanks to Egypt, and other nations in the Middle East are also likely to receive excess U.S. tanks and artillery pieces. Similarly, the Soviet Union is reportedly seeking customers in Asia and the Middle East for some of the weapons it is withdrawing from

Used by permission of Michael T. Klare. This chapter was written especially for this book.

Eastern Europe. These transfers are occurring, moreover, at a time when the other major arms producers are vigorously pursuing new military markets in the Third World and as many Middle Eastern nations—alarmed by Iraq's aggressive moves in the Persian Gulf area—have sought to expand and enhance their military capabilities. As a result of these endeavors and an improving world economic climate, the 1990s are likely to witness a significant increase in military exports to the developing countries.

It would be very unwise, of course, to make overly specific predictions about the future magnitude of the arms traffic, given all the fluctuations that have occurred in recent years. The 1980s began with a tremendous surge in arms buying, as numerous Third World governments sought to equip their defense forces with modern tanks, missiles, and jet aircraft. In the mid-1980s, however, the international "debt crisis" produced a virtual freeze in bank lending to the Third World, and thus many developing nations have had to curtail their purchases of costly new weapons. The outbreak of peace in several areas also put a damper on the arms traffic. As a result, arms sales dropped from their peak levels of $50–60 billion per year in the early 1980s to a more modest $30–$40 billion per year at the end of the decade.

As we enter the 1990s, several factors point to a marked upturn in arms sales to the Third World. First, the Iraqi invasion of Kuwait has sparked a new round of arms buying by Middle Eastern countries. Second, the scarcity of credit has begun to ease as the world economy improves and as Third World governments proceed with plans for the restructuring of their debts. Third, the newly industrialized nations of the Pacific Rim have begun a drive for military modernization that will generate billions of dollars worth of new arms orders over the next few years. Finally, a number of the larger and more developed Third World countries—among them, Brazil, Egypt, India, Iraq, Israel, Pakistan, Syria, and Turkey—have apparently embarked on determined efforts to enter the 21st century as major military powers.

If these factors do prevail in the 1990s, it is likely that international arms sales will again reach the peak levels of the early 1980s. But while the dollar value of military exports may return to previous levels, we are not likely to see a complete restoration of the arms trade patterns that prevailed in the 1970s and early 1980s. During the past decade, the structure of the arms traffic experienced a number of important modifications, affecting the supply side of the trade, the composition of the marketplace, and the types of commodities sold. These modifications can only become more pronounced in the years ahead, producing new patterns of international trade and cooperation. In order to appreciate the nature of these changing patterns, it is useful to examine the basic dimensions of the arms traffic and consider how each has evolved in the recent past.[1]

---

[1] The author first explored these patterns in "Who's Arming Who?" *Technology Review,* May 1990, pp. 43–50.

## SUPPLIERS

Until very recently, the sale of arms to Third World countries was a highly concentrated affair, with the two superpowers and a handful of other industrial powers accounting for a very large percentage of the total North-to-South traffic. Thus, from 1975 to 1982, six nations—the United States, the Soviet Union, Great Britain, France, West Germany, and Italy—together supplied 84 percent (in dollar terms) of all munitions ordered by Third World countries. Within this exclusive group, moreover, the two superpowers enjoyed an especially privileged position, accounting together for approximately two-thirds of all military sales to the developing countries.[2]

As the decade progressed, however, the market share enjoyed by the "Big Six" began to shrink as other producers, eager to cash in on the booming arms business, offered comparable systems at competitive prices. Thus, according to the Congressional Research Service (CRS) of the Library of Congress, the portion of total Third World orders claimed by the Big Six declined somewhat in the mid-1980s, to about 75 percent.[3] Dividing up the remaining one-fourth of the market were a number of "second-tier" suppliers in Europe—notably Belgium, Czechoslovakia, East Germany, Poland, the Netherlands, Spain, Sweden, and Switzerland, along with several emerging producers in the Third World. These smaller suppliers cannot always compete with the Big Six in all categories of high-technology munitions, but they have succeeded in producing less-sophisticated variants that are well suited to Third World needs and budgets.

Probably the most dramatic development of the past decade was the emergence of Brazil and China as world-class military suppliers. While both had supplied some arms to other Third World countries in earlier years, it was only in the 1980s that they became a significant factor in the international arms traffic. Thus, according to the U.S. Arms Control and Disarmament Agency (ACDA), military sales by Brazil grew from $670 million in 1976–81 to $2.6 billion in 1982–87 (an increase of 288 percent), while sales by China soared from $1.25 billion to $7.8 billion (a 524 percent increase).[4] Both of these countries now export a wide range of basic combat systems—armored vehicles, artillery pieces, rockets and missiles, light combat aircraft—and both have pursued a common strategy of offering reliable, unsophisticated weapons at prices way below those charged by the traditional suppliers for similar items. While not quite in the same league as Brazil and China, several other Third World producers posted significant export gains in the 1980s. Notable examples include North

---

[2] Richard F. Grimmett, *Trends in Conventional Arms Transfers to the Third World by Major Supplier, 1975–1982* (Washington: Congressional Research Service, 1983), p. 10. (Hereinafter cited as CRS, *Trends 75–82.*)

[3] CRS, *Trends 81–88*, p. 34.

[4] U.S. Arms Control and Disarmament Agency, *World Military Expenditures and Arms Transfers 1988* (Washington: U.S. Government Printing Office, 1989), pp. 77, 80 (all figures in current dollars). (Hereinafter cited as ACDA, *WMEAT 1988.*)

Korea and Israel (each with 1982–87 sales of $2.4 billion), South Korea (with sales of $2.1 billion), and Egypt (with sales of $770 million).[5]

As we enter the 1990s, it is apparent that the supply side of the weapons traffic has become much more complex—and crowded—than was the case in previous decades. What we are seeing, in fact, is the emergence of a multi-tiered supply system, with both old and new producers striving to expand, or at least to preserve, their existing share of the international market.

At the apex of this system—occupying the first "tier"—are to be found the two superpowers plus the major industrial powers of Europe. Because these countries continue to lead the rest of the world in the development of high-technology weapons, they will continue to find customers for their products among those Third World countries that seek—and can afford to pay for—the most advanced systems available. For the superpowers, this will entail the continued exploitation of indigenous technological capabilities; for the Europeans, this will probably entail increased collaboration across national boundaries as individual companies pool their technical capabilities with those of others in order to enhance their mutual technological competitiveness.

Next in line are the second-tier suppliers, consisting of the smaller European producers which have established a distinctive market "niche" for a particular type of weapons—e.g., anti-aircraft guns in Sweden, naval systems in the Netherlands—plus the emerging Third World producers like China and Brazil that have found a receptive market for low- and medium-technology equipment. Many of these suppliers recorded significant sales gains in the 1980s, but most of them are likely to face increased competition from aggressive newcomers in the 1990s.

Finally, there is a third tier, consisting of private dealers and brokers (some operating on the fringes of the law) that sell second-hand and surplus equipment, and, in some cases, stolen guns and ammunition. These suppliers played a relatively minor role in the international arms traffic prior to 1980, but received an enormous boost from the Iran-Iraq war, which generated a huge demand for black-market arms. Sales have been somewhat sluggish for this group since the end of the Iran-Iraq war, but could rise in the years ahead due to increased demand from insurgent groups in Asia, Africa, and Latin America.

This sales picture is likely to become even more complex in the 1990s, as additional Third World producers seek to carve out a market niche of their own, and as other producers combine forces to better compete in a crowded field. Indeed, several major Third World countries have announced plans to become major exporters in the years ahead, including India, Indonesia, Pakistan, Singapore, Taiwan, and Turkey. Further complicating the picture is the emergence of large multinational consortia designed to pool the resources of many individual companies. Such multinational linkages are already well established

---

[5] Ibid., pp. 83, 89, 91 (all figures in current dollars).

in Europe—witness the European Fighter Aircraft (EFA) program and such joint enterprises as Eurocopter and Euromissile—and are now spreading across oceans, to Latin America and Asia.[6]

## BUYERS

Although more and more Third World countries are producing at least some weapons in domestic factories, most of the developing nations still rely on the international market for a significant share of their military requirements. According to the ACDA, a total of 107 Third World countries each purchased at least $1 million worth of imported arms between 1983 and 1987. Of these, 43 were located in Africa, 24 in Latin America, 16 in the Middle East, 15 in East Asia and the Pacific, and 6 in South Asia.[7]

Despite the relative abundance of recipients, however, the statistics on global arms transfers indicate that a relatively small number of countries are responsible for a very large proportion of the total value of all arms exports to the Third World. Thus, again using ACDA data, we find that just twelve nations—Angola, Cuba, Egypt, Ethiopia, India, Iran, Iraq, Israel, Libya, Saudi Arabia, Syria, and Vietnam—together accounted for two-thirds of all transfers to the developing countries between 1983 and 1987.[8]

An assessment of the major arms-importing countries reveals a number of common features among them. These countries have either engaged in armed combat within the past decade (Angola, Cuba, Ethiopia, Iran, Iraq, Israel, Libya, Syria, Vietnam), and/or participated in a regional arms race with a neighboring rival (India vs. Pakistan; India vs. China; Israel vs. Egypt, Iraq, Syria, and Saudi Arabia; Egypt vs. Libya). In addition, most of these countries possess large supplies of oil or, as in the case of Angola, Ethiopia, Cuba, Egypt, Israel, and Vietnam, receive substantial military subsidies from one or the other of the superpowers. It is this combination of means and motive that propelled these nations to the top of the list of Third World arms importers in the 1980s.

While the arms trade is likely to remain highly concentrated in the years ahead, the composition of the top-ranked group is likely to experience periodic revision in response to changing political and economic conditions. In recent years, the most significant factor in the changing economic environment was the decline in national income experienced by the oil-exporting nations of the Middle East. With a glut in world oil supplies and the resulting drop in prices, most oil-producing nations had far less capital with which to purchase arms in the late 1980s than they did at the beginning of the decade. Thus Saudi Arabia,

---

[6] For discussion, see: Carole A. Shifren, "Lower East-West Tensions May Boost Joint European Defense Projects," and Paul Proctor, "Asian Manufacturers Seek Aircraft Development Share," *Aviation Week and Space Technology,* March 19, 1990, pp. 86–88 and 88–90, respectively.

[7] ACDA, *WMEAT 1988,* pp. 111–14.

[8] Ibid.

which spent $25 billion on its armed forces in 1983, cut its military spending to $10 billion in 1987 as a result of declining oil income.[9] Also inhibiting the demand for arms on the part of some Third World countries was the global debt crisis, which severely constrained the availability of credit for costly arms acquisitions.

The changing political climate has also affected the volume of arms transfers to some Third World countries. Thus the signing of a cease fire between Iran and Iraq—which together spent an estimated $65 billion on imported arms between 1981 and 1988[10]—resulted in a sharp (if temporary) drop in arms transfers to the Persian Gulf region. Similarly, the 1988 peace settlement in Angola reduced the flow of arms to that country, while the merger of North and South Yemen is likely to produce a similar decline in arms transfers to these formerly separate (and antagonistic) nations. The current economic turmoil in the Soviet Union is also likely to affect international arms transfer patterns, since Moscow is expected to curtail its military assistance to such long-term allies as Cuba, Ethiopia, North Korea, and Vietnam.

However, while some countries have been forced to *reduce* their arms spending, we have also seen an *increase* in military spending by a number of other Third World nations. Most noticeable in this regard is the surge in arms spending by the emerging economic powers of the Pacific Rim—notably South Korea, Taiwan, Thailand, Malaysia, and Singapore. As the national income of these nations has risen, they have devoted more and more money to the modernization of their military forces. South Korea, for instance, increased its military spending from $2.9 billion in 1980 to $5.6 billion in 1987, while Taiwan's defense expenditures jumped from $2.8 billion to $4.7 billion. Military spending in Singapore and Malaysia has been rising at an equally brisk pace, pushing defense expenditures in these countries to well over $1 billion per year.[11] As these countries proceed with their ambitious arms-acquisitions programs, the Pacific Rim countries are likely to move way up the list of the major arms-importing nations.[12]

Also fueling the arms trade in the 1990s will be the efforts of a number of Third World countries to improve their overall military capabilities, thereby to enhance their status as major regional powers. Especially prominent in this category are Egypt, India, Iraq, Israel, Saudi Arabia, and Turkey—all of which have embarked on ambitious efforts to modernize the combat capabilities of their sizeable military forces. India, which seeks to play a major military role in South

---

[9] Ibid., p. 59.

[10] CRS, *Trends 81–88,* pp. 40–41.

[11] ACDA, *WMEAT 1988,* pp. 38, 49, 52, 60.

[12] For discussion, see: Alex Gliksman, "Arms Production in the Pacific," *National Defense,* December 1989, pp. 41–43; P. Lewis Young, "Strong Southeast Asian Budgets Attracting Widespread Industry Interest," *Armed Forces Journal,* March 1990, p. 38; and *The New York Times,* May 6, 1990.

Asia and the Indian Ocean area, became the world's number one arms importer in the late 1980s, and is likely to remain high on the list of major recipients throughout the 1990s. Iraq and Egypt have both engaged in major military-industrial endeavors (some are joint ventures involving both countries), while Israel and Saudi Arabia have sought new weapons to counter the aggressive military moves of Iraq. And Turkey, which has long been eclipsed by the other powers in NATO, has ordered 120 F-16 fighters from the United States and plans to spend some $10 billion on imported arms and military technology in the next few years.

Also to be found on the list of major recipients in the 1990s will be those Third World countries that are facing major insurgent or ethnic conflicts. Among those likely to be included in this group are countries like Afghanistan, El Salvador, Peru, the Philippines, and the Sudan with continuing conflicts left over from the 1980s, as well as other nations that are just beginning to experience widespread insurgent and ethnic unrest. And while the purchasing power of these countries is likely to be constrained by domestic economic conditions and the diminished military aid programs of the superpowers, they are likely to seek large supplies of infantry arms, helicopters, and other counterinsurgency weapons in the years ahead.

## COMMODITIES

As now configured, the international arms trade encompasses a wide variety of weapons and military systems, ranging from small arms and ammunition at one end of the spectrum to tanks, aircraft, and warships at the other end. Also included in this spectrum are combat-support systems (communications devices, radar systems, transport vehicles, and so on), uniforms and other quartermaster supplies, and technology for the manufacture of arms. Significant sales in all of these categories can usually be found in the tally of world military exports for any given year, but the relative popularity of any given type of weapon or system is likely to change from year to year in response to changing market conditions.

At the beginning of the 1980s, Third World buyers exhibited a strong preference for the acquisition of major front-line systems—heavy tanks, supersonic jet fighters, and large warships. Between 1980 and 1983 alone, the developing countries acquired 7,889 tanks and self-propelled guns (SPGs), 2,258 supersonic combat aircraft, 83 major surface warships, and 1,300 helicopters.[13] Because "big ticket" items of this sort are the costliest items sold on the international arms market, large multiple sales of such products in the early 1980s pushed the annual tally of military exports to record levels.

---

[13] CRS, *Trends 80–87,* p. 65.

By the middle of the decade, however, the demand for major combat systems of this sort had dropped off noticeably. Thus, deliveries of supersonic combat aircraft in the 1984–87 period fell by 47 percent from the 1980–83 figure, to 1,197, while deliveries of tanks and SPGs fell by 49 percent, to 4,006.[14] Because these items account for such a large proportion of the dollar value of arms exports, the declining demand for front-line systems produced a marked reduction in annual trade figures in the later 1980s.

Several factors account for the decline in orders for major front-line systems. Some of these, of course, were economic in nature: as a result of the international debt crisis, many Third World countries were forced to curtail their spending on imported goods of all types, while the drop in oil prices forced the oil-exporting nations to reduce their weapons imports.

Other factors, however, also influenced the demand for these systems. Most significant, perhaps, was the "crisis of absorption" created by the acquisition of so many modern weapons at the same time. While often possessed with considerable ambition, many Third World countries discovered that they lacked the technical military skills needed to operate and maintain all of the sophisticated weapons they ordered in the late 1970s and early 1980s. As a result, these countries have tended to postpone further purchases of major systems while struggling to absorb the equipment already acquired.[15]

The absorption crisis also occurred at a time when many Third World military officials were reassessing the need for sophisticated front-line weapons. To a great extent, this reassessment was the product of the "lessons learned" from the Iran-Iraq war and other armed conflicts of the 1980s. Prior to the onset of the Iran-Iraq conflict, most military analysts tended to assume that future regional conflicts of this type would be decided by short but intense battles utilizing the various high-technology weapons then being purchased in record numbers on the international market. Instead, the Gulf conflict evolved into a prolonged war of endurance in which the *quantity* of arms on each side, rather than their quality, often proved decisive. "The Gulf war quickly stalemated into an infantryman's and an artilleryman's war, reminiscent of World War I," arms analyst Morton S. Miller wrote in 1988. This situation, he noted, "created a market for huge quantities of low-technology arms and combat-consumables."[16] Iran and Iraq each spent many billions of dollars on such hardware during their eight-year war with one another, and other Third World countries, fearful of being caught in a similar situation, have made comparable purchases of their own.

But while these experiences have tended to dampen enthusiasm for imports of some front-line systems, the wars of the 1980s have generated increased demand for at least one category of weapons: modern battlefield missiles. Thus

---

[14] Ibid.

[15] See Morton S. Miller, "Conventional Arms Trade in the Developing World, 1976–86: Reflections on a Decade," in ACDA, *WMEAT 1987*, p. 19.

[16] Ibid., p. 21.

the Falklands conflict, and later the Iran-Iraq war, demonstrated the lethal effectiveness of precision-guided anti-ship missiles like the French *Exocet*—used by Argentina to sink the British destroyer HMS *Sheffield* and later by Iraq to cripple the USS *Stark.* In Afghanistan, the military fortunes of the anti-Soviet *mujahedeen* were reversed almost overnight by the introduction of shoulder-fired *Stinger* anti-aircraft missiles. Much larger (if somewhat less accurate) surface-to-surface missiles were used by both Iran and Iraq during the so-called "war of the cities" to attack each other's civilian populations. These, and other such experiences, have led many Third World countries to place great emphasis on the acquisition of modern missiles, even while cutting back on purchases of other combat systems.

The Iran-Iraq experience also led many Third World countries to place greater emphasis on the acquisition of arms-making *technologies,* as distinct from the purchase of finished military systems. Because Iran was the subject of a global arms embargo organized by the United States, Iranian authorities launched an emergency effort to develop domestic facilities for the manufacture of a wide variety of basic combat systems. This, in turn, has inspired other Third World nations to build up their own capabilities for military production, lest they, too, be caught in such a dilemma. To sustain such efforts, these countries have often cut back on purchases of finished military systems in order to channel funds into the acquisition of blueprints, machine tools, specialized components, and other materials needed for the manufacture of arms.

The character of the arms flow has also been influenced by the growing incidence of insurgency, ethnic conflict, and other forms of "low-intensity conflict" in the Third World. These wars rarely produce major battles of the sort witnessed in the Persian Gulf, but have nevertheless produced significant loss of life in such areas as Central America, sub-Saharan Africa, Lebanon, Afghanistan, and the Philippines. To contain these conflicts, affected governments have ordered vast quantities of small arms, infantry weapons, off-road vehicles, and other types of counterinsurgency equipment.

As a result of all these developments, the arms flow of the 1990s is likely to look rather different from that of the 1970s and early 1980s. While many developing nations will continue to buy major weapons systems from their traditional suppliers in the North—especially when comparable systems are not available from producers in the Third World—such acquisitions will increasingly be accompanied by transfers of materials and technology for the production of armaments. Thus Turkey, which plans to spend some $10 billion on military hardware in the early 1990s, will devote most of this amount to the acquisition of technology for the manufacture of modern weapons, including the F-16 fighter, armored personnel carriers, and multiple-launch rocket systems. India, meanwhile, has made arrangements with the Soviet Union and several Western nations for the transfer of technology for the production of modern tanks, aircraft, missiles, and helicopters.

The 1990s are also likely to witness increased sales—usually through illicit and clandestine channels—of materials and technology for the manufacture of ballistic missiles and weapons of mass destruction (nuclear and/or chemical). According to the Stockholm International Peace Research Institute, at least ten Third World nations—Argentina, Brazil, Egypt, India, Iran, Iraq, Israel, Pakistan, South Korea, and Taiwan—are now engaged in programs for the development of ballistic missiles.[17] In addition, approximately one dozen Third World countries are believed to possess an incipient capability for the production of chemical munitions; a smaller group of nations is thought to possess an ability to manufacture nuclear weapons, or is attempting to acquire such a capability.[18] Which countries will succeed in these various endeavors cannot of course be predicted at this time, but recent disclosures regarding the Iraqi military program illustrate how far some of these efforts have proceeded.

## POLITICAL AND MILITARY IMPLICATIONS

Having examined the dynamics of the weapons trade, what conclusions can we draw about the impact of arms transfers on the global security environment? Militarily, the most pronounced impact of the arms trade is the growing world-wide proliferation of modern weapons of all types. This virtual cornucopia of weapons has made it possible for Third World belligerents to conduct prolonged wars of great intensity and duration. The Iran-Iraq war, for instance, lasted eight years, consumed $65 billion worth of imported arms and ammunition, and resulted in the death or injury of an estimated 1,250,000 people. To satisfy Iran's and Iraq's insatiable hunger for weapons, a total of 41 countries sold at least some weapons to one or the other of the belligerents, and 28 supplied military hardware to both.[19]

Other recent conflicts, while not quite as bloody as the Iran-Iraq war, were also notable for the high levels of destruction engendered by imported weapons. The war in Afghanistan, for instance, is estimated to have produced as many as 500,000 deaths over a ten-year period, and has resulted in the virtual annihilation (through bombing and rocket attacks) of many provincial towns and villages. In Lebanon, heavily armed militias and sectarian armies have produced thousands of casualties each year in a seemingly unquenchable fratricidal conflict. And in Angola, where both sides in a protracted civil war were equipped with modern weapons, the death toll is estimated at well over 25,000.[20]

---

[17] Stockholm International Peace Research Institute, *SIPRI Yearbook 1989* (Oxford and New York: Oxford University Press, 1989), pp. 287–318.

[18] For discussion, see: Leonard S. Spector, *The Undeclared Bomb* (Cambridge, Mass.: Ballinger, 1987); *SIPRI Yearbook 1989*, pp. 99–129.

[19] ACDA, *WMEAT 1988*, pp. 21–23.

[20] For data on casualties in recent wars, see *SIPRI Yearbook 1989*, pp. 339–55.

These and other examples demonstrate that even the so-called "low-intensity" conflicts of the 1990s are likely to entail high levels of violence and bloodshed.

Arms transfers have also contributed to the escalatory potential of regional wars, as graphically demonstrated by the Iran-Iraq conflict. After countless battles failed to produce a decisive victory for either side, both belligerents escalated their military effort in a number of ways. Thus, in an effort to curb their respective adversary's oil deliveries (which produced the income needed to purchase military supplies), both sides attacked ships and oil facilities located far from the front lines of battle, often striking vessels belonging to neutral countries. Both sides, moreover, used ballistic missiles to strike at cities in the enemy's interior, and both used chemical weapons in attacks on military and civilian personnel.

Fortunately, neither Iraq nor Iran took the fateful step of using ballistic missiles to carry chemical warheads in attacks on populated areas—a step that would undoubtedly have produced many thousands of civilian fatalities. It is important to note, however, that the technology to deliver such munitions is in the hands of several potential Middle Eastern belligerents. Syria, for instance, has reportedly developed chemical warheads for its Soviet-supplied Scud-B and SS-21 missiles, and several other countries are believed to possess a similar capability.[21]

Clearly, the introduction of hybrid weapons of this sort poses a very significant threat to regional stability. As it is, Israeli officials have threatened to launch a pre-emptive attack on Syria if they have any reason to believe that Damascus is preparing chemically armed missiles for attacks on Israel.[22] Even more frightening to contemplate is Israel's likely reaction in the event that Syria or Iraq actually struck Israeli cities with chemical weapons. "If, heaven forbid, they dare to employ these means," Israeli Defense Minister Yitzhak Rabin declared in 1988, "the response [by Israel] will be one hundred times stronger"[23]—an obvious allusion to nuclear retaliation.

Nor is an Israeli-Syrian clash the only encounter that could spark nuclear escalation in the decades ahead. The growing proliferation of nuclear weapons, chemical munitions, and high-technology conventional arms is creating a number of incipient "Third World superpowers" capable of conducting military operations on a scale previously reserved for the major industrial powers. At this point, only China, Israel, and India can claim this dubious status; by 1999, it could be held as well by Brazil, Iraq, Pakistan, South Korea, Taiwan, and Turkey. Even now, a major conflict involving any of these emerging powers would risk significant escalation; in just a few more years, that risk could include a regional nuclear conflagration. And because such conflicts could jeop-

---

[21] Robert D. Shuey, et al., *Missile Proliferation* (Washington: Congressional Research Service, 1988), pp. 3, 54, 68.

[22] Ibid., p. 69.

[23] Cited in *Arms Control Today,* December 1988, p. 70.

ardize the vital interests of the superpowers, future wars of this type provide the most plausible scenario one can imagine for the outbreak of World War III.

The emergence of these Third World powers, or "regional hegemons" as they are sometimes called, will slowly but surely transform the global configuration of international relations. Third World countries that were once under the thrall of the great imperial powers of the North will seek to acquire spheres of influence of their own—as vividly demonstrated by the 1990 Iraqi invasion and occupation of Kuwait. Smaller nations that once sought out the Europeans or the superpowers as allies will increasingly seek to align with local powers that dominate their particular region. And new alliances and coalitions may spring up that unite the strength of two or more local hegemons in a continent-spanning power bloc.

Whether this emerging world will prove more violent and chaotic than the one we are leaving is impossible to determine. What does seem likely, however, is that international politics will become increasingly complex, and that the resolution of global and regional problems will require the cooperation of more and more major actors. As suggested by the U.S. Commission on Integrated Long-Term Strategy, a world of many power centers "would confront American strategic planners with a far more complicated environment than does the familiar bipolar competition with the Soviet Union." In such a world, "the United States would have to manage relations with several global powers and form appropriate coalitions with them."[24] The same, of course, would be true for the Soviet Union and the other major industrial powers. Whatever its final configuration, this world will undoubtedly confront the traditional powers with an extraordinary array of risks and challenges.

---

[24] U.S. Commission on Integrated Long-Term Strategy, *Discriminate Deterrence* (Washington: U.S. Government Printing Office, 1988), p. 7.

# 10

# REFLECTIONS ON TERRORISM

## Walter Laqueur

**In this essay, Walter Laqueur examines the nature of the "terrorist menace" of our time. With terrorism representing a relatively new and successful strategy for many political actors (including some national governments), much of the global political agenda has become dominated by the search for ways to confront this threatening practice. Here, the author defines the essence of terrorism and suggests strategies to eradicate it. Laqueur, author of *The Age of Terrorism* (1988) and *The Long Road to Freedom* (1989), is chairman of the research council of the Center for Strategic and International Studies at Georgetown University.**

I

Fifty years hence, puzzled historians will try to make sense of the behavior of Western governments and the media . . . regarding terrorism. They will note that presidents and other leaders frequently referred to terrorism as one of the greatest dangers facing mankind. For days and weeks on end, television networks devoted most of their prime-time news to covering terrorist operations. Publicists referred to terrorism as the cancer of the modern world, growing inexorably until it poisoned and engulfed the society on which it fed.

Reprinted from Walter Laqueur, "Reflections on Terrorism," *Foreign Affairs* 65 (Fall 1986), pp. 86–100. Copyright 1986 by the Council on Foreign Relations, Inc. Reprinted by permission of *Foreign Affairs.* Some footnotes have been deleted; others have been renumbered to appear in consecutive order.

Naturally, our future historian will expect that a danger of such enormity must have figured very highly on the agenda of our period—equal, say, to the dangers of war, starvation, overpopulation, deadly disease, debts and so on. He will assume that determined action was taken and major resources allocated to fight against this threat. But he will be no little surprised to learn that when the Swedish prime minister was killed in 1986, the Swedish government promised a reward for information leading to the apprehension of his killer that amounted to less than ten percent of the annual income of an investment banker or a popular entertainer; that the French government offered even less for its terrorists; that West Germany was only willing to pay a maximum of $50,000 "for the most dangerous" ones. The United States offered up to $500,000, again not an overwhelming sum considering the frequency of the speeches about terrorism and the intensity of the rhetoric. . . .

His confusion will further deepen when he learns that the number of Americans killed inside the United States in 1985 as the result of terrorist attack was two, and that the total number of U.S. civilians killed abroad between 1973 and the end of 1985 was 169. In countless articles and books, our historian will read about the constantly rising number of terrorist attacks. Being a conscientious researcher he will analyze the statistics, which are bound to increase his confusion, for he will find that more American civilians were killed by terrorists in 1974 (22) than in 1984 (16).

On the basis of these and other facts, our historian will lean toward revisionism. He may well reach the conclusion that there was no terrorism, only a case of mass delusion—or that hysteria was deliberately fanned by certain vested interests such as producers of anti-terrorist equipment, perhaps, or the television networks which had established a symbiotic relationship with the terrorists, who provided them with free (or almost free) entertainment for long periods.

These are, of course, the wrong conclusions. The impact of terrorism is measured not only in the number of its victims. Terrorism is an attempt to destabilize democratic societies and to show that their governments are impotent. If this can be attained with a minimum effort, if so much publicity can be achieved on the basis of a few attacks, no greater exertion is needed. Furthermore . . . there have been ominous new developments such as the emergence of narco-terrorism and the occurrence of state-sponsored terrorism on a broader level than before. If terrorism has never been a serious threat as far as America is concerned, let alone other major powers such as the Soviet Union, China or Japan, it is also true that in certain Latin American countries, and in places like Turkey and Italy, it was for a while a real danger.

In short, there has been (and is) a terrorist menace in our time. But the historian of the future will still be right in pointing to the wide discrepancy between the strong speeches and the weak actions of those who felt threatened. And he must be forgiven if he should draw the conclusion that those living in this "age of terrorism" perhaps never quite understood the exact nature of the threat.

## II

What is terrorism? It would be highly desirable if all discussions of terrorism, of its motives and inspiration, its specific character, its modes of operation and long-term consequences, were based on a clear, exact and comprehensive definition. Ideally, there should be agreement as to whether terrorism is violence in general or some particular form of violence; whether the emphasis should be on its political aims or its methods of combat or the extra-normal character of its strategy; whether its purposive, systematic character should be singled out or, on the contrary, its unpredictability and its symbolic aspect or perhaps the fact that so many of its victims are innocents.

Agreement on a definition, alas, does not exist, and there is no reason to assume that it will in the foreseeable future. The author of an excellent research guide to terrorism, published a few years ago, listed 109 different definitions of terrorism provided between 1936 and 1981.[1] There have been more since; the U.S. government alone has provided half a dozen, which are by no means identical. Most experts agree that terrorism is the use or threat of violence, a method of combat or a strategy to achieve certain goals, that its aim is to induce a state of fear in the victim, that it is ruthless and does not conform to humanitarian norms, and that publicity is an essential factor in terrorist strategy.

Beyond this point definitions differ, often sharply, which is by no means surprising, be it only because the character of terrorist groups has been subject to change. There is little, if anything, in common between the Russian terrorists of the nineteenth century and Abu Nidal; a definition trying to cover both as well as others would be either very vague or very misleading. There is no such thing as terrorism pure and unadulterated, specific and unchanging, comparable to a chemical element; rather, there are a great many terrorisms. Historians and sociologists are not in full agreement on what socialism is or fascism was. It would be unrealistic to expect unanimity on a topic so close to us in time. But the absence of an exact definition does not mean that we do not know in a general way what terrorism is; it has been said that it resembles pornography, difficult to describe and define, but easy to recognize when one sees it.

According to one school of thought, "state terrorism" is the all-important issue. It is true that the number of victims and the amount of suffering caused by oppressive, tyrannical governments has been infinitely greater than that caused by small groups of rebels. A Hitler or a Stalin killed more people in one year than all terrorists throughout recorded history.

There are basic differences in motives, function and effect between oppression by the state (or society or religion) and political terrorism. To equate them, to obliterate the differences, is to spread confusion. The study of the Inquisition or the Gestapo or the Gulag is of undoubted importance, but it will shed no light whatsoever on contemporary terrorism.

[1] Alex Schmid, *Political Terrorism: A Research Guide.* New Brunswick, N.J.: Transaction, 1984.

If there has been a significant development during the [contemporary period], it is not oppression by the state but state-sponsored terrorism. This latter is not, of course, a product of the [recent past]; attempts to undermine the political or social order in other countries have been made by ambitious or revengeful rulers since time immemorial. The term "destabilization" may be new, but the use of proxies is as old as the hills. There are, however, certain new features to this old acquaintance that make it both more dangerous and more pervasive than in the past. It has become more frequent because resistance to it has been weak and uncoordinated. It has become more brazen: Mussolini, one of the chief practitioners of state-sponsored terrorism in the 1930s, would reject any imputation of responsibility with great indignation. In full uniform, shedding bitter tears, he attended the service in Rome in honor of Yugoslavia's King Alexander, who had been assassinated at his behest. Today's Qaddafis, on the other hand, do not stick to such proprieties, but claim the right to engage in acts of terror within the territory of other countries. Above all, there is the danger that state-sponsored terrorism will escalate into full military conflict, with the incalculable consequences of all-out war in this age.

Some of the obfuscation concerning terrorism stems from the belief in some circles that contemporary terrorism is basically revolutionary, a reaction against social and national injustice, and therefore worthy of support or at least understanding. But, in fact, terrorism is by no means the monopoly of the extreme left; quite frequently it is used by the extreme right and neo-fascists. Those trying to find mitigating circumstances for "revolutionary terrorism" find themselves sooner or later in the uncomfortable position of performing the same service for their political enemies. Terrorism is not an ideology but a strategy that can be used by people of different political convictions. Contemporary terrorism is certainly not the brainchild of Marxism-Leninism or Muslim fundamentalism, even though proponents of these creeds have made notable contributions to its spread.

Terrorism is neither identical to guerrilla warfare nor a subspecies of it. The term "urban guerrilla" is as common as it is mistaken. Terrorism is indeed urban, but not "guerrilla" in any meaningful sense; the difference is not one of semantics but of quality. A guerilla leader aims at building up ever-growing military units and eventually an army, in order to establish liberated zones in which propaganda can be openly conducted, and eventually to set up an alternative government. All this is impossible in cities. In many instances, guerrilla movements and other insurrectional groups do have footholds in cities, but they are usually not of much consequence, because in the urban milieu there are no opportunities for guerrilla warfare. There is a world of difference between a temporary zone of control and the establishment of an alternative government.

Some Western experts, and especially the media, have great difficulty accepting the basic differences among various forms of violence. "Terrorists," "commandos," "partisans," "urban guerrillas," "gunmen," "freedom fighters," "insurgents" and half a dozen other terms are often used interchangeably, frequently as a result of genuine confusion, sometimes probably with political intent, because the guerrilla has, on the whole, a positive public relations image, which the terrorist clearly does not possess.

Soviet writers on this subject have fewer inhibitions about calling a spade by its rightful name. In a recent study, one of them noted that "urban guerrilla is a fraudulent concept, scheduled to mask ordinary terrorism." Soviet ideologists are by no means opposed to the use of revolutionary violence. On the other hand, they know that terrorism carried out by marginal groups almost always causes more harm than good to the cause it sponsors. It is easy to think of guerrilla movements that defeated the forces opposing them, but it is very difficult to remember more than a few cases in which terrorism has had any lasting effect.

## III

How to eradicate terrorism? Moralists believe that terrorism is the natural response to injustice, oppression and persecution. Hence their seemingly obvious conclusion: remove the underlying causes and terrorism will wither away! This sounds plausible enough, for happy and content people are unlikely to commit savage acts of violence. Although this may be true as an abstract general proposition, it seldom applies in the real world, which is never quite free of conflicts.

The historical record shows that, while in the nineteenth century terrorism frequently developed in response to repression, the correlation between grievance and terrorism in our day and age is far less obvious. The record also shows that in more recent times the more severe the repression, the less terrorism tends to occur. This is an uncomfortable, shocking fact that has therefore encountered much resistance. But it is still true that terrorism in Spain gathered strength only after General Franco died, that the terrorist upsurges in West Germany, France and Turkey took place under social democratic or left-of-center governments, that the same is true with regard to Peru and Colombia, and that more such examples could easily be adduced.

Terrorism has never had a chance in an effective dictatorship, but hardly a major democratic country has entirely escaped it. There is a limit to the perfection of political institutions, and, however just and humane the social order, there will always be a few people deeply convinced that it ought to be radically changed and that it can be changed only through violent action. The murder of Sweden's prime minister, Olof Palme, is just one illustration that shows that "objective factors" cannot account for the actions of a fringe group.

Nationalist-separatist terrorism has been doing better than that of the extreme left and right, and it is not difficult to understand why. National groups and minorities usually have grievances, and some of them may be quite justified. In some instances, they can be put right; in others assuaged, but frequently neither may be possible. In an ideal world, each group of people, however small, claiming the right of full independence and statehood, should receive it. But in some cases, given the lack of national homogeneity and the intermingling of ethnic and religious groups, no basic redress may be feasible.

Even at this late date, it may be possible for the Turks to accept responsibility for the Armenian massacres during World War I, to apologize to the descendants of the victims, and to show contrition. But an Armenian state on Turkish territory (as Asala, the Secret Army for the Liberation of Armenia, demands) would be an absurdity: Armenians no longer live in eastern Turkey, nor do they have any intention of settling there. . . .

The Basque Homeland and Liberty group (ETA) and the Corsican militants are also fighting for independent statehood. But even if these ministates would be viable, which is uncertain, these groups' demands are by no means shared by most of their fellow countrymen, let alone by the majority populations in either the Basque region or Corsica, which are of different ethnic backgrounds (Spanish and French, respectively) from the terrorist groups.

Nor is it certain that the establishment of new, independent states would put an end to terrorism. On the contrary, there could well be an intensification of the struggle between various terrorist groups, between moderates who want to proceed with the business of statehood and radicals who claim that what has been achieved is only a beginning and that the borders of the new state should be expanded. The Tamils in Sri Lanka have been fighting with as much relish against each other as against their common enemy, and there is no reason to assume that this would stop if they were to get a state of their own.

The high tide of PLO activities both on the political and the terrorist level was in the mid-1970s. True, even then much of Middle Eastern terrorism had only a tenuous connection with Israel but was indigenous to the region. Since then this trend has become even more pronounced: some of the terrorist groups, such as Abu Nidal's or Abu Mussa's, serve the highest bidder among the Arab governments. They have killed considerably more Arabs than Israelis. As for Shi'ite terrorism, this never had much to do with Israel except at times when the Israelis happened to get in the Sh'ites' way.

No effort should be spared to pursue the peace process between Arabs and Israelis. But few serious students of this conflict argue that if a Palestinian state were to come into existence in the foreseeable future, terrorism would decrease. No settlement that recognizes Israel would be to the liking of Palestinian radicals. This does not make the search for a solution of the conflict undesirable or unnecessary, but there should be no illusions with regard to its likely consequences so far as the persistence of terrorism is concerned.

## IV

It is frequently argued that there is no defense against extremists willing to sacrifice their lives and that arresting or shooting terrorists cannot solve the problem because the "blood of the martyrs is the seed of the church." Historical experience does not confirm such wisdom.

The number of potential terrorists inside every country is limited. On the basis of a painstaking analysis, a recent study reaches the obvious conclusion that "the more terrorists in prison, the lower the violence level."[2] This does not, of course, apply to a mass insurrection supported by the overwhelming majority of the population, but it is true with regard to terrorist groups.

Shi'ite propensity to engage in terrorist suicide attacks has been very much exaggerated. True, there have been a few cases, but not more than four or five of such operations. Furthermore, this readiness to commit suicide can be found at all times and for many reasons. Ten members of the Irish Republican Army starved themselves to death—despite the express ban of the Catholic church against suicide; members of Baader-Meinhof also killed themselves, not to mention the mass suicide in Jonestown. When the Japanese authorities asked for kamikaze candidates during the last year of the war, many thousands volunteered and some 4,600 were killed. It is not so much a matter of specific religion but of fanaticism, and a psychological predisposition. What Voltaire wrote about the subject seems still relevant today: the entire species (of fanatics) is divided into two classes—the first does nought but pray and die, the second wants to reign and massacre.

Terrorism has been stamped out with great ease not only by modern dictatorships; it has been defeated also by governments that are anything but modern. In 1981, Ayatollah Khomeini's former allies from the left, the mujahedeen and some other groups, turned against the new rulers of Iran. They were many and experienced; within three months they succeeded in killing the prime minister, many chiefs of police, half the government and the executive committee of the ruling party, not to mention dozens of members of parliament. Perhaps never before had a terrorist onslaught been so massive and so successful. Yet within another three months the terrorists either were dead or had escaped abroad. The government acted with great brutality; it killed without discrimination; it extracted information by means of torture; it refused as a matter of principle to extend medical help to injured terrorists. And it broke the back of the terrorist movement. . . .

The power of the state is infinitely greater than that of terrorists, and it will always prevail, provided there is the determination or the ruthlessness to do so. But can a democratic society subdue terrorism without surrendering the values

---

[2] Christopher Hewitt, *The Effectiveness of Anti-Terrorist Policies.* Lanham, Md.: University Press of America, 1984, p. 47.

central to the system? Again, experience shows that it can be done without great difficulty. The Italian authorities defeated the Red Brigades, while acting strictly within the law, by a mixture of overdue political reform, penetration of the terrorist ranks, and the promise of substantial reduction in prison terms to the penitents. Terrorist movements do not have an unlimited life span. If terrorists realize after a few years that the murder of a few politicians (and many innocents) has not brought them any nearer their goals, their resolve weakens.

The nationalist-separatist terrorists hold out longer, for their basis of support is stronger and they may have assistance from foreign countries. But even in Northern Ireland and the Basque region of Spain, the level of violence is lower now than [during the 1970s], and the Armenian Asala has all but disappeared.

A dialectical process seems to dictate the policy of democratic societies toward terrorists. As long as terrorism is no more than a nuisance, a democracy will rightly resist any attempt to curtail its traditional freedoms. Once terrorism becomes more than a nuisance, once the normal functioning of society is affected, there will be overwhelming pressure on the government to defeat the threat by all available means. Hence the paradoxical conclusion that the more successful the terrorists, the nearer their ultimate defeat. There are exceptions to every rule, but in this case they are few and far between.

## V

State-sponsored terrorism is mainly the instrument of dictators with ambitions far in excess of their power base. The chief protagonist of this kind of terrorism between the two world wars was not Hitler but Mussolini, who used various groups of Balkan terrorists to destabilize neighboring countries such as Yugoslavia. The Soviet Union was also active in the field, but its operations were mainly limited to the assassination of emigré political leaders such as Trotsky. Today's mini-Mussolinis in the Middle East and in Central America rule small or relatively weak countries. Libya is an extreme example: but for its investment in terrorism, it would be not much more important than Mauritania or the Yemens. Libyan sponsorship of terrorism has been largely the initiative of one man, Muammar al-Qaddafi. But the balance sheet of a decade of such sponsorship is not impressive: publicity has not resulted in political clout. Qaddafi is still only a minor troublemaker, isolated among the Arabs, distrusted and kept at a distance even by those who support him at the United Nations or take his money. The Syrian and Iranian sponsors of terrorism have been more discriminating in their targets and therefore, within limits, more successful.

The attitude of the Soviet bloc has been ambiguous. It has used terrorism as a weapon to destabilize certain countries, but only as a minor instrument in its general arsenal of political warfare, and this for two reasons. The Soviets will never extend support openly; it has to be carefully laundered through a series of subcontractors and middlemen. But this also means that they cannot have full control over the terrorists; the gunmen may land them in situations that were not planned, and which may be politically harmful. To engage in international terrorism is to play with a fire that is difficult to control.

Mention has already been made of the other reason: Marxist-Leninists believe in mass action rather than individual terror, and past experience tends to show that they are by and large correct. Far from weakening a society, terrorism has quite frequently had the opposite, immunizing effect, bringing about greater internal cohesion. The effect of the murder of the Italian leader Aldo Moro is one example; the consequences of terrorism on the internal situation in Israel is another. Far from diverting resources from national defense, the terrorist threat strengthens the feeling that more ought to be done for national security, which plays into the hands of the forces of law and order. Seen in a wider perspective, systematic terrorism is a mixed blessing from the Soviet point of view. It may [have caused] friction between the United States and its allies, many of which [took] a softer line vis-à-vis international terrorism. But such a rift is not about matters of principle—no one in Europe actually likes international terrorism. . . . It is an embarrassment, bad for the image of the country affected; tourism suffers, and there are all kinds of other negative consequences.

For these consequences the governments of Western Europe to a large extent have to blame themselves. For years they have permitted themselves to be blackmailed, beginning with the establishment of Libyan people's bureaus, which replaced legations and embassies in open contravention of diplomatic practice. Yet the European governments more often than not preferred to close their eyes, as they did when Libyan emigrés and their own nationals were gunned down in broad daylight in their cities.

Appeasement is not reprehensible per se; at one stage or another all countries have made concessions to terrorists. If appeasement had worked, a good case could be made in its favor: why endanger the lives of European nationals in the Middle East; why sacrifice trade and goodwill just because of a few isolated incidents? But appeasement has had no beneficial results. . . .

## VI

As internal terrorism has declined in the Western world [since the 1970s] and as international terrorism has become more frequent, the need for full international cooperation against terrorism has been invoked a great many times. It is a hopeless undertaking, however, as long as some states sponsor, finance, equip and train terrorists and provide sanctuaries for them. Spokesmen for democratic societies will continue to proclaim that terrorism is abhorred and condemned by the whole civilized world. But the civilized world does not extend that far these days, and proceedings in the United Nations have shown that it is very difficult to have terrorism condemned even on paper, unless some of the leading communist or Third World countries just happen to be on the receiving end of terrorist operations—which helps to clear their minds but, unfortunately, not for very long.

These debates will no doubt go on for many years; it may be wrong to pay too much attention to them. International terrorism is an extra-legal activity, and thus the contribution of our legal experts is bound to have a limited effect. Specific bilateral agreements or pacts among several countries may be of certain value; the exchange of information between NATO countries and others has improved . . . and as a result some terrorist attacks have been prevented. Under certain conditions quiet diplomacy, such as issuing unpublicized warnings, has been of help; in other circumstances preemptive publicity has helped. Most sponsors of state terrorism do not want their involvement to become known. They will, at the very least, temporarily scale down their involvement once they realize that what was meant to be a high-value, low-risk undertaking might escalate into an armed conflict in which the risks are high and the value is at best uncertain.

But truly effective concerted action against terrorism is possible only on the basis of the strategy first advocated by the nineteenth-century Russian terrorists. This is "hitting the center," meaning those rulers of countries who are sponsors of international terrorism. But hitting the center may not be easy for a variety of reasons. The responsibility for a certain terrorist action or campaign cannot always be easily proved. The aggrieved party may find it difficult to provide sufficient hard evidence. Smoking guns are seldom left at the scene of the crime in this kind of business. Even if there is evidence, to reveal it would often mean giving away the identity of well-placed intelligence sources in the terrorist hierarchy, of which there are probably not many.

For a country or a group of countries subject to attacks by international terrorism, there are, broadly speaking, three ways to react. Given the natural inertia of democratic governments and the difficulties involved, the obvious reaction is to condemn the attack but to refrain from any physical act of retaliation. As long as these attacks occur relatively rarely and inasmuch as they do not result in many victims, this is a feasible policy. But lack of reaction is usually interpreted as a sign of weakness, in which case the attacks will become more frequent and murderous. The sponsors of international terrorism resemble in many respects children trying to find out by trial and error how far they can go in provoking the adults until punishment will be meted out to them.

If an escalation in international terrorist attacks does take place, the obvious way to retaliate is to pay back the sponsors in their own coin. As General George Grivas, head of the EOKA (the National Organization of Cypriot Combatants) in Cyprus and a man of great experience in the field, once put it: to catch a mouse, one uses a cat, not a tank (or an aircraft carrier). But democratic countries may not have cats, meaning a truly effective covert action capability, or "active measures," to use the well-known Soviet term. Even if they have a capability of this kind, they may find it difficult to use, be it because terrorist acts are much easier to carry out in open societies than in dictatorships or because those who engage in covert action on behalf of a democratic country are not normally permitted to kill enemy leaders. In the United States there is an absolute prohibition by presidential order.

What alternatives exist? In some cases diplomatic action may have some success; on other occasions economic sanctions may have a certain impact, but only if there is agreement between the major Western countries. Otherwise, in the absence of "cats," retaliation takes the form of military action. Such escalation involves risks: innocent people are likely to get killed, and those who retaliate will be blamed for creating a new dangerous situation. This has been the fate of the Israelis, who for a long time combined covert action with surgical air strikes (which, on occasion, hit the wrong target). It was also the fate of the United States after the strike against Libya in April 1986: those who retaliate become attackers, and there will be a great deal of handwringing and dire warnings. No government will lightly take such a course of action. It will only do so if it has good reason to believe that the alternative—refraining from counteraction—would have fateful consequences, and if public opinion at home is so strongly in favor of retaliation that it cannot safely be ignored. This is particularly true with regard to a superpower, whose freedom of action is by necessity more restrained than that of a small country. The more powerful a country, the stronger the constraints to act cautiously, for everything a major power does is important; it may turn a local incident into an international conflict.

## VII

Thus the inclination will still be to wait and see. Terrorism may not outgrow the nuisance stage, but if it does, a one-time, limited application of military force may be sufficient to drive the lesson home. There is a tendency to magnify the importance of terrorism in modern society: society is vulnerable to attack, but it is also astonishingly resilient. Terrorism makes a great noise, but so far it has not been very destructive. Our media resemble the Bedouin warriors described by Lawrence of Arabia, who were sturdy fighters except for their mistaken belief that weapons were dangerous in proportion to the noise they created.

But what if terrorism does outgrow the nuisance stage, and what if the one-time lesson administered is not sufficient? In theory, the state sponsors of terrorism should never let this come to pass. For once they succeed in provoking the superpower, the political calculus changes, and they are bound to lose in a confrontation with a much more powerful nation. Only gross miscalculation can lead them into such a course of action. Unfortunately, it is not certain that rational behavior will always prevail on their part. In this case the victims of state-sponsored terrorism must act. They could bring back General Grivas' cats, which is difficult in a democratic society and perhaps undesirable. Or they can choose deliberate escalation, hitting back with military force against elusive terrorist targets. If there is at the present time a terrorist threat, it is not the one usually adduced, that of destroying societies from within. It is the danger of terrorist provocation leading well beyond the confines of mere terrorism and counterterrorism. This danger cannot be reduced without Soviet cooperation. The Qaddafis and Assads will act much more cautiously when they know that they cannot count on automatic Soviet help, once their transgressions lead to retribution. Terrorism, in other words, may not be very important, but like some minor diseases, it can have unpleasant and even dangerous consequences if neglected.

# 11

# THE CHANGING NATURE OF WORLD POWER

## Joseph S. Nye, Jr.

**In this essay Joseph S. Nye, Jr. draws fundamental distinctions among three concepts—power, the balance of power, and hegemony—and evaluates how their meaning has changed given the revolutionary changes that have swept world politics since 1990. Nye is Clarence Dillon Professor of International Affairs at Harvard University. The author of numerous books and articles on international affairs, Nye has recently written *Bound to Lead: The Changing Nature of American Power* (1990).**

## THE CHANGING SOURCES OF POWER

. . . Some observers have argued that the sources of power are, in general, moving away from the emphasis on military force and conquest that marked earlier eras. In assessing international power today, factors such as technology, education, and economic growth are becoming more important, whereas geography, population, and raw materials are becoming less important. Kenneth Waltz argues that a 5-percent rate of economic growth in the United States for three years would add more to American strength than does our alliance with Britain.[1] Richard Rosecrance argues that since 1945, the world has been poised between a territorial system composed of states that view power in terms of land mass, and a trading system "based in states which recognize that self-sufficiency is an illu-

This article draws on material from Joseph S. Nye, Jr., *Bound to Lead: The Changing Nature of American Power* (New York: Basic Books, 1990). Some footnotes have been deleted and others have been renumbered to appear in consecutive order. Used by permission of Joseph S. Nye, Jr.

[1] Kenneth N. Waltz, *Theory of International Politics* (Reading, Mass.: Addison-Wesley, 1979), 172.

sion." In the past, says Rosecrance, "it was cheaper to seize another state's territory by force than to develop the sophisticated economic and trading apparatus needed to derive benefit from commercial exchange with it."[2]

If so, perhaps we are in a "Japanese period" in world politics. Japan has certainly done far better with its strategy as a trading state after 1945 than it did with its military strategy to create a Greater East Asian Co-Prosperity sphere in the 1930s. But Japan's security vis-à-vis its large military neighbors—China and the Soviet Union—depends heavily on U.S. protection. In short, even if we can define power clearly, it still has become more difficult to be clear about the relationship of particular resources to it. Thus, we cannot leap too quickly to the conclusion that all trends favor economic power or countries like Japan.

Like other forms of power, economic power cannot be measured simply in terms of tangible resources. Intangible aspects also matter. For example, outcomes generally depend on bargaining, and bargaining depends on relative costs in particular situations and skill in converting potential power into effects. Relative costs are determined not only by the total amount of measurable economic resources of a country but also by the degree of its interdependence in a relationship. If, for example, the United States and Japan depend on each other but one is less dependent than the other, that asymmetry is a source of power. The United States may be less vulnerable than Japan if the relationship breaks down, and it may use that threat as a source of power.[3] Thus, an assessment of Japanese and American power must look not only at shares of resources but also at the relative vulnerabilities of both countries.

Another consideration is that most large countries today find military force more costly to apply than in previous centuries. This has resulted from the dangers of nuclear escalation, the difficulty of ruling nationalistically awakened populations in otherwise weak states, the danger of rupturing profitable relations on other issues, and the public opposition in Western democracies to prolonged and expensive military conflicts. Even so, the increased cost of military force does not mean that it will be ruled out. To the contrary, in an anarchic system of states where there is no higher government to settle conflicts and where the ultimate recourse is self-help, this could never happen. In some cases, the stakes may justify a costly use of force. And, as recent episodes in Grenada and Libya have shown, not all uses of force by great powers involve high costs.

Even if the direct use of force were banned among a group of countries, military force would still play an important political role. For example, the American military role in deterring threats to allies, or of assuring access to a crucial resource such as oil in the Persian Gulf, means that the provision of protective force can be used in bargaining situations. Sometimes the linkage may be

---

[2] Richard N. Rosecrance, *The Rise of the Trading State* (New York: Basic Books, 1986), 16, 160.

[3] Robert O. Keohane and Joseph S. Nye, Jr., *Power and Interdependence* (Boston: Little, Brown, 1977), chap. 1. . . .

direct; more often it is a factor not mentioned openly but present in the back of statesmen's minds.

In addition, there is the consideration that is sometimes called "the second face of power."[4] Getting other states to change might be called the directive or commanding method of exercising power. Command power can rest on inducements ("carrots") or threats ("sticks"). But there is also an indirect way to exercise power. A country may achieve the outcomes it prefers in world politics because other countries want to follow it or have agreed to a system that produces such effects. In this sense, it is just as important to set the agenda and structure the situations in world politics as it is to get others to change in particular situations. This aspect of power—that is, getting others to want what you want—might be called indirect or co-optive power behavior. It is in contrast to the active command power behavior of getting others to do what you want.[5] Co-optive power can rest on the attraction of one's ideas or on the ability to set the political agenda in a way that shapes the preferences that others express. Parents of teenagers know that if they have structured their children's beliefs and preferences, their power will be greater and will last longer than if they had relied only on active control. Similarly, political leaders and philosophers have long understood the power that comes from setting the agenda and determining the framework of a debate. The ability to establish preferences tends to be associated with intangible power resources such as culture, ideology, and institutions. This dimension can be thought of as soft power, in contrast to the hard command power usually associated with tangible resources like military and economic strength.[6]

---

[4] Peter Bachrach and Morton S. Baratz, "Decisions and Nondecisions: An Analytical Framework," *American Political Science Review* 57 (September 1963): 632–42. See also Richard Mansbach and John Vasquez, *In Search of Theory: A New Paradigm for Global Politics* (Englewood Cliffs, N.J.: Prentice Hall, 1981).

[5] Susan Strange uses the term *structural power,* which she defines as "power to shape and determine the structures of the global political economy" in *States and Markets* (New York: Basil Blackwell, 1988), 24. My term, *co-optive power,* is similar in its focus on preferences but is somewhat broader, encompassing all elements of international politics. The term *structural power,* in contrast, tends to be associated with the neo-realist theories of Kenneth Waltz.

[6] The distinction between hard and soft power resources is one of degree, both in the nature of the behavior and in the tangibility of the resources. Both types are aspects of the ability to achieve one's purposes by controlling the behavior of others. Command power—the ability to change what others *do*—can rest on coercion or inducement. Co-optive power—the ability to shape what others *want*—can rest on the attractiveness of one's culture and ideology or the ability to manipulate the agenda of political choices in a manner that makes actors fail to express some preferences because they seem to be too unrealistic. The forms of behavior between command and co-optive power range along this continuum:

| Command | coercion | inducement | agenda-setting | attraction | Co-optive |
| power | | | | | power |

Further, soft power resources tend to be associated with co-optive power behavior, whereas hard power resources are usually associated with command behavior. But the relationship is imperfect. For example, countries may be attracted to others with command power by myths of invincibility, and command power may sometimes be used to establish institutions that later become regarded as legitimate. But the general association is strong enough to allow the useful shorthand reference to hard and soft power resources.

Robert Cox argues that the nineteenth-century *Pax Britannica* and the twentieth-century *Pax Americana* were effective because they created liberal international economic orders, in which certain types of economic relations were privileged over others and liberal international rules and institutions were broadly accepted. Following the insights of the Italian thinker Antonio Gramsci, Cox argues that the most critical feature for a dominant country is the ability to obtain a broad measure of consent on general principles—principles that ensure the supremacy of the leading state and dominant social classes—and at the same time to offer some prospect of satisfaction to the less powerful. Cox identifies Britain from 1845 to 1875 and the United States from 1945 to 1967 as such countries.[7] Although we may not agree with his terminology or dates, Cox has touched a major point: soft co-optive power is just as important as hard command power. If a state can make its power legitimate in the eyes of others, it will encounter less resistance to its wishes. If its culture and ideology are attractive, others will more willingly follow. If it can establish international norms that are consistent with its society, it will be less likely to have to change. If it can help support institutions that encourage other states to channel or limit their activities in ways the dominant state prefers, it may not need as many costly exercises of coercive or hard power in bargaining situations. In short, the universalism of a country's culture and its ability to establish a set of favorable rules and institutions that govern areas of international activity are critical sources of power.[8] These soft sources of power are becoming more important in world politics today.

Such considerations question the conclusion that the world is about to enter a Japanese era in world politics. The nature of power is changing and some of the changes will favor Japan, but some of them may favor the United States even more. In command power, Japan's economic strength is increasing, but it remains vulnerable in terms of raw materials and relatively weak in terms of military force. And in co-optive power, Japan's culture is highly insular and it has yet to develop a major voice in international institutions. The United States, on the other hand, has a universalistic popular culture and a major role in international institutions. Although such factors may change in the future, they raise an important question about the present situation: What resources are the most important sources of power today? A look at the five-century-old modern state system shows that different power resources played critical roles in different periods. (See Table 1.) The sources of power are never static and they continue to change in today's world.

In an age of information-based economies and transnational interdependence, power is becoming less transferable, less tangible, and less coercive. However,

[7] Robert W. Cox, *Production, Power, and World Order* (New York: Columbia University Press, 1987), chaps. 6, 7.
[8] Stephen D. Krasner, *International Regimes* (Ithaca, N.Y.: Cornell University Press, 1983).

**TABLE 1**
LEADING STATES AND MAJOR POWER RESOURCES, 1500s–1900s

| PERIOD | LEADING STATE | MAJOR RESOURCES |
|---|---|---|
| Sixteenth century | Spain | Gold bullion, colonial trade, mercenary armies, dynastic ties |
| Seventeenth century | Netherlands | Trade, capital markets, navy |
| Eighteenth century | France | Population, rural industry, public administration, army |
| Nineteenth century | Britain | Industry, political cohesion, finance and credit, navy, liberal norms, island location (easy to defend) |
| Twentieth century | United States | Economic scale, scientific and technical leadership, universalistic culture, military forces and alliances, liberal international regimes, hub of transnational communication |

the transformation of power is incomplete. The twenty-first century will certainly see a greater role for informational and institutional power, but military force will remain an important factor. Economic scale, both in markets and in natural resources, will also remain important. As the service sector grows within modern economies, the distinction between services and manufacturing will continue to blur. Information will become more plentiful, and the critical resource will be the organizational capacity for rapid and flexible response. Political cohesion will remain important, as will a universalistic popular culture. On some of these dimensions of power, the United States is well endowed; on others, questions arise. But even larger questions arise for the other major contenders—Europe, Japan, the Soviet Union, and China. But first we need to look at the patterns in the distribution of power—balances and hegemonies, and how they have changed over history, . . .

## BALANCE OF POWER

International relations is far from a precise science. Conditions in various periods always differ in significant details, and human behavior reflects personal choices. Moreover, theorists often suffer from writing in the midst of events, rather than viewing them from a distance. Thus, powerful theories—those that are both simple and accurate—are rare. Yet political leaders (and those who seek to explain behavior) must generalize in order to chart a path through the apparent chaos of changing events. One of the longest-standing and most frequently used concepts is balance of power, which eighteenth-century philosopher David Hume called "a constant rule of prudent politics." For centuries, balance of power has been the starting point for realistic discussions of international politics.

To an extent, balance of power is a useful predictor of how states will behave; that is, states will align in a manner that will prevent any one state from developing a preponderance of power. This is based on two assumptions: that states exist in an anarchic system with no higher government and that political leaders will act first to reduce risks to the independence of their states. The policy of balancing power helps to explain why in modern times a large state cannot grow forever into a world empire. States seek to increase their powers through internal growth and external alliances. Balance of power predicts that if one state appears to grow too strong, others will ally against it so as to avoid threats to their own independence. This behavior, then, will preserve the structure of the system of states.

However, not all balance-of-power predictions are so obvious. For example, this theory implies that professions of ideological faith will be poor predictors of behavior. But despite Britain's criticism of the notorious Stalin-Hitler pact of 1939, it was quick to make an alliance with Stalin's Soviet Union in 1941. As Winston Churchill explained at the time, "If I learned that Hitler had invaded Hell, I would manage to say something good about the Devil in the House of Commons." Further, balance of power does not mean that political leaders must maximize the power of their own states in the short run. Bandwagoning—that is, joining the stronger rather than the weaker side—might produce more immediate spoils. As Mussolini discovered in his ill-fated pact with Hitler, the danger in bandwagoning is that independence may be threatened by the stronger ally in the long term. Thus, to say that states will act to balance power is a strong generalization in international relations, but it is far from being a perfect predictor.

Proximity and perceptions of threat also affect the way in which balancing of power is played out. A small state like Finland, for instance, cannot afford to try to balance Soviet power. Instead, it seeks to preserve its independence through neutrality. Balance of power and the proposition that "the enemy of my enemy is my friend" help to explain the larger contours of current world politics, but only when proximity and perceptions are considered. The United States was by far the strongest power after 1945. A mechanical application of power balance might seem to predict an alliance against the United States. In fact, Europe and Japan allied with the United States because the Soviet Union, while weaker in overall power, posed a proximate threat to its neighbors. Geography and psychology are both important factors in geopolitics.

The term *balance of power* is sometimes used not as a prediction of policy but as a description of how power is distributed. In the latter case, it is more accurate to refer to the distribution of power. In other instances, though, the term is used to refer to an evenly balanced distribution of power, like a pair of hanging scales. The problem with this usage is that the ambiguities of measuring power make it difficult to determine when an equal balance exists. In fact, the major concerns in world politics tend to arise from inequalities of power, and particularly from major changes in the unequal distribution of power.

## HEGEMONY IN MODERN HISTORY

No matter how power is measured, an equal distribution of power among major states is relatively rare. More often the processes of uneven growth, which realists consider a basic law of international politics, mean that some states will be rising and others declining. These transitions in the distribution of power stimulate statesmen to form alliances, to build armies, and to take risks that balance or check rising powers. But the balancing of power does not always prevent the emergence of a dominant state. Theories of hegemony and power transition try to explain why some states that become preponderant later lose that preponderance.

As far back as ancient Greece, observers attempting to explain the causes of major world wars have cited the uncertainties associated with the transition of power. Shifts in the international distribution of power create the conditions likely to lead to the most important wars. However, while power transitions provide useful warning about periods of heightened risk, there is no iron law of hegemonic war. If there were, Britain and the United States would have gone to war at the beginning of this century, when the Americans surpassed the British in economic and naval power in the Western Hemisphere. Instead, when the United States backed Venezuela in its boundary dispute with British Guyana in 1895, British leaders appeased the rising American power instead of going to war with it.

When power is distributed unevenly, political leaders and theorists use terms such as *empire* and *hegemony.* Although there have been many empires in history, those in the modern world have not encompassed all major countries. Even the British Empire at the beginning of this century encompassed only a quarter of the world's population and Britain was just one of a half-dozen major powers in the global balance of power. The term *hegemony* is applied to a variety of situations in which one state appears to have considerably more power than others. For example, for years China accused the Soviet Union of seeking hegemony in Asia. When Soviet leader Mikhail Gorbachev and Chinese leader Deng Xiaoping met in 1989, they pledged that "neither side will seek hegemony in any form anywhere in the world."

Although the word comes from the ancient Greek and refers to the dominance of one state over others in the system, it is used in diverse and confused ways. Part of the problem is that unequal distribution of power is a matter of degree, and there is no general agreement on how much inequality and what types of power constitute hegemony. All too often, hegemony is used to refer to different behaviors and degrees of control, which obscures rather than clarifies that analysis. For example, Charles Doran cites aggressive military power, while Robert Keohane looks at preponderance in economic resources. Robert Gilpin sometimes uses the terms *imperial* and *hegemonic* interchangeably to refer to a situation in which "a single powerful state controls or dominates the lesser states in the system."[9] British hegemony in the nineteenth century is commonly cited even though Britain ranked third behind the United States and Russia in GNP and third behind Russia and France in military expenditures at the peak of its relative power around 1870. Britain was first in the more limited domains of manufacturing, trade, finance, and naval power.[10] Yet theorists often contend that "full hegemony requires productive, commercial, and financial as well as political and military power."[11]

Joshua Goldstein usefully defines hegemony as "being able to dictate, or at least dominate, the rules and arrangements by which international relations, political and economic, are conducted. . . . Economic hegemony implies the ability to center the world economy around itself. Political hegemony means being able to dominate the world militarily."[12] However, there are still two important questions to be answered with regard to how the term *hegemony* is used. First, what is the scope of the hegemon's control? In the modern world, a situation in which one country can dictate political and economic arrangements has been extremely rare. Most examples have been regional, such as Soviet power in Eastern Europe, American influence in the Caribbean, and India's control over its small neighbors—Sikkim, Bhutan, and Nepal. In addition, one can find instances in which one country was able to set the rules and arrangements governing specific issues in world politics, such as the American role in money or trade in the early postwar years. But there has been no global, system-wide hegemon during the past two centuries. Contrary to the myths about *Pax Britannica* and *Pax Americana,* British and American hegemonies have been regional and issue-specific rather than general.

Second, we must ask what types of power resources are necessary to produce a hegemonic degree of control. Is military power necessary? Or is it enough to have preponderance in economic resources? How do the two types of power relate to each other? Obviously, the answers to such questions can tell us a great deal about the future world, in which Japan may be an economic giant and a military dwarf while the Soviet Union may fall into the opposite situation. A careful look at the interplay of military and economic power raises doubt about the degree of American hegemony in the postwar period.

[9]Charles F. Doran, *The Politics of Assimilation: Hegemony and Its Aftermath* (Baltimore: Johns Hopkins University Press, 1971), 70; Robert O. Keohane, *After Hegemony* (Princeton, N.J.: Princeton University Press, 1984), 32; Robert Gilpin, *War and Change in World Politics* (New York: Cambridge University Press, 1981), 29.

[10]Bruce M. Russett, "The Mysterious Case of Vanishing Hegemony; or, Is Mark Twain Really Dead?" *International Organization* 39 (Spring 1985): 212.

[11]Robert C. North and Julie Strickland, "Power Transition and Hegemonic Succession" (Paper delivered at the meeting of the International Studies Association, Anaheim, Calif., March–April 1986), 5.

[12]Joshua S. Goldstein, *Long Cycles: Prosperity and War in the Modern Age* (New Haven, Conn.: Yale University Press, 1988), 281.

**TABLE 2**
MODERN EFFORTS AT MILITARY HEGEMONY

| STATE ATTEMPTING HEGEMONY | ENSUING HEGEMONIC WAR | NEW ORDER AFTER WAR |
| --- | --- | --- |
| Hapsburg Spain | Thirty Years' War, 1618–1648 | Peace of Westphalia, 1648 |
| Louis XIV's France | Wars of Louis XIV | Treaty of Utrecht, 1713 |
| Napoleon's France | 1792–1815 | Congress of Vienna, 1815 |
| Germany (and Japan) | 1914–1945 | United Nations, 1945 |

*Source*: Charles F. Doran, *The Politics of Assimilation: Hegemony and Its Aftermath* (Baltimore: Johns Hopkins University Press, 1971), 19–20.

### Theories of Hegemonic Transition and Stability

General hegemony is the concern of theories and analogies about the instability and dangers supposedly caused by hegemonic transitions. Classical concerns about hegemony among leaders and philosophers focus on military power and "conflicts precipitated by the military effort of one dominant actor to expand well beyond the arbitrary security confines set by tradition, historical accident, or coercive pressures."[13] In this approach, hegemonic preponderance arises out of military expansion, such as the efforts of Louis XIV, Napoleon, or Hitler to dominate world politics. The important point is that, except for brief periods, none of the attempted military hegemonies in modern times has succeeded. (See Table 2.) No modern state has been able to develop sufficient military power to transform the balance of power into a long-lived hegemony in which one state could dominate the world militarily.

More recently, many political scientists have focused on economic power as a source of hegemonic control. Some define hegemonic economic power in terms of resources—that is, preponderance in control over raw materials, sources of capital, markets, and production of goods. Others use the behavioral definition in which a hegemon is a state able to set the rules and arrangements for the global economy. Robert Gilpin, a leading theorist of hegemonic transition, sees Britain and America, having created and enforced the rules of a liberal economic order, as the successive hegemons since the Industrial Revolution.[14] Some political economists argue that world economic stability requires a single stabilizer and that periods of such stability have coincided with periods of hegemony. In this view, *Pax Britannica* and *Pax Americana* were the periods when Britain and the United States were strong enough to create and enforce the rules for a liberal international economic order in the nineteenth and twentieth centuries. For example, it is often argued that economic stability "historically has

[13] Doran, *Politics of Assimilation,* 15.
[14] Keohane, *After Hegemony,* 32; Gilpin, *War and Change,* 144.

occurred when there has been a sole hegemonic power; Britain from 1815 to World War I and the United States from 1945 to around 1970. . . . With a sole hegemonic power, the rules of the game can be established and enforced. Lesser countries have little choice but to go along. Without a hegemonic power, conflict is the order of the day."[15] Such theories of hegemonic stability and decline are often used to predict that the United States will follow the experience of Great Britain, and that instability will ensue. Goldstein, for example, argues that "we are moving toward the 'weak hegemony' end of the spectrum and . . . this seems to increase the danger of hegemonic war."[16]

I argue, however, that the theory of hegemonic stability and transition will not tell us as much about the future of the United States. Theorists of hegemonic stability generally fail to spell out the causal connections between military and economic power and hegemony. As already noted, nineteenth-century Britain was not militarily dominant nor was it the world's largest economy, and yet Britain is portrayed by Gilpin and others as hegemonic. Did Britain's military weakness at that time allow the United States and Russia, the two larger economies, to remain mostly outside the liberal system of free trade? Or, to take a twentieth-century puzzle, did a liberal international economy depend on post-war American military strength or only its economic power? Are both conditions necessary today, or have modern nations learned to cooperate through international institutions?

One radical school of political economists, the neo-Marxists, has attempted to answer similar questions about the relationship between economic and military hegemony, but their theories are unconvincing. For example, Immanuel Wallerstein defines hegemony as a situation in which power is so unbalanced that

> one power can largely impose its rules and its wishes (at the very least by effective veto power) in the economic, political, military, diplomatic, and even cultural arenas. The material base of such power lies in the ability of enterprises domiciled in that power to operate more efficiently in all three major economic arenas—agro-industrial production, commerce, and finance.[17]

According to Wallerstein, hegemony is rare and "refers to that short interval in which there is simultaneously advantage in all three economic domains." At such times, the other major powers become "*de facto* client states." Wallerstein claims there have been only three modern instances of hegemony—in the Netherlands, 1620–1650; in Britain, 1815–1873; and in the United States, 1945–1967. (See Table 3.) He argues that "in each case, the hegemony was

---

[15]Michael Moffitt, "Shocks, Deadlocks and Scorched Earth: Reaganomics and the Decline of U.S. Hegemony," *World Policy Journal* 4 (Fall 1987): 576.

[16]Goldstein, *Long Cycles,* 357.

[17]Immanuel M. Wallerstein, *The Politics of the World-Economy: The States, the Movements, and the Civilizations: Essays* (New York: Cambridge University Press, 1984), 38, 41.

TABLE 3
A NEO-MARXIST VIEW OF HEGEMONY

| HEGEMONY | WORLD WAR SECURING HEGEMONY | PERIOD OF DOMINANCE | DECLINE |
|---|---|---|---|
| Dutch | Thirty Years' War, 1618–1648 | 1620–1650 | 1650–1672 |
| British | Napoleonic Wars, 1792–1815 | 1815–1873 | 1873–1896 |
| American | World Wars I and II, 1914–1945 | 1945–1967 | 1967– |

*Source:* Immanuel Wallerstein, *The Politics of the World Economy* (New York: Cambridge University Press, 1984). 41–42.

secured by a thirty-year-long world war," after which a new order followed—the Peace of Westphalia after 1648; the Concert of Europe after 1815; and the United Nations–Bretton Woods system after 1945.[18] According to this theory, the United States will follow the Dutch and the British path to decline.

The neo-Marxist view of hegemony is unconvincing and a poor predictor of future events because it superficially links military and economic hegemony and has many loose ends. For example, contrary to Wallerstein's theory, the Thirty Years' War *coincided* with Dutch hegemony, and Dutch decline began with the Peace of Westphalia. The Dutch were not militarily strong enough to stand up to the British on the sea and could barely defend themselves against the French on land, "despite their trade-derived wealth."[19] Further, although Wallerstein argues that British hegemony began after the Napoleonic Wars, he is not clear about how the new order in the balance of power—that is, the nineteenth-century Concert of Europe—related to Britain's supposed ability to impose a global free-trade system. For example, Louis XIV's France, which many historians view as the dominant military power in the second half of the seventeenth century, is excluded from Wallerstein's schema altogether. Thus, the neo-Marxist historical analogies seem forced into a Procrustean ideological bed, while other cases are left out of bed altogether.

Others have attempted to organize past periods of hegemony into century-long cycles. In 1919, British geopolitician Sir Halford Mackinder argued that unequal growth among nations tends to produce a hegemonic world war about every hundred years. More recently, political scientist George Modelski proposed a hundred-year cyclical view of changes in world leadership. (See Table 4.) In this view, a long cycle begins with a major global war. A single state then emerges as the new world power and legitimizes its preponderance with postwar peace treaties. (Preponderance is defined as having at least half the resources available for global order-keeping.) The new leader supplies security and order for the international system. In time, though, the leader loses legitimacy, and

---

[18] Ibid.
[19] Goldstein, *Long Cycles,* 317.

TABLE 4
LONG CYCLES OF WORLD LEADERSHIP

| CYCLE | GLOBAL WAR | PREPONDERANCE | DECLINE |
|---|---|---|---|
| 1495–1580 | 1494–1516 | Portugal, 1516–1540 | 1540–1580 |
| 1580–1688 | 1580–1609 | Netherlands, 1609–1640 | 1640–1688 |
| 1688–1792 | 1688–1713 | Britain, 1714–1740 | 1740–1792 |
| 1792–1914 | 1792–1815 | Britain, 1815–1850 | 1850–1914 |
| 1914– | 1914–1945 | United States, 1945–1973 | 1973– |

*Source:* George Modelski, *Long Cycles in World Politics* (Seattle: University of Washington Press, 1987), 40, 42, 44, 102, 131, 147.

deconcentration of power leads to another global war. The new leader that emerges from that war may not be the state that challenged the old leader but one of the more innovative allies in the winning coalition (as, not Germany, but the United States replaced Britain). According to Modelski's theory, the United States began its decline in 1973.[20] If his assumptions are correct, it may be Japan and not the Soviet Union that will most effectively challenge the United States in the future.

Modelski and his followers suggest that the processes of decline are associated with long waves in the global economy. They associate a period of rising prices and resource scarcities with loss of power, and concentration of power with falling prices, resource abundance, and economic innovation.[21] However, in linking economic and political cycles, these theorists become enmeshed in the controversy surrounding long cycle theory. Many economists are skeptical about the empirical evidence for alleged long economic waves and about dating historical waves by those who use the concept.[22] . . .

Vague definitions and arbitrary schematizations alert us to the inadequacies of such grand theories of hegemony and decline. Most theorists of hegemonic transition tend to shape history to their own theories by focusing on particular power resources and ignoring others. Examples include the poorly explained relationship between military and political power and the unclear link between decline and major war. Since there have been wars among the great powers during 60 percent of the years from 1500 to the present, there are plenty of candi-

[20]George Modelski, "The Long Cycle of Global Politics and the Nation-State," *Comparative Studies in Society and History* 20 (April 1978): 214–35; George Modelski, *Long Cycles in World Politics* (Seattle: University of Washington Press, 1987).

[21]William R. Thompson, *On Global War: Historical Structural Approaches to World Politics* (Columbia: University of South Carolina Press, 1988), chaps. 3, 8.

[22]Richard N. Rosecrance, "Long Cycle Theory and International Relations," *International Organization* 41 (Spring 1987): 291–95. An interesting but ultimately unconvincing discussion can be found in Goldstein, *Long Cycles.*

dates to associate with any given scheme.[23] Even if we consider only the nine general wars that have involved nearly all the great powers and produced high levels of casualties, some of them, such as the Seven Years' War (1755–1763), are not considered hegemonic in any of the schemes. As sociologist Pitirim Sorokin concludes, "no regular periodicity is noticeable."[24] At best, the various schematizations of hegemony and war are only suggestive. They do not provide a reliable basis for predicting the future of American power or for evaluating the risk of world war as we enter the twenty-first century. Loose historical analogies about decline and falsely deterministic political theories are not merely academic: they may lead to inappropriate policies. The real problems of a post-cold-war world will not be new challenges for hegemony, but the new challenges of transnational interdependence.

[23]Jack S. Levy, "Declining Power and the Preventive Motivation for War," *World Politics* 40 (October 1987): 82–107. See also Jack S. Levy, *War in the Modern Great Power System, 1495–1975* (Lexington: University of Kentucky Press, 1983), 97.

[24]Pitirim Aleksandrovich Sorokin, *Social and Cultural Dynamics: A Study of Change in Major Systems of Art, Truth, Ethics, Law and Social Relationships* (1957; reprint, Boston: Porter Sargent, 1970), 561.

PART **TWO**

# DISCORD AND COLLABORATION

States necessarily must direct their attention and resources toward the quest for security, for the threat of war is an ever-present danger in an anarchical society. Issues relating to arms and influence therefore occupy a prominent place on the foreign policy agendas of nation-states, and the pursuit of national security— defined especially in terms of military policy and strategy—seems in today's insecure world to constitute the very essence of international politics. Hence the issues treated in Part One of *The Global Agenda* appropriately command central importance.

Compelling as this realist perspective is, it is at best a caricature of international politics if it fails to acknowledge the broad range of issues and objectives that motivate states' behavior, even in their quest for security. The high politics of peace and security entails both issues and strategies that lie beyond arms and war, deterrence, and the raw exercise of influence. It also includes activities of states that often have little or nothing to do with armaments or the threat of war; and it includes many activities motivated by the desire to collaborate with others so as to derive mutual benefits.

Indeed, contrary to the Hobbesian perspective of some observers, international politics is not exclusively a "war of all against all." States are not normally straining at the leash to attack one another. Nor do they allocate the bulk of their time, on a day-to-day basis, to planning the use of force against their perceived adversaries. The texture of world politics is shaped by more varied national interests and activities.

Part Two of *The Global Agenda* directs attention to issues and perspectives that involve some of the relatively routine and continuing interactions of states as they seek to promote their national interests. No assumption is made that under normal conditions relations among states are conducted without conflict. Conflict is endemic to all those relations—like politics, it is unavoidable. But we *can* assume that the manner in which states usually respond to conflict includes activities that do not involve preparations for war and the threat or use of force.

By extension, this way of looking at international politics in Part Two begins with the assumption that states respond to a perceived need not only for power but also for order. Accordingly, interstate interaction is characterized by both cooperation and conflict, by collaboration as well as discord. Nation-states value a stable international environment, and therefore seek and support not just a strong defense but also common institutions, rules, and procedures that contribute to the creation of a more orderly world. In short, states engage in cooperation as well as conflict to realize their preferred objectives.

What factors influence whether amity or enmity will dominate the pattern of interaction among states? Clearly, there are many. Underlying all of them, it may be argued, are states' perceptions of reality. Reality is partially subjective—what states perceive it to be—and consequently actions are influenced strongly by images of reality as well as by objective facts. Whether states see the world as fearful and hostile or as holding out opportunities for collaboration to realize preferred futures will influence the postures they assume toward global issues and their reactions to the challenges and options those issues present.

How international politics and the policies of states toward one another are pictured is shaped by our images and world views of the global system's dominant characteristics. To organize perceptions about these subjects, social scientists have developed abstract models that describe and explain various properties of international relations. To assist us in developing a frame of reference, Ole R. Holsti, in "Models of International Relations: The Realist and 'Complex Interdependence' Perspectives on Conflict and Cooperation," describes and summarizes two models scholars have fashioned to organize research and theorizing on world politics. These are, respectively, the classical and modern versions of "realism," and the "complex interdependence" or "global society" model of transnational interactions. His discussion elucidates the assumptions and conclusions about relations among nations suggested by these two models and provides a basis for understanding the diverse ways discord and collaboration manifest themselves in world affairs.

The varying utility of alternate models of international politics is made especially evident in efforts to interpret the evolving relationship between the United States and the Soviet Union. The East-West conflict, which throughout the post–World War II era was clearly the world's most threatening global contest, has undergone substantial changes recently. As the expectation of discord has receded and the prospects for great-power cooperation have concomitantly expanded, a new era has come into being in which issues other than the Cold War now command greater attention. From the transformation of this relationship may be extracted various, potentially incompatible, lessons about discord and collaboration in international affairs. The accuracy of these lessons will depend, however, on the adequacy of the models and theoretical perspectives that structure the conclusions drawn.

Indeed, images of the prospects for global collaboration may hinge on how the evolving relationship between the United States and the Soviet Union is viewed. The relationship is the subject of considerable controversy, because the intentions and external behavior of each superpower have varied and resist precise definition. For more than four decades, the expectation of superpower discord remained high, and the possibilities for lasting cooperation appeared remote, in large measure because of the distrust, ideological rivalry, and misperceptions that fueled the superpowers' animosity during the Cold War.

But in late 1989 and 1990 this antagonism came abruptly to an apparent end. Many observers and policymakers now accept that, as William G. Hyland's 1990 book title proclaimed, *The Cold War Is Over* (although they differ about the processes through which this hostile relationship was reconciled). As we look to the future, the probable consequences of this revolutionary development for world politics are at issue.

In "U.S.–Soviet Relations: Threshold of a New Era," Arnold L. Horelick evaluates the diverse ways in which the transformation of a conflictual relationship to an embryonically collaborative one is likely to impact on the superpowers' future relations. As Horelick demonstrates, now that managing the East-West conflict is no longer a necessary preoccupation, the newly found (if fragile) harmony between the superpowers provides an opportunity to address a wide range of long-neglected global issues. But as "policymakers in both capitals face a new international politics in which their bipolar competition will no longer provide the dominant framework for ordering the system and disciplining the behavior of states," they are nonetheless left with many remaining as well as many new challenges, including how to construct a new architecture for European order, negotiate agreements for the reduction and control of nuclear arsenals, and forge political institutions to supplement or replace the Cold War military alliances. Horelick inventories the issues of this transitional era in a survey that underscores the diminished influence and control both superpowers can now exert in shaping the post–Cold War world, while showing why the adjustment for the United States, although difficult, is likely to be incomparably less so than for the Soviet Union.

The Cold War began in Europe, and to many it came to an apparent end there. If this achievement is not temporary or illusory, then the fate of Europe in the wake of the Cold War's end becomes a highly important if uncertain question. In "Europe After the Superpowers: Why We Will Soon Miss the Cold War," John J. Mearsheimer examines Europe's ability to play an independent role now that Germany is united and the Soviets and Americans have begun to withdraw. Those who contend that armed conflicts among the European nations are no longer possible—that the two world wars extinguished the appetites of European states for war—are, Mearsheimer warns, likely to prove mistaken. "The theories of peace that implicitly undergird this optimism are notably shallow constructs," he argues, because "they stand up to neither logical nor historical analysis." Instead, he warns that the conditions that have made for decades of peace in the West are fast disappearing, as Europe faces a return to the multipolar system that between 1648 and 1945 bred destructive conflicts with monotonous regularity.

Constructing three scenarios of the nuclear future in Europe that could materialize, Mearsheimer shows that under conditions in which (1) nuclear weapons are removed from Europe, (2) a nuclear-free zone is created in Central Europe, or (3) nuclear weapons proliferate on the continent, the probable outcome will be the same: war will eventually erupt. Mearsheimer maintains that Europe experienced peace for almost five decades for two principal reasons: bipolar systems like that extant during the Cold War tend to be stable, and the existence of nuclear weapons has bred caution. But if these restraints are lifted and Europe reverts to multipolarity, a new era of major crises and wars will follow. Whereas some feel that European economic interdependence will anchor stability and peace will be strengthened further because liberal democracies do not wage wars against one another, Mearsheimer suggests that these theories are not applicable to an emergent multipolar world. He also predicts that more European countries, including possibly the united Germany, will seek nuclear arsenals if the superpowers reduce their presence in the continent. Hence, if not carefully managed, turbulent and possibly violent times may lie in Europe's future.

During most of the post–World War II era, the issues that defined the East–West conflict understandably dominated discussions of world politics (especially among the contestants in the European theater). But another important set of issues has centered on the North–South conflict between the "core" and the "periphery"—on relations between the rich nations of the First World and poor nations of the Third, and on the efforts of the latter to extract concessions and aid from the former. In "First World, Third World, Which World? The Future of the Less Developed Countries," Mark Falcoff explores the Third World countries' future. As a point of departure, he notes that during the Cold War Third World nations attempted to exploit the East–West rivalry to gain concessions through the practice of "nonalignment." By playing one superpower off against the other, they managed to elicit assistance when the Cold War antagonists competed with each other for allies in the Third World. But now the circumstances have radically changed with the end of the Cold War. The "postcolonial era" has come to an end, and this means that the superpowers' competition for foreign clients will cease. "For with no Cold War," Falcoff explains, foreign assistance is likely to decline because "there can be no 'Third

World,' or rather, no 'Third Worldism.' And with no alignment—no sharp bipolarity within the international system—there can be no nonalignment, either." Hence the efforts of the "marginalized" Third World to wield political leverage and obtain resources will be greatly reduced. Falcoff concludes that the destiny of the Third World lies in the hands of Third World leaders themselves, who alone must attack their internal and external problems. Given their desire to escape the constraints imposed by what they perceive as an international economic order that made them dependent on the rich nations of the North, the Third World has the opportunity for the first time in four decades to address its problems without the obtrusive interference of the great powers.

Conflict has been especially recurrent and deadly in the world's most visible troublespot, the Middle East. In "The Volatile Middle East: The Roots of Muslim Rage," Bernard Lewis examines the struggle between Islam and the West that for fourteen centuries has consisted "of a long series of attacks and reprisals, jihads and crusades, conquests and reconquests." Today, as in the past, the Muslim world is animated by an intensely violent resentment of the West. "Suddenly," Lewis observes, for many Muslims "America had become the archenemy, the incarnation of evil, the diabolic opponent of all that is good." The purpose of his essay is to explain why this is the case—an explication that goes far in enabling us to understand why conflict in the Middle East erupts so recurrently and why Muslim rage rooted in religious precepts, memories of a glorious Muslim past now lost, and recollections of humiliation at the hands of the industrialized (and imperialist?) West have embittered the Muslim world and made the United States the focus of its hatred. The accusations underlying the rising tide of Muslim rage against the West are multiple, as Lewis' inventory demonstrates. Because these accusations are deeply felt, they are likely to cast their spell over future relations between the Middle East and the West.

One way states have sought to reduce tensions is through negotiated arms control agreements. Arms control and disarmament efforts have a long (albeit disappointing) history. When successful, they have contributed to a dampening of the risks that weapons themselves contribute to political conflict, and therefore, in the eyes of some observers, to the reduced probability of war. A willingness to engage in and abide by arms control agreements thus constitutes one means by which states can collaborate in order to enhance their mutual security.

Joseph S. Nye, Jr. evaluates the future prospects for arms control in "Arms Control After the Cold War." Now that the Cold War has passed from the scene, the improved superpower relationship, Nye avers, has reduced international anxieties and improved the prospects for reaching and ratifying new agreements. But, he warns, many obstacles remain, because, ironically, the relaxed political climate has lessened the urgency of framing new arms control initiatives.

Nye's review of arms control successes and failures during the past three decades illuminates these continuing barriers and provides a summary of the major issues that surround debate among policymakers and students of the subject about the benefits and costs of arms control. In addition, Nye surveys the new challenges to controlling the proliferation of weapons, including those evident in the escalating arms race through the diffusion of power and the spread of technology. Examples of such threats include a new generation of chemical and biological weapons and ballistic missiles in the conflict-prone Third World. Nonetheless, the current period of improved superpower relations provides a historic opportunity to make real progress in the control of weapons, Nye observes, especially if multilateral institutions such as the United Nations are permitted to play a more active role. Thus Nye concludes that the post–Cold War period poses both unparalleled peril and promise for arms control. Because negotiated arms control agreements are inherently "part of a political process," they offer perhaps the best evidence of the capacity of nations to bargain in order to collaboratively restrain threats to their mutual security.

In addition to arms control agreements, the potential for either discord or collaboration is illustrated vividly by the uses to which states have put another policy instrument: alliances. Coalitions and the treaties of alliance that formalize them are voluntary associations created to enable allies to collaborate among themselves for defense (and to wage war) against those with whom they are in conflict. Today, because of the destructiveness of nuclear weapons, the political role of alliances—that of making more credible the commitment of one state to the defense of others—is perhaps more important than their strictly military function, that of aggregating power. Thus, as "latent war communities," alliances are inherently and simultaneously institutions for conflict *and* for cooperation. Their successful management is, therefore, necessarily an important issue in world politics.

The next reading selection in *The Global Agenda* examines the formation, maintenance, and functions of alliances in world politics. In "Alliances in Theory and Practice: What Lies Ahead?" Stephen M. Walt examines the factors that are likely to shape defense pacts in the new global environment of the 1990s. Looking theoretically at the geostrategic and domestic conditions that prompt states to ally, Walt notes that historically it has been the existence of an external threat that has driven nations together. If a durable U.S.–Soviet détente develops, Walt predicts, "a significant decrease in alliance cohesion . . . is likely." Nonetheless, he concludes, "such a development is less worrisome than it might appear" because, as threats to national security recede, so will the collective defense requirements of states and the pressures on alliance members. To buttress this prediction, Walt traces the structural changes that have occurred recently in world affairs, and evaluates their implications for existing alliance systems and for the capacity of alliances to inhibit war in the multipolar world on the horizon.

Problem solving in international affairs also requires the creation of effective institutions to cope with global problems. Since its birth at the end of World

War II, the United Nations has represented to many perhaps the greatest hope (and most bitter disappointment) for responding to human needs. In "The Future and the United Nations," Secretary-General of the United Nations Javier Perez de Cuellar turns an eye toward the institution his secretariat manages and assesses its potential for carrying out the multiple missions the UN charter assigns it. The secretary-general's perspective on the world organization frames well the problems and prospects of the United Nations in a global environment where nation-states remain the principal actors, and where disputes between states often have a greater impact on international institutions than those institutions have on the parties to those disputes.

But this circumstance shows signs of changing. Respect for the United Nations was given impetus by the world organization's success in 1989 and 1990 at resolving a number of international conflicts. Perez de Cuellar was credited with brokering an end to the eight-year Iran–Iraq war and the withdrawal of Soviet troops from Afghanistan, and the UN successfully supervised Nicaragua's first free elections as well as those in Namibia. Then, in the wake of Iraq's brutal invasion of Kuwait, it was through the UN Security Council that the world community organized a trade embargo against the renegade Iraqi dictator Saddam Hussein and later authorized the use of force against Iraq. The achievement was realized because the superpowers acted in concert rather than, as had been their custom throughout the Cold War, using their power to veto any action that might benefit their adversary. As the concept of collective security, which had been the original purpose of the United Nations, was revived through joint U.S.–Soviet action, the United Nations was freed from paralysis and began to emerge as an important force for peace.

The recent achievements of the United Nations suggest that it has finally begun to fulfill its original promise. But, as Perez de Cuellar notes, even in the post–Cold War atmosphere of superpower collaboration, many long-standing disputes continue "to resist positive trends towards conciliation," and in the new "relatively benevolent international climate" in which the Security Council shows signs of performing as "a responsive, collegial body," many new global problems—drug trafficking, the deterioration of the environment, the widening gap between the rich and the poor—have pushed their way onto the global agenda and demand attention. His essay explains why the United Nations may remain the most effective vehicle for the "vast and painstaking cooperative work required."

The response of nations comprising the international system to the problem of managing international discord and collaboration is exhibited by yet another of the system's structural features: its legal system. In "The Reality and Relevance of International Law," Christopher C. Joyner examines a wide spectrum of viewpoints regarding the functions of international law in world affairs. He concludes that, despite its limitations, many of which are exaggerated by those uninformed about its principles and procedures, international law succeeds in doing what states ask of it, not the least of its functions being maintenance of the order, stability, and predictability that states prize.

As we look to the future, will nation-states approach the issues they face on the global agenda in a collaborative manner? Or will the tendency toward conflict command more attention? It is to this question that Robert Axelrod and Robert O. Keohane bring insight in the concluding selection of Part Two of *The Global Agenda*. Using the primary structural feature of the international system as their point of reference—namely, that world politics takes place in an anarchy, without supranational regulation—Axelrod and Keohane show in "Achieving Cooperation Under Anarchy: Strategies and Institutions" how cooperation occurs even under conditions where it might appear most unlikely. Cooperation (and discord) in world politics are explained, they argue, by three factors: the interaction of mutual interests, "the shadow of the future" coloring states' images of subsequent behavior by those with whom they interact, and the number of parties to transnational cooperative ventures. In helping us to understand the success of attempts at cooperation in both military-security relations and political-economic relations, Axelrod and Keohane highlight the ways in which new institutions and norms can contribute to the development and maintenance of cooperation, as well as the strategies and background conditions that most foster these practices. Whether discord or collaboration will be greater or lesser ingredients in the future of world politics will be influenced considerably, they suggest, by the ways states reciprocate the cooperative acts of others and encourage these collaborative practices by cultivating institutions and norms to support their continuation. Despite the reality of anarchy and discord, Axelrod and Keohane conclude, beneficial forms of international cooperation can be promoted, particularly in the low politics realm of political economy but also in the realm of high politics where security is at stake.

# 12

# MODELS OF INTERNATIONAL RELATIONS: PERSPECTIVES ON CONFLICT AND COOPERATION

Ole R. Holsti

**Two models that have been developed to describe and explain different properties of discordant and accommodative relations in world politics are described by Ole R. Holsti: classical and modern "realism" and the "global society/complex interdependence" models. Each provides a basis for understanding many of the forces that shape interstate relations and the issues that confront the multifarious actors in the international system. Holsti is George V. Allen Professor of International Affairs at Duke University, and is a former president of the International Studies Association. He is the author of many books and articles dealing with international affairs generally and, more specifically on American elite opinion on foreign policy issues including (with James N. Rosenau) *American Leadership in World Affairs: Vietnam and the Breakdown of Consensus* (1984).**

This essay [describes] two "models" that political scientists have used in their research on international relations during recent decades. . . .

Because "classical realism" is the most venerable and persisting model of international relations, it provides a good starting point and baseline for compar-

Adapted for the second edition of this book by K. J. Holsti and reprinted from K. J. Holsti, "Change in the International System: Interdependence, Integration, and Fragmentation," in Ole R. Holsti, Randolf M. Siverson and Alexander L. George, eds., *Change in the International System* (Boulder, Colo.: Westview Press, 1980), pp. 23–53. Copyright © 1980 by Westview Press. Some footnotes have been deleted; others have been renumbered to appear in consecutive order. Used by permission of Westview Press.

ison with competing models. . . . Following a discussion of classical realism, an examination of "modern realism" will identify the continuities and differences between the two approaches. The essay then turns to several models that [challenges] one or more core premises of both classical and modern realism: . . . [namely] Global-Society/Complex-Interdependence . . .

There have always been Americans, such as Alexander Hamilton, who viewed international relations from a realist perspective, but its contemporary intellectual roots are largely European. Three important figures of the interwar period probably had the greatest impact on American scholarship: the historian E. H. Carr, the geographer Nicholas Spykman, and the political theorist Hans J. Morgenthau. Other Europeans who have contributed significantly to realist thought include John Herz, Hedley Bull, Raymond Aron, and Martin Wight, while notable Americans of this school include scholars Arnold Wolfers and Norman Graebner, as well as diplomat George F. Kennan, journalist Walter Lippmann, and theologian Reinhold Niebuhr.[1]

Although realists do not constitute a homogeneous school—any more than do any of the others discussed in this essay—most of them share at least five core premises about international relations. To begin with, they view as central questions the causes of war and the conditions of peace. They also regard the structure of the international system as a necessary if not always sufficient explanation for many aspects of international relations. According to classical realists, "structural anarchy," or the absence of a central authority to settle disputes, is the essential feature of the contemporary system, and it gives rise to the "security dilemma": in a self-help system one nation's search for security often leaves its current and potential adversaries insecure, any nation that strives for absolute security leaves all others in the system absolutely insecure, and it can provide a powerful incentive for arms races and other types of hostile interactions. Consequently, the question of relative capabilities is a crucial factor. Efforts to deal with this central element of the international system constitute the driving force behind the relations of units within the system; those that fail to cope will not survive. Thus, unlike "idealists" or "liberal internationals," classical realists

---

[1]Among the works that best represent their realist perspectives are E. H. Carr, *Twenty Years' Crisis* (London, 1939); Nicholas Spykman, *America's Strategy in World Politics: The United States and Balance of Power* (New York, 1942); Hans J. Morgenthau, *Politics among Nations: The Struggle for Power and Peace,* 5th ed. (New York, 1973); John Herz, *International Politics in the Atomic Age* (New York, 1959); Hedley Bull, *The Anarchical Society: A Study of Order in World Politics* (London, 1977); Raymond Aron, *Peace and War* (Garden City, NY, 1966); Martin Wight, "The Balance of Power and International Order," in *The Bases of International Order: Essays in Honor of C. A. W. Manning,* ed. Alan James (London, 1973); Arnold Wolfers, *Discord and Collaboration* (Baltimore, 1962); Norman A. Graebner, *America as a World Power: A Realist Appraisal from Wilson to Reagan* (Wilmington, DE, 1984); George F. Kennan, *American Diplomacy, 1900–1950* (Chicago, 1951); Walter Lippmann, *U.S. Foreign Policy: Shield of the Republic* (Boston, 1943); and Reinhold Niebuhr, *The Children of Light and the Children of Darkness* (New York, 1945).

view conflict as a natural state of affairs rather than a consequence that can be attributed to historical circumstances, evil leaders, flawed sociopolitical systems, or inadequate international understanding and education.

A third premise that unites classical realists is their focus on geographically based groups as the central actors in the international system. During other periods the major entities may have been city states or empires, but at least since the Treaties of Westphalia (1648), states have been the dominant units. Classical realists also agree that state behavior is rational. The assumption behind this fourth premise is that states are guided by the logic of the "national interest," usually defined in terms of survival, security, power, and relative capabilities. To Morgenthau, for example, "rational foreign policy minimizes risks and maximizes benefits." Although the national interest may vary according to specific circumstances, the similarity of motives among nations permits the analyst to reconstruct the logic of policymakers in their pursuit of national interests—what Morgenthau called the "rational hypothesis"—and to avoid the fallacies of "concern with motives and concern with ideological preferences."[2]

Finally, the nation-state can also be conceptualized as a *unitary* actor. Because the central problems for states are starkly defined by the nature of the international system, their actions are primarily a response to external rather than domestic political forces. At best, the latter provide very weak explanations for external policy. According to Stephen Krasner, for example, the state "can be treated as an autonomous actor pursuing goals associated with power and the general interest of the society."[3] However, classical realists sometimes use domestic politics as a residual category to explain deviations from rational policies.

Realism has been the dominant model of international relations during at least the past five decades, perhaps in part because it seemed to provide a useful framework for understanding World War II and the Cold War. Nevertheless, the classical versions articulated by Morgenthau and others have received a good deal of critical scrutiny. The critics have included scholars who accept the basic premises of realism but who found that in at least four important respects these theories lacked sufficient precision and rigor.

Classical realism usually has been grounded in a pessimistic theory of human nature, either a theological version (e.g., St. Augustine and Reinhold Niebuhr), or a secular one (e.g., Machiavelli, Hobbes, and Morgenthau). Egoism and self-interested behavior are not limited to a few evil or misguided leaders, as the idealists would have it, but are basic to *homo politicus* and thus are at the core of a realist theory. But according to its critics, because human nature, if it means anything, is a constant rather than a variable, it is an unsatisfactory explanation

---

[2]Morgenthau, *Politics*, 7, 5.

[3]Stephen D. Krasner, *Defending the National Interest: Raw Materials Investment and U.S. Foreign Policy* (Princeton, 1978), 33. Krasner's study compares realist, interest-group liberal, and Marxist theories.

for the full range of international relations. If human nature explains war and conflict, what accounts for peace and cooperation? In order to avoid this problem, most modern realists have turned their attention from human nature to the structure of the international system to explain state behavior.

In addition, critics have noted a lack of precision and even contradictions in the way classical realists use such concepts as "power," "national interest," and "balance of power." They also see possible contradictions between the central descriptive and prescriptive elements of classical realism. On the one hand, nations and their leaders [as Hans Morgenthau put it,] "think and act in terms of interests defined as power," but, on the other, statesmen are urged to exercise prudence and self-restraint, as well as to recognize the legitimate national interests of other nations. Power plays a central role in classical realism, but the correlation between the relative power balance and political outcomes is often less than compelling, suggesting the need to enrich analyses with other variables. Moreover, the distinction between "power as capabilities" and "useable options" is especially important in the nuclear age.

While classical realists have typically looked to history and political science for insights and evidence, the search for greater precision has led many modern realists to look elsewhere for appropriate models, analogies, metaphors, and insights. The discipline of choice is often economics, from which modern realists have borrowed a number of tools and concepts, including rational choice, expected utility, theories of firms and markets, bargaining theory, and game theory. Contrary to the assertion of some critics, however, modern realists *share* rather than reject the core premises of their classical predecessors.

The quest for precision has yielded a rich harvest of theories and models, and a somewhat less bountiful crop of supporting empirical applications. Drawing in part on game theory, Morton Kaplan described several types of international systems—for example, balance-of-power, loose bipolar, tight bipolar, universal, hierarchical, and a unit-veto system in which any action requires the unanimous approval of all its members. He then outlined the essential rules that constitute these systems. For example, the rules for a balance-of-power system are: "(1) increase capabilities, but negotiate rather than fight; (2) fight rather than fail to increase capabilities; (3) stop fighting rather than eliminate an essential actor; (4) oppose any coalition or single actor that tends to assume a position of predominance within the system; (5) constrain actors who subscribe to supranational organizational principles; and (6) permit defeated or constrained essential actors to re-enter the system."[4] . . .

Kenneth Waltz's *Theory of International Politics,* the most prominent effort to develop a rigorous and parsimonious model of "modern" or "structural" realism, has tended to define the terms of a vigorous debate during the past decade. It follows and builds upon another enormously influential book in which Waltz

---

[4]Morton Kaplan, *System and Process in International Politics* (New York, 1957).

developed the Rousseauian position that a theory of war must include the system level (what he called the "third image") and not just first (theories of human nature) or second (state attributes) images. Why war? Because there is nothing in the system to prevent it.[5]

*Theory of International Relations* is grounded in analogies from microeconomics; international politics and foreign policy are analogous to markets and firms. Oligopoly theory is used to illuminate the dynamics of interdependent choice in a self-help anarchical system. Waltz explicitly limits his attention to a structural theory of international systems, eschewing the task of linking it to a theory of foreign policy. Indeed, he doubts that the two can be joined in a single theory and he is highly critical of many system-level analysts, including Morton Kaplan, Stanley Hoffmann, Richard Rosecrance, Karl Deutsch and J. David Singer, and others, charging them with various errors, including "reductionism"; that is, defining the system in terms of the attributes or interactions of the units.

In order to avoid reductionism and to gain rigor and parsimony, Waltz erects his theory on the foundations of three core propositions that define the structure of the international system. The first concentrates on the principles by which the system is ordered. The contemporary system is anarchic and decentralized rather than hierarchical; although they differ in many respects, each unit is formally equal.[6] A second defining proposition is the character of the units. An anarchic system is composed of similar sovereign units and therefore the functions that they perform are also similar rather than different; for example, all have the task of providing for their own security. In contrast, a hierarchical system would be characterized by some type of division of labor, as is the case in domestic politics. Finally, there is a distribution of capabilities among units in the system. Although capabilities are a unit-level attribute, the distribution of capabilities is a system-level concept.

A change in any of these elements constitutes a change in system structure. The first element of structure as defined by Waltz is a quasiconstant because the ordering principle rarely changes, and the second element drops out of the analysis because the functions of units are similar as long as the system remains anarchic. Thus, the last of the three attributes, the distribution of capabilities, plays the central role in Waltz's model.

Waltz uses his theory to deduce the central characteristics of international relations. These include some non-obvious propositions about the contemporary international system. For example, with respect to system stability (defined as maintenance of its anarchic character and no consequential variation in the number of major actors) he concludes that because the present bipolar system

---

[5]Kenneth Waltz, *Theory of International Politics* (Reading, MA, 1979); idem, *Man, the State, and War* (New York, 1959).

[6]Because Waltz strives for a universal theory that is not limited to any era, he uses the term "unit" to refer to the constituent members of the system. In the contemporary system these are states, but in order to reflect Waltz's intent more faithfully, the term "unit" is used here.

reduces uncertainty, it is more stable than alternative structures; interdependence has declined rather than increased during the twentieth century, a tendency that has actually contributed to stability; and the proliferation of nuclear weapons may contribute to rather than erode system stability.[7]

Unlike some system-level models, Waltz's effort to bring rigor and parsimony to realism has stimulated a good deal of further research, but it has not escaped controversy and criticism.[8] Leaving aside highly charged polemics—for example, that Waltz and his supporters are guilty of engaging in a "totalitarian project of global proportions"—most of the vigorous debate has centered on four alleged deficiencies relating to interests and preferences, system change, misallocation of variables between the system and unit levels, and an inability to explain outcomes.

Specifically, a spare structural approach suffers from an inability to identify completely the nature and sources of interests and preferences because these are unlikely to derive solely from the structure of the system. Ideology or domestic considerations may often be at least as important. Consequently, the model is also unable to specify adequately how interests and preferences may change. The three defining characteristics of system structure are too general, moreover, and thus they are not sufficiently sensitive to specify the sources and dynamics of system change. The critics buttress their claim that the model is too static by pointing to Waltz's assertion that there has only been a single structural change in the international system during the past three centuries.

Another drawback is the restrictive definition of system properties, which leads Waltz to misplace, and therefore neglect, elements of international relations that properly belong at the system level. Critics have focused on his treatment of the destructiveness of nuclear weapons and interdependence. Waltz labels these as unit-level properties, whereas some of his critics assert that they are in fact attributes of the system.

Finally, the distribution of capabilities explains outcomes in international affairs only in the most general way, falling short of answering the questions that are of central interest to many analysts. For example, the distribution of power at the end of World War II would have enabled one to predict the rivalry that emerged between the United States and the Soviet Union, but it would have been inadequate for explaining the pattern of relations between these two nations—the Cold War rather than withdrawal into isolationism by either or both, a division of the world into spheres of influence, or World War III. In order to do so, it is necessary to explore political processes *within* states—at minimum within the United States and the USSR—as well as *between* them.

[7]Waltz, "The Myth of National Interdependence," in *The International Corporation,* ed. Charles P. Kindleberger (Cambridge, MA, 1970); Waltz, "The Spread of Nuclear Weapons: More May Be Better," *Adelphi Papers,* no. 171 (1981).

[8] . . . The best single source for the various dimensions of the debate is Robert Keohane, ed., *Neorealism and Its Critics* (New York, 1986).

Robert Gilpin shares with Waltz the core assumptions of modern realism, but his study of *War and Change in World Politics* [9] also attempts to cope with some of the criticism leveled at Waltz's theory by focusing on the dynamics of system change. Drawing upon both economic and sociological theory, his model is based on five core propositions. The first is that the international system is stable—in a state of equilibrium—if no state believes that it is profitable to attempt to change it. Second, a state will attempt to change the status quo of the international system if the expected benefits outweigh the costs; that is, if there is an expected net gain for the revisionist state. Related to this is the proposition that a state will see a change through territorial, political, and economic expansion until the marginal costs of further change equal or exceed the marginal benefits. Moreover, when an equilibrium between the costs and benefits of further change and expansion is reached, the economic costs of maintaining the status quo (expenditures for military forces, support for allies, etc.) tend to rise faster than the resources needed to do so. An equilibrium exists when no powerful state believes that a change in the system would yield additional net benefits. Finally, if the resulting disequilibrium between the existing governance of the international system and the redistribution of power is not resolved, the system will be changed and a new equilibrium reflecting the distribution of relative capabilities will be established.

Unlike Waltz, Gilpin includes state-level processes in order to explain change. Differential economic growth rates among nations—a structural-systemic level variable—play a vital role in his explanation for the rise and decline of great powers, but his model also includes propositions about the law of diminishing returns on investments, the impact of affluence on martial spirits and on the ratio of consumption to investment, and structural change in the economy. Table 1 summarizes some key elements of realism. It also contrasts them to . . . [an]other system-level [model] of international relations—the Global-Society/Complex-Interdependence [model], to which we now turn our attention.

Just as there are variants of realism, there are several Global-Society/Complex-Interdependence (GS/CI) models, but this discussion focuses on two common denominators; they all challenge the first and third core propositions of realism identified earlier, asserting that inordinate attention to the war/peace issue and the nation-state renders it an increasingly anachronistic model of global relations.[10] The agenda of critical problems confronting states

---

[9][(Cambridge, 1981.)]

[10]Robert Keohane and Joseph S. Nye, Jr., *Power and Interdependence: World Politics in Transition* (Boston, 1977); Edward Morse, *Modernization and the Transformation of International Relations* (New York, 1967); James N. Rosenau, *The Study of Global Interdependence* (London, 1980); Richard Mansbach and John Vasquez, *In Search of Theory: A New Paradigm for Global Politics* (New York, 1981); Andrew M. Scott, *The Dynamics of Interdependence* (Chapel Hill, 1982); Rosenau, *Turbulence in World Politics* [Princeton, 1990].

**TABLE 1**
TWO MODELS OF THE INTERNATIONAL SYSTEM

| | REALISM | COMPLEX INTERDEPENDENCE |
|---|---|---|
| *Type of model* | Classical: descriptive and normative<br>Modern: deductive | Descriptive and normative |
| *Central problems* | Causes of war<br>Conditions of peace | Broad agenda of social, economic, and environmental issues arising from gap between demands and resources |
| *Conception of current international system* | Structural anarchy | Global society<br>Complex interdependence (structure varies by issue-area) |
| *Key actors* | Geographically based units (tribes, city-states, nation-states, etc.) | Highly permeable nation-states *plus* a broad range of nonstate actors, including IOs, IGOs, NGOs, and individuals |
| *Central motivations* | National interest<br>Security<br>Power | Human needs and wants |
| *Loyalties* | To geographically based groups (from tribes to nation-states) | Loyalties to nation-state declining<br>To emerging global values and institutions that transcend those of the nation-state and/or to subnational groups |
| *Central processes* | Search for security and survival | Aggregate effects of decisions by national and nonnational actors<br>How units (not limited to nation-states) cope with a growing agenda of threats and opportunities arising from human wants |
| *Likelihood of system transformation* | Low (basic structural elements of system have revealed an ability to persist despite many other kinds of changes) | High in the direction of the model (owing to the rapid pace of technological change, etc.) |
| *Sources of theory, insights, and evidence* | Politics<br>History<br>Economics (especially "modern" realists) | Broad range of social sciences<br>Natural and technological sciences |

has been vastly expanded during the twentieth century. Attention to the issues of war and peace is by no means misdirected, according to proponents of a GS/CI perspective, but concerns for welfare, modernization, the environment, and the like are today no less potent sources of motivation and action. The diffusion of knowledge and technology, combined with the globalization of communications, has vastly increased popular expectations. The resulting demands have outstripped resources and the ability of existing institutions—notably the sovereign nation-state—to cope effectively with them. Interdependence arises from an inability of even the most powerful states to cope, or to do so unilaterally or at acceptable levels of cost and risk, with issues ranging from trade to AIDS, and immigration to environmental threats.

Paralleling the widening agenda of critical issues is the expansion of actors whose behavior can have a significant impact beyond national boundaries; indeed, the cumulative effects of their actions can have profound consequences for the international system. Thus, although nation-states continue to be important international actors, they possess a declining ability to control their own destinies. The aggregate effect of actions by multitudes of non-state actors can have potent effects that transcend political boundaries. These may include such powerful or highly visible non-state organizations as Exxon, the Organization of Petroleum Exporting Countries, or the Palestine Liberation Organization. On the other hand, the cumulative effects of decisions by less powerful or less visible actors may also have profound international consequences. For example, decisions by thousands of individuals, mutual funds, banks, pension funds, and other financial institutions to sell securities on 19 October 1987 not only resulted in an unprecedented "crash" on Wall Street, but also within hours its consequences were felt throughout the entire global financial system. Governments might take such actions as loosening credit or even closing exchanges, but they were largely unable to contain the effects of the panic.

The widening agenda of critical issues, most of which lack a purely national solution, has also led to creation of new actors that transcend political boundaries; for example, international organizations, transnational organizations, non-government organizations, multinational corporations, and the like. Thus, not only does an exclusive focus on the war/peace issue fail to capture the complexities of contemporary international life but it also blinds the analyst to the institutions, processes, and norms that permit cooperation and significantly mitigate some features of an anarchic system. In short, according to GS/CI perspectives, an adequate understanding of the emergent global system must recognize that no single model is likely to be sufficient for all issues, and that if it restricts attention to the manner in which states deal with traditional security concerns, it is more likely to obfuscate than clarify the realities of contemporary world affairs.

The GS/CI models have several important virtues. They recognize that international behavior and outcomes arise from a multiplicity of motives, not merely security, at least if security is defined solely in military or strategic terms. They also alert us to the fact that important international processes and conditions originate not only in the actions of nation-states but also in the aggregated behavior of other actors. These models not only enable the analyst to deal with a broader agenda of critical issues but, more importantly, they force one to contemplate a much richer menu of demands, processes, and outcomes than would be derived from power-centered realist models. Stated differently, GS/CI models are more sensitive to the possibility that politics of trade, currency, immigration, health, the environment, and the like may significantly and systematically differ from those typically associated with security issues.

On the other hand, some GS/CI analysts underestimate the potency of nationalism and the durability of the nation-state. Two decades ago one of them wrote that "the nation is declining in its importance as a political unit to which allegiances are attached."[11] Objectively, nationalism may be an anachronism but, for better or worse, powerful loyalties are still attached to nation-states. The suggestion that, because even some well-established nations have experienced independence movements among ethnic, cultural, or religious minorities, the sovereign territorial state may be in decline is not wholly persuasive. Indeed, that evidence perhaps points to precisely the opposite conclusion: In virtually every region of the world there are groups which seek to create or restore geographically based entities in which its members may enjoy the status and privileges associated with sovereign territorial statehood. Evidence from Poland to Palestine, Spain to Sri Lanka, Estonia to Eritrea, Armenia to Afghanistan, and elsewhere seems to indicate that obituaries for nationalism may be somewhat premature.

The notion that such powerful non-national actors as major multinational corporations (MNC) will soon transcend the nation-state seems equally premature. International drug rings do appear capable of dominating such states as Colombia and Panama. However, the pattern of outcomes in confrontations between MNCs and states, including cases involving major expropriations of corporate properties, indicates that even relatively weak nations are not always the hapless pawns of the MNCs. Case studies . . . indicate that MNC-state relations yield a wide variety of outcomes.

Underlying the GS/CI critique of realist models is the view that the latter are too wedded to the past and are thus incapable of dealing adequately with change. At least for the present, however, even if global dynamics arise from multiple sources (including non-state actors), the actions of nation-states and their agents would appear to remain the major sources of change in the international system. . . .

At the risk of ending on a platitude, it seems clear that . . . neglect of foreign policy decision making not only leaves one unable to explain the dynamics of international relations, but many important aspects of a nation's external behavior will be inexplicable. Advocates of the realist model have often argued its superiority for understanding the "high" politics of deterrence, containment,

---

[11]Rosenau, "National Interest," [*International Encyclopedia of the Social Sciences,* Vol. 11 (New York, 1968)] 39. A more recent statement of this view may be found in Richard Rosecrance, *The Rise of the Trading State* (New York, 1986). See also John H. Herz, "The Rise and Demise of the Territorial State," *World Politics* 9 (July 1957): 473–93; and his reconsideration in "The Territorial State Revisited: Reflections on the Future of the Nation-State," *Polity* 1 (Fall 1968): 12–34.

alliances, crises, and wars, if not necessarily for "low" politics. But there are several rejoinders to this line of reasoning. First, the low politics of trade, currencies, and other issues that are almost always highly sensitive to domestic pressures are becoming an increasingly important element of international relations. Second, the growing literature on the putative domain *par excellence* of realism, including deterrence, crises, and wars, raises substantial doubts about the universal validity of the realist model even for these issues. Finally, exclusive reliance on realist models and their assumptions of rationality may lead to unwarranted complacency about dangers in the international system. Nuclear weapons and other features of the system have no doubt contributed to the "long peace" between major powers. At the same time, however, a narrow focus on power balances, "correlations of forces," and other features of the international system will result in neglect of dangers—for example, the command, communication, control, intelligence problem or inadequate information processing—that can only be identified and analyzed by a decision-making perspective.

At a very general level, this conclusion parallels that drawn three decades ago by the foremost contemporary proponent of modern realism: the "third image" (system structure) is necessary for understanding the context of international behavior, whereas the first and second images (decision makers and domestic political processes) are needed to understand dynamics within the system.[12] But to acknowledge the existence of various levels of analysis is not enough. *What* the investigator wants to explain and the *level of specificity and comprehensiveness* to be sought should determine which level(s) of analysis are relevant and necessary. In this connection, it is essential to distinguish two different dependent variables: foreign policy decisions by states, on the one hand, and the outcomes of policy and interactions between two or more states, on the other. If the goal is to understand the former—foreign policy decisions—Harold and Margaret Sprout's notion of "psychological milieu" is relevant and sufficient; that is, the objective structural variables influence the decisions via the decision maker's perception and evaluation of those "outside" variables.[13] However, if the goal is to explain outcomes, the "psychological milieu" is quite inadequate; the objective factors, if misperceived or misjudged by the decision maker, will influence the outcome. Political scientists studying international relations are increasingly disciplining their use of multiple levels of analysis in studying outcomes that cannot be adequately explained via only a single level of analysis.

Which of these models and approaches are likely to be of [the most] utility . . . ? Clearly there is no one answer; political scientists are unable to agree on a single multilevel approach to international relations and foreign policy; thus they are hardly in a position to offer a single recommendation. . . . In the

---

[12]Waltz, *Man, the State, and War,* 238.

[13]Harold and Margaret Sprout, "Environmental Factors in the Study of International Politics," *Journal of Conflict Resolution* 1 (December 1957): 309–28.

absence of the often-sought but always-elusive unified theory of human behavior that could provide a model for all seasons and all reasons, one must ask at least one further question: A model for what purpose? For example, in some circumstances, such as research on major international crises, it may be important to obtain systematic evidence on the beliefs and other intellectual baggage that key policymakers bring to their deliberations. Some of the approaches described above should prove very helpful in this respect. Conversely, there are many other research problems for which [we] would quite properly decide that this type of analysis requires far more effort than could possibly be justified by the benefits to be gained.

. . . Those who focus on security issues can hardly neglect [classical realism's] central premises and concepts. On the other hand, modern or structural realism of the Waltz variety is likely to have rather limited appeal . . . if we take seriously his doubts about being able to incorporate foreign policy into it. It may perhaps serve to raise consciousness about the importance of the systemic context within which international relations take place, but that may not be a major gain—after all, such concepts as "balance of power" have long been a standard part of the [diplomats'] vocabulary. Gilpin's richer approach, which employs both system- and state-level variables to explain international dynamics, may well have greater appeal. . . .

The Global-Society/Complex-Interdependence models will be helpful to [those] with an interest in evolution of the international system and with the growing disjuncture between demands on states and their ability to meet them— the "sovereignty gap." One need not be very venturesome to predict that this gap will grow rather than narrow in the future. [Students] of all kinds of international and transnational organizations are also likely to find useful concepts and insights in these models. . . .

# 13

# U.S.–SOVIET RELATIONS: THRESHOLD OF A NEW ERA

## Arnold L. Horelick

**In this essay Arnold L. Horelick evaluates the consequences of the Cold War's end for the future of the two superpowers' relations in particular and for international security in general. Horelick is Senior Corporate Fellow in Soviet Affairs at the RAND Corporation and professor of political science at the University of California, Los Angeles. He served as the U.S. National Intelligence Officer for the U.S.S.R. and Eastern Europe from 1977 to 1980, and has authored *U.S.–Soviet Relations: The Next Phase* (1986) and co-authored *Managing U.S.–Soviet Relations in the 1990s* (1989).**

I

As the decade of the 1980s closed, the United States and the Soviet Union appeared finally to have mastered their forty-year-old conflict. At the 1989 Malta summit between Presidents George Bush and Mikhail Gorbachev, the convergence of American and Soviet positions on most agenda items was unprecedented. Their relationship seemed likely to develop with minimum tension, low risk and, prospectively, at greatly reduced cost.

But precisely at the moment when they seem to have perfected their methods for managing the conflicts of the cold war era, that era has abruptly ended. The

From *Foreign Affairs* (America and the World 1989–1990). Copyright 1989 by the Council on Foreign Relations. Used by permission of *Foreign Affairs*. Some section headings have been deleted and others have been renumbered to appear in consecutive order—

finely honed instruments of conflict management face early obsolescence. Instead, policymakers in both capitals face a new international politics in which their bipolar competition will no longer provide the dominant framework for ordering the system and disciplining the behavior of states. For the United States the adjustment will surely be difficult, but incomparably less so than for the Soviet Union.

By every measure of conventional postwar scorekeeping, 1989 was the year in which the West won the cold war. . . . Moscow, moreover, seemed helpless or unwilling to prevent the sudden deterioration of its most sensitive geopolitical position. The Soviet Union was immersed in a profound domestic crisis that threatened both the political stability and the territorial integrity of the state. The Soviet economy was in a shambles. Discontent and pessimism were endemic. In Moscow, supporters and critics competed in making estimates of how many months Gorbachev still had left in which to deliver on perestroika's promise before a "revolution from below," a military coup or a hard-line conservative backlash swept both him and his program away, or compelled him to suspend *demokratizatsia* and glasnost.

In foreign policy, according to the old calculus, Gorbachev may have gained some breathing space for the beleaguered Soviet Union, but only at a high cost: surrendering the "socialist gains" in Eastern Europe, abandoning Third World friends and clients to U.S.-supported counterrevolution, and making an uninterrupted series of grossly asymmetrical arms control concessions, which after five years still had not been seriously reciprocated by the West. Thus, when he arrived at Malta for his first meeting with the new American president, Gorbachev held the weakest geopolitical hand any Soviet leader has had to play in a summit meeting. To a Soviet "old thinker," Bush's praise of Gorbachev and his suspension of a few minor discriminatory economic restrictions were merely the cosmetic part of "rollback with a human face." . . .

Ironically, viewed against the background of Gorbachev's forthcoming and welcome departures in foreign policy, his troubles at home helped him abroad. They encouraged the evolution of the Bush Administration's policy from skeptical, watchful waiting to broad engagement with the Soviet Union. The president finally endorsed both Gorbachev and his policies. Amid mounting evidence that perestroika might be failing, Bush claimed to be second to none in supporting it.

## II

During the waning years of President Reagan's second term, the running battle over how to deal with Gorbachev's Soviet Union was finally resolved. There were those centered in the office of the secretary of defense who had been the "squeezers." They opposed any relaxation of competitive pressure on the Soviet Union, which they saw as the key to forcing the Kremlin into global retreat and compelling it to choose between outright abandonment of communism or collapse. There was another group, in the State Department, the "dealers," who saw the shifting global correlation of forces and Gorbachev's preoccupation with internal reform as an opportunity to reach arms control and regional agreements on unprecedentedly favorable terms. As Soviet reforms deepened, the "dealers" even grew prepared for such agreements to help Gorbachev as well. By the end of the Reagan Administration, the president's own growing confidence in Gorbachev and Secretary of State George Shultz's persistent efforts to overcome right-wing attachment to the militantly anti-Soviet stance of Reagan's first term had prevailed. "Squeezing" Gorbachev had effectively dropped out of the operative spectrum.

By the time George Bush took office . . . virtually the entire American foreign policy establishment, including its most prominent conservative members, were "dealers" of one kind or another. . . . This reflected the administration's recognition that it was in the West's interest to move expeditiously toward concluding the arms control agreements . . . under negotiation, regardless of the uncertainty about the future of Gorbachev and perestroika. If Gorbachev survived and perestroika prospered, the groundwork would be laid for moving further toward institutionalizing a much more stable and less confrontational military relationship. Once the Soviet Union had destroyed nuclear weapons and withdrew or dismantled conventional forces as required by the agreements, it would be difficult, costly and time-consuming for any future Soviet leadership, even one more hostile or assertive, to reverse the process. The stage thus was set . . . ; the Bush Administration had made its choice.

The collapse of communist domination of Eastern Europe had made a crucial difference. It provided dramatic, tangible evidence of a change both in the policies and geopolitical position of the U.S.S.R. that could not possibly be explained away as a ruse or a temporary tactical retreat which might leave the Soviet Union free to resume the old struggle after a respite. The crisis in Eastern Europe reinforced a Western perception that real strategic opportunities lay ahead, not only in arms control but in political arrangements that could fundamentally improve European security—the principal area of competition and the heart of the cold war. It suddenly became critical for the West to see Eastern Europe through a period of free elections and in the process to reassure Moscow that its security would not be threatened.

III

It was not surprising that at [the December 1989] Malta [summit] both Bush and Gorbachev used almost identical language in proclaiming that their two countries were "at the threshold of a new era." . . . Going into Malta, the Soviet and American leaders had slogans, not visions, and much less blueprints, for a new European order. While Gorbachev had surrounded his longstanding call for a "Common European Home" with thousands of words, there was not much more substance to his theme than to President Bush's [subsequent] call for a "Europe Whole and Free." . . .

Gorbachev himself had inspired the change in Eastern Europe, which he subsequently acknowledged as inevitable. What he clearly had hoped for was to spread perestroika to Eastern Europe, where a wave of reform would be instituted by rejuvenated and restructured Communist parties that would "renew socialism." His vision was a voluntary community of Eastern states pursuing common socialist agendas and led by like-minded reformers. Those states would still be linked, but far more loosely than in the past. For enduring geopolitical and economic reasons, the alliance with the Soviet Union would continue, but in a less militarized and more politicized grouping that would occupy the Eastern wing of the European "common home."

This vision had already been upset by the transfer of power to Solidarity in Poland, and had been completely overtaken by events in East Germany and Czechoslovakia. Gorbachev acknowledged that the Communists had "lost" the confidence of the people. The hope that some vague common commitment might still emerge to a democratized version of socialism may not have been entirely abandoned in Moscow, but the prospects were poor, and fading. Moscow had to look more and more to a geopolitical rationale for maintaining security ties between Eastern Europe and the Soviet Union. Its policy had to be to make such a rationale persuasive and acceptable to its allies. To do that Gorbachev had to rely on the West's shared concern about stability and enlist Western support for a "calm and peaceful" transition in Eastern Europe.

At some point, Gorbachev may have had a game plan for meshing the interrelated processes of demilitarization in the West and reform in the East. The revolt of Eastern Europe, however, destroyed whatever balance Gorbachev had hoped to maintain between these two aims. Gorbachev must surely have understood that his unmistakable support for reform in Eastern Europe, together with his unilateral force reductions and proposed CFE cuts, would produce more independent allies and weaken Soviet control of the Warsaw Pact—a trend confirmed by the evolution of events in Poland and Hungary.

But earlier, in December 1988 when he announced the decision to cut troops unilaterally, Gorbachev probably hoped—not implausibly—that rapid changes in the West's perception of a Soviet threat would stimulate a comparable weakening of NATO's military efforts and cohesion. By the summer and fall of 1989 changes in Eastern Europe were completely outstripping the more careful arms reduction process on which Gorbachev may have been relying. Moreover, by November it was clear that the issue of German reunification would have to be faced not at the end of a gradual process of change but at a much earlier stage, and under conditions in which the security structures of the East were disintegrating while NATO remained wholly intact. Once the issue of German reunification was raised, it became even more crucial for Gorbachev to emphasize to the uneasy Western allies of the F.R.G. [West Germany] their common interest with Moscow in maintaining stability in Europe during the transition, and to encourage a multilateral approach to the German question such that Moscow would not be obliged to be the sole naysayer.

## IV

The emergence of the German question must have caused second thoughts in Moscow about continuing the Soviet campaign to dissolve the opposing alliances and to seek the withdrawal of foreign forces from Europe. In such a reappraisal, Gorbachev was no doubt encouraged by reassuring evidence that the United States and its allies were not seeking to undercut Moscow during its time of troubles in Eastern Europe, and that they too preferred a stable orderly transition, rather than a precipitous upheaval, to end the division of Europe. In the West as well as in the East there was a clear preference for stability: "This is not the time," Gorbachev told the French foreign minister, "to destroy the established international political institutions."

While the superpowers did in fact have certain common interests in a stable process, their objectives were a mix of overlapping interests and potential new conflicts.

For the West the approach to a new European security order is likely to be to preserve and strengthen Western institutions that have proved so effective during the cold war, and to ensure that the democratic Eastern countries that may emerge have an opportunity for broader and deeper relations with the West. The Western design [seeks to ensure that the reunified Germany will] remain strongly anchored in the West. . . .

[Arms] control, if given time to unfold, would tend to perpetuate the two alliances in Europe. . . . Gorbachev . . . explicitly argued for retaining existing institutions in formulations that do not distinguish between NATO and the Warsaw Pact. Officially, the United States has taken no position on the desirability of the Warsaw Pact's survival. Nevertheless, the CFE process that the United States and NATO endorsed serves to stabilize the Warsaw Pact and give it a rationale that democratic governments in Eastern Europe might also be able to accept and use to defend against nationalist anti-Soviet electoral pressures at home.

On the other hand, both Moscow and Washington have talked, in strikingly similar language, about the transformation of their alliances from military organizations to more "political" ones. For both this is a means of giving their alliances, and their leading roles in them, a new dispensation in a world in which the alliances' primary military functions are waning in importance.

But prospects for a political NATO and a political Warsaw Pact are quite different. NATO is necessarily a political alliance. While there may be some resistance, especially from the French, to permitting Atlanticist NATO to intrude on the political prerogatives of the European Community, the transformation of

NATO into an alliance with growing political functions faces no profound obstacles.

To transform the Warsaw Pact into a more "political" organ is a much more dubious proposition. As Soviet European specialists have acknowledged, the political infrastructure of the Warsaw Treaty Organization is poorly developed. It lacks a permanent political staff headquarters; its highest political organs meet only rarely and for largely ceremonial purposes; and its most important political decisions in the past were made in party, not state, channels—a practice that has been overtaken by the collapse of ruling Communist parties in Eastern Europe. . . .

## V

Neither Moscow nor Washington can yet see what will replace the cold-war system. The 1990s are likely to be a transitional period for relations between the two superpowers. In the multipolar world now emerging, they are likely to have more parallel and convergent interests than before. The Soviet Union, however, will find itself in radically altered circumstances that are still evolving and that could change even more radically. It now prefers gradualism and preserving existing institutions, but desperation could lead to more risky strategies. As for the United States, it needs to consult with its allies to work out a Western position before further engaging the Soviet Union on a new "architecture" for Europe.

It is misleading to conclude, however, that these new circumstances will place the superpowers on the sidelines because they no longer control events and no longer dominate their alliances. So long as large Soviet forces remain in Eastern Europe, [some] significant potential for reversing policy in Eastern Europe, by a different Soviet regime, will persist.

In this light, it is the United States alone among all NATO members that is capable of leading the Western effort to negotiate the Soviet Union out of Europe as a military presence. Reciprocal military moves to compensate Moscow will have to come chiefly from Washington. The nuclear dimension is still almost exclusively a U.S.-Soviet issue to negotiate. Finally, the United States is best positioned to broker a Western consensus . . . and to lead in negotiating it with the Soviets.

As the United States and the Soviet Union reach the threshold of a new era in their relations, their roles in shaping the post–cold war world will be different from those they played in managing the East-West conflict, but no less crucial. Both will have to adapt their policies and behavior to environments in which they will have substantially diminished control and influence. In making this adjustment, the United States can draw on its own democratic institutions and traditions and on its long experience in heading an alliance of free and often contentious partners. For the Soviet Union, this will be an entirely new experience for which the history of its foreign relations and its domestic political traditions have poorly prepared it. In the long run, its success in adjusting to a new and constructive international role will depend on its success in transforming the Soviet system itself. It is in this sense above all that the success of perestroika is in the fundamental interest of the Western world as well as of the peoples of the Soviet Union.

# 14

# EUROPE AFTER THE SUPERPOWERS: WHY WE WILL SOON MISS THE COLD WAR

John J. Mearsheimer

**This essay explores the consequences for Europe likely to result now that the United States and the Soviet Union have moved past the bitter confrontation that dominated their relations for forty years of Cold War rivalry. Examining the effects of a scenario under which the Cold War comes to a complete end and the Soviet Union withdraws its forces from Eastern Europe, leaving the states in that region fully independent, John J. Mearsheimer forsees great danger in that the conditions that for centuries made conflict and war in Europe recurrent are likely to be recreated. Mearsheimer is professor and chair of the department of political science, University of Chicago, and has written widely; among his books are *Conventional Deterrence* (1983) and *Liddell Hart and the Weight of History* (1989).**

. . . We may . . . wake up one day lamenting the loss of the order that the Cold War gave to the anarchy of international relations. For untamed anarchy is what Europe knew in the forty-five years of this century before the Cold War, and untamed anarchy—Hobbes's war of all against all—is a prime cause of armed conflict. Those who think that armed conflicts among the European states are now out of the question, that the two world wars burned all the war out of Europe, are projecting unwarranted optimism onto the future. . . . The prospect of major crises, even wars, in Europe is likely to increase dramatically now that

Used by permission of John J. Mearsheimer.

158

the Cold War is receding into history. The next forty-five years in Europe . . . are likely to be substantially more violent than the past forty-five years, the era that we may someday look back upon not as the Cold War but as the Long Peace, in John Lewis Gaddis's phrase.

This pessimistic conclusion rests on the general argument that the distribution and character of military power among states are the root causes of war and peace. Specifically, the peace in Europe since 1945—precarious at first, but increasingly robust over time—has flowed from three factors: the bipolar distribution of military power on the Continent; the rough military equality between the polar powers, the United States and the Soviet Union; and the ritualistically deplored fact that each of these superpowers is armed with a large nuclear arsenal. . . . What will keep the peace in the future? Specifically, what new order is likely to emerge if NATO and the Warsaw Pact dissolve, which they will do if the Cold War is really over, and the Soviets withdraw from Eastern Europe and the Americans quit Western Europe, taking their nuclear weapons with them—and should we welcome or fear it?

One dimension of the new European order is certain: it will be multipolar. Germany, France, Britain, and perhaps Italy will assume major-power status. The Soviet Union will decline from superpower status, not only because its military is sure to shrink in size but also because moving forces out of Eastern Europe will make it more difficult for the Soviets to project power onto the Continent. They will, of course, remain a major European power. The resulting four-or-five-power system will suffer the problems endemic to multipolar systems—and will therefore be prone to instability. The other two dimensions—the distribution of power among the major states and the distribution of nuclear weapons—are less certain. Indeed, who gets nuclear weapons is likely to be the most problematic question facing the new Europe. Three scenarios of the nuclear future in Europe are possible.

## THE "EUROPE WITHOUT NUCLEAR WEAPONS" SCENARIO

Many Europeans (and some Americans) seek to eliminate nuclear weapons from Europe altogether. Fashioning this nuclear-free Europe would require that Britain, France, and the Soviet Union rid themselves of these talismans of their sovereignty—an improbable eventuality, to say the least. Those who wish for it nevertheless believe that it would be the most peaceful arrangement possible. In fact a nuclear-free Europe has the distinction of being the most dangerous among the envisionable post–Cold War orders. The pacifying effects of nuclear weapons—the caution they generate, the security they provide, the rough equality they impose, and the clarity of the relative power they create—would be lost. Peace would then depend on the other dimensions of the new order—the number of poles and the distribution of power among them. The geometry of power in Europe would look much as it did between the world wars—a design for tension, crisis, and possibly even war.

The Soviet Union and [the] unified Germany would likely be the most powerful states in a nuclear-free Europe. A band of small independent states in Eastern Europe would lie between them. These minor Eastern European powers would be likely to fear the Soviets as much as the Germans, and thus would probably not be disposed to cooperate with the Soviets to deter possible German aggression. In fact, this very problem arose in the 1930s, and the past forty-five years of Soviet occupation have surely done little to mitigate Eastern European fears of a Soviet military presence. Thus scenarios in which Germany uses force against Poland, Czechoslovakia, or even Austria enter the realm of the possible in a nuclear-free Europe.

Then, too, the Soviet withdrawal from Eastern Europe hardly guarantees a permanent exit. Indeed, the Russian presence in Eastern Europe has surged and ebbed repeatedly over the past few centuries. In a grave warning, a member of President Mikhail Gorbachev's negotiating team at the [1990] Washington summit said, "You have the same explosive mixture you had in Germany in the 1930s. The humiliation of a great power. Economic troubles. The rise of nationalism. You should not underestimate the danger."

Conflicts between Eastern European states might also threaten the stability of the new European order. . . . Warfare in Eastern Europe . . . might widen to include the major powers, especially if disorder created fluid politics that offered opportunities for expanded influence, or threatened defeat for states friendly to one or another of the major powers. During the Cold War both superpowers were drawn into Third World conflicts across the globe, often in distant areas of little strategic importance. Eastern Europe is directly adjacent to both the Soviet Union and Germany, and it has considerable economic and strategic importance. Thus trouble in Eastern Europe would offer even greater temptations to these powers than past conflicts in the Third World offered to the superpowers. Furthermore, Eastern European states would have a strong incentive to drag the major powers into their local conflicts, because the results of such conflicts would be largely determined by the relative success of each party in finding external allies.

It is difficult to predict the precise balance of conventional military power that will emerge in post–Cold War Europe. The Soviet Union might recover its strength soon after withdrawing from Eastern Europe. In that case Soviet power would outmatch German power. But centrifugal national forces might pull the Soviet Union apart, leaving no remnant state that is the equal of a unified Germany. Finally, and probably most likely, Germany and the Soviet Union might emerge as powers of roughly equal strength. The first two geometries of power, with their marked military inequality between the two leading countries, would be especially worrisome, although there would be cause for concern even if Soviet and German power were balanced.

A non-nuclear Europe, to round out this catalogue of dangers, would likely be especially disturbed by hypernationalism, since security in such an order would rest on mass armies, which . . . often cannot be maintained without a mobilized public. The problem would probably be most acute in Eastern Europe, with its uncertain borders and irredentist minority groups. But there is also potential for trouble in Germany. The Germans have generally done an admirable job of combating hypernationalism over the past forty-five years, and of confronting the dark side of their past. Nevertheless, a portent like the recent call of some prominent Germans for a return to greater nationalism in historical education is disquieting.

For all these reasons, it is perhaps just as well that a nuclear-free Europe, much as it may be longed for by so many Europeans, does not appear to be in the cards.

## THE "CURRENT OWNERSHIP" SCENARIO

Under this scenario Britain, France, and the Soviet Union retain their nuclear weapons, but no new nuclear powers emerge in Europe. This vision of a nuclear-free zone in Central Europe, with nuclear weapons remaining on the flanks of the Continent, is also popular in Europe, but it, too, has doubtful prospects.

Germany will prevent it over the long run. The Germans are not likely to be willing to rely on the Poles or the Czechs to provide their forward defense against a possible direct Soviet conventional attack on their homeland. Nor are the Germans likely to trust the Soviet Union to refrain for all time from nuclear blackmail against a non-nuclear Germany. Hence they will eventually look to nuclear weapons as the surest means of security, just as NATO has done.

The small states of Eastern Europe will also have strong incentives to acquire nuclear weapons. Without them they would be open to nuclear blackmail by the Soviet Union, or by Germany if proliferation stopped there. Even if those major powers did not have nuclear arsenals, no Eastern European state could match German or Soviet conventional strength.

Clearly, then, a scenario in which current ownership continues, without proliferation, seems very unlikely.

## THE "NUCLEAR PROLIFERATION" SCENARIO

The most probable scenario in the wake of the Cold War is further nuclear proliferation in Europe. This outcome is laden with dangers, but it also might just provide the best hope for maintaining stability on the Continent. Everything depends on how proliferation is managed. Mismanaged proliferation could produce disaster; well-managed proliferation could produce an order nearly as stable as that of the Long Peace. . . .

I am pessimistic that proliferation can be well managed. The members of the nuclear club are likely to resist proliferation, but they cannot easily manage this tricky process while at the same time resisting it—and they will have several motives to resist. The established nuclear powers will be exceedingly chary of helping the new nuclear powers build secure deterrents, simply because it goes against the grain of state behavior to share military secrets with other states. After all, knowledge of sensitive military technology could be turned against the donor state if that technology were passed on to adversaries. Furthermore, proliferation in Europe will undermine the legitimacy of the 1968 Nuclear Non-Proliferation Treaty, and this could open the floodgates of proliferation worldwide. The current nuclear powers will not want that to happen, and so they will probably spend their energy trying to thwart proliferation, rather than seeking to manage it.

The best time for proliferation to occur would be during a period of relative international calm. Proliferation in the midst of a crisis would obviously be dangerous, since states in conflict with an emerging nuclear power would then have a powerful incentive to interrupt the process by force. However, the opposition to proliferation by citizens of the potential nuclear powers would be so vociferous, and the external resistance from the nuclear club would be so great, that it might take a crisis to make those powers willing to pay the domestic and international costs of building a nuclear force. All of which means that proliferation is likely to occur under international conditions that virtually ensure it will be mismanaged.

## IS WAR OBSOLETE?

Many students of European politics will reject my pessimistic analysis of post–Cold War Europe. They will say that a multipolar Europe, with or without nuclear weapons, will be no less peaceful than the present order. Three specific scenarios for a peaceful future have been advanced, each of which rests on a well-known theory of international relations. However, each of these "soft" theories of peace is flawed.

Under the first optimistic scenario, a non-nuclear Europe would remain peaceful because Europeans recognize that even a conventional war would be horrific. Sobered by history, national leaders will take care to avoid war. This scenario rests on the "obsolescence of war" theory, which posits that modern conventional war had become so deadly by 1945 as to be unthinkable as an instrument of statecraft. War is yesterday's nightmare.

The fact that the Second World War occurred casts doubt on this theory: if any war could have persuaded Europeans to forswear conventional war, it should have been the First World War, with its vast casualties. The key flaw in this theory is the assumption that all conventional wars will be long and bloody wars of attrition. Proponents ignore the evidence of several wars since 1945, as well as several campaign-ending battles of the Second World War, that it is still possible to gain a quick and decisive victory on the conventional battlefield and avoid the devastation of a protracted conflict. Conventional wars can be won rather cheaply; nuclear war cannot be, because neither side can escape devastation by the other, regardless of what happens on the battlefield. Thus the incentives to avoid war are of another order of intensity in a nuclear world than they are in a conventional world.

There are several other flaws in this scenario. There is no systematic evidence demonstrating that Europeans believe war is obsolete. The Romanians and the Hungarians don't seem to have gotten the message. However, even if it were widely believed in Europe that war is no longer thinkable, attitudes could change. Public opinion on national-security issues is notoriously fickle and responsive to manipulation by elites as well as to changes in the international environment. An end to the Cold War, as we have seen, will be accompanied by a sea change in the geometry of power in Europe, which will surely alter European thinking about questions of war and peace. It is not possible, for example, that German thinking about the benefits of controlling Eastern Europe will change markedly once American forces are withdrawn from Central Europe and the Germans are left to provide for their own security? Is it not possible that they would countenance a conventional war against a substantially weaker Eastern European state to enhance their position vis-à-vis the Soviet Union? Finally, only one country need decide that war is thinkable to make war possible.

## IS PROSPERITY THE PATH TO PEACE?

Proponents of the second optimistic scenario base their optimism about the future of Europe on the unified European market coming in 1992—the realization of the dream of the European Community. A strong EC, they argue, ensures that the European economy will remain open and prosperous, which will keep the European states cooperating with one another. Prosperity will make for peace. The threat of an aggressive Germany will be removed by enclosing the newly unified German state in the benign embrace of the EC. Even Eastern Europe and the Soviet Union can eventually be brought into the EC. Peace and prosperity will then extend their sway from the Atlantic to the Urals.

This scenario is based on the theory of economic liberalism, which assumes that states are primarily motivated by the desire to achieve prosperity and that leaders place the material welfare of their publics above all other considerations, including security. Stability flows not from military power but from the creation of a liberal economic order.

A liberal economic order works in several ways to enhance peace and dampen conflict. In the first place, it requires significant political cooperation to make the trading system work—make states richer. The more prosperous states grow, the greater their incentive for further political cooperation. A benevolent spiral relationship sets in between political cooperation and prosperity. Second, a liberal economic order fosters economic interdependence, a situation in which states are mutually vulnerable in the economic realm. When interdependence is high, the theory holds, there is less temptation to cheat or behave aggressively toward other states, because all states can retaliate economically. Finally, some theorists argue, an international institution like the EC will, with ever-increasing political cooperation, become so powerful that it will take on a life of its own, eventually evolving into a superstate. . . .

This theory has one grave flaw: the main assumption underpinning it is wrong. States are not primarily motivated by the desire to achieve prosperity. Although economic calculations are hardly trivial to them, states operate in both an international political and an international economic environment, and the former dominates the latter when the two systems come into conflict. Survival in an anarchic international political system is the highest goal a state can have.

Proponents of economic liberalism largely ignore the effects of anarchy on state behavior and concentrate instead on economic motives. When this omission is corrected, however, their arguments collapse for two reasons.

Competition for security makes it difficult for states to cooperate, which, according to the theory of economic liberalism, they must do. When security is scarce, states become more concerned about relative than about absolute gains. They ask of an exchange not "Will both of us gain?" but "Who will gain more?" They reject even cooperation that will yield an absolute economic gain if the other state will gain more, from fear that the other might convert its gain to military strength, and then use this strength to win by coercion in later rounds. Cooperation is much easier to achieve if states worry only about absolute gains. The goal, then, is simply to ensure that the overall economic pie is expanding and that each state is getting at least some part of the increase. However, anarchy guarantees that security will often be scarce; this heightens states' concerns about relative gains, which makes cooperation difficult unless the pie can be finely sliced to reflect, and thus not disturb, the current balance of power.

Interdependence, moreover, is as likely to lead to conflict as to cooperation, because states will struggle to escape the vulnerability that interdependence creates, in order to bolster their national security. In time of crisis or war, states that depend on others for critical economic supplies will fear cutoff or blackmail; they may well respond by trying to seize the source of supply by force of arms. There are numerous historical examples of states' pursuing aggressive military policies for the purpose of achieving economic autarky. One thinks of both Japan and Germany during the interwar period. And one recalls that during the Arab oil embargo of the early 1970s there was much talk in America about using military force to seize Arab oil fields. . . .

We certainly see a correlation in the Cold War between interdependence and stability, but that does not mean that interdependence has caused cooperation among the Western democracies. More likely the Cold War was the prime cause of cooperation among the Western democracies, and the main reason that intra-EC relations have flourished.

A powerful and potentially dangerous Soviet Union forced the Western democracies to band together to meet a common threat. This threat muted concerns about relative gains arising from economic cooperation among the EC states by giving each Western democracy a vested interest in seeing its alliance partners grow powerful. Each increment of power helped deter the Soviets. Moreover, they all had a powerful incentive to avoid conflict with one another while the Soviet Union loomed to the East, ready to harvest the grain of Western quarrels.

In addition, America's hegemonic position in NATO, the military counterpart to the EC, mitigated the effects of anarchy on the Western democracies and induced cooperation among them. America not only provided protection against the Soviet threat; it also guaranteed that no EC state would aggress against another. . . .

Take away the present Soviet threat to Western Europe, send the American forces home, and relations among the EC states will be fundamentally altered. Without a common Soviet threat or an American night watchman, Western European states will do what they did for centuries before the onset of the Cold War—look upon one another with abiding suspicion. Consequently, they will worry about imbalances in gains and about the loss of autonomy that results from cooperation. Cooperation in this new order will be more difficult than it was during the Cold War. Conflict will be more likely.

In sum, there are good reasons for being skeptical about the claim that a more powerful EC can provide the basis for peace in a multipolar Europe.

## DO DEMOCRACIES REALLY LOVE PEACE?

Under the third scenario war is avoided because many European states have become democratic since the early twentieth century, and liberal democracies simply do not fight one another. At a minimum, the presence of liberal democracies in Western Europe renders that half of Europe free from armed conflict. At a maximum, democracy spreads to Eastern Europe and the Soviet Union, bolstering peace. The idea that peace is cognate with democracy is a vision of international relations shared by both liberals and neoconservatives.

This scenario rests on the "peace-loving democracies" theory. Two arguments are made for it.

First, some claim that authoritarian leaders are more likely to go to war than leaders of democracies, because authoritarian leaders are not accountable to their publics, which carry the main burdens of war. In a democracy the citizenry, which pays the price of war, has a greater say in what the government does. The people, so the argument goes, are more hesitant to start trouble, because it is they who must pay the bloody price; hence the greater their power, the fewer wars.

The second argument rests on the claim that the citizens of liberal democracies respect popular democratic rights—those of their countrymen, and those of people in other states. They view democratic governments as more legitimate than others, and so are loath to impose a foreign regime on a democratic state by force. Thus an inhibition on war missing from other international relationships is introduced when two democracies face each other.

The first of these arguments is flawed because it is not possible to sustain the claim that the people in a democracy are especially sensitive to the costs of war and therefore less willing than authoritarian leaders to fight wars. In fact the historical record shows that democracies are every bit as likely to fight wars as are authoritarian states, though admittedly, thus far, not with other democracies.

Furthermore, mass publics, whether in a democracy or not, can become deeply imbued with nationalistic or religious fervor, making them prone to support aggression and quite indifferent to costs. The widespread public support in post-Revolutionary France for Napoleon's wars is just one example of this phenomenon. At the same time, authoritarian leaders are often fearful of going to war, because war tends to unleash democratic forces that can undermine the regime. In short, war can impose high costs on authoritarian leaders as well as on their citizenry.

The second argument, which emphasizes the transnational respect for democratic rights among democracies, rests on a secondary factor that is generally overridden by other factors such as nationalism and religious fundamentalism. Moreover, there is another problem with the argument. The possibility always exists that a democracy, especially the kind of fledgling democracy emerging in Eastern Europe, will revert to an authoritarian state. This threat of backsliding means that one democratic state can never be sure that another democratic state will not turn on it sometime in the future. Liberal democracies must therefore worry about relative power among themselves, which is tantamount to saying that each has an incentive to consider aggression against another to forestall trouble. Lamentably, it is not possible for even liberal democracies to transcend anarchy. . . .

While the spread of democracy across Europe has great potential benefits for human rights, it will not guarantee peaceful relations among the states of post–Cold War Europe. Most Americans will find this argument counterintuitive. They see the United States as fundamentally peaceloving, and they ascribe this peacefulness to its democratic character. From this they generalize that democracies are more peaceful than authoritarian states, which leads them to conclude that the complete democratization of Europe would largely eliminate the threat of war. This view of international politics is likely to be repudiated by the events of coming years.

## MISSING THE COLD WAR

The implications of my analysis are straightforward, if paradoxical. Developments that threaten to end the Cold War are dangerous. The West has an interest in maintaining peace in Europe. It therefore has an interest in maintaining the Cold War order, and hence has an interest in continuing the Cold War confrontation. The Cold War antagonism could be continued at lower levels of East-West tension than have prevailed in the past, but a complete end to the Cold War would create more problems than it would solve.

The fate of the Cold War is mainly in the hands of the Soviet Union. The Soviet Union is the only superpower that can seriously threaten to overrun Europe, and the Soviet threat provides the glue that holds NATO together. Take away that offensive threat and the United States is likely to abandon the Continent; the defensive alliance it has headed for forty years may well then disintegrate, bringing an end to the bipolar order that has kept the peace of Europe for the past forty-five years. . . .

# 15

# FIRST WORLD, THIRD WORLD, WHICH WORLD? THE FUTURE OF THE LESS DEVELOPED COUNTRIES

Mark Falcoff

**The collapse of the Cold War and the end of the postcolonial era have dramatically changed the circumstances and postures of the Third World countries—and eroded the basis for their "Third Worldism" ideology and "nonalignment" strategy, Mark Falcoff argues. As the Third World's "value as pieces on the strategic and ideological chessboard" has receded, Falcoff shows why the less developed countries face a plethora of new challenges and uncertainties, including the threat of being ignored by their relatively more powerful and wealthy former beneficiaries to the North. Falcoff, a Resident Fellow at the American Enterprise Institute, has co-authored *The Communist Challenge in the Caribbean and Central America* (1987) and written *Chile: Prospects for Democracy* (1988).**

Nineteen eighty-nine, the most pivotal year since World War II, marked a drastic, radical shift in the world's political and military geography. The only date in recent history to which it is comparable is 1945, which saw the destruction of the German and Japanese empires, the emergence of the United States and the Soviet Union as the global superpowers, and the end of the colonial era in Africa and Asia. In some ways, in fact, 1989 closed the cycle begun in 1945. It marked the end of the Cold War: the collapse of the Soviet empire in Eastern Europe,

Used by permission of Mark Falcoff.

the virtual dissolution of the Warsaw Pact, and the devastation of the Marxist idea, both as a political faith and an economic doctrine.

What many people have failed to notice, however, is that 1989 signified the end of the postcolonial era as well. For with no Cold War, there can be no "Third World," or rather, no "Third Worldism." And with no alignment—no sharp bipolarity within the international system—there can be no nonalignment, either. The countries are still there, of course—some 77 non-Western nations, including most of the Latin American republics. But their value as pieces on the strategic and ideological chessboard has significantly depreciated. What will these regimes use in place of the "double blackmail" (a term from the French magazine *L'Express*) by which they have obtained political leverage and resources from both East and West for 40 years or more? The answer is, probably nothing.

Of course, there will be some sort of relationship between the former Third World and the erstwhile First and Second, but it will be very different from the past. First, because the fundamental centers of power will be more concerned with devising methods of cooperation than competing for dubious foreign clients, the capacity of peripheral societies to disrupt the system as a whole will be greatly diminished. This means no more Sarajevos, no more Vietnams—and no more Lebanons, either.

There will still be disorder in such places; in fact, conflict is likely to persist or even grow in much of the non-Western world, as it often has in the past when colonial or tutelary forces have been withdrawn. Wars will continue to occur between countries (Iran and Iraq, Ethiopia and Somalia) or within societies (the Sendero Luminoso guerrilla movement in Peru, the civil strife in El Salvador, the divided island of Cyprus). But without the larger framework of the East-West struggle, the causes at issue—religious and ethnic conflict, millenarian ideologies, irredentism—will seem strange and irrelevant to the United States, Europe, the Soviet Union, and Japan and the outcome therefore virtually meaningless. John P. Roche, former dean of the Fletcher School at Tufts University and former adviser to President Lyndon Johnson, provides pithy counsel for the regional influentials of the future: "Never get mixed up in the religious wars of other people's churches." He adds, "We simply have to realize that while we can blow up the world, we simply can't persuade Azerbaijanis to be lovable toward Armenians or vice versa."

Second, these countries will find it increasingly difficult to extract concessions and resources from Western governments. Now that political influence in the former Third World is no longer a commodity worth bidding for, it will be possible to admit publicly something economists have known all along—that the majority of "developing countries" (a United Nations' euphemism) are not developing at all and never have been. In fact, those non-Western countries that have succeeded in getting on the escalator of growth (the so-called NICs, newly industrializing countries—Korea, Taiwan, Malaysia, Singapore) have done so without massive foreign economic assistance from us or anyone else.

Even if this were not the case, the prospects for Africa, Latin America, and parts of South Asia would not be particularly good—Western European governments will be preoccupied with budget decisions on aid to East Germany, Poland, Hungary, and Czechoslovakia, and in the long term, perhaps the Baltic republics and even the Soviet Union. The U.S. foreign-assistance budget (. . . estimated [in 1991 at $14.9] billion, most of it to five or six countries) will have to survive competing pressures to reduce the deficit or to reallocate defense resources to social spending (the "peace dividend"). The truth is that foreign aid has never been popular with the American people, who believe—repeated polls show—that you can't buy friends; Americans also think (not wrongly) that little foreign aid reaches the people for whom it is intended. Nothing less than a life-and-death struggle with the Soviet Union these past 40 years could have overruled these sentiments; now that the war is over, however, [America's] principal clients will compete for benefits with the very people who pay the bills. The outcome is not difficult to predict. As Congressman David Obey (D-Wisc.) recently put it, "The [United States] is not going to get very excited about aid to anywhere if it comes at the expense of job training, health care, and other things at home."

Third, we can expect that many non-Western societies will simply drop out of the race for economic development because their own domestic political environment renders impossible the implementation of market-oriented economic reforms, or because they do not have the requisite stability, or both. Lacking minimal public order in some of their cities and provinces, and unable to obtain even short lines of commercial credit, such countries will probably have to establish trading entrepôts at their ports or in heavily fortified air and rail termini and deal by barter or for cash. (This has already happened in Iran and Iraq and will probably happen soon in Peru.) The major Western countries and Japan will probably find it necessary to devise a kind of international economic triage, offering credit to only those countries whose policies render them likely to succeed (Chile, Costa Rica) and dispensing outright charity (called charity, not "development assistance") to the most tragic cases of failure (Ethiopia).

### RICH WORLD?

Leaders of the former Third World have no reason to accept this analysis of the future, and in fact many of them are struggling to resist it. As Venezuelan President Carlos Andrés Pérez put it [in 1990], the Latin American countries "own more-or-less half the planet's resources. It would be crazy if the industrialized world forgot us." Ivory Coast President Houphouet-Boigny put it even more categorically: "If the Western Europeans were to allow themselves to abandon Africa, they would inflict enormous damage to themselves." He too mentioned "formidable resources of raw materials"—as though these could not be purchased for ready money rather than as part of a complicated political and economic relationship.

What these leaders fail to grasp is that the [developed world] is no longer living in the nineteenth century when raw materials and abundant inexpensive labor were the principal factors of national wealth. Modern economies depend on technology, research, organizational skills, education, and social mobility, which define the developed world and by their absence establish the boundaries of the underdeveloped world as well. Even from a military point of view, the major powers no longer require, as they did 50 or 100 years ago, an extensive network of overseas bases to project their presence abroad. What most industrial countries will need in the future will not be bases or constabulary facilities but effective airlift capability and elite small-infantry units to periodically rescue beleaguered nationals from disorder in remote or inhospitable foreign locales.

The non-Western world can, of course, threaten to disrupt the order of the center—in fact, it is already doing so with the specter of drugs, uncontrolled immigration, damage to the environment, even nuclear weapons. But what this points to is not a massive program of resource transfers but, as Suzan George of the Transnational Institute recently remarked, an eventual "*cordon sanitaire . . .* around the North, while the South, forgotten, will sink into poverty and instability." There is no reason why Western countries and Japan cannot restrict the entry of drugs and illegal immigration if they decide to do so; the problem is merely one of political will. As for nuclear weapons, while some non-Western societies are apparently close to nuclear capability (or, like India, already possess it), they are far from having adequate delivery systems. They may develop them, of course. . . .

There is a solution to the problems of what used to be called the Third World. It has already been offered by Brazilian Senator Roberto Campos: "The time has arrived for us to reach a choice for wealth—preferring to be the last member of the Jockey Club instead of the first member of the dance hall"—in other words, to choose to be a winner, not a loser. To be winners, these countries must embrace free markets and democracy, the very things that have made what used to be called the First World what it is. One hopes that many countries will make this choice, and to the extent that they do, their societies will be better, safer places. But thanks to the geopolitical changes of 1989, nobody is going to make that choice for them—or even want to try—much less subsidize failure if they do not.

# 16

# THE VOLATILE MIDDLE EAST: THE ROOTS OF MUSLIM RAGE

Bernard Lewis

In the 1990s the Muslim world is braced for conflict with the West—and the United States in particular—inspired by intense resentments. The reasons America and the West are perceived as the incarnation of evil, and the implications of this image for the future of world politics, are explored in Bernard Lewis' probing account of Muslim rage. Lewis is a professor emeritus of Near Eastern Studies at Princeton University. He is the author of numerous books on the Middle East, including *The Political Language of Islam* (1988) and *Race and Slavery in the Middle East: An Historical Enquiry* (1990).

. . . Islam is one of the world's great religions. . . . Islam has brought comfort and peace of mind to countless millions of men and women. It has given dignity and meaning to drab and impoverished lives. It has taught people of different races to live in brotherhood and people of different creeds to live side by side in reasonable tolerance. It inspired a great civilization in which others besides Muslims lived creative and useful lives and which, by its achievement, enriched the whole world. But Islam, like other religions, has also known periods when it inspired in some of its followers a mood of hatred and violence. It is [the West's] misfortune that part, though by no means all or even most, of the Muslim world is now going through such a period, and that much, though again not all, of that hatred is directed against [it].

© by Bernard Lewis. Distributed by New York Times Syndication Sales; used by permission.

We should not exaggerate the dimensions of the problem. The Muslim world is far from unanimous in its rejection of the West, nor have the Muslim regions of the Third World been the most passionate and the most extreme in their hostility. . . . But there is a Libya, an Iran, and a Lebanon, and a surge of hatred that distresses, alarms, and above all baffles Americans.

At times this hatred goes beyond hostility to specific interests or actions or policies or even countries and becomes a rejection of Western civilization as such, not only what it does but what it is, and the principles and values that it practices and professes. These are indeed seen as innately evil, and those who promote or accept them as the "enemies of God."

This phrase, which recurs so frequently in the language of the Iranian leadership, in both their judicial proceedings and their political pronouncements, must seem very strange to the modern outsider, whether religious or secular. The idea that God has enemies, and needs human help in order to identify and dispose of them, is a little difficult to assimilate. It is not, however, all that alien. The concept of the enemies of God is familiar in preclassical and classical antiquity, and in both the Old and New Testaments, as well as in the Koran. A particularly relevant version of the idea occurs in the dualist religions of ancient Iran, whose cosmogony assumed not one but two supreme powers. The Zoroastrian devil, unlike the Christian or Muslim or Jewish devil, is not one of God's creatures performing some of God's more mysterious tasks but an independent power, a supreme force of evil engaged in a cosmic struggle against God. This belief influenced a number of Christian, Muslim, and Jewish sects, through Manichaeism and other routes. The almost forgotten religion of the Manichees has given its name to the perception of problems as a stark and simple conflict between matching forces of pure good and pure evil.

The Koran is of course strictly monotheistic, and recognizes one God, one universal power only. There is a struggle in human hearts between good and evil, between God's commandments and the tempter, but this is seen as a struggle ordained by God, with its outcome preordained by God, serving as a test of mankind, and not, as in some of the old dualist religions, a struggle in which mankind has a crucial part to play in bringing about the victory of good over evil. Despite this monotheism, Islam, like Judaism and Christianity, was at various stages influenced, especially in Iran, by the dualist idea of a cosmic clash of good and evil, light and darkness, order and chaos, truth and falsehood, God and the Adversary, variously known as devil, Iblis, Satan, and by other names.

## THE RISE OF THE HOUSE OF UNBELIEF

In Islam the struggle of good and evil very soon acquired political and even military dimensions. Muhammad, it will be recalled, was not only a prophet and a teacher, like the founders of other religions; he was also the head of a polity and of a community, a ruler and a soldier. Hence his struggle involved a state and its armed forces. If the fighters in the war for Islam, the holy war "in the path of God," are fighting for God, it follows that their opponents are fighting against God. And since God is in principle the sovereign, the supreme head of the Islamic state—and the Prophet and, after the Prophet, the caliphs are his vicegerents—then God as sovereign commands the army. The army is God's army and the enemy is God's enemy. The duty of God's soldiers is to dispatch God's enemies as quickly as possible to the place where God will chastise them—that is to say, the afterlife.

Clearly related to this is the basic division of mankind as perceived in Islam. Most, probably all, human societies have a way of distinguishing between themselves and others: insider and outsider, in-group and out-group, kinsman or neighbor and foreigner. These definitions not only define the outsider but also, and perhaps more particularly, help to define and illustrate our perception of ourselves.

In the classical Islamic view, to which many Muslims are beginning to return, the world and all mankind are divided into two: the House of Islam, where the Muslim law and faith prevail, and the rest, known as the House of Unbelief or the House of War, which it is the duty of Muslims ultimately to bring to Islam. But the greater part of the world is still outside Islam, and even inside the Islamic lands, according to the view of the Muslim radicals, the faith of Islam has been undermined and the law of Islam has been abrogated. The obligation of holy war therefore begins at home and continues abroad, against the same infidel enemy.

Like every other civilization known to human history, the Muslim world in its heyday saw itself as the center of truth and enlightenment, surrounded by infidel barbarians whom it would in due course enlighten and civilize. But between the different groups of barbarians there was a crucial difference. The barbarians to the east and the south were polytheists and idolaters, offering no serious threat and no competition at all to Islam. In the north and west, in contrast, Muslims from an early date recognized a genuine rival—a competing world religion, a distinctive civilization inspired by that religion, and an empire that, though much smaller than theirs, was no less ambitious in its claims and aspirations. This was the entity known to itself and others as Christendom, a term that was long almost identical with Europe.

The struggle between these rival systems has now lasted for some fourteen centuries. It began with the advent of Islam, in the seventh century, and has continued virtually to the present day. It has consisted of a long series of attacks and counterattacks, jihads and crusades, conquests and reconquests. For the first thousand years Islam was advancing, Christendom in retreat and under threat. The new faith conquered the old Christian lands of the Levant and North Africa, and invaded Europe, ruling for a while in Sicily, Spain, Portugal, and even parts of France. The attempt by the Crusaders to recover the lost lands of Christendom in the east was held and thrown back, and even the Muslims' loss of southwestern Europe to the Reconquista was amply compensated by the Islamic advance into southeastern Europe, which twice reached as far as Vienna. For the past three hundred years, since the failure of the second Turkish siege of Vienna in 1683 and the rise of the European colonial empires in Asia and Africa, Islam has been on the defensive, and the Christian and post-Christian civilization of Europe and her daughters has brought the whole world, including Islam, within its orbit.

For a long time now there has been a rising tide of rebellion against this Western paramountcy, and a desire to reassert Muslim values and restore Muslim greatness. The Muslim has suffered successive stages of defeat. The first was his loss of domination in the world, to the advancing power of Russia and the West. The second was the undermining of his authority in his own country, through an invasion of foreign ideas and laws and ways of life and sometimes even foreign rulers or settlers, and the enfranchisement of native non-Muslim elements. The third—the last straw—was the challenge to his mastery in his own house, from emancipated women and rebellious children. It was too much to endure, and the outbreak of rage against these alien, infidel, and incomprehensible forces that had subverted his dominance, disrupted his society, and finally violated the sanctuary of his home was inevitable. It was also natural that this rage should be directed primarily against the millennial enemy and should draw its strength from ancient beliefs and loyalties. . . .

[During the 1980s the Islamic leaders of this] widespread and widening religious revival sought out and identified their enemies as the enemies of God, and gave them "a local habitation and a name" in the Western Hemisphere. Suddenly, or so it seemed, America had become the archenemy, the incarnation of evil, the diabolic opponent of all that is good, and specifically, for Muslims, of Islam. Why?

## SOME FAMILIAR ACCUSATIONS

. . . If we [focus on] the specific, there is no lack of individual policies and actions, pursued and taken by individual Western governments, that have aroused the passionate anger of Middle Eastern and other Islamic peoples. Yet all too often, when these policies are abandoned and the problems resolved, there is only a local and temporary alleviation. The French have left Algeria, the British have left Egypt, the Western oil companies have left their oil wells, the westernizing Shah has left Iran—yet the generalized resentment of the fundamentalists and other extremists against the West and its friends remains and grows and is not appeased.

The cause most frequently adduced for anti-American feeling among Muslims today is American support for Israel. This support is certainly a factor of importance, increasing with nearness and involvement. But here again there are some oddities, difficult to explain in terms of a single, simple cause. In the early days of the foundation of Israel, while the United States maintained a certain distance, the Soviet Union granted immediate *de jure* recognition and support, and arms sent from a Soviet satellite, Czechoslovakia, saved the infant state of Israel from defeat and death in its first weeks of life. Yet there seems to have been no great ill will toward the Soviets for these policies, and no corresponding good will toward the United States. In 1956 it was the United States that intervened, forcefully and decisively, to secure the withdrawal of Israeli, British, and French forces from Egypt—yet in the late fifties and sixties it was to the Soviets, not America, that the rulers of Egypt, Syria, Iraq, and other states turned for arms; it was with the Soviet bloc that they formed bonds of solidarity at the United Nations and in the world generally. More recently, the rulers of the Islamic Republic of Iran have offered the most principled and uncompromising denunciation of Israel and Zionism. Yet even these leaders, before as well as after the death of Ayatollah Ruhollah Khomeini, when they decided for reasons of their own to enter into a dialogue of sorts, found it easier to talk to Jerusalem than to Washington. At the same time, Western hostages in Lebanon, many of them devoted to Arab causes and some of them converts to Islam, are seen and treated by their captors as limbs of the Great Satan.

Another explanation, more often heard from Muslim dissidents, attributes anti-American feeling to American support for hated regimes, seen as reactionary by radicals, as impious by conservatives, as corrupt and tyrannical by both. This accusation has some plausibility, and could help to explain why an essentially inner-directed, often anti-nationalist movement should turn against a foreign power. But it does not suffice, especially since support for such regimes has been limited both in extent and—as the Shah discovered—in effectiveness.

Clearly, something deeper is involved than these specific grievances, numerous and important as they may be—something deeper that turns every disagreement into a problem and makes every problem insoluble.

This revulsion against America, more generally against the West, is by no means limited to the Muslim world; nor have Muslims, with the exception of the Iranian mullahs and their disciples elsewhere, experienced and exhibited the more virulent forms of this feeling. The mood of disillusionment and hostility has affected many other parts of the world, and has even reached some elements in the United States. It is from these last, speaking for themselves and claiming to speak for the oppressed peoples of the Third World, that the most widely publicized explanations—and justifications—of this rejection of Western civilization and its values have of late been heard.

The accusations are familiar. We of the West are accused of sexism, racism, and imperialism, institutionalized in patriarchy and slavery, tyranny and exploitation. To these charges, and to others as heinous, we have no option but to plead guilty—not as Americans, nor yet as Westerners, but simply as human beings, as members of the human race. In none of these sins are we the only sinners, and in some of them we are very far from being the worst. The treatment of women in the Western world, and more generally in Christendom, has always been unequal and often oppressive, but even at its worst it was rather better than the rule of polygamy and concubinage that has otherwise been the almost universal lot of womankind on this planet.

Is racism, then, the main grievance? Certainly the word figures prominently in publicity addressed to Western, Eastern European, and some Third World audiences. It figures less prominently in what is written and published for home consumption, and has become a generalized and meaningless term of abuse—rather like "fascism," which is nowadays imputed to opponents even by spokesmen for one-party, nationalist dictatorships of various complexions and shirt colors.

Slavery is today universally denounced as an offense against humanity, but within living memory it has been practiced and even defended as a necessary institution, established and regulated by divine law. The peculiarity of the peculiar institution, as Americans once called it, lay not in its existence but in its abolition. Westerners were the first to break the consensus of acceptance and to outlaw slavery, first at home, then in the other territories they controlled, and finally wherever in the world they were able to exercise power or influence—in a word, by means of imperialism.

Is imperialism, then, the grievance? Some Western powers, and in a sense Western civilization as a whole, have certainly been guilty of imperialism, but are we really to believe that in the expansion of Western Europe there was a quality of moral delinquency lacking in such earlier, relatively innocent expansions as those of the Arabs or the Mongols or the Ottomans, or in more recent expansions such as that which brought the rulers of Muscovy to the Baltic, the Black Sea, the Caspian, the Hindu Kush, and the Pacific Ocean? In having practiced sexism, racism, and imperialism, the West was merely following the common practice of mankind through the millennia of recorded history. Where it is distinct from all other civilizations is in having recognized, named, and tried, not entirely without success, to remedy these historic diseases. And that is surely a matter for congratulation, not condemnation. We do not hold Western medical science in general, or Dr. Parkinson and Dr. Alzheimer in particular, responsible for the diseases they diagnosed and to which they gave their names.

Of all these offenses the one that is most widely, frequently, and vehemently denounced is undoubtedly imperialism—sometimes just Western, sometimes Eastern (that is, Soviet) and Western alike. But the way this term is used in the literature of Islamic fundamentalists often suggests that it may not carry quite the same meaning for them as for its Western critics. In many of these writings the term "imperialist" is given a distinctly religious significance, being used in association, and sometimes interchangeably, with "missionary," and denoting a form of attack that includes the Crusades as well as the modern colonial empires. One also sometimes gets the impression that the offense of imperialism is not—as for Western critics—the domination by one people over another but rather the allocation of roles in this relationship. What is truly evil and unacceptable is the domination of infidels over true believers. For true believers to rule misbelievers is proper and natural, since this provides for the maintenance of the holy law, and gives the misbelievers both the opportunity and the incentive to embrace the true faith. But for misbelievers to rule over true believers is blasphemous and unnatural, since it leads to the corruption of religion and morality in society, and to the flouting or even the abrogation of God's law. . . . Fundamentalist leaders [see] in Western civilization the greatest challenge to the way of life that they wish to retain or restore for their people.

## A CLASH OF CIVILIZATIONS

The origins of secularism in the West may be found in two circumstances—in early Christian teachings and, still more, experience, which created two institutions, Church and State; and in later Christian conflicts, which drove the two apart. Muslims, too, had their religious disagreements, but there was nothing remotely approaching the ferocity of the Christian struggles between Protestants and Catholics, which devastated Christian Europe in the sixteenth and seventeenth centuries and finally drove Christians in desperation to evolve a doctrine of the separation of religion from the state. Only by depriving religious institutions of coercive power, it seemed, could Christendom restrain the murderous intolerance and persecution that Christians had visited on followers of other religions and, most of all, on those who professed other forms of their own.

Muslims experienced no such need and evolved no such doctrine. There was no need for secularism in Islam. . . .

At first the Muslim response to Western civilization was one of admiration and emulation—an immense respect for the achievements of the West, and a desire to imitate and adopt them. . . . In our own time this mood of admiration and emulation has, among many Muslims, given way to one of hostility and rejection. In part this mood is surely due to a feeling of humiliation—a growing awareness, among the heirs of an old, proud, and long dominant civilization, of having been overtaken, overborne, and overwhelmed by those whom they regarded as their inferiors. In part this mood is due to events in the Western world itself. . . . For vast numbers of Middle Easterners, Western-style economic methods brought poverty, Western-style political institutions brought tyranny, even Western-style warfare brought defeat. It is hardly surprising that so many were willing to listen to voices telling them that the old Islamic ways were best and that their only salvation was to throw aside the pagan innovations of the reformers and return to the True Path that God had prescribed for his people.

Ultimately, the struggle of the fundamentalists is against two enemies, secularism and modernism. The war against secularism is conscious and explicit, and there is by now a whole literature denouncing secularism as an evil neo-pagan force in the modern world and attributing it variously to the Jews, the West, and the United States. The war against modernity is for the most part neither conscious nor explicit, and is directed against the whole process of change that has taken place in the Islamic world in the past century or more and has transformed the political, economic, social, and even cultural structures of Muslim countries. Islamic fundamentalism has given an aim and a form to the otherwise aimless and formless resentment and anger of the Muslim masses at the forces that have devalued their traditional values and loyalties and, in the final analysis, robbed them of their beliefs, their aspirations, their dignity, and to an increasing extent even their livelihood.

There is something in the religious culture of Islam which inspired, in even the humblest peasant or peddler, a dignity and a courtesy toward others never exceeded and rarely equalled in other civilizations. And yet, in moments of upheaval and disruption, when the deeper passions are stirred, this dignity and courtesy toward others can give way to an explosive mixture of rage and hatred which impels even the government of an ancient and civilized country—even the spokesman of a great spiritual and ethical religion—to espouse kidnapping and assassination, and try to find, in the life of their Prophet, approval and indeed precedent for such actions.

The instinct of the masses is not false in locating the ultimate source of these cataclysmic changes in the West and in attributing the disruption of their old way of life to the impact of Western domination, Western influence, or Western precept and example. And since the United States is the legitimate heir of European civilization and the recognized and unchallenged leader of the West, the United States has inherited the resulting grievances and become the focus for the pent-up hate and anger. Two examples may suffice. In November of 1979 an angry mob attacked and burned the U.S. Embassy in Islamabad, Pakistan. The stated cause of the crowd's anger was the seizure of the Great Mosque in Mecca by a group of Muslim dissidents—an event in which there was no American involvement whatsoever. Almost ten years later, in February of 1989, again in Islamabad, the USIS center was attacked by angry crowds, this time to protest the publication of Salman Rushdie's *Satanic Verses.* Rushdie is a British citizen of Indian birth, and his book had been published five months previously in England. But what provoked the mob's anger, and also the Ayatollah Khomeini's subsequent pronouncement of a death sentence on the author, was the publication of the book in the United States.

It should by now be clear that we are facing a mood and a movement far transcending the level of issues and policies and the governments that pursue them. This is no less than a clash of civilizations—the perhaps irrational but surely historic reaction of an ancient rival against our Judeo-Christian heritage, our secular present, and the worldwide expansion of both. It is crucially important that we on our side should not be provoked into an equally historic but also equally irrational reaction against that rival. . . .

# 17

## ARMS CONTROL AFTER THE COLD WAR

Joseph S. Nye, Jr.

**Even though the Cold War has waned, bilateral U.S.–Soviet arms control cannot be divorced from the multilateral arms control problem that, Joseph S. Nye warns, is as urgent as ever. Maintaining that the future is likely to necessitate more rather than less attention to the political role of arms control, Nye takes a broad, critical view of the magnitude of the challenge facing the global community. Nye is Clarence Dillon Professor of International Affairs at Harvard University. Among many other books, he has recently written *Nuclear Ethics* (1988).**

### I

For the past 30 years, arms control has been central to the U.S.-Soviet relationship. Now, if the cold war is over, what will be the role of arms control? On the one hand, the relaxed political climate improves the prospects for reaching and ratifying agreements. On the other, improved U.S.-Soviet relations also reduce anxiety about nuclear weapons and urgency about arms control initiatives. . . .

Geopolitical analysts warn about the diffusion of power in world politics; the spread of chemical and ballistic missile technologies to some 20 nations in the next decade will pose a new type of security threat. . . . The new twist for the time ahead is that the United States and the Soviet Union,

This article draws on material from Joseph S. Nye, Jr., *Bound to Lead: The Changing Nature of American Power* (New York: Basic Books, 1990). Footnotes have been deleted and section headings have been renumbered. Used by permission of Joseph S. Nye, Jr.

though remaining antagonists on the traditional agenda, will find themselves to be partners in some of the emerging problems of arms control.

## II

The 1980s began with a sharp debate about the merits of arms control. Many officials in the Reagan Administration contended that arms control was more of a problem than a solution; it lulled public opinion in Western democracies into accepting Soviet strategic superiority. While the pressure of public opinion brought the administration back to arms control negotiations within its first year, little was accomplished until 1986. Then, in its last two years, the Reagan Administration signed an Intermediate-range Nuclear Forces (INF) agreement, causing consternation among many of the president's most ardent supporters. In addition, the administration made substantial progress toward a treaty in the Strategic Arms Reduction Talks (START).

Some conservatives were outraged by Ronald Reagan's new views. Howard Phillips called him a speech-reader for appeasers. But other conservatives base their skepticism on a more general critique of arms control. Irving Kristol, for example, . . . reiterated his charge that arms control agreements do not lead to enduring settlements of conflicts but instead

> tend to be slow, tedious and conducted in an atmosphere of skepticism and suspicion. As a result, agreements are likely to have limited scope. Moreover, technological innovations in weaponry, to say nothing of changes in national leadership, will always make an arms control treaty vulnerable to conflicting interpretations or outright indifference.

Some aspects of this case against arms control have merit. Weapons are symptoms rather than basic causes of hostility. The legalistic approach to seeking compliance with treaties can lead to disproportionate responses in a period of extreme distrust. Arms control negotiations may sometimes slow the process of change. For example, [during the 1980s] NATO . . . reduced short-range nuclear weapons based in the front lines of Europe. It is quite plausible that efforts to negotiate these reductions in the context of formal arms control agreements would have hindered this stabilizing change. Similarly, some Soviets say that Mikhail Gorbachev announced a unilateral reduction of conventional forces in 1988 at the United Nations rather than at the bargaining table for fear that negotiations would slow the process.

Even some of the founding fathers of modern arms control, such as Thomas Schelling, have expressed skepticism about too much reliance on formal agreements. Many strategists believe that types of weapons, their vulnerability and their susceptibility to central control are more important than their numbers. Reductions are not good per se, but must be judged in light of these characteristics. At low numbers, deceptive practices, hidden weapons and breakouts from treaty constraints could have a greater impact on security than at higher levels. However, given the high levels of existing arsenals, reductions would have to be much deeper than currently foreseen before such factors become a serious security problem.

A careful study of the U.S.-Soviet arms control record in the pre-Gorbachev era concluded that critics' fears that arms control agreements would lull the public and weaken the defenses of democracies have not been borne out. On the other hand, the hopes of proponents that arms control would save money and lead to dramatic reductions were not borne out either. . . . In the past three decades, arms control agreements were concluded only when neither side had an appreciable advantage; agreements were not reached when either side had a strong preference for development of a new weapon. Based on this modest record, critics argue that arms control contributes little to international stability.

Critics, however, miss the point: arms control is part of a political process. Too often the experts judge arms control proposals on their technical details rather than on their political significance. For example, the INF agreement was militarily insignificant. In fact one could argue that, in terms of stability, by first removing longer-range nuclear missiles from Europe rather than starting with the short-range artillery, the INF agreement seized the wrong end of the stick concerning command and control of weapons during crises. But the political significance of the INF agreement—the improvement in the U.S.-Soviet relationship in the second half of the Reagan Administration—far outweighed the technical problems related to the details of military doctrine. . . .

In a sense, all of arms control is a confidence- and security-building measure. By increasing transparency and communication among adversaries, worst case analyses are limited and security dilemmas are alleviated. It may be that the most important aspects of the two Strategic Arms Limitation Talks (SALT) agreements were the provisions on open skies for satellite reconnaissance, the agreed counting rules for various types of weapons and the establishment of a Standing Consultative Commission to discuss alleged violations and misunderstandings. In that sense, informal operational arms control and formally negotiated reductions are not exclusive alternatives; they can complement one another.

The agreements on incidents at sea, crisis centers, confidence- and security-building measures in Europe and the . . . agreement on the Prevention of Dangerous Military Activities have been scorned by some experts as the "junk food" of arms control. But the classical distinctions between reductions in arms and measures to build confidence and security have begun to blur. Both structural and operational arms control are parts of a larger process of political reassurance among adversaries. . . .

The opportunities presented by the current political climate and the possibility of a return to cold war relations reinforce the argument for reaching good agreements now: their institutional effects will linger and ameliorate our security problems if relations deteriorate in the future between the United States and the

Soviet Union. While Gorbachev's glasnost may have increased transparency and communications beyond the arms control process, both formal reductions (such as the asymmetrical reductions in conventional forces in Europe) and informal agreements that provide access to information (such as exchanges among military officers and visits to Soviet facilities) can help lock in gains for Western security.

Skeptics also neglect a further political role of arms control: the establishment of international security regimes. By treating the military relations among states as a problem of common security, arms control agreements help legitimize some activities and discourage others. These international regimes cannot be kept in separate watertight compartments. For example, the long-term management of nuclear proliferation would be impossible in the context of a totally unconstrained U.S.-Soviet nuclear arms race. Similarly, it is difficult to imagine the United States and the Soviet Union managing the diffusion of chemical and biological weapons technology if these two countries were engaged in unconstrained developments in those fields.

Skeptics point out that most states develop nuclear and chemical weapons because of security problems with their neighbors, not because the United States or the Soviet Union promise to disarm. This argument is largely correct. The existence of Article Six of the Nonproliferation Treaty (NPT), in which the superpowers promise to reduce their arsenals, did not deter Pakistan, South Africa or Israel in their nuclear policies. On the other hand, a renewal of the NPT in 1995 will be harder if it must take place in the context of a sharp U.S.-Soviet nuclear arms competition. As one looks further down the road and contemplates the diffusion of destructive power and technology to poor countries and transnational groups, bilateral U.S.-Soviet arms control cannot be divorced from the multilateral arms control problem. On the contrary, the management of international security in the future is likely to require more, not less, attention to the political role of arms control.

## III

While debate continues on a prudent response in the bilateral relationship, other analysts argue for more attention to a different aspect of the current era, the diffusion of power in world politics. So long as an intense superpower hostility blanketed world politics, the gradual diffusion of power in world politics was not readily noticeable. With the diminished Soviet threat in the Gorbachev era and Soviet withdrawal from some of its Third World positions, other changes in the nature of world politics have become more visible.

Some, such as Yale historian Paul Kennedy [in *The Rise and Fall of the Great Powers*,] portray such changes as a decline of American hegemony, but the concept of decline is a misleading way to portray the situation. The United States is not in decline in relation to such powers as the Soviet Union, the

European Community or China. Nor is it accurate to refer to the emerging situation as "multipolar," if that means returning to a balance among a number of nations with roughly equal power resources, analogous to the period before 1945.

The word "polycentrism" comes closer to describing the current diffusion of power. As world politics becomes more complex, all major states are less able to achieve their purposes. Although the United States has leverage over particular countries, it has far less leverage over the complex system as a whole. But it is not alone in this situation. All great powers today are less able to use traditional power resources to achieve their purposes because private actors and smaller states have become more important in many issues.

While several trends contributing to the diffusion of power are economic, at least three are related to the use of force. One trend is the process of modernization in developing countries. Increased social awareness and nationalism make military intervention and external rule more costly. In 1953 the United States restored the shah of Iran to his throne with a minor covert action. It is hard to imagine, however, how many troops would have been needed to restore the shah in the socially mobilized and nationalistic Iran of 1979. Similarly, the defeats of the United States in Vietnam and of the Soviet Union in Afghanistan were less the result of the increased power of a weak state than the increased cost for outsiders of ruling socially mobilized and nationalistic populations.

Another trend in the diffusion of power is the spread of technology, which enhances the capabilities of less developed states. While the superpowers maintain a large lead in military technology, the forces that many Third World states will be able to deploy in the 1990s will make regional superpower intervention more costly than it was in the 1950s. In addition, at least a dozen Third World states have developed a significant capability to export arms, and more countries are acquiring sophisticated weapons capabilities. Twenty countries could now make chemical weapons and 15 Third World nations could be producing their own ballistic missiles in the 1990s. In addition to the five states that had the bomb when the NPT was signed in 1968, India, Pakistan, Israel and South Africa now have a nuclear capability and others may follow. Although a small nuclear capability does not make these states contenders for global power, it does increase the potential cost of regional intervention by larger powers. Technology also enhances the power of private groups. For instance, handheld antiaircraft missiles helped guerrillas in Afghanistan and new plastic explosives are effective tools for terrorists.

Finally, the changing nature of the issues in world politics is diminishing the ability of great powers to control their environment. An increasing number of issues do not simply pit one state against another; in some issues, all states try to control private, transnational non-state actors. The solutions to many issues of transnational interdependence will require collective action and cooperation among states. Areas for global action include ecological changes such as acid rain and global warming, health epidemics such as AIDS, and illicit trade in drugs and control of terrorists. While force may sometimes play a role, traditional instruments of power are rarely sufficient in dealing with such issues. New power resources, such as effective communication and use of multilateral institutions, may prove more relevant. . . . The ability of the great powers to . . . get what they want in the 1990s is likely to be less than traditional indicators of military power would suggest. . . .

If this portrait of current trends is even partially correct, the bipolar focus of the past will not be sufficient. . . . In fact, on many of these issues, the United States and the Soviet Union will find themselves on the same side.


## IV

Concern over the proliferation of technology is not new. The NPT has been in force for two decades, and in 1995 the majority of the states party to the treaty must vote on extending its duration. What is new, however, are the interactions between nuclear, chemical, biological and ballistic missile technology, the increase in the number of states involved and the new threats posed for national security. A critical question is what role the arms control process can play in coping with these new threats.

Technology spreads with time, and many technologies of mass destruction have a long duration. Modern chemical weaponry, for example, is a 75-year-old technology. Nuclear technology is now half-a-century old and intercontinental ballistic missiles have been with us for some three decades. Nonetheless, one should not be fatalistic about the spread of technology. Policy can make a difference in the rate and conditions under which it spreads. For example, in 1963 President Kennedy foresaw a world in the 1970s with some 25 nuclear states; today the number is only a third of what he predicted.

In a world in which self-defense is a recognized right of states, it is remarkable that some 140 states have signed a treaty by which they deny themselves access to the most destructive weaponry. The broad nonproliferation regime—the NPT, the International Atomic Energy Agency (IAEA), the nuclear suppliers' guidelines and various bilateral agreements—has not solved the problem of nuclear proliferation but it has alleviated it by placing added burdens on the proliferator. Clever bureaucrats and military officers find obstacles in their way. Political leaders must face the fact that developing nuclear weaponry may have too great a political cost. While some countries have not adhered to the treaty, the regime has so far constrained the problem of nuclear proliferation to a handful of problem countries.

The very success of the nonproliferation regime, however, has driven potential proliferators underground into covert actions. The important new developments in nuclear proliferation are the existence of the four covert or de facto nuclear states—Israel, India, Pakistan and South Africa—and the prevalence of efforts to use clandestine facilities dedicated to military purposes rather than the misuse of commercial nuclear energy sources, the major problem in the 1970s. . . .

In a complicated world of covert proliferation, the danger of mistakes grows. Since many of the states acquiring new nuclear capabilities lack the political and technological capacity to control nuclear weaponry, the risk of leakages to terrorist groups or of unauthorized use during political turmoil will also increase.

The question of chemical weapons proliferation differs from nuclear proliferation in several ways. First, there are more countries—20 is a frequently cited number—suspected of having or trying to develop chemical weapons. In addition, the technology is relatively simple and it lacks the difficulties of control and monitoring associated with radiation. The dual uses of chemical technologies for fertilizers, pesticides and herbicides as well as weapons is even closer than the overlap between commercial and military nuclear facilities. Thus far, the proliferation of chemical weaponry has not seriously infected Latin America or Africa, but in the Middle East and Southeast Asia it has involved some of the world's poorest countries. In that sense, the aphorism that chemical weaponry is the poor country's atom bomb has some justification. What is more, in the Middle East the taboo against use of chemical weapons has been broken in the Iran-Iraq War; Iraq even used chemicals against its own Kurdish population.

After World War I, the 1925 Geneva Protocol prohibited the first use of chemical weapons but permitted their production and stockpiling. The Geneva Protocol remains the principal international constraint, although it has been supplemented in recent years by an informal institution, the "Australia group." Nineteen chemical suppliers met under Australian auspices in 1985 to discuss tougher export controls on chemicals that are precursors to the manufacture of weapons. The group has agreed to require formal licenses on eight specific chemicals and has a warning list for 30 more in hopes that industry will voluntarily alert national governments to any suspicious foreign interest in those substances.

In addition, since 1980, the U.N. Conference on Disarmament has been engaged in negotiations on a chemical weapons convention (CWC) that would place a complete and total ban on chemical weapons in all states. The ban would prohibit the production or stockpiling of chemical weapons and would require the destruction of all existing chemical weapons stocks.

Verification remains the most difficult issue. A small chemical weapons plant could be hidden within a larger industrial infrastructure or built in a remote area. These verification problems might be addressed (though not fully solved) through ad hoc inspections of non-declared facilities. In addition, commercial chemicals that could be used in the manufacturing of weapons must be monitored at both the production and consumption end points. . . .

Biological weapons are of slightly less immediate concern than chemical weapons. According to American government officials, there are about ten countries with current or developing capabilities to employ living organisms (such as anthrax, lassa fever or typhus, as opposed to inert toxins). Biological weapons, however, have limited military utility since their dispersal mechanisms are difficult to manage; a change of wind can make them as lethal to the attacker as they are to the defender. Moreover, it is difficult to sustain the living organisms in biological weapons in hot climates for long periods. For these reasons, biological weapons are better suited for mass destruction than as precise military instruments. This lack of military utility may have thus far slowed their development. In addition, since 1972, a biological weapons convention has banned the use or possession of these weapons. Research continues, however, since the convention allows the development of antidotes against biological weaponry. . . .

## V

In the post cold war era, arms control may lead to major reductions in the forces of the superpowers. Even in this new era, however, military forces will still be needed because of the normal course of great power politics and because of the new diffusion of destructive power. Moreover, there is always the prospect that the changes in the Soviet Union could be reversed. . . .

It has become fashionable to speak of the recent end of the cold war and even of the "end of history." When the cold war ended may well be a matter of semantics: strictly defined, as a period of intense hostility and little communication, it probably ended in the 1960s. The "little cold war" of the early 1980s was mostly rhetorical. More important is the fact that the cold war and the division of Europe produced four decades of relative stability, albeit at a high price for East Europeans.

Rather than the end of history, we are now seeing the return of history in Europe with its ethnic tensions and the unsolved problem of Germany's role, which Bismarck put on the international agenda in 1870. The peaceful evolution of new arrangements in Europe will make reassurance more necessary than ever. Arms control can play a large part in that reassurance by reducing and restructuring force levels in the conventional arms negotiations and by establishing a variety of confidence-building measures in the Conference on Security and Cooperation in Europe. Negotiating gradual changes in the overall European security framework can help to alleviate the anxieties and overreactions that would otherwise derail economic evolution and integration of the continent.

. . . [The] current period of improved bilateral relations provides an important opportunity for the United States and the Soviet Union to work together with other countries to reinforce and establish regimes for dealing with the diffusion of power. Here too there are gains to be locked in. Such multilateral arms control regimes will have to be considered in a broader context of security. For example, the superpowers have already rediscovered the value of U.N. peacekeeping forces, itself a confidence- and security-building measure. They may also rediscover the wisdom of the early postwar architects of the U.N. Charter and particularly of the U.N. Security Council. In an era when the great powers are reducing their involvement in the Third World, other countries may develop greater interest in measures for the regional constraint of force. . . .

Arms control will never provide all the answers to national security. In some cases, it might even do more harm than good. In all cases, it will have to be integrated with other dimensions of policy and other policy instruments. But the changing nature of world politics suggests both new roles and new importance for arms control. If an arms control process did not exist, we would assuredly have to invent it.

# 18

# ALLIANCES IN THEORY AND PRACTICE: WHAT LIES AHEAD?

Stephen M. Walt

In this essay Stephen M. Walt surveys the causes of alliance formation and dissolution in order to understand theoretically and provide a basis for predicting how current global trends will affect the likely evolution of contemporary alliance systems in the emerging post–Cold War multipolar system of the twenty-first century. Walt is associate professor of political science at the University of Chicago. He has published a number of articles on international politics and security affairs, and has authored *The Origins of Alliances* (1987).

## THE COLD WAR ALLIANCES IN A CHANGING WORLD

More than anything else, the Cold War between the United States and the Soviet Union has been a competition for allies. Constrained from a direct test of strength by the danger of nuclear war and the sheer physical difficulty of either superpower conquering the other, the United States and Soviet Union devoted their efforts to recruiting and supporting a variety of allies and clients. In some cases bound by formal treaty, in others linked through informal but no less significant commitments, the two superpowers established alliance relationships with states in virtually every area of the globe. These alliances were intended primarily to enhance the members' security, either through a deterrent guarantee (i.e., the "nuclear umbrella") or by increasing the ally's own defense capabili-

Used by permission of Stephen M. Walt. This chapter was adapted especially for this book from an article that was originally published in the Summer 1989 issue of the *Journal of International Affairs*.

ties. Enlisting allies was also seen as a way to demonstrate the superiority of each superpower's social system and to advance their competing political and ideological values.

The resulting arrangements were remarkably stable, in at least two different senses. First, each of the main alliance networks was unusually long-lived. NATO celebrated its 40th birthday in 1989—probably the record for a modern multilateral alliance—and its Soviet counterpart, the Warsaw Pact, is nearly as old (though now virtually defunct). Although there have been important defections from each bloc (e.g., Iraq, China, Libya, Egypt, Ethiopia, Somalia, Nicaragua and Iran), most of the ties between the superpowers and their client states showed an impressive durability. When realignments occurred, they were usually due to internal upheavals rather than external changes. Moreover, past realignments often canceled each other out (for example, Ethiopia's shift toward the Soviet Union led to Somalia's realignment with the United States). As a result, the relative power of each superpower's alliance network remained relatively constant over the past four decades.

Second, the alignment of the strongest states into opposing blocs lent predictability to the central strategic competition and minimized rivalries within each superpower's sphere of influence. Thus unlike the unstable alliance commitments that helped cause the First World War, the post–World War II alliance systems made war among the great powers less likely.

The impressive stability of postwar alliance networks contrasts sharply with the perennial belief that alliances are relatively unimportant in a bipolar, nuclear world. In the 1960s, for example, some experts predicted that the bipolar competition between the United States and the Soviet Union would encourage neutralism, or suggested that the superpowers' commanding positions made their alliance commitments increasingly irrelevant. Other commentators argued that the invention of nuclear weapons made traditional alliances obsolete, because no nation would risk its own destruction in order to save another. And ever since NATO was founded, recurring disputes within the alliance led critics to predict its imminent demise. Yet despite the various attempts to dismiss alliances as an unimportant phenomenon in contemporary international politics, the desire to enhance security through alignment with others remains an important aspect of statecraft. The bipolar competition between the superpowers did permit some countries to use nonalignment as a strategy for obtaining aid from both, but few nations have been willing to dispense entirely with allied support. Both superpowers competed eagerly to acquire additional clients, and even avowedly nonaligned states like India sought explicit allied support when necessary. Thus, despite the "nuclear revolution" and the emergence of bipolarity, alliances have remained a central feature of international politics.

Will the future be like the past? Are the alliance structures that have dominated the international landscape for the past four decades likely to endure into the 21st century? It seems certain that they will not. First, the relative decline of

U.S. power, together with the emergence of Japan and Western Europe as important economic rivals, heralds the end of what Robert Gilpin has called the "American System": the grand coalition of advanced industrial countries that emerged after World War II. Though still some distance away, a gradual return to multipolarity will restore both greater flexibility and greater uncertainty to future alliance commitments. Moreover, economic competition within the Western alliance presents an obvious challenge to continued cooperation, and one that is likely to grow. Second, the recent improvements in Soviet-American relations—largely due to domestic reforms in the Soviet Union and Gorbachev's innovative diplomacy—is making existing alliance commitments less necessary. Indeed, current alliance relationships may even be an impediment to a further relaxation of East-West tensions. For both reasons, the United States is likely to be less willing to maintain its present overseas commitments, especially if the Soviet threat continues to decline. Similarly, traditional U.S. allies will be less inclined to follow U.S. guidance.

The waning of the Soviet-American rivalry—and especially in its ideological aspects—will have major effects on alliance relations in the developing world as well. The end of the Cold War will reduce the ability of Third World clients to extract support from either superpower, and will force present clients to seek other arrangements to preserve their security. Moreover, if the superpowers worry less about defending clients against threats from the opposing bloc, their ability to work together to resolve existing regional conflicts should increase. Recent evidence of this trend includes the Afghanistan settlement and the December 1988 agreement on Namibia, as well as joint U.S.-Soviet opposition to Iraq's seizure of Kuwait.

In sum, the emergence of a durable Soviet-American detente will exert far-reaching effects on a wide range of international political relationships. Most importantly, the two major alliance networks that have been a central feature of international politics for the past 40 years can no longer be taken for granted. Given the importance of these potential changes, understanding the likely evolution of existing international alliances is a critical task. To gauge the impact of these trends, it is necessary first to ask why states form alliances in the first place. Only by understanding the causes of alignments is it possible to understand how current trends will affect present alliance structures. In short, what do different theories of alliance formation reveal about the likely evolution of contemporary alliance relations?

## THEORIES OF ALLIANCE FORMATION

Although several motives can be identified, the principal reason to form an alliance is to balance against an external threat. The rationale for this tendency is straightforward: in the anarchic world of international politics, where no supreme authority exists to protect states from each other, states facing an external threat will join forces with others in order to amass sufficient power to deter or defeat an attack.

This explanation for alliances is usually associated with balance-of-power theory: states with lesser capabilities are presumed to ally against the stronger. According to this view, alliances form because states do not want others to achieve a dominant position. As a result, strong states eventually provoke others to ally against them, solely because their superior capabilities present a danger to weaker powers.

Although this explanation for alliances is both elegant and parsimonious, it neglects several other factors that statesmen will consider when making alliance choices. For example, states may choose to ally with the stronger of two powers, if the weaker side is more dangerous for other reasons. Thus, by focusing solely on capabilities, balance-of-power theory cannot explain why balances often fail to form. For example, balance-of-power theory cannot tell us why virtually all of the world's strategically significant states chose to ally with the United States and against the Soviet Union, thereby creating a coalition whose aggregate capabilities dwarfed those of its principal rival.

This deficiency can be corrected by recognizing that states form alliances in order to balance against *threats,* and that power is only one element in their calculations, albeit a very important one. In addition to relative power, statesmen will also consider geographic proximity, offensive capabilities and perceived intentions. Other things being equal, states that are nearby are more dangerous than those that are far away; states that possess offensive military forces pose a greater threat than those with purely defensive capabilities; and states with aggressive intentions will be viewed as more worrisome than states that seek only to preserve the status quo. States possessing all of these traits—large capabilities, close proximity to others, offensive military forces and aggressive intentions—will be especially likely to provoke a countervailing coalition. Thus, balance-of-power theory is something of a misnomer: "balance-of-threat" theory more accurately describes the primary dynamics of alliance formation.

Although the tendency for states to balance against threats has been widely recognized by scholars, two other explanations are often suggested as well. First, for much of the Cold War, many U.S. leaders believed that potential allies were more likely to *bandwagon* than to balance. According to this view, states tend to ally *with* the strongest or most threatening state. This view implied that the United States had to maintain unchallenged credibility and visible military superiority in order to prevent its allies from defecting to the Soviet side. As President John F. Kennedy expressed this concern: "if the United States were to falter, the whole world would inevitably move towards the Communist bloc." More recently, when seeking support for the contras in 1983, President Reagan argued that "if we cannot defend ourselves in Central America . . . then we cannot expect to prevail elsewhere. . . . [Our] credibility will collapse and our alliances will crumble." Despite the dearth of evidence supporting this belief, fear of bandwagoning helped justify the prolonged U.S. effort in Vietnam and the recurring concern over "Finlandization" in Europe. In sharp contrast to the balancing hypothesis, the belief that states tend to bandwagon when choosing allies justifies intense concern over even minor shifts in the distribution of power, and greater willingness to use force in order to maintain one's credibility.

A second rival explanation views alliances as the product of *ideological solidarity.* In this view, states form alliances with nations whose domestic systems or political values resemble their own. Thus, the United States is said to favor liberal democracies while the Soviet Union was believed to attract leftist or Marxist regimes, primarily for ideological reasons. Like the bandwagoning hypothesis, this view has been popular throughout the Cold War. The claim that ideology was a powerful motive for alignment was used to "explain" the allegedly monolithic nature of "International Communism" (an image shattered by the Sino-Soviet split in the early 1960s), and justified U.S. opposition to leftist forces in the developing world. Similar views appeared on the Soviet side as well, both in their optimistic belief that "progressive regimes" (i.e., Marxist or socialist states) would be reliable allies and in their oft-repeated concern for "capitalist encirclement."

Despite the enduring influence that these alternative explanations for alliances exerted upon both Soviet and U.S. foreign policy, there is relatively little evidence to support either one. Although bandwagoning does occur in certain rare circumstances (i.e., when especially weak and isolated states face far more powerful opponents), the available evidence reveals that states usually form alliances to balance against the threats faced. Similarly, although ideological solidarity can reinforce the desire to balance against a shared threat, a common ideology can also be a potent source of conflict and division, as it has been within the communist world.

Among other things, these results lay bare much of the justification for U.S. intervention in far-flung regions of the globe. Because states balance rather than bandwagon, the United States does not need to prove its strength in marginal areas in order to reassure its principal allies. And because ideology is a relatively weak force for alignment, there is little danger that leftist states would become loyal satellites of the Kremlin, unless external opposition (often led by the United States) forced them to seek Soviet assistance in response.

Even more significantly, balance-of-threat theory provides a compelling explanation for the main alliance relationships that have anchored Western security since the onset of the Cold War. Contrary to the recurring fears that the United States and its allies were slipping behind the Soviet bloc, the Western alliance during the Cold War remained well ahead of its main rival on most of the critical indicators of national power (GNP, defense spending, size of armed forces, etc.).

## WHAT IS CHANGING?

This long-standing U.S. advantage may now be in jeopardy. Suddenly, the formerly harsh face of Soviet Russia has been replaced by the smiling face of Mikhail Gorbachev. Moreover, Gorbachev's leadership involves more than a change in expression; the evidence suggests that his desire to transform political and social conditions within the Soviet Union and Soviet relations with the outside world is utterly sincere. Nor have his efforts to date been fruitless. Despite continued domestic opposition, Gorbachev's foreign policy initiatives have already produced a Soviet withdrawal from Afghanistan, an agreement eliminating intermediate-range nuclear forces, a host of proposals for arms control and regional security, and most important of all, the end of Communism in Eastern Europe and the reunification of Germany.

Unlike earlier Soviet "peace offensives," Gorbachev's current efforts have been taken seriously by the West. By reducing other states' perceptions of a "Soviet threat," Gorbachev undoubtedly hopes to lessen the array of forces presently confronting the Soviet Union. If successful, such a development would permit the Soviet Union to reduce further the military burdens that have long stifled development of Soviet society and the Soviet economy. Perhaps even more important, such a campaign may eventually succeed in dissolving NATO entirely, and provide the Soviet Union with far greater access to Western technology and capital.

## IMPLICATIONS FOR EXISTING ALLIANCES

Let us assume that new thinking in foreign policy continues to guide Soviet initiatives, and that the various proposals for reducing the Soviet threat to Western Europe are implemented. Let us also assume that the relative power of the United States does not change dramatically and that Soviet-American relations continue the warming trend begun during the last year of the Reagan administration. The question thus becomes: how will a reduction in the Soviet threat and a concomitant improvement in Soviet-American relations affect existing alliance commitments?

## EVOLUTION IN THE WESTERN ALLIANCE

By definition, the end of the Cold War implies a diffusion of threats. In contrast to the heyday of U.S.-Soviet rivalry, it will be less clear which states pose the greatest danger to other states' interests; as a result, international alignments will be more ambiguous and less durable than they were throughout the Cold War. As balance-of-threat theory predicts, the declining Soviet threat will permit the West to worry less about deterring a direct military challenge. Cooperation with the former Soviet bloc will increase, while relations within the Western alliance will become more difficult.

In particular, optimistic rhetoric about maintaining NATO in its present from should be viewed with skepticism. A total Soviet withdrawal from Eastern Europe is now virtually certain, and without a clear and present Soviet threat, neither European politicians nor U.S. taxpayers are likely to support a large U.S. military presence in Europe. To be sure, NATO's elaborate institutional structure will slow the pace of devolution somewhat, and new institutions may provide a framework for consultation and collaboration among the advanced industrial countries. Over time, however, only a dramatic resurgence of the Soviet threat is likely to preserve NATO's traditional structure and rationale. And shorn of U.S. protection and the unifying effects of the Soviet threat, the advanced industrial countries (including Japan) will find cooperation more difficult to sustain, especially in areas where tensions are already evident (such as trade policy). If present trends continue, however, a significant decrease in alliance cohesion and a lessening of the Western military effort is likely. Such a development is not as worrisome as it might appear. If the Soviet Union is in fact less dangerous, the United States and its allies do not need to work as hard to protect themselves. Indeed, far from being a source of concern, a real reduction in the Soviet threat is precisely the goal that NATO has sought since the strategy of containment was first outlined.

Because history suggests that global conflict is more likely when the United States withdraws from world affairs, the devolution of existing alliance structures should be undertaken with some caution. Ideally, the United States would retain an important role in any post–Cold War security arrangements, if only to provide a detached, stabilizing presence. But as its present allies will have less need for U.S. protection, the United States must recognize that its influence over them will decline rapidly. Thus, although the waning of the Soviet threat undoubtedly increases U.S. security, it is also creating a world where friends and foes will be more difficult to distinguish and U.S. influence will be smaller.

## SUPERPOWER COMMITMENTS IN THE DEVELOPING WORLD

Given the inherent stability in superpower relations with the industrial powers, the developing world has been the principal arena of superpower rivalry for most of the Cold War. Not only has the Third World been the principal locus of global conflict, it is also where the major realignments have occurred. Both trends are likely to continue, but with a crucial difference. After four decades of competition, both superpowers are learning that the stakes in most Third World conflicts are not worth major efforts. For the United States, the key event was Vietnam, for the Soviet Union, Afghanistan provided the crucial lesson. As each superpower recognizes the limits of its own power and the low strategic value of much of the developing world, its willingness to devote substantial resources to the support of weak and unreliable allies is likely to decline even further. It is worth noting, for example, that even the Reagan administration chose to conduct its Third World policy "on the cheap" by using proxy forces like the contras or the UNITA guerrillas in Angola. For its part, the Soviet Union has steadily reduced its verbal and material support for many of the "progressive regimes" it recruited in the 1970s, while revising its previously optimistic forecasts regarding the prospects for significant strategic gains in these regions. Soviet writers now call for the "de-ideologization" of the superpower competition, implying the end of efforts to attract additional converts to socialism. Similarly, the United States ended the contra war, opened talks with the Palestine Liberation Organization and renewed its efforts to fashion regional settlements in Indochina, southern Africa and Afghanistan. All of these developments testify to an overdue sense of realism regarding the low strategic stakes in the developing world. (The Persian Gulf remains the obvious exception to this rule, as the Kuwait crisis revealed.)

Neither superpower will abandon all of its Third World allies, but a substantial improvement in U.S.-Soviet relations will make it more difficult for states in the developing world to obtain the same level of support they enjoyed in the past. Previously, even relatively weak client states extracted large concessions from their patron, by threatening either to realign or to damage their patron's prestige by collapsing. So long as the superpowers placed a high value on even relatively weak allies, either for ideological reasons or because they believed their credibility was at stake, even marginal allies found such tactics effective. But if the superpowers recognize that most clients cost more than they are worth, the leverage that clients can exercise will decline sharply.

A decline in the superpower competition in the developing world will exert powerful effects on these states. Although most of their security problems will remain, a gradual disengagement by the superpowers will encourage developing countries to make alternative arrangements. One possibility is greater reliance on alternative military suppliers such as France, Israel, Italy and Third World exporters like Brazil. Another option is the creation of independent regional security associations. Both trends are already evident. And as balance-of-threat theory predicts, the emergence of a clear regional threat will cause otherwise unlikely allies to join forces. The broad-based international coalition that formed to counter Iraq's seizure of Kuwait (which included the United States, the Soviet Union, Saudi Arabia, Kuwait, Egypt, Syria and several European states) is the obvious recent example.

It remains to be seen, however, whether these trends will reduce or increase the level of conflict in the developing world. In particular, declining great power involvement will remove some of the constraints on Third World conflict. To note but one example, the Iran-Iraq war broke out after Iran and Iraq had reduced or severed ties with their respective superpower allies, and Iraq's invasion of Kuwait may reflect the greater latitude that regional powers may perceive as the Cold War order erodes. Contrary to the view that superpower involvement has fueled conflict in the developing world, a decline in superpower involvement and the emergence of Soviet-American detente could just as easily lead to greater tensions. That possibility is another reason why joint superpower initiatives to deal with festering regional conflicts should be a major item on the Soviet-American diplomatic agenda.

# 19

# THE FUTURE AND THE UNITED NATIONS

Javier Perez de Cuellar

**Javier Perez de Cuellar, secretary-general of the United Nations, summarizes the UN's role in coping with world problems. In discussing the improved climate for concerted action by the world organization for addressing long-standing problems, the secretary-general focuses on the UN as an instrument for conflict management and resolution and as a mechanism for the improvement of global welfare, and explains why the United Nations has begun to make a number of meaningful contributions toward fulfilling the mission the UN Charter set for it.**

In all we do at the United Nations, we must be constantly aware that we live in a rapidly changing—indeed revolutionary—period. The [late 1980s] witnessed almost unimaginable changes in the attitudes of governments, in the perception of what our real problems are and in the nature and development of those problems. Despite our heavy day-to-day preoccupations, we must make a constant and conscious effort to remain on the crest of this great wave of change.

[In] accepting the Nobel Peace Prize in Oslo [in 1989] on behalf of UN Peacekeeping Forces, I said that the prospects of realizing the vision expressed in the Charter of the United Nations seemed better than at any time since the Organization was founded. A broad agreement seems to be emerging over where we are and what our priority work must be. The early tentative hopes [in 1989]

From *The Harvard International Review* (Winter 1990). Used by permission of the United Nations Secretariat and the *Harvard International Review*.

have been replaced by a confident consensus that there is indeed a new pragmatism, openness and flexibility in international relations. The improved understanding and cooperation among the major powers certainly deserves much of the credit for this. However, it is also the result of changes such as the worldwide diffusion of economic and political power from a few nations to many. A growing willingness to use multilateral approaches and actions to address world problems has accompanied and accelerated these changes.

While the hopeful view I expressed [in 1989] has been encouragingly confirmed, I want to emphasize the word "prospects." For while it is true that the international climate is exceptionally favorable, an immense task lies before us if we are to take advantage of it.

The effects of the new climate have so far been most striking in the realm of international peace and security. Some—but sadly not all—long-standing disputes and conflicts have been regulated, at least to the point where actual fighting has stopped. In most of these cases, however, a basic settlement has still to be reached, and constant effort and vigilance will be required if we are to avoid new disasters. Much remains to be done. Some areas of conflict such as the Middle East and Cambodia, for example, have so far continued to resist positive trends towards conciliation.

One of the most encouraging features of the past two years has been the development of the Security Council as a responsive, collegial body. The close cooperation between the Council and the Secretary General has also been a most helpful development of great potential importance, especially in difficult or dangerous times.

We are, however, still far from the collective system for international peace and security envisaged in the Charter. That system was supposed to create the context not only for dealing with aggressors, but for the peaceful settlement of all disputes and for a large degree of disarmament. Although this has proved to be an unrealistic vision in the conditions of the post-[World War II] period, a number of recent developments indicate that governments may not find it so unrealistic after all, as they reconsider the current state of the world. I believe, therefore, that we must use the present climate and the improvements that have already taken place as a starting point for new efforts to make the Security Council the center of a more effective system of international peace and security.

It is a matter of the utmost importance that an international atmosphere be established in which nations in danger will feel confident in entrusting their fate to the Security Council rather than desperately going it alone. We need to develop the Council's influence as a benevolent and positive element in encouraging conflicting parties to make concessions necessary for the settlement of great problems. We should aspire to an international system which really can relieve humanity of the crippling and deadly burden of armaments. We must develop peacekeeping as an increasingly reliable and effective servant of the purposes of the Security Council. We should see such developments as going hand in hand with the development of the rule of law, which in the long run is vital to the future of the human race.

In this relatively benevolent international climate, various new threats to peace and stability are emerging. Terrorism of all sorts has, unfortunately, been with us for many years. [In recent years] we have also seen how other destructive forces like the international drug trade can threaten both the stability and authority of governments as well as international security in its broadest sense. We have to consider urgently how the United Nations can best be used to counter these threats. One of the obvious needs is a means to co-ordinate the resources and efforts of all nations in dealing with the drug menace.

I said earlier that it is the function of the United Nations to keep abreast of peaceful change, indeed to anticipate it as best as human foresight can. Nowhere is this more necessary than in the vast and complex realm of socioeconomic affairs—or to put it less bureaucratically, the realm of ordinary people's everyday lives. Here the pace of change has been relentless. It has in many fields outstripped our capacity to analyze problems, to devise relevant policies and to take action.

The technological revolution has both good and dangerous sides. The threat to the environment at the moment looms large in the world's priorities. That is well and good, provided we see that problem as part of a vast complex of problems. Our concern for the environment must not allow us to forget the related problem of a widening gulf between rich and poor, and the need to face up on a global level to this old problem which is getting worse. A world in which a significant part is doomed to live in poverty, bitterness and disappointment is not only morally unacceptable; it will be dangerously unstable. We are still a very long way from dealing effectively with this fundamental problem which was, incidentally, an important part of the vision of the Charter.

I would hope that in the 1990s we shall develop a capacity for the maintenance of peace and security consistent enough to allow the United Nations to concentrate its members' energy and resources on the vast problems and possibilities of the future. [In 1987] this would have seemed to many to be an idle dream, an unrealistic and escapist piece of idealism. Today it is the major challenge to the United Nations. It is also a practical possibility, provided—and this is a large qualification—that governments as well as non-governmental and private sectors are prepared for the vast and painstaking cooperative work required. . . .

Dag Hammarskjöld once referred to the United Nations as an organization "not created in order to bring us to heaven, but in order to save us from hell." I wonder what he would have thought of our present situation. There has recently been vast improvement in relations between the Security Council's Permanent Members (China, France, UK, US and the USSR). The greatest menace of all—

the threat of nuclear war—appears to be receding, and a view of the world as a challenge to cooperative effort seems to be taking its place.

At another level, however, conflict is rife. The deployment of new weapons and new military techniques, as well as a vast buildup of armaments is an ominous reminder that we have not yet made the concept of common security the basis of a workable system.

At yet another level, vast problems—some old and some new—affect the lives of people all over the world and cast awesome shadows on the future. The challenges to the international community for constructive action have never been so urgent or so complex as now. Nor have the benevolence of the political climate and the general will to pragmatic action ever been so evident.

I very much hope that some of our great problems are behind us and that we have learned some lessons from them. I have no doubt, however, that the greatest challenges—and the greatest prizes—are still ahead. My ambition for the United Nations is that it can proceed into the 1990s as a strong and confident player and leader in this historic and fateful process.

# 20

# THE REALITY AND RELEVANCE OF INTERNATIONAL LAW

Christopher C. Joyner

**International law reflects the need for order, predictability, and stability in international relations. The functions and impact of international law are analyzed by Christopher C. Joyner, who emphasizes both the strengths and limitations of legal norms as instruments for managing conflicts and promoting collaboration in world politics. Joyner is professor of political science at George Washington University. He is the editor of *The Persian Gulf War* (1990) and *The Antarctic Legal Regime* (1988) and has published numerous articles, notes, and reviews on international legal issues.**

It is difficult to open up any major newspaper on any day without seeing numerous stories devoted to issues having important international legal implications: the arms trade, chemical weapons, transnational pollution, terrorism, international trade and commerce, acid rain, oil prices, Libya, Iraq, Iran, South Africa, the Middle East, German reunification, and European Community integration, to mention only a few. Yet, students of international relations rightly continue to ask certain fundamental questions about the nature and purpose of international law. Is international law really "law?" Or is it nothing more than "positive morality?" How can international law work in a modern state system dictated by considerations of national interests and power politics? Is international law more

This essay was written especially for this book. WHOI Contribution No. 6476. Used by permission of Christopher C. Joyner.

of a restraint on national policy, or is it merely a policy instrument wielded by governments to further their own ad hoc purposes to gain legitimacy? In sum, what is the reality and relevance of international law to contemporary world politics? This essay seeks to address these inquiries and in the process to explore the role of international law in contemporary international affairs.

## CONCEPTUAL BASES OF INTERNATIONAL LAW

International law, often described as public international law or the law of nations, refers to the system of law that governs relations between states. States traditionally were the only subjects with rights and duties under international law. In the modern era, however, the ambit of international law has been greatly expanded to where it now encompasses many actors other than states, among them international organizations, multinational corporations, and even individual persons. Nevertheless, states remain the primary concern and focus of international law in world politics.[1]

It is important at the outset to note that the initial reaction of many students and laymen alike to the notion of international law is one of skepticism. A prevalent view holds that national governments have scant respect for international law, and therefore they have little or no incentive to obey it, given the absence of a supranational system armed with sanctions capable of being enforced against a lawbreaker. In short, a popular belief is that international law is not really law.

However, the reality as demonstrated through their behavior is that states do accept international law as law and, even more significant, in the vast majority of instances they usually obey it. Though it is certainly true that international law is sometimes disobeyed with impunity, the same observation is equally true of any domestic legal system. For example, do local laws prevent traffic violations from occurring? Do municipal (i.e., domestic) laws against murder, rape, burglary, or assault and battery prevent those crimes from being committed? Put simply, does the presence of "enforced" law ipso facto insure compliance or even apprehension and prosecution? Clearly, in the real world, the answer is no. Richard Falk put it well when he observed,

> The success of domestic law does not rest in its capacity to solicit the respect of its subjects; the incidence of homicide and civil violence, and even of rebellion, is high. International law is a weak legal system not because it is often or easily flouted by

---

[1] See generally Wolfgang Friedmann, *The Changing Structure of International Law* (New York: Columbia University Press, 1964); Wolfgang Friedmann, *Law in a Changing Society* (New York: Columbia University Press, 1972); R. P. Anand, *New States and International Law* (Delhi: Vikas, 1972); and James Crawford, *The Creation of States in International Law* (Oxford: Clarendon Press, 1979).

powerful states, but because certain violations, however infrequent, are highly destructive and far-reaching in their implications.[2]

International law is not violated more often, or to a higher degree, than the law of other legal systems. Yet why does the contrary misconception persist? Two general reasons may offer much of the explanation. First, there is sensationalism; people tend to hear only about international law when blatant violations make the news. When states attack each other (or, for that matter, when a person is murdered), it becomes a newsworthy event. If the law is obeyed, and international relations between states proceed uninterrupted by violence, those affairs usually go unreported. The second reason for the misimpression that international law is frequently violated is the tendency of many people to presume that the mere existence of a transnational dispute automatically signifies that some law has been breached. This, of course, is not true; the fact that a dispute between states has arisen ought not to be taken to mean that a breach of international law has occurred, just as a civil dispute involving two individuals is not necessarily indicative of a breach in municipal law. Disputes between states may arise over many concerns, none of which may involve violations of law. For example, there may exist a genuine uncertainty about the facts of a case or uncertainty about the law itself; there may be need for new law to meet changing international conditions; or there may even occur the resort to unfriendly but legal acts (called retorsion) by one state against another. While these situations may be unfortunate and perhaps in some instances regrettable, they do not perforce constitute violations of the law.

Most criticism about international law can be generally categorized. First, there are those who view the law of nations as something that can never work and is therefore ignored by states, groups, or individuals. Law, in effect, becomes an "orphan" within the international community. On the other hand, there is the group that sees international law as an instrument of purpose, a "harlot" as it were, to be used, abused, or discounted in accord with one's own moment of convenience, interest, or capability. Still other critics perceive the law as not having any "teeth" or power of enforcement. The absence of an executive authority or international policeman thereby renders all values, norms, and rules subject to mere voluntary accession. International law in this instance becomes a "jailer." Perhaps more cynical is the view which asserts that international law does not exist and that it cannot exist until either all states agree to cooperate and coordinate the creation of mutually acceptable legal codes or this condition is imposed upon them. In this scenario, international law must assume the role of a magician. Prevalent in the hard-line realist school of international politics, this perception suggests that international law provides nothing more than a utopian dream. That is, governments that place heavy emphasis upon

---

[2] Richard A. Falk, *The Status of Law in International Society* (Princeton, N.J.: Princeton University Press, 1970), p. 29.

inserting morality in foreign policy considerations live in a world of idealism, naively hoping for the mythical attainment in international affairs where law will govern supremely and man will be saved from a system of international anarchy. For these critics, proponents of international law thus represent a "never-never land" school of thought.[3]

The reality of international law does not fit either neatly or aptly into any of these perceptions. John Austin, who dominated jurisprudential thinking in Great Britain during the nineteenth century, contributed much in the way of theory suggesting the frailties of international law. Austin reasoned that for a legal system to exist in fact, three indispensable elements were essential: (1) There had to exist a clearly identifiable superior, or sovereign, who was capable of issuing (2) orders or commands for managing society, and (3) there had to be punitive sanctions capable of enforcing those commands. For Austin, law thus was defined as the general command emanating from a sovereign, supported by the threat of real sanctions. Since international law had neither a sovereign nor the requisite enforcement authority, Austin concluded that it was not really "law"; international law, he believed, ought to be considered merely as "positive morality."[4] The Austinian concept involves the relatively uncomplicated contention that genuine law has its rules laid down by a superior power (the executive), and that they are enforced by another superior power (the police). At first blush, this line of thinking may seem logically attractive. However, in the real world, it becomes intellectually simplistic to assume that law exists only when and where formal structures exist; moreover, it is likewise faulty to confuse characteristics of a legal system as being those prerequisites necessary to define law's existence. The remainder of this essay addresses these contentions.

## NATURE OF INTERNATIONAL LAW

Generally speaking, the function of law is to preserve order. That is, law embodies a system of sanctioned regularity, a certain order in itself, which conveys the notion of expectations. Law provides for the regularity of activities that can be discerned, forecast, and anticipated in a society. Through law, the attempt is made to regulate behavior in order to insure harmony and maintain a society's values and institutions.[5]

In this connection, a system of law should have three basic characteristics. First, a statement of a prescribed pattern of behavior must be evident. Second, an

---

[3] These schools critical of international law are proposed in John H. E. Fried, "International Law—Neither Orphan Nor Harlot, Neither Jailer Nor Never-Never Land," in Karl Deutsch and Stanley Hoffmann, eds., *The Relevance of International Law* (New York: Doubleday, 1971), pp. 124–176.

[4] John Austin, *The Province of Jurisprudence Determined and the Uses of the Study of Jurisprudence* (London: Weidenfeld and Nicolson, 1954), pp. 121–126, 137–144.

[5] See Myres S. McDougal and Florentino P. Feliciano, *Law and Minimum World Order* (New Haven: Yale University Press, 1961).

obligational basis approved by the society must be present. And third, some process for punishing unlawful conduct in the society must be available. As essential facets, the measure of how well these elements interact will in large part determine the effectiveness of the legal system as a whole as well as the extent of its actual existence and performance.

Given these general observations, what significance can be attached to the nature of international law? Expressed in an Austinian sense, can a bona fide legal system that fulfills these objectives exist in the absence of a formal government structure, i.e., without a centralized system of law creation, law application, and law enforcement? The answer clearly is yes. International law does qualify as a legal system, albeit a somewhat primitive and imperfect one. International law consists of a set of norms that prescribe international behavior, although those patterns may at times seem vaguely defined. International law furnishes a principled foundation for policy decisions, albeit adherence to principle often becomes justifiable if it can be shown to be practical. Relatedly, reasons do exist for states to obey international law; i.e., an obligatory basis does in fact exist to support international law's operation in world affairs. Finally, a system of sanctions is available in international law, and it contributes to coercive enforcement of the law. To appreciate these observations more fully, it is worthwhile to examine the evolutionary nature and sources of international law, the obligational basis for its operation, and the enforcement process available for punishing illegal behavior in the international community.

## SOURCES OF INTERNATIONAL LAW

No legal system flashes into existence fully panoplied. All orders of law, from the most primitive to the most sophisticated, have their roots in the society they govern. International law is no different. The modern law of nations has undergone a process of evolution as old as the nation-state system itself, owing its direct origins to the Treaty of Westphalia in 1648. Importantly in this regard, over the past three centuries, specific sources for the creation of new international law have become widely acknowledged in and accepted by the international community.[6]

Foremost among the sources of international law are international conventions and treaties.[7] When ratified by a substantial number of states, some multilateral conventions may be deemed tantamount to an international legal statute

---

[6] See generally Clive Parry, *The Sources and Evidences of International Law* (Dobbs Ferry, N.Y.: Oceana, 1965). The following enumeration of sources is based upon the priority set out in Article 38 of the Statute of the International Court of Justice, appended to the Charter of the United Nations.

[7] T. O. Elias, *The Modern Law of Treaties* (Leiden: Sijhoff, 1974); I. M. Sinclair, *The Vienna Convention on the Law of Treaties* (Dobbs Ferry, N.Y.: Oceana, 1973); Shabati Rosenne, *The Law of Treaties: A Guide to the Legislative History of the Vienna Convention* (Dobbs Ferry, N.Y.: Oceana, 1971); and Jonathan I. Charney, "International Agreements and the Development of International Law," *Washington Law Review,* Vol. 61 (1986), pp. 971–996.

and are aptly labeled "lawmaking" treaties. Examples of these types of treaties include the four 1958 Geneva Conventions on the Law of the Sea, the 1969 Vienna Convention on the Law of Treaties, and the 1967 Outer Space Treaty. Also, general multilateral treaties can create the organizational machinery through which new international law can be developed. For example, specialized agencies of the United Nations, such as the World Health Organization, International Civil Aviation Organization, Universal Postal Union, and International Telecommunication Union—all of which were created by specific international treaties—have themselves become sources of rules and regulations throughout the international community. Thus international organizations that were created by international law contribute to the growth of additional law through the purpose of their functional operation.[8]

The second major source of international law is custom. In the eighteenth and nineteenth centuries, when interaction among states was relatively sporadic and less complex than today, certain habitual patterns of behavior often emerged to form obligatory rules. That is, through widespread adherence and repeated use, certain customary practices by governments became accepted as law, with normatively binding constraints.[9] Prominent among laws evolving from customary state practice were those pertaining to the law of the sea, in particular those regulations establishing the 3-mile territorial limit, the definition of piracy, and proper division of the spoils of war. Today, however, due to the increasing interdependence and complexity of modern international relations coupled with the spread of the traditional Eurocentric legal system beyond the borders of the Western world, custom as a body of unwritten though clearly recognized norms seems to be diminishing as a source of international law. Much of customary international law developed in the era of nineteenth century colonialism. Largely for this reason, it is now viewed with suspicion or held in disrepute by many of the newly independent states in the Third World. Another critical weakness of custom as a contemporary source of law is couched in the traditional requirement that customary law must grow into acceptance slowly, through a gradual, evolutionary process over many decades, perhaps even hundreds of years. This requisite for gradual evolution and slow acceptance of an emergent customary norm leaves that rule vulnerable to become archaic or anachronistic even before it can become accepted as law. This likelihood undoubtedly is at work today as rapid advances in technology play havoc with traditional legal parameters and

---

[8] See generally Rosalyn Higgins, *The Development of International Law through the Political Organs of the United Nations* (London: Oxford University Press, 1963). Significantly, however, resolutions adopted by the United Nations General Assembly are deemed only to be recommendations and are not lawfully binding upon the membership. See Christopher C. Joyner, "The U.N. General Assembly Resolutions and International Law: Rethinking the Contemporary Dynamics of Norm-Creation," *California Western International Law Journal,* Vol. 11, No. 3 (Summer 1981), pp. 445–478.

[9] See Anthony A. D'Amato, *The Concept of Custom in International Law* (Ithaca, N.Y.: Cornell University Press, 1971); and H. W. A. Thirlway, *International Customary Law and Codification* (Leiden: Sijhoff, 1972).

jurisdictional designs—a reality that makes imperative the constant need for international law to keep pace with technological developments.

The third primary source of international law is the general principles of law recognized by civilized nations.[10] Often general principles are associated with the Roman notion of *jus gentium,* the law of peoples. These principles of law, derived largely from municipal experience, hold relevant legal connotations for the international realm; consequently, they have been assimilated into the corpus of international law. General principles of law—which include notions such as "equity" (justice by right), "comity" (voluntary courtesy), and *pacta sunt servanda* ("pacts made in good faith are binding," the underpinning precept for treaty agreement)—serve as sources by analogy for the creation and perfection of international legal norms. Yet general principles of international law are encumbered by the difficulty of being framed as sources of law in terms of morality and justice. "Morality" and "justice" remain highly subjective concepts, susceptible to disparate interpretations; thus, in their application, general principles may be vulnerable to vagaries perceived in the situation or the particular context in which they are set.

The final source of modern international law is twofold and deemed to be secondary and indirect as compared to treaties, custom, and general principles. This source, first, encompasses judicial decisions of courts—both national and international—and, second, teachings and writings of the most qualified jurists and publicists. Two important points merit mention here. The first is that for international law, court decisions are principally employed as guidelines; they cannot set precedents. There is no *stare decisis* in the law of nations; accordingly, a decision by any court or tribunal, inclusive of the International Court of Justice, cannot be held as binding authority for subsequent judicial decisions. The second point is that while writings by scholars and jurists supply a rich seedbed for opinions on the law, they too carry no binding legal authority. Text writers by themselves cannot create or codify international law; however, their importance as sources of the law may become amplified to the extent that governments may adopt suggestions and interpretations in the application of international law to foreign policy.[11]

International law is broad in scope and far-reaching in content; for convenience, it may be divided into laws of peace and laws of war. Under the realm of peace, international law provides norms for stipulating its subjects and sets out the process of recognition for states and governments: the rights and duties of

[10] See generally Wolfgang Friedmann, "The Uses of 'General Principles' in the Development of International Law," *American Journal of International Law,* Vol. 57 (April 1963), pp. 279–299; Arnold McNair, "The General Principles of Law Recognized by Civilized Nations," *British Yearbook of International Law,* Vol. 33 (1957), pp. 1–19; and Georg Schwarzenberger, *The Dynamics of International Law* (South Hackensack, N.J.: Rothman, 1976).

[11] See, e.g., Herbert C. Merillat, ed., *Legal Advisers and Foreign Affairs* (Dobbs Ferry, N.Y.: Oceana, 1964).

states, how title to territory is acquired, how national boundaries are determined, and various regulations for use of ocean, air, and outer space. Also in this respect is the international law pertinent to individuals. It not only encompasses rules affecting nationality, diplomatic agents, resident aliens, and extradition but also more recent norms pertaining to international criminal law, refugees, and the protection of human rights. Within the ambit of laws relating to war, much ground is likewise covered. Included here are those laws and procedures promoting peaceful settlement of disputes; techniques available for self-help short of war; the legal nature of and requirements for belligerency; the laws of armed conflict on land, on sea, and in the air; conditions for neutrality; and the treatment and definition of war crimes.[12] Important to remember here is that these international legal considerations have been integrated into states' national laws, usually by treaty but also through specific legislation, judicial decisions, or executive fiat. This realization, however, should not imply that international law is thus rendered subservient to domestic laws. It is not, either in theory or in factual application.[13]

Though made up of a wide-ranging body of norms, international law has no specific codes or statutes. The closest approximations to municipal legal codes are called digests in international law. These digests, each of which usually entails a series of several volumes, are compendia containing selections from court decisions, international treaties, foreign policy statements, government memoranda, juridical opinions, scholarly publications, and other like materials that furnish detailed views on international legal matters. While held as important comments on the law, digests are not regarded in and of themselves to be definitively authoritative or legally binding in their contents.[14]

Notwithstanding doubts and skepticism, then, the unmistakable fact remains that international law has definite sources and exists as a body, a reality that mirrors the fundamental conviction by states that such law is necessary. The law of

---

[12] The texts available on international law are manifold. For representative samples, see William W. Bishop, ed., *International Law: Cases and Materials,* 3rd ed. (Boston: Little Brown, 1971); Michael Akehurst, *A Modern Introduction to International Law,* 6th ed. (London; Allen & Unwin, 1987); Mark W. Janis, *An Introduction to International Law* (Boston: Little, Brown & Co., 1988); Gerhard von Glahn, *Law Among Nations: An Introduction to Public International Law,* 5th ed. (New York: Macmillan, 1986); and Werner Levi, *Contemporary International Law: A Concise Introduction,* 2nd ed. (Boulder, Colo.: Westview, 1991). The classic modern treatise on international law is L. F. L. Oppenheim, *International Law: A Treatise:* Vol. 1, *Peace,* 8th ed., edited by Hersch Lauterpacht (New York: Longmans Green, 1955) and Vol. 2, *Disputes, War and Neutrality,* 7th ed., edited by Hersch Lauterpacht (New York: Longmans Green, 1952).

[13] At least one prominent scholar of international law has cogently argued to the contrary, namely that the law of nations in fact represents a higher order than domestic or national law. See Hans Kelsen, *Principles of International Law,* 2nd ed. (New York: Holt, Rinehart & Winston, 1966).

[14] For examples, see the following: Green H. Hackworth, *Digest of International Law,* 8 vols. (Washington, D.C.: U.S. Government Printing Office, 1940–1944); John Bassett Moore, *A Digest of International Law,* 8 vols. (Washington, D.C.: U.S. Government Printing Office, 1906); and Marjorie M. Whiteman, *Digest of International Law,* 15 vols. (Washington, D.C.: U.S. Government Printing Office, 1963–1973).

nations has evolved over nearly four centuries into a body of treaty-based and customary rules, undergirded by general principles of law and explicated through judicial decisions as well as in the writings of prominent jurists and publicists. Intimately connected to this are the attendant realizations that an obligatory basis exists for international law and that, in substantial measure, the law is obeyed.

## BASIS OF OBLIGATION IN INTERNATIONAL LAW

Perhaps the archfiction of international law is the notion of absolute sovereignty. Such sovereignty embodies the idea of totality and completeness; as a legal creation, sovereignty consequently becomes a paradox, if not an impossibility, when placed into the interdependent complexities of the modern state system. More significantly, unlimited sovereignty has become unacceptable today as the preeminent attribute of states, a fact which national governments have increasingly recognized as more and more of their sovereignty has been relinquished to international commitments. For example, traditionally in international law, absolute, unfettered sovereignty allowed for states to exercise free national will in deciding whether or not to resort to war. Given the incredible power of military capability today, the costs of this license could literally lead to destruction of the entire international community; as a consequence, through international legal instruments promoting arms control and national restraint, such sovereignty has been diminished by states themselves for the sake of international security. Recent examples clearly demonstrating this trend include the 1987 INF Treaty and the 1972 Anti-Ballistic Missile Treaty between the United States and the Soviet Union, the 1972 Biological Weapons Convention, and the 1968 Treaty on the Non-Proliferation of Nuclear Weapons.

The above observations prompt the obvious question concerning why states should obey international law. That is, what is the obligatory basis upon which the rule of law is founded in contemporary world affairs? The answer is plain and undeniable: It is in the states' fundamental interest to do so. States are the lawgivers in the international community. Agreement upon a legal norm and the effectiveness of its application clearly rest in how it affects each state's own national interests. Consent therefore remains the keystone to international law's efficacy because it appeases the desire of states to maintain their relative freedom of action in the name of national sovereignty. In short, states obey international law because they agree to do so. But why should they? Several plausible reasons may be proffered: National governments recognize the utility of the law; they prefer some degree of order and expectation over unpredictable anarchy; obedience is less costly than disobedience; a certain sense of justice may motivate their willingness to obey; or, habit and customary practice in international dealings over many years have operated to promote obedience.

More significant than any of these explanations, however, is the recognition that reciprocity contributes to the efficacy of international law and, correspondingly, to more regularized patterns of behavior in the international system. Put simply, states accept and obey international law because governments find it in their national interest to do so. It serves a state's national interest to accept international legal norms if other states also accept these norms, and this reciprocal process can give rise to predictive patterns of interstate conduct in international relations. States, like individual persons, have discovered that consent to be bound by and obligated to certain rules can serve to facilitate, promote, and enhance their welfare and opportunities in the society. Contemporary international law consequently has come to embody a consensus of common interests—a consensus which plainly indicates that international law works efficiently and most often when it is in the national interest of states to make it work.[15]

## ENFORCEMENT OF INTERNATIONAL LAW

The third critical consideration in determining the effectiveness of international law—the quality of its enforcement—is still left hanging: What happens when states fail to obey the law, when they violate the agreed-upon norms? How is the law to be enforced or, put differently, how are violators of international law to be punished? International law does supply means for both sanction and enforcement, although, to be sure, these means are primitive in comparison to municipal procedures. Despite development over the past seventy years of relatively sophisticated, universalistic, sanctions-equipped international organizations—namely, the League of Nations[16] and the United Nations[17]—the world community still relies primarily upon the principle of self-help to enforce international legal sanctions.

The principle of self-help permits sanctions to be applied by one party in reaction to perceived illegal conduct committed by another party. Self-help has

---

[15] See generally Arthur Larson et al., eds., *Sovereignty within the Law* (Dobbs Ferry, N.Y.: Oceana, 1965); Charles de Visscher, *Theory and Reality in Public International Law* (Princeton, N.J.: Princeton University Press, 1968); and Arthur Nassbaum, *A Concise History of the Law of Nations* (New York: Macmillan, 1954).

[16] The League of Nations Covenant, which was incorporated as Part I of the Treaty of Versailles (1919), contained in Article 16 sanction provisions that would subject a member "who committed an act of war" against another member to "the severance of all trade or financial relations, the prohibition of all intercourse between their nationals and the nationals of the Covenant-breaking State, and the prevention of all financial, commercial or personal intercourse between the nationals of the Covenant-breaking State and the nationals of any other State, whether members of the League or not."

[17] After determining "the existence of any threat to the peace, breach of the peace or act of aggression" as authorized in Article 39 of the United Nations Charter, the Security Council is empowered under Article 42 to "take such action by air, sea, or land forces as may be necessary to maintain or restore international peace and security. Such action may include demonstrations, blockade, and other operations by air, sea, or land forces of Members of the United Nations."

emerged as the major means for effecting sanctions in the international community.[18] Not only must states perceive when their rights have been violated; they must also confront the state that allegedly has committed that illegal act and must compel the state to make restitution for its wrongdoing. Techniques for applying self-help range from diplomatic protest to economic boycott to embargo to war. Consequently, in international law, states literally *must* take the law into their own hands to protect their legal rights and to get the law enforced. It is not surprising, then, that international law is often characterized as being primitive.

In assessing the sanctions process in international law, it is fair to conclude that as international disputes become more serious and are viewed by governments as placing national prestige or survival increasingly at risk, the principle of limited self-help as a sanctioning process is likely to make the legal system correspondingly less effective. Absent a centralized agency for approving and supervising the sanctioning action, self-help may be rendered subject to prevalent conditions in the environment. In sum, self-help's prominent role in international law places a major limitation upon that legal system's effectiveness. As revealed in the international legal order, resort to self-help for law enforcement represents a necessary but limiting compromise between a sanctioning process required by international law and the desires by states to retain their independence, i.e., their sovereignty. Self-help thus highlights the observation that international law is a relatively weak, decentralized, and primitive legal system. The fact remains, however, that international law still enjoys the status of being a legal system—one that works effectively nearly all the time and for nearly all situations when its participant member states want it to do so.

On balance, the performance of international law is hampered by disabilities within those very elements that generally contribute to the effectiveness of legal systems. First, there is a lack of international institutions for clarifying and communicating legal norms; that is, modern international law is still characterized by an imperfect process of norm creation. Second, there is no central, generally recognized belief system to serve as an obligatory authority for international law. The obligatory basis for international law lies with the states themselves. Third, and perhaps most debilitating, international law is without an efficient, corporate process for perceiving and punishing illegal behavior in the world community. Resort by states to self-help remains the principal means for sanctioning international wrongdoing.

Yet, what appears really faulty with international law does not stem from these weaknesses in the international legal process. Rather, it derives from the

---

[18] Even so, specific legal limitations have been set on the use of force, i.e., the degree and kind of "self-help" exercised. See, e.g., Benjamin Ferencz, *Defining International Aggression: The Search for World Peace,* 2 vols. (Dobbs Ferry, N.Y.: Oceana, 1975); Sydney D. Bailey, *Prohibitions and Restraints in War* (London: Oxford University Press, 1972); and Peter D. Trooboff, ed., *Law and Responsibility in Warfare: The Vietnam Experience* (Chapel Hill: University of North Carolina Press, 1975).

decentralized international community which that law is attempting to regulate. In short, that the operation of contemporary international law may be less than wholly effective can be attributed mainly to the condition that there does not presently exist sufficient international consensus among states to demand that the law be made more effective in its application.

All this should not be inferred to mean that international law is either surrealistic or irrelevant in today's world. It certainly is neither. To rush to the conclusion that international law's frailties leave it with little real function in international relations today would be not only superficial but also shortsighted. It would overlook the hundreds of decisions made by national and international tribunals aimed at settling claims and setting arbitration awards. It ignores the thousands of international law cases affecting contractual relations between corporations and governments. It fails to account for the constant, pervasive process of international intercourse that goes on involving states, organizations, and individual persons. In a modern age of satellite telecommunications, worldwide transportation, and interdependent global commerce, international law has become indispensable. Setting frequencies for telecommunication broadcasts, flight routes for aircraft, conditions for international postage and media communication, monetary exchange rates, navigation transit by ocean vessels carrying goods in trade—all these activities and myriad others are made possible only through the channels afforded by international legal agreement, i.e., through international law. International law codifies ongoing solutions for persistent international problems. The law of nations has become in effect the lubricant that permits transnational commerce, communication, transportation, and travel to operate smoothly and on course in the global community.[19]

## CONCLUSION

Law prescribes the conduct of a society's members and makes coexistence and the survival of that society possible. Not surprisingly, then, the law of nations is pervasive and fundamental. It not only seeks to regulate or lessen possibilities for conflict but also works to promote international exchange and cooperation on a broad, multifaceted scale. International law is man-made; governments of states in the international society can in large part determine the nature of that society and formulate laws to meet those ends. Hence, the ingredients of international law are neither preordained nor immutable.

International law is law. It is not some form of diplomatic maneuvering or rhetorical camouflage. International law has form and substance: there exists a clearly identifiable corpus of rules and regulations which have been generally accepted by states in their dealings with one another. International law has

---

[19] For a thoughtful treatment of this situation, see Marvin S. Soroos, *Beyond Sovereignty: The Challenge of Global Policy* (Columbia: University of South Carolina Press, 1986).

specific sources from which legal norms can be derived, and self-imposed sanctions are available to states to punish illegal behavior. Yet international law should not be construed as being pure law; in other words, it is not apolitical, nor is it wholly comprised of normativism or legalism. International law cannot be so because the very components of that legal system—states—are highly politicized actors in their own right.[20]

International law is crafted not accidentally or capriciously but carefully and intentionally by the states themselves. The law of nations is a product of the times and of the national governments that operate in the international milieu. It can change, adapt, and evolve. International law is not static; it is a dynamic and evolutionary process that is shaped by events and influences events. Contemporary international law reflects the nature of the changing world because it must be responsive to that evolving reality. Flexibility therefore remains one of international law's chief strengths. Even so, ironically, it is sometimes blamed for fostering one of the law's greatest weaknesses: namely, the lack of a centralized, formal structure for codifying international norms, an omission that invites distortions in legal interpretation as well as self-serving policy positions.

International law must not be regarded as a panacea for prohibiting unlawful international conduct nor as a brake on incorrigible governments. It does, however, provide internationally acceptable ways and means of dealing with these situations. Modern international law may not satisfy all national governments all of the time, nor can it supply every answer for all the international community's ills. Nevertheless, it remains far preferable to the alternative of no law at all and, similarly, it is far wiser for national governments to appreciate the existence and function of this international legal system than to overlook the mutual advantages it affords. International law remains the best touchstone and only consistent guide for state conduct in a complex, multicultural world.[21]

With the passing of the Cold War and East–West ideological rivalry, grave global problems have emerged as foci for serious international concern in the 1990s. The Third World debt crisis, international armed conflict, transnational terrorism, overpopulation, deforestation, global warming, AIDS, deterioration of the ozone layer, drug trafficking, and proliferation of chemical weapons—none of these issues are amenable to domestic or unilateral resolution. If politically viable solutions are to be reached, international cooperation is essential. The law of nations supplies proven ways and means to facilitate these collaborative international efforts. Indeed, in the search for global solutions to global problems,

---

[20] On this theme, see Francis Anthony Boyle, *World Politics and International Law* (Durham: Duke University Press, 1985).

[21] For discussion on this point, see Christopher C. Joyner and John C. Dettling, "Bridging the Cultural Chasm: Cultural Relativism and the Future of International Law," *California Western International Law Journal*, Vol. 20, No. 2 (1989–1990), pp. 275–314.

international law supplies the best opportunities for accommodating national interests with international priorities.

In the final analysis, international law does not fail in contemporary world society. Instead, it is the states themselves that fail the law whenever they choose not to adhere to its basic norms. Thus the need to surmount this fundamental obstacle of self-serving, sovereign-state interests must remain as the pre-eminent challenge on international law's global agenda in the next century. To be sure, given the profound lessons of state conduct in the past, it will not be an easy task.

# 21

## ACHIEVING COOPERATION UNDER ANARCHY: STRATEGIES AND INSTITUTIONS

### Robert Axelrod and Robert O. Keohane

In this essay Robert Axelrod and Robert Keohane weave together the various strands of thinking about the means by which international cooperation occurs under conditions of anarchy. Arguing that collaboration occurs even in circumstances that discourage it and instead encourage competition, the authors analyze the structural properties of the international system that make this outcome less improbable than might be otherwise imagined, identify the preconditions necessary for achieving interstate cooperation, and discuss how new institutions and norms might facilitate significant levels of cooperation in the international system. Axelrod is professor of political science and public policy at the University of Michigan; his most recent book is *The Evolution of Cooperation* (1984). Keohane is professor of government and an associate of the Center for International Affairs at Harvard University; he has written *After Hegemony: Cooperation and Discord in the World Political Economy* (1984) and *International Institutions and State Power* (1989).

Achieving cooperation is difficult in world politics. There is no common government to enforce rules, and by the standards of domestic society, international institutions are weak. Cheating and deception are endemic. Yet, . . . coopera-

Used by permission of Robert O. Keoshane and Robert Axelrod. Footnotes have been deleted.

tion is sometimes attained. World politics is not a homogeneous state of war: cooperation varies among issues and over time.

. . . Cooperation is not equivalent to harmony. Harmony requires complete identity of interests, but cooperation can only take place in situations that contain a mixture of conflicting and complementary interests. In such situations, cooperation occurs when actors adjust their behavior to the actual or anticipated preferences of others. Cooperation, thus defined, is not necessarily good from a moral point of view.

Anarchy also needs to be defined clearly. As used here, the term refers to a lack of common government in world politics, not to a denial that an international society—albeit a fragmented one—exists. Clearly, many international relationships continue over time, and engender stable expectations about behavior. To say that world politics is anarchic does not imply that it entirely lacks organization. Relationships among actors may be carefully structured in some issue-areas, even though they remain loose in others. Likewise, some issues may be closely linked through the operation of institutions while the boundaries of other issues, as well as the norms and principles to be followed, are subject to dispute. Anarchy, defined as lack of common government, remains a constant; but the degree to which interactions are structured, and the means by which they are structured, vary.

It has often been noted that military-security issues display more of the characteristics associated with anarchy than do political-economic ones. . . . This does not mean, however, that analysis of these two sets of issues requires two separate analytical frameworks. . . .

[Two] dimensions . . .—the shadow of the future, and the number of players—help us to understand the success and failure of attempts at cooperation in both military-security and political-economic relations. . . .

## THE SHADOW OF THE FUTURE

. . . Concern about the future helps to promote cooperation. . . . Specific factors that help to make the shadow of the future an effective promoter of cooperation . . . include:

1. long time horizons;
2. regularity of stakes;
3. reliability of information about the others' actions;
4. quick feedback about changes in the others' actions.

The dimension of the shadow of the future seems to differentiate military from economic issues more sharply than does the dimension of payoffs. Indeed, its four components can be used to analyze some of the reasons why issues of international political economy may be settled more cooperatively than issues of international security, even when the underlying payoff matrices are similar. . . . Most important is a combination of the first two factors: long time horizons and regularity of stakes. In economic relations, actors have to expect that their relationships will continue over an indefinite period of time; that is, the games they play with each other will be iterated. Typically, neither side in an economic interaction can eliminate the other, or change the nature of the game decisively in a single move. In security affairs, by contrast, the possibility of a successful preemptive war can sometimes be a tempting occasion for the rational timing of surprise. Another way to put this is that, in the international political economy, retaliation for [nonreciprocated cooperation] will almost always be possible. . . . In security affairs, it may be [difficult] to limit or destroy the opponent's capacity for effective retaliation. . . .

The length of the shadow of the future . . . is not necessarily dictated by the objective attributes of a situation. On the contrary, . . . expectations are important. International institutions may therefore be significant, since institutions embody, and affect, actors' expectations. Thus institutions can alter the extent to which governments expect their present actions to affect the behavior of others on future issues. The principles and rules of international regimes make governments concerned about precedents, increasing the likelihood that they will attempt to punish defectors. In this way, international regimes help to link the future with the present. That is as true of arms control agreements, in which willingness to make future agreements depends on others' compliance with previous arrangements, as it is in the General Agreement on Tariffs and Trade, which embodies norms and rules against which the behavior of members can be judged. By sanctioning retaliation for those who violate rules, regimes create expectations that a given violation will be treated not as an isolated case but as one in a series of interrelated actions.

## NUMBER OF ACTORS: SANCTIONING PROBLEMS

The ability of governments to cooperate . . . is affected . . . also by the number of players [in an interactive relationship] and by how their relationships are structured . . . Reciprocity can be an effective strategy to induce cooperation among self-interested players. . . . However, . . . when there are many actors, . . . it may be impossible to identify, much less to punish, [non-cooperation]; even if it is possible, none of the cooperators may have an incentive to play the role of policeman. Each cooperator may seek to be a free-rider on the willingness of others to enforce the rules.

We may call the difficulty of preventing defection through decentralized retaliation the "sanctioning problem." [This can occur as an result of] the inability to identify defectors, . . . [or] when [states] are unable to focus retaliation on [non-cooperaters, or] when some members of a group lack incentives to punish [such actors]. This obstacle to cooperation often arises where there are many actors, some of which fail to cooperate in the common effort to achieve some collective good. . . . When sanctioning problems are severe, cooperation is in danger of collapsing. One way to bolster it is to restructure the situation so that sanctioning becomes more feasible.

## THE CONTEXT OF INTERACTION

Whether cooperation can take place without central guidance depends . . . . also on the context within which interaction takes place. Context may, of course, mean many different things. Any interaction takes place within the context of norms that are shared, often implicitly, by the participants. [Political scientist] John Ruggie has written of the "deep structure" of sovereignty in world politics, and also of the way in which shifting values and norms of state intervention in society—the emergence and legitimation of the welfare state—affected the world political economy between 1914 and 1945. . . .

Interactions also take place within the context of institutions. . . . Institutions alter the payoff structures facing actors, they may lengthen the shadow of the future, and they may enable [conflicts] to be broken down into [conflicts] with smaller numbers of actors. . . .

## GROPING TOWARD NEW INSTITUTIONS AND NORMS

[We] began with a set of hypotheses about how specific features of an international setting would affect the chances for the development of cooperation. Factors included were . . . the shadow of the future and the number of actors. These hypotheses [are] supported by a broad set of cases that . . . [cover] trade disputes, monetary policy, and debt rescheduling as well as arms races, the outbreak of war, and diplomatic concerts. [These two] factors [can be shown to] help to account for both cooperation and conflict.

We [discover from a reading of history] that . . . the actors [are] not satisfied with simply selecting strategies based upon the situation in which they [find] themselves. In many cases we [can observe] deliberate efforts to change the very structure of the situation by changing the context in which each of them would be acting. Decision makers themselves [perceive] (more or less consciously) that some aspects of the situations they [face tend] to make cooperation difficult. So they worked to alter these background conditions. Among the problems they [encounter are] the following:

**1.** how to provide incentives for cooperation so that cooperation would be rewarded over the long run, and defection punished;

**2.** how to monitor behavior so that cooperators and defectors could be identified;

**3.** how to focus rewards on cooperators and retaliation on defectors;

**4.** how to link issues with one another in productive rather than self-defeating ways and, more generally, how to play multilevel games without tripping over their own strategies.

A fundamental strategic concept in attaining these objectives is that of reciprocity. Cooperation in world politics seems to be attained best not by providing benefits unilaterally to others, but by conditional cooperation. Yet reciprocity encounters many problems in practice. . . . Reciprocity requires the ability to recognize and retaliate against a defection. And retaliation can spread acrimoniously.

Actors in world politics seek to deal with problems of reciprocity in part through the exercise of power. Powerful actors structure relationships so that countries committed to a given order can deal effectively with those that have lower levels of commitment. This is done by establishing hierarchies. . . .

Another way to facilitate cooperation is to establish international regimes. Regimes can be defined as "sets of implicit or explicit principles, norms, rules, and decision-making procedures around which actors' expectations converge in a given area of international relations." International regimes have been extensive in the post-1945 international political economy, as illustrated by the international trade regime (centered on the GATT [General Agreement on Tariffs and Trade]) and the international monetary regime (including the [International Monetary Fund] as well as other organizations and networks). Since the use of power can facilitate the construction of regimes, this approach should be seen as complementary to, rather than in contradiction with, an emphasis on hierarchical authority. Regimes do not enforce rules in a hierarchical sense, but they do change patterns of transaction costs and provide information to participants, so that uncertainty is reduced. . . .

International regimes do not substitute for reciprocity; rather, they reinforce and institutionalize it. Regimes incorporating the norm of reciprocity delegitimize defection [from cooperative ventures] and thereby make it more costly. Insofar as they specify precisely what reciprocity means in the relevant issue-area, they make it easier to establish a reputation for practicing reciprocity consistently. Such reputations may become important assets, precisely because others will be more willing to make agreements with governments that can be expected to respond to cooperation with cooperation. Of course, compliance is difficult to assure; and international regimes almost never have the power to enforce rules. Nevertheless, since governments with good reputations can more easily make agreements than governments with bad ones, international regimes can help to facilitate cooperation by making it both easier and more desirable to acquire a good reputation.

International regimes may also help to develop new norms. . . . Major banks today are trying mightily to strengthen norms of repayment (for debtors) and of relending (for banks), but it is not at all clear that this will be successful. Better examples of creating norms may be provided by the evolution of thinking on chemical and biological warfare, and by the development, under GATT, of norms of nondiscrimination—which are now . . . under pressure. Evidently, it is difficult to develop new norms, and they often decay in reaction to conspicuous violations.

Establishing hierarchies, setting up international regimes, and attempting to gain acceptance for new norms are all attempts to change the context within which actors operate by changing the very structure of their interaction. It is important to notice that these efforts have usually not been examples of forward-looking rationality. Rather, they have been experimental, trial-and-error efforts to improve the current situation based upon recent experience. Like other forms of trial-and-error experimentation, they have not always worked. . . .

Eventually, any institution is likely to become obsolete. The question is under what conditions international institutions—broadly defined as "recognized patterns of practice around which expectations converge"—facilitate significant amounts of cooperation for a period of time. Clearly, such institutions can change the incentives for countries affected by them, and can in turn affect the strategic choices governments make in their own self-interest. . . .

The experimental groping by policy makers does not necessarily lead to stronger and ever more complex ways of achieving cooperation. The process proceeds by fits and starts. The success of each step is uncertain, and there is always danger that prior achievements will come unstuck. New experiments are often tried only under obvious pressure of events (as in debt rescheduling). And they are often dependent upon the active leadership of a few individuals or states who feel a serious need for change and who have the greatest resources. . . .

But . . . states are often dissatisfied with the structure of their own environment. . . . Governments have often tried to transform the structures within which they operate so as to make it possible for the countries involved to work together productively. Some of these experiments have been successful, others have been stillborn, and still others have collapsed before fully realizing the dreams of their founders. We understand the functions performed by international regimes, and how they affect strategies pursued by governments, better than we did a number of years ago . . . Even within a world of independent states that are jealously guarding their sovereignty and protecting their power, room exists for new and better arrangements to achieve mutually satisfactory outcomes, in terms both of economic welfare and military security.

This does not mean that all endeavors to promote international cooperation will yield good results. Cooperation can be designed to help a few at the expense of the rest; and it can accentuate as well as alleviate injustice in an imperfect world. Yet the consequences of failure to co-operate—from warfare to the intensification of depressions—make us believe that more cooperation is often better than less. If governments are prepared to grope their way toward a better-coordinated future, scholars should be prepared to study the process. And, in a world where states have often been dissatisfied with international anarchy, scholars should be prepared to advance the learning process—so that despite the reality of anarchy, beneficial forms of international cooperation can be promoted.

# PART THREE

## POLITICS AND MARKETS

During recent years the global agenda has included issues relating to international trade protectionism, balance-of-payments adjustments, and international monetary instability. These have been matched on the domestic agendas of many nations with issues relating to inflation, unemployment, deficits, debts, and economic stagnation. The two sets of issues are not unrelated. Under conditions of global interdependence—defined as a condition of *mutual sensitivity* and *mutual vulnerability*—decisions made in one nation often have important implications and consequences for other nations. Efforts to control inflation at home, for example, can affect the value of national currencies used for international trade and capital transactions, which in turn may affect different nations' balance-of-payments positions, that is, the state of their financial transactions with the rest of the world.

Interdependence, by blurring the distinctions between foreign policy and domestic policy and between national security policy and foreign economic policy, raises important questions about the problems that have long dominated world politics. Traditionally, issues relating to economics have been regarded as matters of *low politics*. While the *high politics* of peace and security issues engaged the attention of nations' policy-making elites, the *low politics* of more routinized international economic affairs could be left to the lower-level bureaucrats. Today, as controversies over the distribution of wealth and the processes and institutions that govern it affect everyone, transnational economic issues are among the most important political issues on the global agenda, and they now

**223**

compete with traditional national security issues for the attention of top-level elites. Indeed, as the Cold War between the United States and the Soviet Union and their erstwhile allies recedes into history, it has become commonplace to argue that geo-economics will replace geopolitics as the motive force behind states' struggle for preeminence in a new world era. In this new environment commercial advantage, not military might, will determine who commands power and who will exercise influence over whom.

The term "political economy" highlights the intersection of politics and economics. It draws attention to the facts that economic linkages between nations affect their political affairs, and that the nature of their political ties influences their economic exchanges. Thus politics (the exercise of power and influence) and economics (the distribution of material wealth) have a reciprocal impact on one another.

The high politics–low politics distinction has always been overdrawn, perhaps, but the complexity and urgency of political economy issues—fueled by the expansion of world trade since World War II and the globalization of production and finance via multinational corporations and transnational banks—are now more apparent than ever. Thus it is no exaggeration to argue that some of the most important issues on the global agenda are affected by the interplay of political and economic forces, and that an answer to the classic question of politics—Who gets what, when, and how?—must be sought in this interplay. Political economy thus provides a conceptual focus designed to accommodate the complex realities of the contemporary global environment.

As noted, the issues on the global agenda that comprise the political economy issue-area are numerous. It is not surprising, therefore, that a number of analytical perspectives compete with one another in an effort to bring insight and meaning to them. It is useful to begin with a discussion of some of these contending perspectives and schools of thought. Robert Gilpin does this admirably in the first essay in Part Three, "Can the Interdependent World Political Economy Survive? Three Perspectives on the Future." Writing from a neorealist perspective, Gilpin evaluates the merits and limitations of three paradigms, or approaches, to understanding international political economy. These are the liberal, Marxist, and economic nationalist schools of thought. The first sees the future affected most by challenges to the nation-state posed by increasing economic interdependence and technological advances; it is termed the *sovereignty-at-bay* model. The second envisions the future influenced most by the continuing struggle between haves and have-nots in a hierarchical system that, consistent with Marxist thought, is seen as inherently exploitative; it is termed the *dependencia* model to emphasize the pattern of inequality and exploitation that this view ascribes to the international political economy. This perspective, like the liberal one, emphasizes the role of multinational corporations in the world political economy. The third, by contrast, sees the future determined primarily by the way in which nation-states pursue their national interests; appropriately, it is labeled the *mercantilist* model. Gilpin's essay not only usefully describes and evaluates these alternative perspectives, but also offers some inviting propositions about the implications of interdependence for the world's future.

With this theoretical orientation as a background, the next four essays in *The Global Agenda* focus on the challenges of changes in the global political economy and on the costs and opportunities policymakers in different national settings now face. We begin with an essay on "The International Political Economy" in which the author, Miles Kahler, examines sea changes in the global political economy that occurred coincidentally with the tidal wave of changes that engulfed politico-military affairs at the end to the 1980s, albeit sea changes that took place often outside the limelight of popular and media attention. They include structural changes involving Japan, the developing countries, the European Community, and some of the centrally planned economies of Eastern Europe and the Soviet Union. Embracing elements of both the liberal and economic nationalist perspectives outlined by Gilpin, Kahler also examines the ever-tightening interconnectedness of international markets, most recently financial markets, and what this means for transnational economic entities as well as nation-states. Finally, he also notes how poorly adapted to the changing global political economy existing mechanisms of international management remain. Thus, "internationalized though they may be, markets will continue to confront fragmented political authority. Whatever the sea-changes in the international economy, they will take place within these deeply embedded features of international relations, for they have not yet transformed them."

Is Europe the exception? In 1985 the European Community (EC) adopted the Single European Act, which sought boldly to jump-start momentum for the integration of the twelve Western European countries comprising the EC. The target date for realization of a single, continent-wide European common market is 1992. Donald J. Puchala examines the expectations and implications associated with Europe 1992 in our next essay, "The New Meaning of European Unity." Necessarily the process of creating a single common market involves political decisions designed to remove economic barriers; non-state actors, such as multinational corporations, are also playing an important role in the integrative process. What Europe 1992 ultimately portends economically and politically for the rest of the world may, however, be the most important if the most elusive question.

Puchala's perspective on the meaning of Europe 1992 clearly reflects the liberal or "sovereignty-at-bay" model of the future. In contrast, Robin Broad and John Cavanagh embrace the *dependencia* model in their essay, "No More NICs." The newly industrializing countries (NICs)—most notably Hong Kong, Singapore, South Korea, and Taiwan—have enjoyed an unusual degree of economic growth in recent decades by pursuing an export-led path to economic development. The strategy itself is a reflection of the *neomercantilist* policies toward economic matters now practiced by many states.

Neomercantilism refers to the use of state power to maintain domestic production and employment by reducing imports, stimulating domestic production, and promoting exports. Broad and Cavanagh argue that while that strategy may have worked for some developing nations, and while the World Bank and others have promoted widespread use of the strategy, for a variety of reasons it cannot work for others. Principal among the reasons is the changing nature of the global political economy and the role of developing nations in the emerging international division of labor. "The changing world economy has created a desperate need to rethink the kinds of adjustments that will produce growth and development," they argue. "At the very least, the adjustment strategies must be built on realistic assumptions. The NICs were the product of a radically different world economy. That they cannot be replicated . . . is an indication of how much the world economy has changed."

The changed and changing world economy has affected the powerful as well as the weak. The United States emerged from World War II as the world's undisputed leader in economics as well as politics. It became the hegemonic power of the postwar era. Now, however, its leadership is under challenge at home and abroad, as the costs of leadership have become burdensome and the benefits doubtful. In the view of many, the United States is a hegemonic power in decline.

The global political economy that came into being following World War II can be described as a liberal international economic order (LIEO) in which the capitalist nations of the Western world, led by the United States, sought to promote the free flow of goods and capital across national boundaries unfettered by politically imposed barriers. The neomercantilist challenge to the LIEO became increasingly evident in the United States and elsewhere in the industrialized world during the 1980s; this challenge, embodied in the rise of protectionist sentiment and cries for *fair* trade rather than *free* trade, is in part a response to nations' loss of control over their own well-being. It reflects a penchant for dealing aggressively and unilaterally with the costs of complex interdependence which, ironically, resulted from the success that the United States, as the hegemonic power in the postwar political economy, and its politico-military allies and economic partners had realized in promoting the LIEO. What the declining power of the United States portends for the future has been the subject of ongoing debate because of its effects not only on the United States itself, but also on the rest of the world.

A primary unraveling of the LIEO is occurring in the international trade regime, and developments within the United States have spurred its denouement. Although the United States has been a primary advocate of the most-favored-nation principle of non-discrimination in international trade, its own behavior as well as policy proposals advanced in Congress and in other policy-making and academic circles belie that commitment. Bilateralism, not multilateralism, and managed trade, not free trade, have sometimes been policy, not just prescription.

In "Trade Policy at a Crossroad," Robert E. Litan and Peter O. Suchman explore the reasons within the United States and within the larger framework of the General Agreement on Tariffs and Trade (GATT) that have given rise to the ebbing of the U.S. commitment to an open, liberal trade regime. Paramount among those reasons are the seemingly intractable twin deficits of the United States—in the budget of its federal government and in its trade with the rest of the world—that the United States has experienced since the mid-1980s. Litan and Suchman conclude that the problems the United States faces cannot be solved through the strategies advocated by critics of the liberal trade regime; instead, solutions must be sought domestically, with the adjustments in U.S. relations with other states pursued through the operation of the free-floating exchange rate system extant since the early 1970s. Simultaneously, a U.S. recommitment to GATT is in order, as the rules-oriented, multilateral trade system remains the best hope not only for prosperity but also, if the 1930s are a guide, to global peace and security.

The imperative that the United States rethink its current policies is vividly underscored by Walter Russell Mead in his essay, disturbingly entitled "On the Road to Ruin." Mead recounts how the United States emerged preeminent from the ravages of World War II, but he also emphasizes that "Western Europe and Japan are back, and their preferences are beginning once again to shape the world's economy." The world Mead foresees consists of three rival economic blocs: "a Euro-bloc based on the Western European nations of the Common Market and now expanding to include . . . Eastern Europe; an East Asian bloc dominated by Japan and including . . . the other free-market industrializing nations of the region; and the American bloc, dominated by the United States, augmented by Canada, and incorporating Latin America." It is a world inimical to U.S. interests, as the American bloc "is the weakest and most troubled." In the end, unless the United States undertakes radically new thinking, the three-bloc world portends that the United States will plummet from its position as the world's hegemonic power to a position akin to that of Argentina—"A rich country . . . in many ways similar to ours . . . [whose] economy alternates between hyperinflation and depression; its politics, between anarchy and dictatorship."

Among the changes that Mead finds troublesome as he contemplates the present and future position of the United States in world affairs is that U.S. "oil production is no longer adequate for our own uses." Domestic oil production in the United States has fallen continuously for nearly two decades or more. Ominously, domestic consumption, after falling in response to the two oil price shocks of the 1970s induced by the Organization of Petroleum Exporting Countries (OPEC), has also risen in recent years. The result is growing U.S. dependence on foreign sources of energy on a scale unmatched since the crisis years of the 1970s. This in turn will propel greater U.S. dependence on a small coterie of oil exporters concentrated in the volatile Persian Gulf region, whose ability to extract monopoly prices for their scarce resources will multiply.

These are among the developments discussed by James Schlesinger in "Oil and Power in the Nineties." Concern for the balance of Soviet and American interests and power projection capabilities in the Middle East—"assuming that the Soviet Union can surmount its current 'time of troubles'"—adds to the uncertain future Schlesinger considers. Schlesinger could not have foreseen the invasion of Kuwait by Iraq in August 1990 when he wrote his essay—few did; nor could he have predicted the response to the invasion mounted by the United States in concert with the Soviet Union and other nations—few also predicted this. In the face of these unexpected developments, Schlesinger's arguments hold up remarkably well: the combination of economic and political trends spotlights the Middle East now and will likely do so for years to come.

Each of the three previous essays builds its argument in whole or in part on the alleged decline of American power. Empirically there is evidence to support the proposition that the preeminent role of the United States in the global political economy is not what it once was. There are also historical analogies. Britain is widely reputed to have been the hegemonic power of the nineteenth century whose mantle passed to the United States in the twentieth. But do the data in fact support the interpretations advanced by those who use them? And are the forces that led to Britain's decline now applicable to the United States? Will Germany or Japan emerge as the hegemonic power in the twenty-first century in the same way and as a consequence of the same misguided policies alleged to have sealed Britain's fate?

These questions are at the center of a heated debate in the United States and abroad in part as a consequence of the provocative treatise by the historian Paul Kennedy, *The Rise and Fall of the Great Powers,* published in 1987, in which the author draws on the historical record spanning centuries to understand the forces surrounding the rise and decline of hegemonic powers. The questions are all the more urgent because of the policy prescriptions they imply. "Although the United States is at present still in a class of its own economically and perhaps even militarily," Kennedy writes, "it cannot avoid confronting the two great tests which challenge the *longevity* of every major power that occupies the 'number one' position in world affairs: whether, in the military/strategical realm, it can preserve a reasonable balance between the nation's perceived defense requirements and the means it possesses to maintain those commitments; and whether . . . it can preserve the technological and economic bases of its power from relative erosion in the face of ever-shifting patterns of global production." The danger, he warns, is similar to that faced by hegemonic powers in earlier historical periods, notably the Spanish at the turn of the seventeenth century and the British at the turn of the twentieth. "The United States now runs the risk . . . of . . . 'imperial overstretch': that is to say, decision-makers in Washington must face the awkward and enduring fact that the sum total of the United States' global interests and obligations is nowadays far larger than the country's power to defend them all simultaneously."

Joseph S. Nye, Jr., is among those who have challenged Kennedy's thesis. His essay is an appropriate conclusion to Part III of *The Global Agenda,* as its title—"The Misleading Metaphor of Decline"—conveys the message that Nye disagrees with Kennedy and other "declinists." Drawing sometimes explicitly, sometimes implicitly on the changing concept of power that he elaborates in Part I of this book (see selection 11), Nye is especially concerned that a misreading of historical and contemporary evidence could lead to misguided policy choices. The United States *is* different from Britain, he argues, and there is much evidence that calls into question that the decline of the United States "has been either precipitous or continuous." In consequence, seeing the problems the United States faces "as American decline and drawing analogies to Britain is misleading, for this directs attention away from the real problems arising out of long-term changes in world politics and suggests remedies that would weaken rather than strengthen America's standing."

# 22

# CAN THE INTERDEPENDENT WORLD POLITICAL ECONOMY SURVIVE? THREE PERSPECTIVES ON THE FUTURE

Robert Gilpin

**In this essay Robert Gilpin summarizes and critically analyzes three perspectives on international political economy: the liberal, the Marxist, and the mercantilist/nationalist. He utilizes these comparative assessments to reflect on the probable future course of international economic relations. Gilpin is Dwight D. Eisenhower Professor of International Affairs at Princeton University. His publications include *War and Change in World Politics* (1981) and *The Political Economy of International Relations* (1987).**

Edward Hallet Carr observed that "the science of economics presupposes a given political order, and cannot be profitably studied in isolation from politics."[1] Throughout history, the larger configurations of world politics and state interests have in large measure determined the framework of the international economy. Succeeding imperial and hegemonic powers have sought to organize and maintain the international economy in terms of their economic and security interests.

From this perspective, the contemporary international economy was the creation of the world's dominant economic and military power, the United States.

Reprinted from Robert Gilpin, "Three Models of the Future," *International Organization* 29 (Winter 1975), pp. 37–60 by permission of The MIT Press, Cambridge, Massachusetts. © 1975 by the Regents of the University of Wisconsin System. Some footnotes have been deleted; others have been renumbered to appear in consecutive order.

[1]Edward Hallet Carr, *The Twenty Years' Crisis 1919–1939* (London: Macmillan and Co., 1951), p. 117.

At the end of the Second World War, there were efforts to create a universal and liberal system of trade and monetary relations. After 1947, however, the world economy began to revive on the foundations of the triangular relationship of the three major centers of noncommunist industrial power: the United States, Western Europe, and Japan. Under the umbrella of American nuclear protection and connected with the United States through military alliances, Japan and Western Europe were encouraged to grow and prosper. In order to rebuild these industrial economies adjacent to the Sino-Soviet bloc, the United States encouraged Japanese growth, led by exports, into the American market and, through the European Economic Community's (EEC) common external tariff and agricultural policy, also encouraged discrimination against American exports.

Today, the triangular relationship of the noncommunist industrial powers upon which the world economy has rested is in disarray. The signs of decay were visible as early as the middle 1960s, when President John F. Kennedy's grand design failed to stem the coalescence of an inward-looking European economic bloc and to achieve its objective of an economic and political community extending from Scandinavia to Japan and pivoted on the United States.

Believing that the world trading and monetary system was operating to America's disadvantage, the administration of Richard Nixon took up the challenge with a completely different approach. On 15 August 1971, former President Nixon announced a new foreign economic policy for the United States. In response to the first trade deficit since 1893 and to accelerating attacks on the dollar, the president imposed a surcharge on American imports, suspended the convertibility of the dollar, and took other remedial actions. Subsequently the dollar was devalued twice (December 1971 and February 1973); the world moved toward a system of flexible exchange rates; and intense negotiations were initiated to create a new international monetary and trading system.

A new economic policy was necessary for several reasons. The United States believed an overvalued dollar was adding significantly to its unemployment rate.[2] American expenditures abroad for military commitments, foreign direct investment, and goods and services required, in the 1970s, greater outlays of foreign exchange than the United States could earn or wished to borrow. The US rapprochement with China, its moves toward détente with the Soviet Union, and President Nixon's announcement of the New Economic Policy appeared to signal the end of the political order that American economic and military supremacy had guaranteed; this political order had been the foundation for the post–World War II world economy. All these policy initiatives were efforts to adjust to the growing economic power of America's partners, Europe and Japan, and to the growing military power of its primary antagonist, the Soviet Union. In

---

[2]C. Fred Bergsten, "The New Economics and U.S. Foreign Policy," *Foreign Affairs* 50 (January 1972): 199–222.

terms of the present article, these economic and political changes raised the question of whether the interdependent world economy could survive in the changing political environment of the 1970s and beyond.

In this brief article I make no attempt to give a definitive answer to this question. Rather, my purpose is to present and evaluate three models of the future drawn from current writings on international relations. These models are really representative of the three prevailing schools of thought on political economy: liberalism, Marxism, and economic nationalism. Each model is an amalgam of the ideas of several writers who, in my judgment (or by their own statements), fall into one or another of these perspectives on the relationship of economic and political affairs.

Each model constitutes an ideal type. Perhaps no one individual would subscribe to each argument made by any one position. Yet the tendencies and assumptions associated with each perception of the future are real enough; they have a profound influence on popular, academic, and official thinking on trade, monetary, and investment problems. One, in fact, cannot really escape being influenced by one position or another.

Following the presentation of the three models, I present a critique that sets forth the strengths and weaknesses of each. On the basis of this critique, I draw some general conclusions with respect to the future of . . . international relations. . . .

## THE SOVEREIGNTY-AT-BAY MODEL

I label the first model *sovereignty at bay,* after the title of Raymond Vernon's influential book on the multinational corporation.[3] According to this view, increasing economic interdependence and technological advances in communication and transportation are making the nation state an anachronism. These economic and technological developments are said to have undermined the traditional economic rationale of the nation state. In the interest of world efficiency and domestic economic welfare, the nation state's control over economic affairs will continually give way to the multinational corporation, to the Eurodollar market, and to other international institutions better suited to the economic needs of mankind.

Perhaps the most forceful statement of the sovereignty-at-bay thesis is that of Harry Johnson—the paragon of economic liberalism. Analyzing the international economic problems of the 1970s, Johnson makes the following prediction:

> In an important sense, the fundamental problem of the future is the conflict between the political forces of nationalism and the economic forces pressing for world integration. This conflict currently appears as one between the national government and the

---

[3]Raymond Vernon, *Sovereignty at Bay* (New York: Basic Books, 1971).

international corporation, in which the balance of power at least superficially appears to lie on the side of the national government. But in the longer run economic forces are likely to predominate over political. . . . Ultimately, a world federal government will appear as the only rational method for coping with the world's economic problems.[4]

Though not all adherents of the sovereignty-at-bay thesis would go as far as Johnson, and an interdependent world economy is quite conceivable without unbridled scope for the activities of multinational corporations, most do regard the multinational corporation as the embodiment par excellence of the liberal ideal of an interdependent world economy. It has taken the integration of national economies beyond trade and money to the internationalization of production. For the first time in history, production, marketing, and investment are being organized on a global scale rather than in terms of isolated national economies. The multinational corporations are increasingly indifferent to national boundaries in making decisions with respect to markets, production, and sources of supply.

The sovereignty-at-bay thesis argues that national economies have become enmeshed in a web of economic interdependence from which they cannot easily escape, and from which they derive great economic benefits. Through trade, monetary relations, and foreign investment, the destinies and well-being of societies have become too inexorably interwoven for these bonds to be severed. The costs of the ensuing inefficiencies in order to assert national autonomy or some other nationalistic goal would be too high. The citizenry, so this thesis contends, would not tolerate the sacrifices of domestic economic well-being that would be entailed if individual nation states sought to hamper unduly the successful operation of the international economy.

Underlying this development, the liberal position argues, is a revolution in economic needs and expectations. Domestic economic goals have been elevated to a predominant position in the hierarchy of national goals. Full employment, regional development, and other economic welfare goals have become the primary concerns of political leadership. More importantly, these goals can only be achieved, this position argues, through participation in the world economy. No government, for example, would dare shut out the multinational corporations and thereby forego employment, regional development, or other benefits these corporations bring into countries. In short, the rise of the welfare state and the increasing sensitivity of national governments to the rising economic expectations of their societies have made them dependent upon the benefits provided by a liberal world-economic system.

In essence, this argument runs, one must distinguish between the creation of the interdependent world economy and the consequences of its subsequent

---

[4]Harry G. Johnson, *International Economic Questions Facing Britain, the United States, and Canada in the 70's,* British-North American Research Association, June 1970, p. 24.

dynamics.[5] Though the postwar world economy was primarily a creation of the United States, the system has since become essentially irreversible. The intermeshing of interests across national boundaries and the recognized benefits of interdependence now cement the system together for the future. Therefore, even though the power of the United States and security concerns may be in relative decline, this does not portend a major transformation of the international economy and political system.

The multinational corporation, for example, is now believed to be sufficiently strong to stand and survive on its own. The flexibility, mobility, and vast resources of the corporations give them an advantage in confrontations with nation states. A corporation always has the option of moving its production facilities elsewhere. If it does, the nation state is the loser in terms of employment, corporate resources, and access to world markets. Thus the multinationals are escaping the control of nation states, including that of their home (source) governments. They are emerging as sufficient powers in their own right to survive the changing context of international political relations.

On the other hand, it is argued that the nation state has been placed in a dilemma it cannot hope to resolve.[6] It is losing control over economic affairs to transnational actors like the multinational corporation. It cannot retain its traditional independence and sovereignty and simultaneously meet the expanding economic needs and desires of its populace. The efforts of nation states to enhance their security and power *relative* to others are held to be incompatible with an interdependent world economy that generates *absolute* gains for everyone. In response to the growing economic demands of its citizens, the nation state must adjust to the forces of economic rationality and efficiency.

In the contemporary world, the costs of disrupting economic interdependence, of territorial conquest, and of risking nuclear warfare are believed to be far greater than any conceivable benefits. The calculus of benefits and risks has changed, and "the rational relationship between violence as a means of foreign policy and the ends of foreign policy has been destroyed by the possibility of all-out nuclear war."[7] In contrast to the nineteenth century, the cost of acquiring territory is viewed as having simply become too great. In the contemporary world, there is more to be gained through economic cooperation and an international division of labor than through strife and conflict. Thus, in the opinion of Saburo Okita, formerly president of the Japan Economic Research Center, the exercise of force for economic gain or to defend economic interests is an anachronism:

[5]Samuel Huntington, "Transnational Organizations in World Politics," *World Politics* 25 (April 1973): 361.

[6]Edward Morse, "Crisis Diplomacy, Interdependence, and the Politics of International Economic Relations," *World Politics* 24, supplement (Spring 1972): 123–50.

[7]Hans Morgenthau, "Western Values and Total War," *Commentary,* October 1961, p. 280.

We are living in a century when such military action is no longer viable. To build up military power just to protect overseas private property is rather absurd in terms of cost-benefit calculations. The best course for the Government in case of nationalization or seizure of overseas private Japanese assets is to compensate Japanese investors directly in Japan rather than to spend very large amounts of money to build up military strength.[8]

Just as the nuclear revolution in warfare now inhibits the exercise of military power, the revolution in economic relations now inhibits the national exercise of economic power by increasing the cost. Advances in transportation and communications have integrated national economies to the point where many believe it is too costly to threaten the severance of economic relations in order to achieve particular political and economic goals. Economically as well as militarily in the contemporary world, nations are said to be mutually deterred from actions that would disrupt the interdependent economy. This mutual vulnerability of necessity limits and moderates the economic and political struggle among nation states. It provides the necessary minimum political order where the multinational corporations of all the major industrial powers can flourish and bring benefits to the whole of mankind.

The sovereignty-at-bay view also envisages a major transformation of the relationships among developed and underdeveloped countries. The multinational corporations of the developed, industrial economies must not only produce in each other's markets, but the locus of manufacturing industry will increasingly shift to underdeveloped countries.[9] As the economies of developed countries become more service oriented, as their terms of trade for raw materials continue to deteriorate, and as their labor costs continue to rise, manufacturing will migrate to lesser-developed countries. United States firms already engage in extensive offshore production in Asia and Latin America. Western Europe has reached the limits of importing Mediterranean labor, which is the functional equivalent of foreign direct investment. Japan's favorable wage structure and undervalued currency have eroded. With the end of the era of cheap energy and of favorable terms of trade for raw materials, the logic of industrial location favors the underdeveloped periphery. Increasingly, the multinational corporations of all industrial powers will follow the logic of this manufacturing revolution. Manufacturing, particularly of components and semiprocessed goods, will migrate to lesser-developed countries.

This vision of the future has been portrayed most dramatically by Norman Macrae, in an issue of *The Economist*, who foresees a world of spreading affluence energized perhaps by "small transnational companies run in West

---

[8]Quoted in *New York Times Magazine*, 29 October 1972, p. 58.
[9]John Diebold, "Multinational Corporations—Why Be Scared of Them?" *Foreign Policy*, no. 12 (Fall 1973): 79–95.

Africa by London telecommuters who live in Honolulu?"[10] New computer-based training methods and information systems will facilitate the rapid diffusion of skills, technologies and industries to lesser-developed countries. The whole system will be connected by modern telecommunications and computers; the rich will concentrate on the knowledge-creating and knowledge-processing industries. More and more of the old manufacturing industries will move to the underdeveloped world. The entire West and Japan will be a service-oriented island in a labor-intensive global archipelago. Thus, whereas the telephone and jet aircraft facilitated the internationalization of production in the Northern Hemisphere, the contemporary revolution in communications and transportation will encompass the whole globe.

"The logical and eventual development of this possibility," according to management consultant John Diebold, "would be the end of nationality and national governments as we know them."[11] This sovereignty-at-bay world, then, is one of voluntary and cooperative relations among interdependent economies, the goal of which is to accelerate the economic growth and welfare of everyone. In this model, development of the poor is achieved through the transfer of capital, technology, and managerial know-how from the continually advancing developed lands to the lesser-developed nations; it is a world in which the tide of economic growth lifts all boats. In this liberal vision of the future, the multinational corporation, freed from the nation state, is the critical transmission belt of capital, ideas, and growth.

## THE DEPENDENCIA MODEL

In contrast to the sovereignty-at-bay vision of the future is what may be characterized as the *dependencia* model.[12] Although the analysis underlying the two approaches has much in common, the dependencia model challenges the partners-in-development motif of the sovereignty-at-bay model. Its Marxist conception is one of a hierarchical and exploitative world order. The sovereignty-at-bay model envisages a relatively benevolent system in which growth and wealth spread from the developed core to the lesser-developed periphery. In the dependencia model, on the other hand, the flow of wealth and benefits is seen as moving—via the same mechanisms—from the global, underdeveloped periphery to the centers of industrial financial power and decision. It is an exploitative system

---

[10]"The Future of International Business," *The Economist,* 22 January 1972.

[11]Diebold, p. 87.

[12]The literature on dependencia, or underdevelopment, has now become legend. One of the better statements of this thesis is Osvaldo Sunkel, "Big Business and 'Dependencia': A Latin American View," *Foreign Affairs* 50 (April 1972): 517–31. For an excellent and critical view of the dependencia thesis, see Benjamin J. Cohen, *The Question of Imperialism—The Political Economy of Dominance and Dependence* (New York: Basic Books, 1973), chapter 6.

that produces affluent development for some and dependent underdevelopment for the majority of mankind. In effect, what is termed transnationalism by the sovereignty-at-bay advocates is considered imperialism by the Marxist proponents of the dependencia model.

In the interdependent world economy of the dependencia model, the multinational corporation also reigns supreme. But the world created by these corporations is held to be far different from that envisaged by the sovereignty-at-bay school of thought. In the dependencia model the political and economic consequences of the multinational corporation are due to what Stephen Hymer has called the two laws of development: the law of increasing firm size, and the law of uneven development. The law of increasing firm size, Hymer argues, is the tendency since the Industrial Revolution for firms to increase in size "from the *workshop* to the *factory* to the *national* corporation to the *multidivisional corporation* and now to the multinational corporation."[13] The law of uneven development, he continues, is the tendency of the international economy to produce poverty as well as wealth, underdevelopment as well as development. Together, these two economic laws are producing the following consequence:

> . . . a regime of North Atlantic Multinational Corporations would tend to produce a hierarchical division of labor within the firm. It would tend to centralize high-level decision-making occupations in a few key cities in the advanced countries, surrounded by a number of regional sub-capitals, and confine the rest of the world to lower levels of activity and income, i.e., to the status of towns and villages in a new Imperial system. Income, status, authority, and consumption patterns would radiate out from these centers along a declining curve, and the existing pattern of inequality and dependency would be perpetuated. The pattern would be complex, just as the structure of the corporation is complex, but the basic relationship between different countries would be one of superior and subordinate, head office and branch office.[14]

In this hierarchical and exploitative world system, power and decision would be lodged in the urban financial and industrial cores of New York, London, Tokyo, etc. Here would be located the computers and data banks of the closely integrated global systems of production and distribution; the main computer in the core would control subsidiary computers in the periphery. The higher functions of management, research and development, entrepreneurship, and finance would be located in these Northern metropolitan centers. "Lower" functions and labor-intensive manufacturing would be continuously diffused to the lesser-developed countries where are found cheap pliable labor, abundant raw materials, and an indifference to industrial pollution. This global division of labor between higher and lower economic functions would perpetuate the chasm

---

[13]"The Multinational Corporation and the Law of Uneven Development," in *Economics and World Order–From the 1970's to the 1990's,* ed. Jagdish Bhagwati (New York: The Macmillan Co., 1972), p. 113 and passim.
[14]Ibid., p. 114.

between the affluent northern one-fifth of the globe and the destitute southern four-fifths of the globe.

The argument of the dependencia thesis is that the economic dependence of the underdeveloped periphery upon the developed core is responsible for the impoverishment of the former. Development and underdevelopment are simultaneous processes; the developed countries have progressed and have grown rich through exploiting the poor and making them poorer. Lacking true autonomy and being economically dependent upon the developed countries, the underdeveloped countries have suffered because the developed have a veto over their development:

> By dependence we mean a situation in which the economy of certain countries is conditioned by the development and expansion of another economy to which the former is subjected. The relation of interdependence between two or more economies, and between these and world trade, assumes the form of dependence when some countries (the dominant ones) can expand and be self-sustaining, while other countries (the dependent ones) can do this only as a reflection of that expansion, which can have either a positive or negative effect on their immediate development.[15]

Though this particular quotation refers to trade relations, much of the dependence literature is addressed to the issue of foreign direct investment. In content, most of this literature is of a piece with traditional Marxist and radical theories of imperialism. Whether because of the falling rate of profit in capitalist economies or the attraction of superprofits abroad, multinational corporations are believed to exploit the underdeveloped countries. Thus, Paul Baran and Paul Sweezy see the multinational necessarily impelled to invest in lesser-developed countries.[16] Constantine Vaitsos has sought to document the superprofits available to American corporations in Latin America.[17] The message conveyed by this literature is that the imperialism of free investment has replaced the imperialism of free trade in the contemporary world.

## THE MERCANTILIST MODEL

A key element missing in both the sovereignty-at-bay and the dependencia models is the nation state. Both envisage a world organized and managed by powerful North American, European, and Japanese corporations. In the beneficial corporate order of the first model and the imperialist corporate order of the second, there is little room for nation states, save as servants of corporate power and

---

[15]Quoted in Cohen, pp. 190–91.

[16]*Monopoly Capital—An Essay on the American Economic and Social Order* (New York: Monthly Review Press, 1966).

[17]Constantine Vaitsos, "Transfer of Resources and Preservation of Monopoly Rents," Economic Development Report No. 168, Development Advisory Service, Harvard University, 1970. (Mimeographed.)

ambition. In opposition to both these models, therefore, the third model of the future—the mercantilist model—views the nation state and the interplay of national interests (as distinct from corporate interests) as the primary determinants of the future role of the world economy.[18]

According to this mercantilist view, the interdependent world economy, which has provided such a favorable environment for the multinational corporation, is coming to an end. In the wake of the relative decline of American power and of growing conflicts among the capitalist economies, a new international political order less favorable to the multinational corporation is coming into existence. Whether it is former President Nixon's five-power world (US, USSR, and China, the EEC, and Japan), a triangular world (US, USSR, and China), or some form of American-Soviet condominium, the emergent world order will be characterized by intense international economic competition for markets, investment outlets, and sources of raw materials.

By *mercantilism* I mean the attempt of governments to manipulate economic arrangements in order to maximize their own interests, whether or not this is at the expense of others. These interests may be related to domestic concerns (full employment, price stability, etc.) or to foreign policy (security, independence, etc.).

This use of the term *mercantilism* is far broader than its eighteenth-century association with a trade and balance-of-payments surplus. The essence of mercantilism, as the concept is used in this article, is the priority of *national* economic and political objectives over considerations of *global* economic efficiency. The mercantilist impulse can take many forms in the contemporary world: the desire for a balance-of-payments surplus; the export of unemployment, inflation, or both; the imposition of import and/or export controls; the expansion of world market shares; and the stimulation of advanced technology. In short, each nation will pursue economic policies that reflect domestic economic needs and external political ambitions without much concern for the effects of these policies on other countries or on the international economic system as a whole.

The mercantilist position in effect reverses the argument of the liberals with respect to the nature and success of the interdependent world economy. In contrast to the liberal view that trade liberalization has fostered economic growth, the mercantilist thesis is that several decades of uninterrupted economic growth permitted interdependence. Growth, based in part on relatively cheap energy and other resources as well as on the diffusion of American technology abroad, facil-

---

[18]See, for example, David Calleo and Benjamin Rowland, *America and the World Political Economy* (Bloomington, Ind.: Indiana University Press, 1973). Mercantilism is also the real theme of Ernest Mandel's *Europe vs. America—Contradictions of Imperialism* (New York: Monthly Review Press, 1970).

itated the reintroduction of Japan into the world economy and the development of a closely linked Atlantic economy. Now both cheap energy and a technological gap, which were sources of rapid economic growth and global interdependence, have ceased to exist.

International competition has intensified and has become disruptive precisely because the United States has lost much of its technological lead in products and industrial processes. As happened in Britain in the latter part of the nineteenth century, the United States no longer holds the monopoly position in advanced technologies. Its exports must now compete increasingly on the basis of price and a devalued dollar. As was also the case with Great Britain, the United States has lost the technological rents associated with its previous industrial superiority. This loss of industrial supremacy on the part of the dominant industrial power threatens to give rise to economic conflict between the rising and declining centers of industrial power.

From the mercantilist perspective, the fundamental problem of modern international society has been how to organize an industrial world economy. This issue arose with the spread of industrialism from Great Britain and the emergence of several competing capitalist economies in the latter part of the nineteenth century. In the decades prior to the First World War, the issue of how to organize a world economy composed of several competing industrial economies was at the heart of international politics. The resulting commercial and imperial struggle was a major factor in the subsequent outbreak of the First World War.

The issue was never resolved during the interwar period. During the Second World War, the organization of the world economy was regarded, at least in the United States, as a central question for the postwar era. Would it be a universal liberal system or a fragmented system of regional blocs and preference arrangements? With the outbreak of the cold war and the undisputed hegemony of the United States over other capitalist economies, however, the issue faded into the background. Former President Nixon's 15 August 1971 speech signaled to mercantilist writers that with the easing of the cold war the issue has once again moved to the fore.

These mercantilist writers tend to fall into the two camps of malevolent and benign mercantilism. Both tend to believe the world economy is fragmenting into regional blocs. In the wake of the relative decline of American power, nation states will form regional economic alliances or blocs in order to advance their interests in opposition to other nation states. International trade, monetary arrangements, and investment will be increasingly interregional. This regionalization of economic relations will replace the present American emphasis on multilateral free trade, the international role of the dollar, and the reign of the American multinational corporation.

Malevolent mercantilism believes regionalization will intensify international economic conflict. Each bloc centered on the large industrial powers—the

United States, Western Europe, Japan, and the Soviet Union—will clash over markets, currency, and investment outlets. This would be a return to the lawlessness and beggar-thy-neighbor policies of the 1930s.

Benign mercantilism, on the other hand, believes regional blocs would stabilize world economic relations.[19] It believes that throughout modern history universalism and regionalism have been at odds. The rationale of regional blocs is that one can have simultaneously the benefits of greater scale and interdependence and minimal accompanying costs of economic and political interdependence. Though the material gains from a global division of labor and free trade could be greater, regionalism is held to provide security and protection against external economic and political forces over which the nation state, acting alone, has little influence or control. In short, the organization of the world economy into regional blocs could provide the basis for a secure and peaceful economic order.

Benign mercantilism derives from the view of John Maynard Keynes and other Englishmen who were highly critical of an increasingly interdependent world economy. The loss of national self-sufficiency, this more benign view of mercantilism holds, is a source of economic-political insecurity and conflict.[20] Liberalism, moreover, is detrimental to national cultural and political development. Therefore, this benign mercantilist position advocates a regionalization of the world economy as the appropriate middle road between a declining American-centered world economy and a global conflict between the capitalist economies. An inevitable clash between industrial economies can be prevented through the carving out of regional spheres of influence and the exercise of mutual self-restraint among them.

In the opinion of benign mercantilism, the thrust of much domestic and international economic policy, especially since the end of the First World War, has in fact been away from interdependence. Nations have placed a higher priority on domestic stability and policies of full employment than on the maintenance of international links; they have sought to exert national control over their monetary and other economic policies. This is what the Keynesian revolution and its emphasis on management of the domestic economy is said to be all about. The same desire for greater latitude in domestic policy underlies the increasing popularity today of flexible over fixed exchange rates and the movement toward regional blocs. Mercantilists point out that in many industrialized economies there is, in fact, a renewed questioning of whether the further benefits of trade liberalization and interdependence are worth the costs. Interdependence accentuates domestic economic adjustment problems as economic instabilities in one economy spill over into others. It causes labor dislocations, may accentuate

---

[19]Calleo and Rowland.

[20]This paradox is analyzed by Eugene Staley, *World Economy in Transition* (New York: Council on Foreign Relations, 1939), chapter 6, especially p. 15.

inequalities of income distribution, and makes national planning more difficult. In short, according to these mercantilists, the world has reached the limits of interdependence and loss of national self-sufficiency.


## A CRITIQUE OF THE THREE MODELS

In this section . . . I evaluate the three models and draw from each what I consider to be important insights into the nature of contemporary international economic relations. This critique is not meant to cover all the points of each model but only those most directly relevant to this essay.


### Sovereignty at Bay

Fundamentally, the sovereignty-at-bay thesis reduces to a question of interests and power: Who has the power to make the world economy serve its interests? This point may be best illustrated by considering the relationship of the multinational corporation and the nation state. In the writings I identified with the sovereignty-at-bay thesis, this contest is held to be most critical.

On one side of this contest is the host nation state. Its primary source of power is its control over access to its territory, that is, access to its internal market, investment opportunities, and sources of raw material. On the other side is the corporation with its capital, technology, and access to world markets. Each has something the other wants. Each seeks to maximize its benefits and minimize its costs. The bargain they strike is dependent upon how much one wants what the other has to offer and how skillfully one or the other can exploit its respective advantages. In most cases, the issue is how the benefits and costs of foreign investments are to be divided between the foreign corporation and the host economy.

The sovereignty-at-bay thesis assumes that the bargaining advantages are and always will be on the side of the corporation. In contrast to the corporation's vast resources and flexibility, the nation state has little with which to bargain. Most nation states lack the economies of scale, indigenous technological capabilities, or native entrepreneurship to free themselves from dependence upon American (or other) multinational corporations. According to this argument, the extent to which nation states reassert their sovereignty is dependent upon the economic price they are willing to pay, and it assumes that when confronted with this cost, they will retreat from nationalistic policies.

In an age of rising economic expectations, the sovereignty-at-bay thesis rests on an important truth: A government is reluctant to assert its sovereignty and drive out the multinational corporations if this means a dramatic lowering of the standard of living, increasing unemployment, and the like. But in an age when the petroleum-producing states, through cooperation, have successfully turned the tables on the multinational corporations, it becomes obvious that the sovereignty-at-bay thesis also neglects the fact that the success of the multinational corporation has been dependent upon a favorable political order. As this order changes, so will the fortunes of the multinationals.

This political order has been characterized by an absence of unity on the part of the economies that have been host to American and other corporations. The divisions between and within the host countries themselves, and the influence of the American government, left the host countries with little power to bargain effectively or to increase their relative benefits from foreign investments in their countries. Thus, in the case of Canada, the competition between the provinces and particularly between English Canada and Quebec greatly weakened Canada's position vis-à-vis American investors. Similarly, nationalistic competition for investment has weakened attempts, such as the Andean Pact, that have tried to develop a common policy toward foreign corporations. But the importance of political factors in the overseas expansion of American corporations may be best illustrated by the case of Western Europe and Japan.

American corporations coveted both the Japanese and Western European markets; they have been able to establish hundreds of subsidiaries in the latter but only a few in the former. The reason for this difference is largely political. Whereas the former has one central government controlling access to Japan's internal market of 100 million population, six [now twelve] political centers have controlled access to the European Common Market. By interposing itself between powerful American corporations and intensely competitive Japanese firms that desired American capital and technology, the Japanese government has been able to prevent the latter from making agreements not desired by the government. As a consequence, the Japanese home market has been protected as the almost exclusive domain of Japanese industry. American firms have had, therefore, a strong incentive to license their technology to the Japanese or to form corporate arrangements in which the American firms were no more than a minor partner.

What the Japanese succeeded in doing was to break up the package of capital, technology, and entrepreneurship that foreign direct investment entails. The Japanese did not need the capital; they got the technology without managerial control by American corporations; entrepreneurship remained in the hands of Japanese. This Japanese example of untying the package and obtaining the technology, and in many cases the capital, required for development without loss of control has become an inspiration for economic nationalists in Latin America, Canada, and elsewhere.

In Western Europe, on the other hand, an American firm denied the right to establish a subsidiary in one Common Market country has had the option of trying another country and thereby still gaining access to the whole Market. Moreover, the strong desire of individual European countries for American investment has enabled American corporations to invest on very favorable terms. In certain cases, the firms have followed a divide-and-conquer strategy.

Denied permission by President de Gaulle to invest in France, General Motors established in Belgium one of the largest automobile assembly plants in the Common Market. Through this route, the corporation gained access to the French market as well as to other European markets.

In response to this situation, de Gaulle sought to obtain West German cooperation against American investment in EEC countries. Together these two most powerful of the Six could dictate a policy the others would be forced to accept. Through the instrumentality of the Franco-German Friendship Treaty of 1963, therefore, de Gaulle sought to form a Bonn-Paris axis directed against American hegemony in Western Europe.

Although there was sentiment in West Germany favorable to taking measures to limit the rapidly growing role of American subsidiaries in EEC countries, the West German government refused to take any action that might weaken the American commitment to defend Western Europe. The United States government not only reminded the West Germans that a continued American military presence was dependent upon West German support of measures to lessen the American balance-of-payments deficit, but it also pressured West Germany to increase its military purchases from the United States and to avoid competitive arrangements with France. Largely as a result of these American pressures, the Friendship Treaty was, in effect, aborted. The first serious counteroffensive of the nation state against the multinational corporation collapsed. It is clear, however, that the outcome of this tale would have been altogether different if West Germany had desired greater military and economic independence from the United States. In short, the American corporate penetration of the European Common Market [was] dependent upon the special security relationship of the United States and West Germany.

One could extend this type of analysis for the whole of American overseas investment. American investment in the Middle East, Africa, Latin America, Canada, and elsewhere has benefited from America's dominant position in the world. This position is now seriously challenged not only by the Soviet Union but by Japan, Western Europe, China, the Arabs, and Brazil in Latin America. Throughout these areas, economic nationalism is on the rise, threatening American investments and the income they bring to the United States. The thrust of this attack has been to break up the package of capital, technology, and management in order to acquire the first two without the third; the goal is greater local control through joint ventures, nationalization, and other policies. While the host countries are unlikely to "kill off" the American multinational corporations, they will increasingly make them serve local interests. This in turn will undoubtedly make direct investment abroad less attractive to American corporations.

A reversal of fortunes has already been seen in the case of the oil multinationals. The significance of the offensive by the oil-producing states against the large international oil companies is not merely that the price of oil to the United

States and to the rest of the world has risen but also that the United States may lose one of its most lucrative sources of investment income. The oil crisis and Arab oil boycott which followed the 1973 Arab-Israeli war was a profound learning experience for Europe, Japan, and even the United States. The oil boycott and the behavior of the oil multinationals set into motion a series of events that [helped to] transform national attitudes and policies toward the oil multinationals. The sudden appreciation of how vulnerable governments were to the policies of the oil multinationals and how far their "sovereignty" had been compromised awakened them to the inherent dangers of overdependence on the corporations and their policies. . . .

. . .[W]hen the multinationals were perceived as no longer supportive of the national interests of the United States, there was a reassertion of national sovereignty.

The case of oil and the oil multinationals is perhaps unique. Yet it does suggest that nation states have not lost their power or their will to act when they believe the multinational corporations are threatening their perceived national interests and sovereignty. The experience of the oil boycott and the role of the multinationals in carrying it out reveal the extent to which the operators and the success of these corporations have been dependent upon American power. With the relative decline of American power and the rise of governments hostile to American interests and policies, this case history at least raises the question of how the weakening of the Pax Americana will affect the status of other American multinational corporations throughout the world.

### Dependencia

The weakness of the dependencia, or ultraimperialism, model is that it makes at least three unwarranted assumptions. In the first place, it assumes much greater common interest among the noncommunist industrial powers—the United States, Western Europe, and Japan—than is actually the case. Secondly, it treats the peripheral states of Asia, Africa, Latin America, Canada, and the Middle East solely as objects of international economic and political relations. Neither assumption is true. As the first assumption is considered in more detail in the next section, let us consider the second for a moment.

After nearly two centuries, the passivity of the periphery is now past. The Soviet challenge to the West [during the Cold War] and the divisions among the capitalist powers themselves [gave] the emerging elites in the periphery room for maneuver. These nationalist elites are no longer ignorant and pliable colonials. Within the periphery, there [were] coalescing centers of power that will weigh increasingly in the future world balance of power: China, Indonesia, India, Iran, Nigeria, Brazil, and some form of Arab oil power. Moreover, if properly organized and led, such centers of power in control over a vital resource, as the experience of the Organization of Petroleum Exporting Countries (OPEC) demonstrates, may reverse the tables and make the core dependent upon the periphery. For the moment at least, a perceptible shift appears to be taking place in the global balance of economic power from the owners of capital to the owners of natural resources.[21]

The third unwarranted assumption is that a quasi-Marxist theory of capitalist imperialism is applicable to the relationship of developed and lesser-developed economies today. Again, I illustrate my argument by considering the role of the multinational corporation in the lesser-developed countries, since its allegedly exploitative function is stressed by almost all dependencia theorists.

The dependencia theory undoubtedly has a good case with respect to foreign direct investment in petroleum and other extractive industries. The oil, copper, and other multinationals have provided the noncommunist industrial world with a plentiful and relatively cheap supply of minerals and energy. The dramatic reversal of this situation by the oil-producing countries in 1973-74 and the steady rise of prices of other commodities support the contention that the producing countries were not getting the highest possible price and possibly not a just price for their nonrenewable resources. But what constitutes the just price for a natural endowment that was worthless until the multinationals found it is not an easy issue to resolve.

With respect to foreign direct investment in manufacturing, the case is far more ambiguous. Even if technological rents are collected, does the foreign corporation bring more into the economy in terms of technology, capital, and access to world markets than it takes out in the form of earnings? The research of Canadian, Australian, and other economists, for example, suggests that it does. They find no differences in the corporate behavior of domestic and foreign firms; on the contrary, foreign firms are given higher marks in terms of export performance, industrial research and development, and other economic indicators. Nonetheless, it would be naive to suggest that no exploitation or severe distortions of host economies have taken place.

On the other hand, it may not be unwarranted to suggest that a strong presumption exists for arguing that in terms of economic growth and industrial development, foreign direct investment in *manufacturing* is to the advantage of the host economy. A major cause of foreign direct investment is the sector-specific nature of knowledge and capital in the home economy.[22] In order to prevent a fall in their rate of profits through overinvesting at home or diversifying into unknown areas, American corporations frequently go abroad to guard

---

[21]See C. Fred Bergsten, "The Threat From the Third World," *Foreign Policy,* no. 11 (Summer 1973): 102–24.

[22]This point is developed in US Congress, Senate Committee on Labor and Public Welfare, *The Multinational Corporation and the National Interest* (report prepared for the Committee), 93rd Cong., 1st sess., 1973, Committee print.

against a lower rate of profit at home rather than because the superprofits abroad are attractive. Insofar as this is true, and there is sufficient evidence to warrant its plausibility, foreign direct investment benefits both the corporation and the host economy at a cost to other factors of production in the home economy. Thus, though the Marxists may be right in saying that there is an imperative for capitalism to go abroad, the effect is not to exploit but to benefit the recipient economy—a conclusion, by the way, that Marx himself would have accepted.[23]

While it is true that, in general, lesser-developed countries are economically dependent upon developed countries, the conclusions to be drawn from this fact are not self-evident. Are the countries underdeveloped because they are dependent, as dependencia theorists assume, or are they dependent because they are underdeveloped? China is underdeveloped, but it is not dependent upon any external power (though one could argue a historical case). As Benjamin Cohen has pointed out, the critical question is whether the poor are worse off economically because of this dependence.[24] Does dependence upon the developed countries entail a new loss, or foreclose opportunities of greater benefit to the economy of the undeveloped country? While the opportunity to exploit may be there, is it exercised? These are empirical questions to which no general answers can be given. Whether foreign direct investment is exploitative or beneficial depends on the type of investment, its terms, and the policies of the recipient economy itself.

The dependencia argument that foreign direct investment by multinational corporations preempts the emergence of an indigenous entrepreneurial middle class and creates a situation of technological dependence provides a clue to what is the central concern of dependence theory. Though most frequently couched solely in economic terms, the concepts of underdevelopment and dependence are more political than economic in nature. They involve an assessment of the political costs of foreign investment. They refer both to the internal political development of the recipient country and its external relations. As one of the better dependence theorists has put it, the problem "is not so much growth, i.e., expansion of a given socio-economic system, as it is 'development,' i.e., rapid and fundamental politico-socio-economic transformation."[25] In other words, foreign direct investment fosters an international division of labor that perpetuates underdevelopment and politico-economic dependencia.

This distinction between *growth* and *development* is crucial.[26] Economic growth is defined by most development economists simply as an increase in out-

---

[23]Karl Marx, "The Future Results of British Rule in India," in *Karl Marx on Colonialism and Modernization,* ed. Shlomo Avineri (Garden City, N.Y.: Doubleday, 1968), pp. 125–31.

[24]Cohen, chapter 6.

[25]This distinction is developed by Keith Griffin, *Underdevelopment in Spanish America* (Cambridge, Mass.: The M.I.T. Press, 1969), p. 117.

[26]For a more detailed analysis of the distinction, see J. D. Gould, *Economic Growth in History* (London: Methuen and Co., 1972), chapter 1.

put or income per capita; it is essentially a positive and quantitative concept. The concepts of development and underdevelopment as used by dependence theorists are primarily normative and qualitative; they refer to structural changes internal to the lesser-developed economy and in external relations with the developed world. Dependencia theory really calls for a change in the current international division of labor between the core and the periphery of the international economy, in which the periphery is a supplier of raw materials and whose industries are branch plants of the core's multinational corporations.

Whatever its economic merits, the dependencia model will continue to generate opposition against the structure of the contemporary world economy and the multinational corporation throughout the underdeveloped periphery of the world economy. As these peripheral societies grow in power, one can anticipate that they will undertake initiatives that attempt to lessen their dependence upon developed countries.

### Mercantilism

It seems to me that mercantilists either ignore or ascribe too little significance to certain primary facts. Although the relative power of the United States has declined, the United States remains the dominant world economy. The scale, diversity, and dynamics of the American economy will continue to place the United States at the center of the international economic system. The universal desire for access to the huge American market, the inherent technological dynamism of the American economy, and America's additional strength in both agriculture and resources—which Europe and Japan do not have—provide a cement sufficient to hold the world economy together and to keep the United States at its center.[27]

Furthermore, the United States can compensate for its loss of strength in one issue area by its continued strength in another. For example, the American economic position has indeed declined relative to Europe and Japan. Yet the continued dependence of Europe and Japan on the United States for their security provides the United States with a strong lever over the economic policies of each.

Thus, the fundamental weakness of the mercantilist model is the absence of a convincing alternative to an American-centered world economy. Western Europe, the primary economic challenger to the United States, remains internally divided; it is as yet unable to develop common policies in such areas as industry and energy or with respect to economic and monetary union. It is merely a customs union with a common agricultural policy. Moreover, like Japan, it continues to be totally dependent upon the United States for its security. As long as

---

[27]A forceful statement of this position is Raymond Vernon's "Rogue Elephant in the Forest: An Appraisal of Transatlantic Relations," *Foreign Affairs* 51 (April 1973): 573–87.

both Europe and Japan lack an alternative to their military and economic dependence on the United States, the mercantilist world of regional blocks lacks credibility.

The so-called energy crisis . . . affirmed this assessment. In the first place, the Arab oil boycott revealed the fragility of European unity. Threatened with the loss of vital supplies of Middle Eastern Oil, every nation fended for itself. But subsequently, despite their reluctance, both Europe and Japan participated in the American-sponsored Washington energy conference. The American purpose in calling the conference was in part to reinforce its Middle Eastern diplomacy. But the purpose was also to reassert America's influence over its allies and to forestall policies such as competitive currency depreciation, creation of new trade barriers, and bilateral deals that would tend to fragment the world economy. No doubt, too, as the French and others charged, the United States hoped to find a solution to the energy crisis that did not threaten the position of the American oil multinationals.

Calling for cooperation from its European and Japanese allies, the United States reminded them that their security still rested on American goodwill. Moreover, in the event of a conflict over oil, America's economic weapons were far superior. Thus chastened and reminded where power continued to rest, all but the French fell into line. For the time being at least, the United States demonstrated that it retained sufficient power to maintain intact an American-centered world economy.

Yet sufficient tensions and conflict of interests remain within this world economy to prevent one from dismissing so quickly the mercantilist thesis. Undoubtedly, the interstate conflict that will be the most vexing is the growing demand and competition for raw materials, particularly petroleum. . . . In the longer term, these changes have put the industrial powers in competition for . . . limited resources. They are also competing for export markets in order to finance these vital imports and for the capital the oil-producing states now have to invest. Thus, whereas in the past America's virtual control over the noncommunist world's supply of petroleum was a source of unity, today the United States is struggling with other industrial powers to insure its own position in a highly competitive environment.

In fact, one witnesses in the contemporary world the reemergence of the neo-Malthusian and Social Darwinist fears that swept industrial society and were so disruptive in the latter part of the nineteenth century. A common factor in the several imperialisms that burst forth after 1880 and fragmented the world economy was the growing fear of the potential consequences of exclusion from resources and markets. With expanding populations and productive industries believed to be dependent on foreign sources of food and raw materials, the insecurity of European states was magnified by the loss of their former relative self-sufficiency. The paradox of an interdependent world economy is that it creates sources of insecurity and competition. The very dependence of one state on another and the necessity for access to external markets and sources of raw materials cause anxieties and suspicions that exacerbate international relations.

The other reason for believing that there may be some validity in the mercantilist vision of the future is the weakening of political bonds between the United States, Western Europe, and Japan. During the height of the cold war, the foreign economic policies of these three countries were complementary. Potential conflicts over economic matters were subordinated to the necessity for political unity against the Soviet Union and China. The United States encouraged export-led growth and accepted anti-American trade discrimination in order to enable Japan and Europe to rebuild their shattered economies. Reciprocally, Japan and Europe supported the international position of the dollar. Through foreign direct investment, American corporations were able to maintain their relative share of world markets. Neither the Europeans nor the Japanese challenged America's dominant position with respect to the industrial world's access to vital raw materials, particularly Middle Eastern petroleum.

Until the early 1970s, the political benefits of this arrangement were regarded as outweighing the economic costs to each partner. With the movement toward détente and with the revival of the European and Japanese economies, however, the political benefits have receded in importance and the concern over costs has increased. As a consequence, the United States and its industrial partners now desire reforms of the world's trading and monetary systems that would enable each to pursue its own particular set of interests and to limit that of the others. For example, the United States has proposed reforms of the trade and monetary systems that would limit the ability of the Europeans and the Japanese to run up huge trade surpluses. Europe and Japan, for their part, desire to preserve this scope and to limit the privileges of the United States as world banker.

Regardless of the outcome of the negotiations over the future of the international monetary system, one thing is certain: whatever privilege is retained by the dollar will not be sufficient to enable the United States to behave as it has in the past. Gone are the days when the United States could run an immense balance-of-payments deficit in order to support foreign commitments, to buy up foreign assets, and at the same time pursue a full employment policy at home. It will no longer be able to expand overseas at a relatively low cost to the American standard of living. Having already lost its technological superiority and technological rents, the United States will have to finance its economic and military position abroad through currency devaluation and a current account surplus. Thus the cost of any effort to maintain US political and economic hegemony will bear upon the American people themselves. The weight and popular appreciation of this cost will profoundly alter American attitudes toward

America's world role and towards its European and Japanese allies. These changes in political interests and perceptions cannot but help to push the world in a mercantilistic direction. . . .

## CONCLUSION

In conclusion, what does this redistribution of world power imply for the future of the interdependent world economy? Today, the liberal world economy is challenged by powerful groups (especially organized labor) within the dominant economy; the dominant economy itself is in relative decline. With the decline of the dominant economic power, the world economy may be following the pattern of the latter part of the nineteenth century and of the 1930s and may be fragmenting into regional trading and monetary blocs. This would be prevented, of course, if the United States, as it is presently trying to do, were to reassert its waning hegemony over Western Europe, Japan, and the rest of the noncommunist world economy.

In the wake of the decline of American power and the erosion of the political base upon which the world economy has rested, the question arises whether the wisest policy for the United States is to attempt to reassert its dominance. May not this effort in the areas of trade, money, investment, and energy exacerbate the conflicts between the United States, Western Europe, and Japan? If so, a future that could be characterized increasingly by benign mercantilism could well be transformed into its more malevolent relative. If this were to happen, the United States and its allies would be the losers.

This admonition suggests that the United States should accept a greater regionalization of the world economy than it has been wont to accept in the past. It implies greater representation and voice for other nations and regional blocs in international economic organizations. While such a policy of retrenchment would no doubt harm the interests of American corporations and other sectors of the American economy, the attempt to hold on to rather than adjust to the shifting balance of world power could be even more costly for the United States in the long run.

In a world economy composed of regional blocs and centers of power, economic bargaining and competition would predominate. Through the exercise of economic power and various trade-offs, each center of the world economy would seek to shift the costs and benefits of economic interdependence to its own advantage. Trade, monetary, and investment relations would be the consequence of negotiations as nation states and regional blocs sought to increase the benefits of interdependence and to decrease the costs. This in fact has been the direction of the evolution of the international economy, from a liberal to a negotiated system, since the rise of large and rival economic entities in the latter part of the nineteenth century.

Therefore, debate and policy planning today should not focus on economic independence or dependence but on the nature and consequences of economic interdependence. Economic interdependence may take many forms; it may affect the welfare of nations in very different ways. Some will emphasize security; others, efficiency, low rates of inflation, or full employment. The question of how these benefits and costs will be distributed is at the heart of the increasingly mercantilistic policies of nation states in the contemporary world.

# 23

# THE INTERNATIONAL POLITICAL ECONOMY

## Miles Kahler

The dramatic changes that occurred in East–West politico-military affairs in the late 1980s masked important changes in the international political economy that are, according to Miles Kahler, "profound in their effects on world politics and irreversible in the medium term." Among them are structural changes, changes in the relationship between states and markets, and changes in the transnational character of markets and production. Kahler is professor in the Graduate School of International Relations and Pacific Studies at the University of California at San Diego and is author of *The Politics of International Debt* (1986).

I

For much of the 1980s, absent upheavals to match the oil price shocks of the 1970s, the international political economy was overshadowed by the volatility of East-West relations. This surface calm disguised sea-changes in international economic relations, changes profound in their effects on world politics and irreversible in the medium term. Some of these changes have been glacial in pace and difficult to discern. Other events that appeared cataclysmic, such as the stock market crash of October 1987, are as difficult to assess as heat light-

From Nicholas X. Rizopoulos, ed., *Sea Changes: American Foreign Policy in a World Transformed* (Council on Foreign Relations Press, 1990), pp. 94–109. Used by permission of the Council on Foreign Relations. Some footnotes have been deleted, and others have been renumbered to appear in consecutive order.

254

ning in a summer sky: an illusory warning or a genuine harbinger of storms to come? . . .

Four sea-changes in the international political economy will be discussed in the first section of this essay. The relative absence of change in the political organization of international economic relations—the dog that has not barked—will be briefly noted in the second section. Third, changes in the relationship between states and markets will be examined, particularly the intensified internationalization of financial markets and the globalization of production. Finally, an assessment will be attempted of the importance of all these changes for . . . the character of world politics. . . .

## II

*Structural Change: Shifts in Power and Place.* Two sea-changes became unmistakably clear in the 1980s—the rise of Japan and the divided economic prospects of the developing countries. The implications of two others—the leap toward further integration of the European Community and a more thoroughgoing incorporation of some centrally planned economies into the international economic order—will be fully apparent only in the next decade.

The rise of Japan has been an almost continuous process since the proclamation of the "Japanese miracle" in the early 1960s, but in its earlier manifestations, Japanese economic might expressed itself principally in a powerful export drive in manufactures. During the 1970s, that drive produced an array of trade disputes with the United States and Europe. In the decade that began with the publication of *Japan as Number One,*[1] however, Japan's economic reach expanded into high-technology industrial sectors and international finance, an expansion that fundamentally changed its bilateral relationship with the United States. As the Reagan administration's strategy of fiscal expansion produced massive American borrowing abroad, it became clear that Japan was home to the largest pool of exportable capital in the world economy. A share of that capital served to finance a yawning American payments deficit; other shares financed both a boom in foreign direct investment (in North America and Southeast Asia) and a more active stance in the debt crisis and development lending.

To some—let us call them the optimists—the new financial clout of Japan, added to an existing manufacturing prowess that increasingly encroaches on U.S. high-tech preserves, is not a serious concern. This group has advanced two broad arguments. A number of commentators claim that Japan's ascendancy is transitory. According to this view, Japan will gradually come to look like other industrialized countries. A stronger yen has already increased the volume of manufactured imports; external pressures (and pressures from its own con-

---

[1] Ezra Vogel, *Japan as Number One* (Cambridge, Mass.: Harvard University Press, 1979).

sumers) may force higher public spending, a greater attention to consumer welfare and a weakening of powerful lobbies (such as the agricultural lobby) that would erode Japan's peculiar pattern of policy and its position in the international economy.

A second group of optimists argues that the international implications of Japan's rise have been overstated, since its "power portfolio"—heavily dependent on a cluster of export industries and its capital exports—is not diversified in the fashion of the United States. Hence, Japan will continue to need American military protection and American markets as much as the United States needs Japanese capital and technology. The result: an intensification of interdependence rather than American dependence on Japan.

For many of these observers, the United States must "manage" the bilateral relationship as well as Japan's new role in the world economy until Japan's economic trajectory converges with that of other industrialized economies.

Increasingly, however, a second set of arguments has been heard both in the United States and in Europe. Framed in military metaphors, such as "containment," and hedged by homilies on the importance of U.S.–Japanese ties, these new "revisionist" critics paint a more ambiguous portrait of Japanese aims and capabilities: the ambitious hegemonic power-to-be rather than the acquiescent partner. Japan not only is seen as the first plausible aspirant to that role in the economic sphere since 1945; it also is viewed as a new-model political economy, one that does *not* work like Western economies and one that will remain closed unless more forceful pressure is exerted by its trading partners or an entirely new structure of managed trade is created.[2]

A second sea-change was less apparent . . . in the 1980s: the widening gap in economic performance within the developing world. The 1970s seemed to herald an irreversible push toward economic and political influence on the part of the Third World as a collectivity, as well as on the part of "new influentials," such as Saudi Arabia and Brazil. The 1980s saw the deflation of those hopes with the collapse and only partial recovery of commodity (including oil) prices, the shocks of high real interest rates and an abrupt decline in bank lending in the early 1980s. The lingering debt crisis destroyed the image of the homogeneous Third World, an image that may never have corresponded with reality. In the 1980s heavily indebted countries in Latin America and sub-Saharan Africa experienced the worst decade in terms of economic performance since the Great Depression; the countries of Asia maintained higher growth rates and export performance. The divide is no longer between middle-income and poor developing countries (the Third and Fourth Worlds of the 1970s): India's performance

---

[2]Although the diagnoses and prescriptions of these observers differ considerably, the Japanese have singled out a "Gang of Four" who espouse this more pessimistic view: James Fallows, Chalmers Johnson, Clyde Prestowitz and Karel van Wolferen. For an excellent summary, see Chalmers Johnson, "Rethinking Japanese Politics: A Godfather Reports," *Freedom at Issue* (November-December 1989), pp. 5–11.

in the 1980s was stronger than Peru on most measures; China's better than Brazil's.

Is this new divide the result of indebtedness, taken on in the preceding period of high commodity prices and easy credit, coupled with drastically altered world economic conditions in the early 1980s (high real interest rates, deep recession, plummeting commodity prices) that were beyond the control of developing economies? Or is indebtedness itself a principal symptom of a syndrome of national economic policies that were not successfully altered in the 1980s, an alteration made even more difficult by the burden of debt?

Whatever explanation is advanced, the North-South cleavage changed in the 1980s. Conflicts continue between successful exporters, such as South Korea or Taiwan, and the industrialized countries, responding to their threatened industries. The larger debtors have repeatedly gone to the brink with their creditors, private and public. These patterns of conflict, however, rarely overlap: developing countries no longer aspire to a unified bargaining stance across issue-areas. While some newly industrializing countries confront a transition to rich-country status, other developing countries scramble to escape decades of economic stagnation and an increasingly marginal status in the world economy.

Looking to the immediate future, two sea-changes in the world economy appear likely to occur in the 1990s. The communist states were long excluded (and excluded themselves) from full participation in the institutions of international economic management. The Cold War and the organization of their economies by central planning rather than market principles made integration with the capitalist world economy difficult. Although some socialist states (notably Yugoslavia and Romania) found their way into the International Monetary Fund, the World Bank and the General Agreement on Tariffs and Trade after demonstrating their independence from the Soviet Union, it was not until the entry of Hungary and China into the Bretton Woods institutions in the 1980s that greater participation was clearly linked to a wider program of internal economic reforms. Now Poland has been tipped as a major recipient of IMF and World Bank lending, and the Soviet Union has made clear its own closer integration with the capitalist West.

The significance of renewed momentum toward closer economic integration on the part of the European Community is less clear, and it will depend in part on the future course of events in Eastern Europe and the Soviet Union. The Single European Act will clearly have a substantial impact in the area of "negative integration": removal of remaining barriers to the free movement of goods, capital and labor within the European Community. Its results in other spheres appear more conditional. Movement toward an economic and monetary union, surpassing the relative success of the European Monetary System, could founder on British opposition and German lack of enthusiasm. More important, dramatic changes in Eastern Europe could absorb the energies of Community members, particularly Germany, at a time when the inclusion of new members might slow the motor of integration in any case. In addition, the tug to the East could shift European attention from the international economic sphere, where Community institutions have reinforced common policies, to the political and strategic sphere, where joint positions have been harder to construct.

### III

*The Organization of International Economic Relations: The Weight of the Past.* In contrast to these structural shifts in the centers of international economic power and the continuing evolution of market integration that is considered below, it is worth noting that international institution-building and institutional change have not kept pace. The international organizations that crowned the postwar international economic order remain in place; their persistence symbolizes that the international rules of the game have not collapsed during two decades of economic shock. Nevertheless, their role has been repeatedly questioned and even ignored during the past decade. Even such an apparent exception as the role played by the IMF and the World Bank in managing the debt crisis appears less exceptional in the most recent phase of the crisis, as banks and debtors have moved independently toward debt reduction. . . .

The GATT has served as a useful locus for agreements on trade liberalization; negotiations under its aegis have also served as a means of staving off protectionist demands in the United States and other industrialized countries. Its greatest triumph—dramatic lowering of tariffs among Europe, Japan and the United States—had been accomplished by the end of the 1970s, however, and during the 1980s, crucial trade bargains were often struck outside the GATT. (Voluntary restraints on Japanese automobile exports to the United States were only one example.) Although the most recent trade negotiations, the Uruguay Round, have widened the trade liberalization agenda to include agriculture and services as well as strengthening the GATT, the success of the negotiations remains in doubt.

Official American attitudes toward international economic institutions are certainly warmer now than they were at the beginning of the 1980s; President Bush's proposal to use the World Bank and the IMF to assist Poland is only the latest indication of this trend. Nevertheless, the overall stance of the United States and the other major capitalist countries has been measured for two reasons: their self-proclaimed fiscal bind, which (they claim) makes it increasingly difficult to extract resources from legislatures and electorates to support international institutions, and their ideological resistance to public intervention in international markets.

The most important threat to the institutional fabric, however, is neither a scarcity of resources nor ideological skepticism. The threat arises, paradoxically, from one indicator of institutional success: the growing—and increasingly heterogeneous—membership of these organizations. Developing countries, including such long-standing holdouts as Mexico, are acceding to the GATT in increasing numbers; socialist states have gained entry to the key organizations or, like the Soviet Union, are seeking membership. Apart from the challenges to cooperative solutions that sheer numbers pose for these organizations, heterogeneity of political and economic systems calls into question postwar principles of organization, such as nondiscrimination and liberalization, in a world that is no longer dominated by mixed economies of the "Atlantic" variety. Doubts about the incorporation of Japan and the newly industrializing East Asian countries were noted above; the possibilities for short-term transformation in the Council for Mutual Economic Assistance (COMECON) economies can also be viewed with skepticism.

Can an international order be created with this degree of national diversity? It is a question that was originally avoided by the self-exclusion of many developing countries and the division of the world between American and Soviet blocs. In the 1990s, the question will require an answer.

## IV

*The Power of States and the Force of Markets.* Underlying these concerns over the repositioning of states in the international economy and the efficacy of international institutions are the ongoing integration of international markets and the changing strategies of international corporations. Integration has grown most rapidly in the financial markets, where the growth of international financial transactions has consistently outstripped the growth of world trade. The level of international financial integration was clearly demonstrated in the synchronized crashes that followed Wall Street's plunge in October 1987. The interconnectedness of such markets has existed since the birth of capitalism, but the current speed of transmission, closely tied to advances in computer and telecommunications technology, and the scale of financial flows across national boundaries are clearly unprecedented and deserve the label of sea-change.

The implications of financial integration for the global economy and the international financial system are not clear. . . . For national governments, however, the effects are not obscure: their autonomy in setting economic policies is increasingly constrained, as capital controls become less effective and financial markets read their political and economic missteps with shorter and shorter time lags. Proponents of market perfection view this as a positive development, one that will keep wayward governments on the path of policy rectitude. A less optimistic view would note the blindness of the financial markets in the years preceding the debt crisis, and their tendency to overshoot in both the optimistic and the pessimistic directions on the basis of often incomplete information.

International markets for goods were marked during the 1980s by both liberalization and greater management of trade on the part of governments responding to protectionist pressures. The early years of the decade—years of deep recession, sharp upward movements of the dollar and an unprecedented American current account deficit—witnessed a move toward greater American and European efforts to allocate international market shares in key sectors, such as steel and autos. The often predicted collapse of the trading system did not occur, however; a threat of uncontrollable protectionist pressures in the early 1980s spurred governments to open the Uruguay Round of trade negotiations. Despite rising trade barriers in certain sectors, the growth of world trade resumed after the 1981–1982 recession, and the principal targets of protectionist measures, particularly Japan and the newly industrializing countries, continued their export success. Industrialized governments also moved to lower trade barriers with some of their principal trading partners: the United States and Canada, Australia and New Zealand, the 1992 project of the European Community.

Technology had not undermined closure so clearly as in the financial markets, but governments did confront greater sophistication on the part of traders if their attempts to restrain trade distorted the market too greatly; in developing countries, whole sectors moved to the black market economy in part to evade import and export controls; in such sophisticated sectors as semiconductors, "gray markets" quickly developed to satisfy demand in the United States after the 1986 U.S.–Japan Semiconductor Agreement.

Although the postwar international economic order had always included an ideological commitment by the dominant powers to liberalization in the movement of goods and capital, the free movement of labor has remained a jealously guarded sphere of national authority. In the last decade, however, it has become increasingly clear that better international communication and burgeoning mass tourism have undermined barriers to immigration at a time when the disparities between rich and poor countries remain enormous. Even a society as hostile to immigration as Japan has found it impossible to stop illegal immigration when its own businesses collude to gain cheap labor. Outside the richest countries, brain drains and labor outflows become serious restraints on national governments, particularly in the developing world; economic downturns and political repression no longer produce only the temporarily unemployed or refugees who later return to their homes. Another option, permanent emigration, is now available, as Central America, Peru, China and East Germany have all learned of late.

The differing pace of integration in markets for capital, goods and labor has influenced the increasingly complex strategies of transnational corporations. The global organization of production in certain sectors, such as oil, extends back many decades; but the 1980s was the decade in which the global factory came into its own. Seeking ways to put their capital and rapidly eroding technological advantages together with low-cost labor, firms in the industrialized countries developed suppliers and production sites throughout the world. They attempted to improve their competitive position through cooperative arrangements (such as licensing agreements and joint ventures) with firms that may appear to be their rivals in other settings.

The pursuit of such strategies, by global giants as well as middling firms, has further blurred the distinction between "home" country and "host" country. These cross-cutting corporate interests have also complicated any definition of national economic interest. Should the United States encourage Japanese investment in smaller, American, high-technology firms, for example? Are American corporations in Japan part of the U.S. economy situated abroad, or are they essentially Japanese firms? Such a web of private connections at first appears to create important pressures for liberalization in government policies: the complexity of relations among firms makes efforts at international restriction less likely to be effective or beneficial. On the other hand, nationalist political responses to these new relationships—particularly foreign investment—could provoke a backlash that will create renewed pressure for controls.


## V

*Sea-Changes and the Transformation of World Politics.* That this intensified if uneven integration of markets in capital, goods and labor could be reversed by some future shock—major financial crisis, global economic depression, or war—is a possibility that has haunted liberal memories since the end of World War II. A more pertinent question is whether such dis-integration could arise from the actions of governments, perhaps through unwitting exercises in economic brinksmanship that end up unraveling, in a perverse game of tit for tat, the fabric of economic openness. Few governments are willing to argue any longer for the benefits of economic closure, whatever their skepticism about the stability of markets or the effects of external liberalization on more vulnerable groups or sectors. Governments will certainly continue to shape the rules of the game to protect the interests of politically powerful and less mobile sectors of the economy. Calculated measures in favor of dis-integration, however, seem unlikely.

If the configurations described persist, some might be tempted to argue that they will constitute a sea-change in the very character of world politics, profound enough to contribute to an "end of history." Such predictions would have seemed outlandish at the beginning of the 1980s, when the newest chapter of the Cold War intensified concerns over military dangers. Today, however, one may well ask whether relations among states are not characterized by a permanent shift toward goals of economic welfare and a concomitant rise in the importance of economic resources and economic instruments in interstate competition. Such a change is linked not only to those international economic developments already mentioned, but also to reduction in superpower rivalry and widespread, if not yet universal, internal political liberalization.

Thus . . . we should see changes in the international economy not as producing an inevitable resolution to age-old problems of interstate conflict, but as intimately tied to that conflict, as they have been since the birth of capitalism. The ever changing economic fortunes of nation-states affect their strategic position as well as their perception of national security. Internationalized though they may be, markets will continue to confront fragmented political authority. Whatever the sea-changes in the international economy, they will take place within these deeply embedded features of international relations, for they have not yet transformed them. . . .

# 24

# THE NEW MEANING OF EUROPEAN UNITY

## Donald J. Puchala

**In this essay Donald J. Puchala traces the evolutionary steps that have led to the economic (and, potentially, political) integration of Western Europe. Drawing on the expectations and vision that inspired European leaders to forge a unified economic system by 1992, Puchala assesses, in light of integration theory, the prospects, challenges, and implications of European unity in the 1990s. Puchala is professor and director of the Institute of International Studies at the University of South Carolina. Among his many publications is _Fiscal Harmonization in the European Communities_ (1984).**

Whatever happened to Europessimism? As the twelve countries of the European Community move rapidly to complete their continent-sized common market by the end of 1992, foundations have been laid for even closer economic union, for strengthened Community institutions, and for wider-ranging common positions on issues of global concern. Meanwhile, potential new members are cuing to join the European Community, and the Twelve are leading the way toward bringing their former East European communist neighbors into the capitalist world economy. Some wary pundits are anticipating an eventual bloc of European economic and political power that will dwarf even the United States of America.[1]

Adapted especially for this book from "Integration Theory and the Study of International Relations" in Richard L. Merritt and Bruce M. Russett, eds., from _National Development to Global Community: Essays in Honor of Karl W. Deutsch_ (London: Allen & Unwin, 1981), pp. 145–164. Used by permission of Donald J. Puchala.
[1]Flora Lewis, "The Menace of Trade Blocs," _The New York Times,_ October 23, 1988, p. 23.

What is most surprising about Europe's race toward greater unity in the 1990s is that very few analysts saw it coming. In fact, in the 1970s conventional wisdom had it that Western European integration had run its course. European economic cooperation began in the era of the Marshall Plan between 1948 and 1952, deepened among France, West Germany, Italy, Belgium, the Netherlands and Luxembourg with the opening of the European Coal and Steel Community in 1952, and then deepened further with the European Atomic Energy Community and the multisectoral European Economic Community (EEC) in 1958. In 1967 the executives of the three organizations were merged to create the European Community (EC). Cooperation broadened in 1973 when the United Kingdom, Ireland and Denmark joined the EC.

But then the "double whammy" of the petroleum shocks of the 1970s, which sent EC countries scurrying in different directions for energy security, and the stagflation of the 1970s followed by the world recession of the early 1980s, which again affected EC countries differentially, severely sapped Europeans' capacities to cooperate with each other. From these adversities analysts concluded that EC was after all only a "fair weather" arrangement, that economic integration had not strengthened European economies, or sufficiently cured the "euroscelorsis" of technological backwardness, to carry Europe through world economic storms. European unity, many believed, could not recapture its earlier momentum.

Why the experts were in error in pronouncing the premature demise of Western European integration is complicated. For one thing, academic experts, or integration theorists, including the present author, became intellectual prisoners of their abstract models of "integration processes" and concluded that if Western Europe was not evolving in theoretically prescribed directions then Western Europe was not evolving at all. Obviously, in the 1970s Western Europe was not evolving toward a supranational political federation, nor were Western Europeans shedding their respective nationalities, and from such observations integration theories predicted that Western Europe had to be going nowhere. Actually, it was probably the theories that were going nowhere.[2]

What went largely unnoticed by all but a few observers was that while Western European *capacities* to cooperate during the 1970s and the early 1980s were constrained, Western Europeans' *will* to cooperate was not greatly diminished. Revealingly, the will to unite Western Europe into a political federation never disappeared. During the 1970s it survived in the European Commission, which initiated a series of studies focused on institutional reform in the European Communities, all of which quite predictably concluded that EC institutions needed to be strengthened. Political will to press on with European unity also resided in the European Parliament, particularly among Altiero Spinelli and

---

[2]Ernst B. Haas, *The Obsolescence of Regional Integration Theory* (Berkeley, Calif.: University of California, Institute of International Studies, 1975). *Passim.*

his colleagues of the Crocodile Club who campaigned in 1980 for a new treaty of European Union. Most importantly, political will for greater unity continued in the policies of several governments, notably Italy, Belgium, the Netherlands, France and West Germany, and it was this that produced the Single European Act in 1985 which relaunched European integration. At the same time the European business community and the EC's technological elites refused to retreat into economic nationalism despite the centrifugal pressures of the 1970s. They wanted not to abandon the Common Market but to *complete* it, and their determination along with some British imagination helped to initiate the course of action that has been driving Europe toward and beyond "1992."[3]

### THE IMPLICATIONS OF GREATER EUROPEAN ECONOMIC UNITY

The purpose of this essay is to project some of the likely implications of the relaunching of Western European integration in the 1990s. Assuming that there will not be economic or political shocks in the years immediately ahead that will knock Europe off of its unifying trajectory, greater continental economic and political cohesion will unquestionably enhance Europe's world influence in the early 21st Century. An expanded world economic and political role will be of benefit to Europe, and probably also to the rest of the world, though more about this later.

What the European Community is specifically attempting to do under its 1992 program is to establish a single market by fully integrating the economies of twelve countries. The European Economic Community established by the Treaty of Rome in 1958 created a customs union among six countries—France, West Germany, Italy, Belgium, the Netherlands and Luxembourg—meaning that tariffs and other trading restrictions among these countries were removed and a common external tariff was erected around the group. Later, some steps were taken to open internal borders to flows of labor, agricultural policy was internationalized and some steps were also taken toward internationally harmonizing indirect taxes. In 1973, as noted, the United Kingdom, Ireland and Denmark joined the EC; in 1980 Greece joined and in 1985 Spain and Portugal joined.

However, the main problem with the European Economic Community, as it turned out, was that the Treaty of Rome did not actually create a "common market," because, despite the absence of tariffs, conditions of production, distribution and exchange varied from member-country to member-country. The White Paper drafted by EC Commissioner Arthur Cockfield in 1985 set forth a plan for

---

[3]Pierre-Henri Laurent, "Forging the European Technology Community," in *The Technical Challenges and Opportunities of a United Europe,* Michael Steinberg, ed. (London: Pinter Publishers, 1990), pp. 59–67.

standardizing intra-Community economic conditions by the end of December, 1992.[4] The report set three main objectives for the completion of the common market. It called first for removing physical barriers at intra-Community borders—i.e. customs houses, transshipment points and all of the delay-causing and money-costing bureaucratic procedure that interrupts the smooth flow of intra-Community commerce. Because every member country has its own customs procedures and paperwork requirements for cargoes moving across its frontiers, typical haulings through the Community consume needless hours of stopping and waiting time and reams of redundant paper, all at the expense of speed and efficiency.

Second, the plan for 1992 looked to the removal of countless technical barriers to the flow of goods and services across intra-Community national borders. Here the focus was on almost everything that made the Common Market uncommon: differing national product standards, labelling standards, health and veterinary restrictions, certification requirements, public procurement practices, and countless other nationally peculiar rules, regulations and devices that served deliberately or defacto as non-tariff barriers to intra-Community economic intercourse. According to the liberal rules for the post-1992 European common market, goods, services or marketing conditions that proved to be acceptable anywhere in the EC were thereby rendered acceptable everywhere. This also applied to public procurement practices, where eligibility to bid anywhere became eligibility to bid everywhere.

Third, differing national fiscal systems were to be harmonized. Neutralizing the trade distorting effects of differing national tax structures has long been an aspiration of the European Community. What the 1992 plan mandated was the standardization of rates for the tax on value-added, the Community's common sales tax enacted in 1967. Later would come the standardization of excise taxes and eventually movement toward common income and corporate taxes in the context of a common fiscal policy.

The Commission White Paper was adopted in 1985 and by 1990 the multi-faceted assault on physical barriers, technical barriers and fiscal barriers to the free flow of international commerce in the EC was in full swing. Procedures for international harmonization are being written by the European Commission into a set of "directives," which, after approval by the European Council of Ministers, become mandatory for the member governments. Community authorities in Brussels have prepared some 279 such directives, two-thirds of which had been passed into European Law by the autumn of 1990, and about one-third of which had by that time also been written in national law in respective member-

[4]Commission of the European Communities, "Completing the Internal Market" [White Paper from the Commission to the European Council] COM(85) 310, June 14, 1985. See also the commentary on the White Paper in Michael Calingaert, *The 1992 Challenge: Development of the Community's Internal Market* (Washington: National Planning Association, 1988), pp. 20–29; *Single European Act,* Bull. E.C., Supplement 2/86.

countries.[5] By all indications, the drive to complete the common market by 1992 was running ahead of schedule.

The overall result of executing the 1992 plan will be to greatly facilitate transnational commerce in the European Community. As a result of the international economic integration that the directives will foster in the years after 1992, Western Europe can expect a sharp increase in intra-regional international trade (in both products and services) and ensuing positive impacts on national incomes. The European Commission has estimated an immediate boost in trade by over 20% and a quickly registered 6–7% rise in total Community GNP.[6] These increases in intra-regional economic activity will be differentially felt in different countries and in different industries, but expert consensus now predicts that no countries will be adversely affected. Nationally speaking, everybody is expected to gain something in the aggregate from the initial economic effects of 1992.

Preparing for 1992 and then operating most effectively on the new common market are going to require considerable adjustments in business strategies and behavior. Advantage will accrue for example to firms that are able to realize economies of scale and to firms that are linked into distribution networks in other countries. There will also be advantages to those who produce products that are unaffected by culturally conditioned consumption habits or national tastes. Much of this is to say that advantages will accrue to large, multinationally organized companies. Accordingly, there is presently considerable merger activity afoot in Western Europe. Some firms are merging internationally to operate on the single European market; others are merging intra-nationally to command larger national market segments before the multinationals penetrate after 1992.

There is also the beginning now of a predictable rationalization of production and distribution in Western Europe. Manufacturers are looking to locate their production facilities in the lowest-cost regions of the European Community, with the confidence that barriers to cross-border transport will be minimized and that product standards will be harmonized. At the moment, there is considerable movement toward locating plants in Spain and Ireland in order to take advantage of lower wage rates in these countries. There is also a not unreasonable expectation that the efficiencies realized through economies of scale, rationalized production and distribution, enhanced investment in research and development stemming from bigness and keener marketing strategies required by keener competition will all result in broader choice and lower prices for Western European consumers.

[5]Commission of the European Communities, "Fifth Report of the Commission to the Council and the European Parliament Concerning the Implementation of the White Paper on the Completion of the Internal Market." COM(90) 90 Final, Brussels 28 March 1990; Commission of the European Communities, "A New Community Standards Policy," Brussels, 1988.

[6]Calingaert, *op. cit.,* pp. 66ff; Paolo Cecchini, *The European Challenge 1992* (Aldershot, U.K.: Wildwood House, 1988), Chp. 1 and *passim.*

But the changes that 1992 will bring will also result in some economic dislocation. There will be, for example, imbalances in the supply and demand for labor as the locations of production shift to take advantage of open borders. It is to be expected that some of the poorer EC countries will benefit from increased demand for their lower-wage labor, while some of the better off EC countries may suffer increased unemployment at least in the short run. There is not likely to be very much international labor migration because cultural and linguistic differences have rendered labor relatively immobile in Western Europe. Instead labor movement in response to 1992 will probably take the form of agriculture to industry movement in the southern European Community countries. There could also be a good deal of white collar mobility, and resulting social impermanence, as firms merge and move their production facilities to meet new marketing conditions.

The fate of small and medium-sized firms on the completed common market is uncertain. They could very well benefit generally from the increased consumer demand that the completed common market will generate. They might also find their fortunes enhanced to the extent that they are suppliers to the multinationals. But, small and medium-sized firms could be hurt for the opposite of all of reasons that the new single market is advantageous to the giants. What is probable is that the distribution of costs and gains among differently sized firms will be sector or industry specific, and a good deal will depend upon firms' preparations for 1992.

## POLITICAL COLLABORATION TO 1992 AND BEYOND

The economic consequences of 1992 are only part of what is likely to happen to the European Community in the years ahead. There is a good chance that economic unification of an even farther-reaching nature than that planned for 1992 will emerge in the 1990s. Negotiations were scheduled for late 1990 aimed at the creation of a European Monetary Union (EMU). When established, possibly as early as 1994, the EMU would eventually inaugurate a common European currency, controlled by a European Central Bank, called the Eurofed, and managed by a common monetary policy. Experts contend that EMU can operate successfully only if the national economic policies of the Twelve are also integrated, or at least closely coordinated.

Many in Western Europe today believe that the 1990s will also see further steps toward political unity among the Twelve. In fact, in April 1990, French President François Mitterand and German Chancellor Helmut Kohl jointly called for new steps toward political union among the EC countries. An ensuing summit meeting of EC leaders endorsed the negotiation of a new treaty of political union. Those who seek to push Europe toward greater unity beyond 1992 imagine a sequence of steps that if taken and successful will transform the European Community into a loose confederation of states. It will not be a United

States of Europe with the sovereignty of the separate states superseded and a federal government installed. What might be attainable, however, is a system of continuous, very close coordination among the national governments, facilitated and to some extent orchestrated by a set of stronger central institutions. At the very least the popularly elected European Parliament would be granted greater budgetary powers, and possibly some real legislative prerogatives as well.

Evolution toward a common European foreign policy, in train since 1970, will also continue.[7] The Single European Act of 1985 formally brought the European Commission into the EC foreign policy process, which is called European Political Cooperation (EPC). This is significant because it adds the coordinating and consensus-building skills, plus the staffing resources, of the Commission to the EPC process and in so doing adds to its efficiency. Over the last several years the European Community has arrived at common policies on a broad range of international issues including Palestine and the Middle East, Afghanistan, Central America, Namibia, Cambodia, disarmament and chemical weapons, human rights, the protection of the global environment and relations with Eastern Europe and the Soviet Union. The Twelve also acted in unity in response to the Iraqi invasion of Kuwait in the summer of 1990, which, one foreign minister noted, contributed more to European political integration than years of constitution drafting.

Typically the Twelve announce common foreign policies through appointed spokesmen, promote them through the United Nations and other multilateral channels and stand by them in separate bilateral dealings. The collective stands of the Twelve project the Community as a power in world affairs. The world increasingly recognizes this. Western Europeans know it, and like it. The Twelve, which now embrace a new and more powerful, reunited Germany, appear to have every intention of moving forward in their efforts to formulate Community-wide foreign policy and to project it out into the international system in the 1990s.

Collective Western European defense centered in the European Community is being seriously discussed.[8] For some of those who imagine an eventual loose confederation of Western European states, the completion of a common defense policy is to be the culminating achievement. Presently, though, there remains a certain amount of murkiness surrounding the meaning of Western European security in a post–cold war setting. Among other issues the ongoing dialogue involves the relationship between security policy and disarmament policy, and the relationship between NATO and other frameworks for Western European collective defense and all-European security.

---

[7]Roy H. Ginsberg, *Foreign Policy Actions of the European Community* (Boulder, Colo.: Lynne Rienner Publishers, 1989), pp. 55–116.

[8]John S. Westerlund and Volker F. Fritze, "The Franco-German Brigade," *Defense and Diplomacy,* VII (June, 1989), pp. 24–28; Jacques S. Gansler and Charles Paul Henning, "European Acquisition," *Defense and Diplomacy* VII (June, 1989), pp. 29–35 & 62.

How likely is it that further economic and political steps toward European unity will be taken beyond 1992? As noted, European Monetary Union, the Eurofed, a common currency, a common monetary policy and closely coordinated economic policies are nearly certain to come about.[9] The only question here is how soon? Beyond that, as I wrote elsewhere:

> Expectations have always been somewhat ahead of accomplishment regarding European unity and there is therefore some call for caution. On the other hand, the current relaunching has a great deal supporting it and pushing it forward that was missing earlier. For one thing, the British are on board. Despite persistent opposition to bureaucratization, centralization and over-regulation at the Community level, the current British government is now committed to moving forward toward greater European unity. British support is important, partly because British opposition can be very destructive, and partly because the other major member states are already strongly in favor of pushing forward. Second, Western European public opinion continues to be very much in favor of moving farther, and faster toward greater political unity, albeit in a democratic manner. Third, the current international climate facilitates further progress for "Europe" because there are no major East-West issues presently distracting Western European foreign policy attentions. In addition, the detente climate has opened opportunities for European global diplomacy that, if Western Europe is to take advantage, make greater unity almost imperative. Finally, there is "Europe 1992" itself: not the technicalities of it, but rather the psychology of it. 1992 has thus far been a tremendous confidence-builder for the Western Europeans. As one UN diplomat phrased it 'Europe is on a roll.' Just as surely as movement toward greater unity was impossible during the years of Europessimism, not moving toward greater unity is almost impossible in the current climate of Euro-optimism.[10]

## THE NEW EUROPE AND THE WORLD

There is ample reason to believe that the external impacts of a more economically integrated and politically unified Western Europe will be benign. However, this does not mean that the power and posture of a new Europe will be unchallenging to outsiders.

Early anxieties voiced in the United States and also felt in Japan that post-1992 Europe would be a closed economic fortress have dissipated. Close monitoring of the 1992 directives, and the negotiating away of ambiguities and inequities regarding outsiders, leave most experts assured that access to the post-1992 single market will be relatively free, and that opportunities available for foreign investors and traders will approximate those available to the Europeans themselves. North American and Japanese businessmen are preparing to com-

---

[9] Elke Theil, "From the Internal Market to an Economic and Monetary Union," *Aussenpolitik,* I (1989), pp. 66–75.

[10] Donald J. Puchala, "The Economic and Political Meaning of Europe 1992," in Michael Steinberg (ed.), op. cit., p. 25. On the matter of popular support for moving toward greater unity, see Commission of the European Communities, *Eurobarometer* No. 30, December, 1988, pp. 45–51.

pete on the Europeans' new market, and many will do well. The challenge to outsiders is that European firms, rendered more competitive by the rigors of their new economic environment, will be doing increasingly well on external markets after 1992. North Americans in particular will face much stiffer import competition from EC firms in the future. The Europeans are coming, and economically vulnerable outsiders need to prepare!

Politically, the collective stances of the Twelve on world issues will most likely be more frequent and more forceful as political cohesion intensifies and common foreign policy becomes the norm. If the major themes and emphases thus far exhibited in common EC positions prevail in the years ahead, the world can expect that Europe will be a force for order via multilateral diplomacy and the creation and enforcement of international law. Europe will also be a force for human rights, the furtherance of democracy, the protection of earth's natural environment, and the alleviation of human misery. The moderation and stability that Europe has been collectively projecting into world affairs may prove very important if the world is challenged to respond to economic and political crises in Eastern Europe and to the further decay of the Soviet state.

But, in light of experience thus far, there is no reason to expect that common European positions and the projection of new European power will necessarily serve the interests of the United States in the years ahead. To date, a good many of the EC's collective stances have challenged U.S. policy, as on the issue of Palestine, where the Twelve opposed U.S. ostracism of the PLO, and on the issue of Nicaragua where the Twelve condemned U.S. actions. During the Cold War period, European positions were often politically located between U.S. and Soviet positions, and so too has Europe collectively often come out between the United States and Third World interlocutors. By all indications Europeans will continue to have positions of their own, and many of these will not go down well in Washington.

"As for Western Europe," wrote James Oliver Goldsborough in 1982, "it has today come back from the abyss, culturally, morally, and politically." That Europe is back, and that Europe is strong are among the very few things we can say with certainty about the emerging international political architecture of the twenty-first century. There is now good reason to expect that a politically united and globally interested and active Europe will be a main pillar of this new world architecture.

---

[11]James Oliver Goldsborough, *Rebel Europe: How Can America Live with a Changing Continent?* (New York: Macmillan, 1982), p. 10.

# 25

# NO MORE NICs

## Robin Broad and John Cavanagh

**For many years the export-led path to economic development pursued with great success by the newly industrializing countries (NICs) has been promoted as a model for other developing nations. Robin Broad and John Cavanagh argue the model is of doubtful relevance due to structural changes in the global political economy and the rise of protectionist sentiments in the industrializing countries. Broad has been a Council on Foreign Relations fellow and a resident associate of the Carnegie Endowment. She is author of *Unequal Alliance: The World Bank, the International Monetary Fund, and the Philippines* (1988). John Cavanagh is a former United Nations official and directs the world economy project of the Institute for Policy Studies. He is co-author of *Merchants of Drink: Transnational Control of World Beverages* (1988).**

For more than a decade the most common policy advice to developing countries the world over has been a simple formula: Copy the export-oriented path of the newly industrializing countries, the celebrated NICs. These economies—Brazil, Hong Kong, Mexico, Singapore, South Korea, and Taiwan—burst onto world manufactures markets in the late 1960s and the 1970s. By 1978 these six economies plus India accounted for fully 70 per cent of the developing world's

From *Foreign Policy 72* (Fall 1988). Copyright 1988 by the Carnegie Endowment for International Peace. Used by permission of *Foreign Policy*. Footnotes have been deleted.

272

manufactured exports. Their growth rates for gross national product (GNP) and exports were unequaled.

No wonder the call was sounded for others to follow. Dozens have tried. But with the possible exceptions of Malaysia and Thailand, no country has come close. Why not? The answer lies in far-reaching changes in the global economy—from synthetic substitutes for commodity exports to unsustainable levels of external debt—that have created a glut economy offering little room for new entrants.

Despite these shifts the foremost international development institutions, the World Bank and the International Monetary Fund (IMF), continue to promote the NIC path as the way for heavily indebted developing countries to escape the debt crisis. Yet in 1988, 8 years into a period of reduced growth in world markets, the bankruptcy of this approach should be all too apparent. By the end of the 1970s the World Bank had singled out the four Asian NICs as models to be studied by a second rung of developing countries. Having mastered the production of textiles, clothing, shoes, simple consumer electronics, and other light-manufactured wares, the four NICs were moving into more sophisticated products like automobiles and videocassette recorders. Therefore, the Bank argued, as the NICs' level of industrial development advanced, they would abandon the more basic industries to other countries. . . .

But the World Bank did more than offer the intellectual underpinnings for this development theory. In the late 1970s it positioned itself as a central actor in pushing the would-be NICs up the ladder to the NIC rung. In May 1979 then World Bank President Robert McNamara, in an address to a United Nations Conference on Trade and Development (UNCTAD) meeting in Manila, called for developing countries to "upgrade their export structure to take advantage of the export markets being vacated by more advanced developing countries." McNamara added that the Bank would move to the forefront of this new "program of action." To do so, however, the Bank needed to move beyond its more traditional microlevel project lending with a new instrument that would maximize its leverage with developing countries. Loans for hydroelectric dams, highways, and urban renewal, among other projects, had made the Bank the key international development player; but they did not confer on the Bank adequate leverage for the proposed global restructuring.

Consequently, the Bank turned to a new set of policy prescriptions, dubbed "structural adjustment," the key ingredient of which was structural adjustment loans (SALs). These large balance-of-payments loans—targeted toward broad sectors and heavily conditioned on a recipient's economic reforms—sought to hasten the new international division of labor whereby the would-be NICs would mimic the established NICs' light-manufactures export successes. The SALs were "the World Bank's best weapon yet," as a close aide of McNamara said in 1981.

SALs carried a broad set of policy prescriptions that focused on trade-related economic sectors; they were designed to enhance efficiency and export orientation. . . .

Who are these would-be NICs that the World Bank and the IMF hoped to push up the development ladder? According to various classification systems, including those of the World Bank, this group comprises up to 30 second-tier less developed countries (LDCs) across Africa, Asia, and Latin America.

These would-be NICs largely received the big loans and amplified attention from the Bank during the late 1970s and early 1980s. Of the 9 LDCs rewarded with a structural adjustment loan of more than $50 million as of mid-1982, 7 were would-be NICs and 1 was a NIC. Moreover, the IMF's attention largely complemented the Bank's. Of the 20 LDCs that by mid-1982 had received one of the IMF's extended fund facilities—highly conditioned loans with a 10-year repayment period—of more than $50 million, 12 fell into the would-be NICs grouping and 2 were NICs.

More insight into the Bank's role in the would-be NICs can be gained by looking at one illuminating case, the Philippines. By the end of Ferdinand Marcos's administration in February 1986, the Philippines had borrowed more than $4.5 billion from the World Bank in more than 100 project and program loans. The country was, in the words of Gregorio Licaros, one of Marcos's Central Bank governors, the "guinea pig" for structural adjustment. Indeed, one of the Bank's first SALs was a $200 million loan geared specifically toward restructuring the Philippine industrial sector. . . .

After a record Philippine balance-of-payments deficit of $570 million in 1979, the Bank put together the 1980 SAL package, which was attached not to a specific project but to a group of policies stipulating an export-oriented course for Philippine industry. Former high-ranking Philippine officials, including both proponents and opponents of the reforms, agree that the negotiations marked a critical juncture in the Philippine development path. Tariffs were slashed. Protective import restrictions were lifted. The exchange rate began a steady and steep devaluation, while export- and investment-promotion policies diverted resources from domestically oriented output. New free-trade tax havens, using generous incentives for transnational corporations (TNCs) to exploit low-cost Filipino labor, were established across the archipelago. Individual light-manufacturing industries, such as textiles, cement, food processing, furniture, and footwear, were slated for restructuring according to World Bank specifications.

During this period, similar policies were pushed in other would-be NICs. World Bank SALs to the Ivory Coast, Kenya, Pakistan, Senegal, and Turkey—like the Philippine SAL—all concentrated on improving export incentives and performance. In Thailand, where a Central Bank official vowed in mid-1979 that the World Bank's policies would "never be listened to or followed by top people here," the government implemented economic policy changes almost identical to those of the Philippines a few years and a SAL later. In other cases, notably Chile and Indonesia, would-be NICs followed the Bank's blueprint for development without a formal SAL.

## NIC RIVALRY

In effect the World Bank was helping to create a group of countries that would compete against each other to become NICs. The result was two vicious battles—one to offer cheaper, more docile labor forces and more attractive financial incentives to lure TNC assembly lines away from the other countries, and the other to win scarce export markets.

This competition soon became clear to each would-be NIC. As a deputy governor to the Philippine Central Bank remarked in a 1980 interview: "We've got to always be careful now, always watching, on the lookout for other [developing] nations' next moves. . . . And then we've got to make sure we meet their offer and better it." Sri Lanka's advertisement in the October 16, 1981, issue of the *Far Eastern Economic Review* said it well: "Sri Lanka challenges you to match the advantages of its Free Trade Zone, against those being offered elsewhere. . . . Sri Lanka has the lowest labor rates in Asia." Variations on that appeal were issued by one would-be NIC after another, putting TNCs in a choice position from which to bargain the most lucrative investment or subcontracting deals.

The competition encouraged labor repression and exploitation. One Manila-based TNC executive explained in a 1981 interview: "We tell the [Philippine] government: you've got to clamp down [on labor]. . . . Or we threaten to move elsewhere. And we'll do just that. There's Sri Lanka [and] now China too."

Most of the Bank's public documents sought to play down the problems associated with rivalry among the would-be NICs. But the Bank was not unaware of the potential zero-sum game. In a January 1979 working paper assessing the LDCs' manufacturing export potential, two leading Bank economists, Hollis Chenery and Donald Keesing, forecast that "the increasing number of successful competitors may make it increasingly difficult for newcomers to get established" and that the success of a "few" could leave "too little" opportunity for the rest. . . .

Yet who had set in motion this chain of competition? An October 1979 World Bank report had counseled the Philippines to take advantage of the fact that its wages had "declined significantly relative to those in competing . . . countries," notably Hong Kong and South Korea. Almost simultaneously, as reported in the *Southeast Asia Chronicle* in December 1981, the Bank helped steer Indonesia onto a parallel course, advising that "incentives for firms to locate there rather than in some other Southeast Asian country . . . must be provided." Meanwhile, Sri Lanka received a $20 million World Bank loan to establish a new export platform for apparel subcontracting, and the Bank pushed the

People's Republic of China (PRC), Thailand, and some of the Caribbean Basin countries into the light-manufactures arena as well.

The competition among would-be NICs was further exacerbated by the exporters of an earlier era, the Asian NICs of Hong Kong, Singapore, South Korea, and Taiwan. World Bank theory to the contrary, these countries were not abandoning textiles, apparel, and electronics assembly as they moved into higher stages of industrialization. Indeed, since the 1960s the Asian NICs had been spreading throughout the entire range of industry—from light to heavy, from unsophisticated to sophisticated—leaving little space for would-be NICs. . . .

Another factor also was inhibiting the would-be NICs' economic ascension—new technologies. The more than a decade that separated the NICs' debut from that of the would-be NICs witnessed technological advances in several sectors that changed the very definition of Third World industrialization.

By the late 1970s technological innovations, led by the microprocessor revolution, made the global fragmentation of production highly profitable and desirable. Whereas the original NICs had received complete industrial processes such as shipbuilding and machinery, the would-be NICs won marginal segments of scattered assembly lines for semiconductors and consumer electronics, textiles, and apparel. In Sri Lanka, for example, workers in export-processing zones used basic sewing machines to stitch together garments from imported fabric. In the Philippines, female workers in 1980 were performing only 1 of the 10 major operations of electronic production, attaching hairlike gold wires to silicon chips.

As a result, these new global assembly lines left gaping disparities between the gross value of the would-be NICs' industrial export earnings and the actual value added to the product in the developing country. Consider again the Philippine case. When proclaiming the nontraditional-export strategy's supposed triumphs, the Philippine government naturally focused on . . . the gross value of exports. Yet when stripped of import components' costs, the "value added" by the domestic side of production was but a fraction of the export earnings.

With the Philippines importing cartons for its banana exports, cans for some food exports, and a wide assortment of machinery and component parts for its limited apparel and electronic assembly lines, value added in most Philippine industries was quite low. . . . For every dollar of nontraditional-export earnings, only 25 cents stayed in the Philippines; the rest was siphoned off by import payments. Low value added was a fact of life in the Philippines' part in the new international division of labor.

According to one of the best analyses of electronics subcontracting, the long-term outlook for increasing the amount of value added in developing countries in the industry was bleak. As the December 1981 United Nations Industrial Development Organization report, *Restructuring World Industry in a Period of Crisis,* detailed, the per cent of value added attributable to new LDC microprocessor production lines rose until 1973. By 1977, however, value added in the newest LDC factories already had begun to fall. This downward turn came even as the gross value of semiconductors re-exported to the United States soared ten-fold from 1970 to 1978. Of the seven LDCs studied, the Philippines was the last to start silicon chip assembly. Entering on the downswing of the curve, value added in its factories was the lowest of all.

Since 1977 a growing share of the value was being held in the electronics companies' home countries. The UN report emphasized that, "as the complexity of circuitry increases, more value added is produced in the early wafer-fabrication stage, i.e., in the United States, in Japan, or in some locations in Western Europe. Furthermore, the more complex circuits require much more complex, computerized final testing, which again is usually done in OECD [Organization for Economic Cooperation and Development] locations, particularly in the United States and Japan."

If the production side of the would-be NIC experience offered less than what was advertised, the marketing side was even grimmer. For light-manufactured exports to be the engine of growth for the would-be NICs, world trade—that is, global demand for these products—had to grow each year. There was no way to escape this logic in the aggregate.

But in the late 1970s and early 1980s, at precisely the time when would-be NICs were induced to embark on a nontraditional-export path, these necessary conditions were decidedly absent. Over the decade from 1963 to 1973 the volume of world exports rose at a rapid average annual rate of 8.5 per cent. Beginning in 1973, however, an economic deceleration slowed the average annual expansion to 4 per cent. By 1980 exports were crawling ahead at only 1 per cent per year, and in 1981 they showed no growth. Moreover, 1981 had the dubious distinction of being the first year since 1958 to experience an actual decrease in world trade in current dollar terms, a shrinkage of 1 per cent.

Behind these global trade statistics lurked the domestic stagnation of the industrialized economies. According to IMF figures, from 1976 to 1979 the real GNP of industrialized countries grew at a tolerable average yearly rate of 4 per cent. By 1980, OECD growth was limping ahead at only 1.25 per cent; the next year it increased again by only 1.25 per cent. These 2 years presaged a decade of vastly reduced growth. From 1981 to 1985 world output slowed to an average of 2.7 per cent per year and trade to 2.8 per cent. These aggregate statistics become even more dismal if Eastern Europe and the PRC are excluded: Output over the first half of the 1980s grew at an average annual rate of only 1.4 per cent in developing countries and 2.3 per cent in developed countries.

As more countries battled for the same tepid export markets, prices plunged. Between 1981 and 1985, world prices of food commodities fell at an average annual rate of 15 per cent; agricultural raw materials dropped at an average annual rate of 7 per cent; and minerals and metals fell 6 per cent. The year 1986 proved even dimmer, when a 30 per cent decline in the developing countries' terms of trade (the ratio of prices of developing-country exports to prices of their imports) translated into a staggering $94 billion to the developed world.

Another pitfall facing the LDCs' export-oriented industrialization was the panoply of quantitative restrictions that had spread to cover fully one-half of global trade. Despite official encomiums to "free trade," the OECD countries increasingly were barricading themselves behind what even President Ronald Reagan's Council of Economic Advisers admitted were "neomercantile" policies.

These defensive machinations to moderate the recessionary bite at home were baptized the "new protectionism"—a proliferation of American, European Economic Community, and Japanese trade barriers, notably quotas on LDC-manufactured exports. "New" referred to the dazzling array of nontariff barriers not regulated by the General Agreement on Tariffs and Trade. Voluntary export restraints and orderly marketing arrangements flourished. As the World Bank and the IMF encouraged free-trade policies on LDCs, the major voting blocs within those institutions retreated from any semblance of free trade at home. The retreat of free trade became inextricably meshed with the recession: As OECD growth slackened, quotas were tightened. The more successful a particular LDC export category was, the more restrictive the quota became.

By the calculations of the World Bank's own economists in 1979, the most dangerous of the new protectionist barriers was centered in the apparel, textile, and footwear sectors. Yet it was precisely these sectors—along with furniture, wood products, electronics, and other light-manufactured exports—that the Bank had pinpointed as the engine of growth for the would-be NICs. The restrictive allotments of the Multi-Fiber Arrangement made textiles and apparel perhaps the most heavily controlled sectors in international trade. As a result, the LDCs' share of textile and apparel exports began to shrink in the early 1980s.

Did the Bank adequately address the impact of slow global economic growth and rising protectionism on its policy directives? As early as 1974 the Bank understood certain pitfalls that the 1970s and 1980s might hold for export-oriented industrialization. That year McNamara, in an address to the Board of Governors, noted: "The adverse effect on the developing countries of . . . a reduction in economic growth in their major markets would be great. There is a strong—almost one-to-one—relationship between changes in the growth of OECD countries and that of oil importing nations." . . . And in his May 1979 address to the UNCTAD conference in Manila, McNamara noted that the World Bank had perceived the onset of the new protectionism as early as 1976.

Yet in the late 1970s and early 1980s Bank officials who were planning Third World development strategies continually made assumptions that ignored slow growth and rising protectionism. Their model, grounded in theories of free trade and comparative advantage, posited the absence of such conditions. They opted instead for what was termed "one set of reasonable assumptions" without explaining their legitimacy. The set of "reasonable" assumptions about trade and protectionism that underpinned the Bank's structural adjustment reports and advice to would-be NICs was some permutation of the following: Industrial countries were to grow 4 per cent annually in the 1980s; "worldwide economic recovery" stood on the horizon; and "no major set-backs" would occur in major markets. . . .

The potential effects of this unsubstantiated optimism about the . . . would-be NICs were never seriously considered by Bank officials. The development prescriptions of Bank officials were transformed into a kind of dogma: "The more hostile the external environment, the more urgent" the need for restructuring, an August 1980 *Report and Recommendation* urged. In one instance, a Bank director took the floor at the executive board's final meeting on the Philippine SAL to question the management's scenario of Philippine "dynamic" export-led growth in light of "an adverse environment [including] lower than projected growth rates in industrial countries and increased protectionism." The board chairman's response epitomized the Bank's unquestioning attitude: "If the environment turned out to be more adverse than projected, then the ultimate benefits under the adjustment program would be reduced, but the nature of the adjustment needed would not be changed." But such a response was no more than conjecture. No hard evidence and no computer runs were offered to answer what should have been a basic question: If world trade did not grow, and if key markets became increasingly protected, would export-oriented industrialization be the optimal route to growth? . . .

It was becoming increasingly clear that the World Bank had no vision of development in a world economy of curtailed growth. To a large extent Bank officials had equated growth with development. To them, development did not primarily mean providing adequate food, clean water, clothing, and housing—in short, offering a standard of living consistent with human dignity. Those had become secondary concerns to be met through growth. In the Bank's view, no growth meant no development and therefore could not be considered seriously. . . .

In recent public Bank documents, slow growth in the world economy is still viewed as a short-term or cyclical aberration that does not undermine the basic soundness of the Bank's structural adjustment advice. Indeed, as late as its 1987 *World Development Report,* the Bank was still stressing that the world economy was continuing to "expand," albeit at a "modest and uneven" rate. That outlook enabled the Bank to continue unabashedly to counsel "the outward-oriented trade policies which have proved so successful for the NICs in recent years."

## A NEW WORLD ECONOMY

World Bank forecasts notwithstanding, global stagnation is likely to prove harder to shake than most would like to believe. Aside from protectionism pressures, a series of corporate developments has stunted demand globally, leaving increasing numbers of people at the margins of market activity. Prominent among these developments are the commercial banks' handling of the Third World debt crisis, corporate substitution for Third World raw materials, and labor-saving technological innovations in the developed world.

The debt crisis arose inevitably from the export-oriented development strategies, which depended on heavy borrowing for infrastructure and in many countries fed corruption and capital flight. In the early 1980s, as oil prices and interest rates rose and primary commodity prices fell, country after country announced its inability to service debts owed to banks in the developed world. In rapid succession the creditor banks sent these countries through IMF austerity programs, which prescribed a kind of shock treatment to bring countries' balance of payments out of deficit. Wage freezes, currency devaluations, and government spending cuts reduced imports into the Third World; indeed, many countries wiped out trade and national budget deficits within a few years. But lowered wages and imports also dampened global economic growth.

Technological breakthroughs in substitutes for Third World raw materials also hurt growth performance in the developing world. A single anecdote typifies the impact of longer-term corporate development on commodity markets. Until 1981 the largest consumer of the world's sugar was Coca-Cola. That year, in a move rapidly emulated by other soft drink giants, Coca-Cola began to shift its sweetener from sugar to corn syrup. Western consumers might not have viewed the change as significant to them, but it displaced millions of Third World sugar workers for a product produced within industrial countries.

Advances in plastics, synthetic fibers, food chemistry, and biotechnology are bringing similar far-reaching changes to other raw material and commodity markets. Cumulatively these substitutions have pushed tens of millions of Third World workers into the margins of the marketplace, further curbing global demand.

Likewise, new corporate technologies are transforming developed-country economies. The computer revolution, the major technological breakthrough of the last two decades, is strikingly dissimilar from earlier technological breakthroughs. The advent of electricity and the automobile, for example, generated millions of jobs in related industries and sparked economic booms in the leading countries. The microprocessor revolution has also created millions of jobs. However, applications of microprocessors have spread through almost every manufacturing and service sector in uses that are labor saving. Bank tellers, supermarket check-out clerks, assembly-line workers, and others are all joining the ranks of the unemployed. This phenomenon is reflected in Western Europe, where for 17 straight years the unemployment rate has risen.

The result of these three changes is that all over the world industry is turning out more than consumers can buy. The new global glut economy coexists with billions of people with enormous needs and wants but with little ability to buy.

As world economic growth has slowed, so have the Third World activities of its central private institutions: TNCs and banks. Much of the growth of the 1960s and 1970s was based on a rapid expansion of production around the world by subsidiaries of such TNCs as Ford, John Deere, and Texas Instruments. Western banks followed to provide financing. Then, after 1973, they became major economic actors in the developing world in their own right as recyclers of billions of petrodollars.

This is no longer the case. Banks and corporations go where there is growth and hence profit. Since the early 1980s the Third World basically has stopped growing; many countries have even slipped backward. Consequently, U.S. banks have returned home for new short-term rewards—consumer credit, corporate mergers, and the get-rich-quick gimmicks of financial speculation.

Again, the statistics are stark. In 1983 international bank lending to developing countries, excluding offshore bank centers, totaled $35 billion. By 1985 a mere $3 billion in new lending had trickled in.

Unfortunately, the drop-off in bank and corporate involvement and the factors that spelled a longer-term slowdown did not seem to influence the policy advice of the World Bank and the IMF. . . .

By 1985, however, austerity had bred considerable resistance across the Third World. The United States responded in October 1985 with a plan proposed by Treasury Secretary James Baker. Although it seized the political initiative from the Latin American debtors, the Baker plan offered little that was new. . . .

Yet the changing world economy has created a desperate need to rethink the kinds of adjustments that will produce growth and development. At the very least, the adjustment strategies must be built on realistic assumptions. The NICs were the product of a radically different world economy. That they cannot be replicated . . . is an indication of how much that world economy has changed.

Rather than increasing their reliance on a hostile world environment, developing countries should try to reduce this dependence and to diversify trading partners and products. This approach implies a careful restructuring of trade and financial linkages to conform with a development logic that is driven by internal economic forces.

If economies can no longer be pulled along primarily by external growth, stronger internal buying power must be generated. The great challenge is to transform crushing social needs into effective demand and then to meet that demand by turning first to domestically produced goods and services, next to the region, and only after that to the wider world market. In most developing countries this development framework implies vast internal adjustment quite different from the World Bank's brand of structural adjustment. Most of the Third World's people cannot afford to purchase many goods and services. Wages are locked into rock-bottom subsistence rates; wealth and income are heavily skewed toward a relatively small, wealthy elite. As a result, spreading income more evenly requires, for a start, extensive land reform, progressive taxation policies, and guarantees of worker rights.

To offer more specifics on internal demand-driven development strategies is risky. Vastly different resource bases and social strata among countries suggest that a country-specific approach is essential. Indeed, the sin of universality in development strategies was perhaps the central weakness of IMF and World Bank adjustment programs. Further, the successful implementation of any development strategy depends on its acceptance by entrenched interests in that country. However desirable comprehensive agrarian reform may be in the Philippines, for example, a powerful landowning group has substantial influence in the government and is likely to block serious reform efforts.

These caveats noted, a few general principles for development in a hostile world economy can be sketched out. Most would-be NICs remain predominantly agricultural societies; hence the starting point of internal demand-led development must be in farming. Two undertakings are central to increasing buying power in the countryside: redistributing wealth and raising productivity.

Agrarian reform remains the major means of redistributing wealth and income and thereby increasing the effective purchasing power of the rural population. The people in Third World rural areas are largely either poor tenants or agricultural workers who earn only subsistence wages. They have meager resources to consume in the marketplace. Only through agrarian reform can this population begin to produce a surplus that can be translated into consumption. In economic terms, small farmers have a higher "marginal propensity" to consume than larger ones, and much of their consumption could be satisfied by locally produced products.

Raising productivity depends in large part on upgrading infrastructure—from irrigation and roads to credit institutions and marketing channels. . . .

From this starting point, industrialization based on maximizing industrial linkages with agriculture makes great sense. In particular, three strands of industry could be encouraged:

*Agricultural inputs.* An agricultural sector with rising productivity will need locally produced fertilizer, pesticides, water pumps, and a wide range of tools, from plows to tractors.

*Processing farm products.* From cocoa and coffee to sugar and cotton, increased domestic processing offers more foodstuffs for local consumption and increases the value added of exports.

*Consumer goods.* As purchasing power grows in the countryside, so does the market for locally produced textiles, clothing, shoes, bicycles, refrigerators, and other consumer goods. . . .

The cycle of agriculture-linked industrialization does not stop there. As industry grows, the increased buying power of industrial workers provides an expanding market for farm goods from rural areas. Agriculture and industry would grow in tandem. It is worth pointing out that, popular myths notwithstanding, South Korea pursued this basic strategy in its earliest phase of industrialization. . . .

In a highly interdependent world, such demand-centered development does not and cannot imply autarky. What cannot be produced locally is produced nationally. What cannot be produced nationally is purchased from regional partners—which suggests the importance of revitalizing regional integration institutions. Only for those products for which regional producers cannot satisfy demand is trade necessary with countries on the other side of the globe. Domestic needs should shape trade patterns rather than vice versa. . . .

Beyond domestic market policies in agriculture and industry, development strategies should seek to curtail the wasteful economic activities that are rampant in some countries. These range from large, unproductive landholdings and capital flight to production and export monopolies and cronyism. Rooting out these practices is a monumental political task, threatening as it does entrenched groups of speculators, moneylenders, and landlords and bloated militaries. Development strategies also must pay closer attention to the pressing need to maintain fragile natural resource bases around the world. The disappearance of rain forests, plant and animal species, clean rivers, and clean air has become the dominant trend in too many countries.

. . . Most observers continue to view the Asian NICs as role models. And they offer glowing imagery in support of their view: Asian NICs have "already taken off," and the rest of the noncommunist Southeast Asian countries are "on the runway revving" up to follow, as former Japanese Foreign Minister Saburo Okita has described it.

The would-be NICs have fallen for such prophecies for nearly a decade. Now is the time to demand not imagery but a realistic assessment of options. The debate on adjustment and development should be reopened; strategies that proclaim that the only option is greater dependence on an increasingly hostile and turbulent world economy need to be challenged. It is time to ask whether any more developing countries can really hope to become the South Korea . . . or the Hong Kong of the early 1990s.

# 26

# TRADE POLICY AT A CROSSROAD

## Robert E. Litan and Peter O. Suchman

**Since World War II the United States has been the leading advocate and supporter of the Liberal International Economic Order. Its approach to trade rested on multilateralism and a commitment to rules, particularly nondiscrimination, instead of results. Today both commitments are under attack, as the hegemonic position of the United States in the LIEO has declined and its own economic problems have multiplied. Robert E. Litan and Peter O. Suchman critique alternatives to the rule-based multilateral system that have been advanced; they argue that none of the alternative trade policy regimes offers significant advantages and that, in any case, the resolution of U.S. economic problems will require painful choices at home. The best trade policy lies in a reaffirmation of the rule-based multilateral strategy the United States has pursued since World War II. Litan is a senior fellow in the Economic Studies Programs at the Brookings Institution. Suchman is a partner in charge of international trade law practice at Powell, Goldstein, Frazer, and Murphy in Washington, D.C.**

Since the end of World War II the United States has been perhaps the leading advocate among industrialized nations of liberalized international trade. It was the motivating force behind the General Agreement on Trade and Tariffs (GATT), the seven major trade negotiations pursued under its aus-

Used by permission of Robert E. Litan and Peter O. Suchman. Footnotes, tables, and figures have been deleted.

pices, and the significant reductions in tariffs that these negotiations have produced.

Tariff liberalization, quite predictably, has promoted both trade and interdependence. The ratio of world exports to gross national product (GNP) has climbed throughout the postwar era, especially in the last two decades. . . . This is a healthy development. It implies that nations increasingly have found it cheaper to buy their goods abroad than to produce them at home, affording consumers around the world a wider choice of goods at less cost than if nations had continued to hide behind the high tariffs that they introduced in the 1930s.

Two principles underlie this success. First, the widespread reductions in tariff barriers were made possible only through multilateral bargaining. The industrialized countries formed GATT largely because of the economies in negotiation that could be purchased if a large number of countries reduced their trade barriers simultaneously rather than successively on a bilateral basis over a long period of time. Second, the GATT members agreed on the rules that should govern trade rather than on the results—import and export levels and balances of trade—that individual countries might find desirable or appropriate. In addition, the GATT parties agreed on a framework for resolving bilateral disputes over particular rules.

In the last few years, however, many in the U.S. academic, business, and policy-making communities have raised significant questions about each of these principles. The critics argue that the GATT multilateral framework is no longer viable: it is unsuited for reducing nontariff barriers, it lacks an effective enforcement mechanism, and the members themselves have lost interest in continued negotiations. One prominent economist, Lester Thurow, has even pronounced the GATT to be dead. The preferred alternative is bilateral or regional trade negotiations or even "free trade arrangements" (FTAs), such as those the United States recently completed with Israel and Canada.

Thurow and other critics go one step further. In their view, the new less-than-multilateral negotiations should specify outcomes. Unlike tariffs, which are easily observable and readily monitored, many nontariff barriers can be invisible and inherently difficult, if not impossible, to negotiate away. Results rather than rules should therefore become the centerpiece of trade negotiations.

There are many indications that support within the United States for the rules-oriented, multilateral approach to freer trade is rapidly eroding and that U.S. trade is indeed at a critical crossroad. In this article, we discuss the reasons for this trend, distinguishing along the way fact from myth. We then outline the major shifts in trade policy that critics of the old regime have advanced. We conclude that the critics are wrong. It is in the interest of the United States to vigorously renew its commitment to reducing trade barriers on a multilateral basis without specifying trade outcomes. But [the United States] is unlikely to be successful unless it also undertakes certain measures at home to attack the major sources of current trade tensions.

## SOURCES OF DISSATISFACTION

Four key factors have been undermining the commitment of U.S. policy-makers and business leaders to the GATT framework.

*The trade deficit.* The dominant influence, unrelated to the operation of the GATT, is the dramatic deterioration in U.S. trade performance. From a positive $7 billion balance in 1981, the U.S. current account (which includes trade in both goods and services) fell to a deficit of $154 billion only 6 years later, before improving modestly in 1988 to $144 billion.

As important as the U.S. deterioration is the dramatic improvement in the trade positions of the world's other two industrial leaders, the Federal Republic of Germany (FRG) and Japan. Until 1982 the ratio of the current account to total output in these three countries generally hovered within one percentage point of balance. . . . There has been a sea change since. The U.S. current account has fallen deeply into deficit (more than 3% of GNP); the mirror image is true for Japan and the FRG.

It is no coincidence that in 1985, around the time these trade imbalances became substantial, the U.S. Congress began debating the original version of what eventually became the 1988 Trade Act. Although complex and technical in nature, that proposal essentially was designed to dramatically weaken the U.S. commitment to multilateralism in trade policy. Instead, the bill proposed a uni-lateral tightening of U.S. laws against unfairly traded imports—those that are dumped, unlawfully subsidized, or in violation of our intellectual property laws. Perhaps most controversial was the amendment to the original proposal offered by Richard Gephardt . . . that would have rejected the "rules-oriented" princi-ple of trade law as well. It would have required certain . . . major trading part-ners, notably, the FRG, Japan, and Brazil, to reduce their trade surpluses with [the U.S.] over a 10-year period, or otherwise be subject to U.S. import tariffs and quotas to achieve that objective.

Fearing that a congressional trade initiative would turn strongly protectionist and thus risk a round-robin of retaliatory measures by our trading partners, the Reagan Administration followed a two-part strategy to weaken support for the legislation. First, it displayed a new "get tough" policy on unfair trade by launching complaints against South Korea and Brazil under the prevailing ver-sion of Section 301 of the U.S. trade law, authorizing retaliation against coun-tries that unreasonably discriminate against the importation of U.S. products. Second, abandoning the previous free-market attitude toward exchange rates, newly installed Secretary of the Treasury James Baker negotiated in September 1985 a coordinated depreciation of the dollar against major European and Japanese currencies. The Plaza Accord, as it was called, was designed to reduce the overall U.S. trade deficit by cheapening U.S. exports in terms of foreign cur-rency while raising the dollar price of U.S. imports. In fact, during the following 18 months, until the dollar was stabilized in the Louvre Agreement, the dollar fell by roughly 35% in real terms (adjusted for differences between countries in the rate of inflation) against an average of ten major currencies.

The Administration's initiatives bought valuable time and helped ease the political pressure for a protectionist trade bill. . . . Still, with so much political time and energy invested in trade legislation, Congress was not to be deterred from taking some action, which it did in the summer of 1988.

Significantly, the final bill signed by President Reagan contained a modified version of the original Gephardt amendment that continued to reflect a new unilateral direction in U.S. trade policy. Quickly dubbed "Super 301," this provision requires the U.S. government (not the GATT) to identify the countries that (not the GATT) [believes] most burden [U.S.] exports through their "unreasonable" policies (whether or not they violate GATT or any other international agreement) and then authorizes the President to retaliate against them if they do not agree within a short period to change those policies. Super 301 gets its name from the preexisting Section 301 of the trade law, which contains similar authorization without requiring the President to so publicly identify specific countries as priority "unfair traders."

*Exchange rate pessimism.* The pressure for the United States unilaterally to take even more aggressive actions against trading practices of other countries nevertheless remains and is likely to intensify. The principal reason stems from a phenomenon labeled by some as "exchange rate pessimism," a powerful second force for weakening the long-standing U.S. commitment to a multilateral rules-oriented trade policy.

Simply put, the pessimists submit that movements in exchange rates do not have a significant effect on trade patterns and thus trade rules must be changed to guarantee an improvement in the U.S. trade balance. For example, it is thought in some quarters that the substantial decline of the dollar since 1985 did not "work" because the U.S. trade deficit continued to deteriorate through 1987. Frequently noted is the anti-import bias in Japan relative to other industrialized countries. In 1986, for example, Japan imported only 4.4% of its manufactured goods, compared to 13.8% for the United States and 37.2% for the FRG. This apparent discrimination against imports, it is said, accounts for the fact that despite the near doubling of the value of the yen against the dollar between 1985 and 1988, the U.S. trade deficit with Japan . . . remained stuck at roughly $50 billion.

In fact, economists have repeatedly shown through statistical tests that the pessimists are wrong: trade flows are clearly responsive to changes in prices of both imports and exports. Roughly speaking, these studies demonstrate that for every one percentage point change in prices, the volumes of both exports and imports also change by at least one percentage point. . . .

Why then has the U.S. trade picture brightened so modestly in the face of the substantial dollar depreciation since 1985? The principal answer lies in the mathematics of the trade deficit and the sheer momentum for continuing deficits that the numbers build in. In 1984, before the dollar began to fall, the dollar volume of U.S. imports exceeded U.S. exports by nearly 60%—$346 billion to $224 billion. Thus, even if both exports and imports continued to grow at the same rate thereafter, the trade deficit would have widened simply because imports have been able to advance from a larger base. . . . Similar reasoning explains why the U.S. bilateral trade deficit with Japan has barely moved since 1985. . . .

*A multipolar world.* Perhaps no event in the 1980s [was] more unexpected than the significant easing of East-West tensions. At the same time, U.S. economic hegemony . . . disappeared. The United States is now a net debtor nation, owing increasing sums to Japan, the FRG, Taiwan, and other nations with large trade surpluses. In short, in both economic and political spheres the bipolar world that we lived in before 1980 has been replaced by a world increasingly governed by multiple centers of economic and political strength.

Paradoxically, the emergence of a multipolar world may be weakening commitments to the system of multilateral trade rules and negotiations. The GATT was formed in 1948 very much as the free world economic counterpart to the formal and informal political-military alliances formed between the United States and many other countries after World War II. In particular, at least in its early stages, the GATT was dominated by the United States and was seen in a bipolar context. The Soviet Union was not a founding member and still does not belong today, although recently it has expressed interest in joining.

The thawing of the Cold War and the splintering of economic and political influence around the world weaken the relative importance of the United States and thus subtly undermine continued commitments by other nations to the multilateral trade process. In addition, whereas in the United States freer trade was perceived to be in the interest of many industries because they were more productive than their foreign counterparts and thus wanted access to their markets, now many U.S. industries have lost their competitive edge. In such an environment, freer trade can mean severe disruption, loss of jobs, and lower profits— outcomes that make it politically difficult at home for the United States to continue its leadership of the trade liberalization movement.

*Weaknesses in the GATT.* Finally, the GATT itself has weaknesses. These have existed since the GATT was formed, but they have been seen as more irritating as tariff barriers have been reduced and as other trade tensions have surfaced.

First, the GATT lacks an effective enforcement mechanism. Ironically, it was the U.S. Congress that was primarily responsible for this defect when it rejected the formation of a multilateral enforcement arm for GATT, the International Trade Organization. Second, the GATT fails to cover large areas of trade: agricultural products, services, and textiles (governed by a multicountry system of quotas arranged under the Multi-Fiber Arrangement).

Third, and perhaps most important, an increasing share of trade within the industrialized countries is being burdened by nontariff trade barriers, especially so-called "voluntary restraint agreements" (VRAs) designed to circumvent the letter of the GATT. VRAs are technically legal because they are negotiated "voluntarily" between importing countries, such as the United States (one of the worst offenders in the 1980s, with restrictions on imports of steel and automobiles), and their exporting trading partners. But the "voluntariness" of VRAs is clearly a fiction, and it is widely understood that they run afoul of the spirit of the GATT.

To many, the weaknesses in the GATT highlight the futility of the organization and the multilateral process of negotiation that it represents and encourages. To others, the missing links in the GATT, much like the nuclear weapons stockpiles of the major military powers, represent challenges for future negotiators to overcome. . . .

## OPTIONS FOR U.S. TRADE POLICY

The factors weakening the U.S. commitment to the postwar multilateral, rules-oriented trade regime have prompted a vigorous debate within the political and academic communities in [the United States] about what principles should govern U.S. trade policy in the future. Three schools of thought, somewhat overlapping, have emerged.

The first, and least revolutionary of the alternatives, advocates that the United States itself fill the enforcement void in the GATT by playing the role of "super-cop." The United States has already embarked down this path . . . in adopting the new Super 301 provisions of the 1988 Trade Act. . . .

The second alternative also focuses on rules, but it advocates bilateral FTAs with other like-minded countries—Mexico, South Korea, Taiwan, and even Japan—modeled on the recent FTAs the United States negotiated with Canada and Israel, as well as the more ambitious integration effort now under way in Europe. The FTA policy model, which urges the bilateral negotiation of new rules on many subjects not covered or imperfectly covered by GATT (including investment, services, and agriculture), is thus more forward looking than the "super-cop" approach, which seeks unilateral enforcement of existing rules (that the United States sets) on a case-by-case basis. . . .

The third trade policy alternative would jettison not only the emphasis on multilateral action but on rules as well. Instead, it would "manage trade" by having the United States set bilateral trade targets with our trading partners. The targets could cover only our exports to them or our overall trade balance (as the Gephardt amendment advocated). Similarly, the targets could be set for individual products or industry sectors or could cover all trade.

## A CRITIQUE OF THE CRITICS

Each of the suggested alternatives to the traditional multilateral, rules-based trade policy followed by the United States has its appeal. But each also holds dangers that we think outweigh any benefits they may achieve.

The least risky, but also least promising, alternative is the United States as super-cop. . . . There will always be competing foreign policy objectives that any chief executive must take into account in deciding whether to single out individual countries as "unfair traders." It is widely assumed, for example, that the [Bush] Administration exempted the European Community nations from the priority list [in 1989] primarily in order to avoid exacerbating then-worrisome tensions within the North Atlantic Treaty Organization over an appropriate response to the Soviet Union's nuclear arms reduction proposals.

But even President Bush's minimalist 301 effort has its risks. Several of the practices targeted by the President, notably India's trade-related investment measures and its insurance practices, are not covered by the GATT. If, therefore, [the United States retaliates] against these measures, [its] actions would violate the GATT and entitle the targeted countries lawfully to retaliate against [the United States]. Critics also have been too quick to dismiss the efficacy of the GATT enforcement mechanism. Of the 75 disputes brought before the GATT through September 1985, 88% were settled or dropped by the complaining country. By circumventing the GATT dispute resolution mechanism, [the United States weakens] the commitment of other nations to lawful settlement of trade disputes.

Bilateral or regional FTAs do not offer a much better solution, and conceivably, could produce a worse one. The premise underpinning the case for more FTAs—that GATT negotiations take too long—is questionable. . . .

Moreover, as pioneering as they were, the FTAs with Canada and Israel were relatively limited in scope. Neither dealt with the highly controversial issues . . . discussed in the Uruguay Round [of GATT trade negotiations], including agricultural subsidies, protection of intellectual property rights, and restrictions on services and investment, or the subjects that inevitably would be on the table in future FTA discussions with other countries. Indeed, if the advocates are right that many restrictions against imports are extralegal and thus not amenable to international agreement—such as the complex Japanese distribution system, for example—then FTAs could disadvantage the United States; [the United States] would further open [its] market without meaningful reciprocal concessions.

More FTAs could actually harm world trade. In purely economic terms, such arrangements have two offsetting effects: although they may promote more efficient location of production within the areas covered by the agreements and thus enhance trade and consumer welfare, they may also divert trade from other countries outside the agreement to those inside. . . .

More fundamentally, however, further movement by the United States—the leader of multilateral trade liberalization efforts since the end of World War II—toward bilateral or regional pacts runs a serious risk of undermining, if not unraveling, the GATT. Indeed, given the current inward-looking focus of the Europeans and Canada's new-found partnership with the United States, who would be left to lead the liberalizing process in the GATT if [the United States], too, [abandoned its] commitment to multilateralism? The answer is no one.

Instead, nations would quickly enter a free-for-all to obtain from each other the best deal each could. The world trading system would thus degenerate into a complicated maze of discriminatory bilateral and regional arrangements. Frictions would dramatically increase over "rules of origin" because it would then become all-important to know from which country imports and exports had "originated." In a world of multinational enterprises that often manufacture products in multiple locations, disputes about rules of origin could lead to serious trade rifts and would lead to substantially more red tape and uncertainty for all those involved in international trade.

Finally, the managed trade alternative rests on equally shaky premises and holds perhaps the greatest dangers of all. The principal argument for managed trade—that product-specific bilateral negotiations, especially those with Japan, are worthless—is simply not correct. . . . Between 1985 and 1987, U.S. exports to Japan of medical drugs and equipment, electronics, forest products, and telecommunications—sectors targeted by the U.S. trade negotiators—collectively increased by 47%, or twice the growth of all U.S. exports to Japan during this period.

In any event, the setting of trade targets would be counterproductive. If the targets were bilateral trade balances, it is more than likely that foreign countries would be happy to comply by restricting their exports to the United States rather than liberalizing imports. Like the VRAs that have limited the exports of Japanese cars and steel, these new restrictions would simply raise the price of goods exported to the United States and increase the profits of the foreign producers. Meanwhile, forcing foreign consumers to buy U.S. products they have not voluntarily chosen to purchase can hardly enhance the attractiveness of American goods overseas.

## PREFERRED TRADE POLICY

If none of the alternative trade policy regimes offer significant advantages, what then should be done about America's obvious trade problems—reflected in its $100 billion–plus trade deficit?

The answer most economists have given has been frequently heard, routinely ignored, but still remains correct. In a world of flexible exchange rates, a nation's trade balance—or more accurately, its current account balance—is fundamentally determined not by its trade policies but rather by its spending patterns.

By definition, the current account balance measures the difference between a nation's saving and investment. High-saving countries like Japan that do not invest all of their savings at home export the surplus and invest the proceeds abroad. Low-saving countries like the United States that invest more than they save must import the difference and borrow from abroad to finance their current account deficits. Exchange rates are the primary medium through which shifts in spending patterns influence the trade balance. As a nation increases its saving relative to its investment, its interest rates fall and so does its exchange rate, as investors seek assets denominated in currencies where yields are higher. Conversely, as a nation decreases its saving relative to its investment, its interest rates rise and so does its exchange rate.

Until the 1980s, the United States invested what it saved and thus ran a current account balance near zero. In [the 1980s], however, U.S. savings rates as a share of net national output, both public and private, [fell] dramatically relative to [U.S.] investment rates. . . . The shortfall in domestic saving required for investment . . . required [the United States] to import the difference, both in capital and goods, from abroad.

In short, the cure for [the U.S.] trade imbalance lies in either substantially raising the fraction of national income that is saved or lowering the fraction that is invested. Clearly, the first of these choices is more palatable, if more painful, than the second.

It is not widely appreciated, however, that the removal of foreign trade barriers will have little effect on [the U.S.] trade position. In the short run, lower barriers would permit an increase in [U.S.] exports and thus reduce the overall deficit. But a declining deficit shrinks the available supply of dollars on the market and thus drives up the dollar exchange rate. A higher dollar, in turn, discourages exports and encourages imports. Over the long run, therefore, lower trade barriers have no effect on the trade balance.

By the same reasoning, it is a mistake to blame the deterioration in [U.S.] trade accounts on unfair trade. Between 1981 and 1988, the U.S. trade position declined with every major trading area around the world, except the nations of the Organization of Petroleum Exporting Countries (OPEC). . . . This pattern makes it difficult to believe that a worldwide conspiracy to discriminate against U.S. imports could have suddenly developed only in this decade.

It is, nevertheless, in [the U.S.] interest to remove unfair impediments to [its] exports; doing so will raise the dollar exchange rate at which the United States can achieve balanced trade. A higher value of the dollar, other things being equal, permits American citizens to buy more imports for a given dollar expenditure and thus to enjoy a higher standard of living. The critical trade policy question, therefore, centers on what strategy can best be used to achieve a significant reduction in foreign trade barriers.

In our view, the best approach lies not in abandoning the rules-oriented, multilateral strategy that the United States has pioneered since World War II, but instead in reaffirming the commitment to that strategy and enlisting the vigorous participation of [U.S.] trading partners. At a purely political level, we think that other countries that maintain trade barriers are more likely to lower them in response to international pressure, lawfully applied through the GATT, than solely in response to U.S. complaints. Indeed, [the U.S.] "lone ranger" attitude toward other nations' trade barriers runs a severe risk of tarnishing [its] broader political influence. For example, U.S. relations with both Japan and South Korea have already been severely strained as a result of . . . constant pressure on particular trade issues. Resentment builds, meanwhile, as the United States continues to demonstrate an inability to significantly reduce its national overspending, which other countries think, quite correctly, is the overwhelming reason for their trade surpluses with [the United States].

The United States even runs broader geopolitical risks if it abandons its mantle of leadership on multilateral trade liberalization. It is fitting to recall the history of the period between the two major world wars of this century, when the rise of rival trading blocs contributed significantly to the tensions that led to World War II. Similar tensions led to repeated conflicts in the 17th and 18th centuries. Only when Great Britain, espousing the free trade principles of Adam Smith and David Ricardo, emerged as the dominant world power in the 19th century did these conflicts abate. The United States assumed this mantle of leadership toward free trade after World War II and until now has promoted increased liberalization, more trade, and improvements in living standards around the world.

It would be a severe mistake for the United States to abandon its leadership role simply because of its inability to address the root causes of trade difficulties abroad and its economic weaknesses at home. In the long run, [the United States] should realize that trade is still a positive sum game, not the zero sum game some have now contended. [It] should not be distracted by current tensions into wrecking the multilateral trade system that has helped bring all of the nations that participate in it to unprecedented levels of economic well-being.

# 27

---

# ON THE ROAD TO RUIN

---

Walter Russell Mead

The United States has won the Cold War, but in the process it has lost economic ground to its own allies. So argues Walter Russell Mead, who foresees the emergence of three economic blocs—in Europe, East Asia, and the Western hemisphere—with the United States as the leader of "the weakest and most troubled" of the three. According to Mead, lost American economic supremacy portends a dire future unless significant changes occur in U.S. foreign policy thinking. Mead is a senior fellow in international economics at the World Policy Institute and is author of *Mortal Splendor: The American Empire in Transition* (1987).

The United States has won the Cold War. But the United States has not won this war the way it won World War I and World War II. Each of those wars left the United States richer and thus, in the international arena, more powerful. During World War I we became, for the first time in our history, a creditor nation and a year later played the major role at the Paris Peace Conference; in 1945 we emerged from the war with the world's only healthy industrial economy and soon assumed the mantle of superpower.

From *Harper's Magazine* (March 1990), pp. 59–64. Copyright © 1990 by *Harper's Magazine*. All rights reserved. Used by special permission.

294

The Cold War—the forty-five-year battle to thwart the expansionistic goals of the Soviet Union—is a different story. We have won the Cold War the way Britain won World War I; the Soviet Union has been defeated, but in the struggle the United States lost economic ground to our allies. We had a larger role in the world—economically and politically—in 1950 than we do in 1990. After the Second World War, we were in a position to establish a new world order—and we did. But the post–World War II era is over; the post–Cold War era is beginning. And while the post–World War II order was designed by the United States and served our interests, the new order is being created by others, and it threatens to lock the United States into long-term economic decline. In the era that followed the vanquishing of the Germans and the Japanese, there was no country to challenge the United States; our standard of living knew no precedent or equal. Now it is Japan and Germany who stand to map the post–Cold War world economy; in this new world, the United States may well be the Argentina of the twenty-first century.

It is too often forgotten that the American strategy after World War II had *two* pillars. One was, of course, the policy of containing Soviet expansionism in Europe and the Third World. However, in the years immediately following World War II, the primary goal of our diplomacy—the original foundation of our postwar strategy—was the creation of the international financial system designed at the conference of forty-four states and nations held at the New Hampshire resort of Bretton Woods. It was at Bretton Woods in 1944—more than in Warsaw and Budapest and Bucharest in 1989—that the United States won the Cold War.

In 1944 and the years that followed, Americans had three goals for the postwar economic order. *First,* we insisted that we would be in charge. As we had all the gold and all the goods, this seemed like a reasonable position to take, and those nations that considered it unreasonable were in no position to do much about it. Our *second* demand was for the creation of a truly global trading system. The wholly *international* economy was our idea—a bold, new idea. The nations of Europe had traditionally preferred their own trading blocs to a global system regulated by international rules of trade. Countries like England and France had grown by building overseas empires, carving up the world in a way that guaranteed each imperial power its own source of raw materials and its own markets. American strategists came to believe that such systems blocked economic growth and eventually caused wars. And they were right.

Colonial subjects fought for independence, and countries without colonies fought to get them. The imperial nations used protectionist tariffs to strengthen their own economies at the cost of their colonies and of their nonimperial trade rivals: In both 1914 and 1939, German militarists claimed that the European imperial "haves," Britain and France, were unfairly denying Germany its "place in the sun." Japan felt the same way in the 1930s about the "ABCD" (American,

British, Chinese, and Dutch) powers who had divided up Asia and used their positions against Japan.

Even before the German and Japanese surrenders, the United States implicitly acknowledged that both Germany and Japan had a point. American officials stated, while the war was still being waged, that one of our war aims was the creation of an open international trading system in which all nations could participate on a free and equal basis. After the war, the United States pressed the generally reluctant countries of Western Europe to dismantle their colonial empires and admit the trade of all countries on an equal basis.

Of course, we did not attack the old empires simply out of a sense of fair play. We had powerful, less selfless motives. America is big, stretching from one great ocean to another. We make and consume such a broad range of products that we need markets and suppliers all over the world. History and geography make the United States an economic generalist; after World War II we were able to force all the would-be specialists to see things our way.

The *third* American postwar goal was the establishment of a growth-oriented world economy. Generally speaking, economic policymakers have to choose either slow growth with minimal inflation or faster growth with the risk of greater inflation. Compared with other major countries, the United States wants a little more growth, even if we have to take the inflation. Countries like Germany, on the other hand, are more willing to accept slow growth if it will keep the inflation rate at or near zero.

The United States advocated strong growth after World War II—and continued to in the years that followed—and, to a greater extent than most countries, we fueled growth through debt. Debt is the cornerstone of the American Dream. Debt builds our homes and starts our businesses. American states, cities, and towns are debtors, their capital budgets based on colossal bond issues. American corporations are debtors—and the richest American businessmen tend to be those who make the most creative use of their ability to leverage.

Debtors can tolerate inflation and often welcome it: Inflation means that you get to pay off your debt with cheaper currency. But recessions, when economic growth stalls, are poison to debtors. Heavily indebted businesses can go broke, and all debtors must service their debts out of reduced, not growing, incomes.

Europe, by contrast, is a creditor-oriented society. Its tightly knit national elites have preserved a class system based on inherited wealth, a system that has never quite managed to take hold in the United States. American society is like a Mayan pyramid: a broad top, gently sloping sides, and flights of stairs for easy access to the summit. European societies are more like Egyptian pyramids: narrow tops, steep sides, no steps. Europe's establishments wield power the American establishment can only dream of—and they wield it, generally, in the interests of creditors.

In the 1940s, history gave the United States the opportunity to shape a world economic order to its liking, and we did so. It was global- and growth-oriented—a debtor's paradise. This system worked not only for us; it led to an unprecedented global boom. What was good for the United States turned out to be good for the world. It was as players in this new U.S.-engineered global economy that the nations of Western Europe and Japan rebuilt their shattered economies and reached the position they are in today—one in which they are no longer obliged to accept our leadership.

Western Europe and Japan are back, and their preferences are beginning once again to shape the world's economy. A new world may well be emerging, or rather an old world may be coming back from the dead. I am talking of a world of trading blocs. This would be a world of slow growth. It would be a world in which we would not fit comfortably.

In my darker moments, I envision a world made up of three rival blocs: a Euro-bloc based in the Western European nations of the Common Market and now expanding to include Hungary, Poland, and others in Eastern Europe; an East Asian bloc dominated by Japan and including Korea, Thailand, and the other free-market industrializing nations of the region; and the American bloc, dominated by the United States, augmented by Canada, and incorporating Latin America.

Most of the Euro-bloc countries never really liked the American idea of a global system. The British fought us tooth and nail over "Imperial Preference"—their system of tariff protection to keep their empire together—and with the other nations of Western Europe have been reluctant to open their markets to goods manufactured in the Orient. Europe pressed to keep Japan from becoming a party to the General Agreement on Tariffs and Trade (GATT)—the treaty that, beginning in 1948, laid down a code of international economic conduct aimed at reducing tariffs and opening markets. And even today the nations of Western Europe impose tight restrictions on Japanese-made autos and other imports.

The Europeans have a logical alternative to a global economy, one that becomes more compelling as the Soviet-bloc countries of Eastern Europe move toward market economies. Schematically, it would work like this: Western Europe can import its raw materials from Africa and the Soviet Union, and its fuel, increasingly, not only from the Middle East but also from the USSR. It can place its low-wage industries in the former Soviet-bloc countries. (The average monthly industrial wage in Poland in January 1990 amounted to thirty-seven dollars a month.) The wealthy Western European countries can continue to specialize in high-technology and service industries, marketing these goods and services from the Urals to the Atlantic.

In this new, post–Cold War world, the Western European nations will have very little need of, or interest in, goods and services from Asia or the Americas.

Europe already produces huge agricultural surpluses, and with the increase in agricultural productivity that can be expected with the liberalizing of Eastern Europe, the continent's food supply will only increase. It is true that developments in American and Japanese technology have tended to outpace those of European manufacturers. But the gap has been closing fast. The European consortium that designed and built the Airbus is challenging American dominance of civil aviation; and Europe is also pushing into space. Europe is determined to develop its high-tech industries, and the record of German, French, and British science suggests it will succeed.

On the other side of the world, a new East Asian bloc is rising. Its outlines are already clear. Japan will import raw materials and low-end manufactured products from South Korea, Thailand, and China while exchanging manufactured goods for oil with the Middle East. In addition, Japan will export capital, capital goods, and high-technology products to all these markets—and to some degree to Australia, New Zealand, the United States, and Latin America—in exchange for food and raw materials (and American films and rock videos).

Like the Euro-bloc, the East Asian bloc will aggressively protect its own markets for cutting-edge products, limiting America's role as far as possible to the export of raw materials. Raw materials already form a higher percentage of U.S. exports to Korea than of Korean exports to the United States. This is, from the Asian point of view, an appropriate division of labor and a model for the future transpacific relationship.

The third major bloc is the weakest and most troubled. It is, unfortunately, ours. America's protectionists and neo-isolationists seem to think that a protected Pan-American bloc could strengthen the U.S. economy, but they are sadly mistaken. There aren't enough customers in it. Economically, the United States and Canada are too much like twins to grow rich trading largely with each other. Latin America is in a prolonged economic decline. From 1981 to 1987, to cite just one figure, imports to Argentina, Mexico, and Brazil—the three largest economies in Latin America—fell 36 percent. Latin America is a region of depressed consumption, political instability, and chronic underdevelopment. Moreover, Latin America does not seem particularly eager to tie its future to the United States. The president of Mexico went to Harvard; his children attend the Japanese school in Mexico City. For culture, Latin American elites look not north but to Europe. Britain and Germany have long-standing commercial ties to Argentina, Chile, and Brazil, and these ties will no doubt be strengthened as the remnants of the Cold War recede. In a world of rival blocs, the Asian and European blocs are almost certain to be more appealing to the Latin Americans than one dominated by the gringos; our bloc, along with all its other weaknesses, will be full of defectors and aspiring defectors.

The American bloc has two other large vulnerabilities. The dollar is grossly overextended, and our oil continues to flow principally from the Middle East.

These are weaknesses that could eventually put us at the mercy of the rest of the world.

Despite the fact that the United States is emerging from the Cold War as the world's largest debtor, the dollar remains the key international currency. However, the dollar is but the ghost of its former self. It is worth noting that the countries all over the world that continue to use dollars to settle their accounts, price their commodities, and store their liquid assets (in U.S. government bonds) used to think and deal in pounds, even after the British lost their global supremacy. But not for long.

World trade is shifting out of dollars and into the currencies of the future. The dollar has been falling—usually quietly, sometimes dramatically—against the German mark and the Japanese yen for almost a generation. As the new blocs gain strength, their currencies will be used increasingly in international trade. Already there is the European currency unit (ECU), a weighted average of all the European currencies—a recent survey of European companies found that 50 percent of them said they would use the ECU in the future. Japan, too, is making changes in its financial system that make the yen more useful in international trade. In the 1990s, the dollar will not reign but will be forced to compete as it has not since the Great Depression.

Meanwhile, the United States must go on importing oil. We remain, and will remain, dependent on the Middle Eastern oil producers. It is not, however, clear that they will remain dependent on us.

Most Americans recall little of our successful effort to drive Europe out of the Middle East in the 1940s and 1950s—or how angry this made the Europeans. Britain and France had divided the region between themselves following World War I; after World War II we used our economic prowess to drive them out and keep them out. When Britain and France, with Israel, invaded Egypt in 1956—the Suez Crisis—the United States forced them into a humiliating retreat, primarily by mounting an international attack on the British pound. Today, Europe wants back in to the Middle East, and it will probably get there.

The greatest single support of the dollar today may be OPEC's policy of establishing oil prices in dollars. Since almost every country needs to buy oil, almost every country has a good reason to hold dollars. But why should OPEC assume the risks of holding its assets in a weakening currency? It might be better, economically, for OPEC to shift to yen or marks or, someday, the ECU.

Economics may suggest one policy to the oil states; security, another. The United States' close security relationship with the oil producers is the key to what remains of our international supremacy. The oil states take dollars because they need the U.S.-provided security umbrella. But Europe is increasingly able to offer an umbrella of its own. When the American flotilla entered the mined Persian Gulf in 1987 during the Iran-Iraq War, Europe sent ships as well. The American press read this as a show of loyalty from our trusty allies; it was actually a signal to the states of the region—a second umbrella held out for their consideration.

Also with regard to the Middle East, Europe neither has nor wants a "special relationship" with Israel. It has no Israeli lobby putting arms requests for Saudi Arabia under hostile scrutiny. It increasingly is able to deliver sophisticated weapons to the Arab countries of the Middle East at competitive prices. Already there are signs of a larger European diplomatic role in the region. The countries of Western Europe will soon be in the position of being able to offer interested Middle East states money at least as strong as the dollar and protection at least as secure as anything the United States can offer.

Should the Middle East leave the American orbit, and the oil business leave the dollar zone, the American Century would surely, quickly, draw to an end. The dollar would fall like a meteor, *el peso del norte;* the United States would have to earn foreign exchange to pay its oil bills; our foreign debt would begin to cramp living standards; foreigners would lose interest in supporting the deficit through the purchase of U.S. Treasury bonds. Rich Americans would move their capital out of the United States and into safe havens abroad. We would begin to learn what it means to be a soft-money debtor in a hard-money world.

Fifty years ago, the United States was the wonder of the world: a rare combination of Canada, Saudi Arabia, and Japan. We had enormous quantities of strategic minerals, the largest oil reserves in the world, vast stocks of food, and the most dynamic industrial economy of any nation.

At the end of World War II, other advantages were added to these. We were the only major country whose economy and infrastructure had not been destroyed by the war. No one else had a merchant marine capable of handling such a flow of goods in international trade. We had accumulated an enormous gold reserve. We had the best-equipped army in the world and an unchallengeable navy and air force. We enjoyed an atomic monopoly, made all the more useful by our demonstration that we possessed the will to use the bomb.

These weapons have fallen from our hands. Our oil production is no longer adequate for our own uses. World markets in minerals and food are glutted. Our industrial economy has lost its supremacy—it is, at best, first among equals. We now owe foreigners more than Argentina, Brazil, and Mexico combined; Germany and Japan can set the value of the dollar.

This is the road to Argentina. Argentina is a rich country and in many ways similar to ours. Spacious skies cover its amber waves of grain; purple mountain majesties tower over its plains; it has oil and cowboys in the south and industry in the north. Its talented population is made up of immigrants and their descendants who came to the New World determined to build a better life for themselves and their children.

Fifty years ago, Argentina was part of the First World. It was a European society with living standards comparable to those of Canada and France. Today it is part of the Third World. Its economy alternates between hyperinflation and depression; its politics, between anarchy and dictatorship. . . .

The future does not have to be this bleak. But we will have to change the way we think about foreign policy. For the last fifty years we have waged foreign policy in the spirit of Jeane Kirkpatrick and General Patton; now we need to move in the spirit of Ginger Rogers and Fred Astaire. Peace is a complicated dance in which partners change rapidly. It is a dance at which the United States has never excelled.

In the nineteenth century, we were proud of our wallflower status; we sipped lemonade and heaped scorn on the wrinkled and rouged coquettes waltzing gaily around the European ballroom. After World War I, when it was our turn to preside, we closed down the bar and told the band to play hymns. As Jane Austen might have predicted, the result was more rational but very much less like a ball. Our guests grew impatient; French premier Georges Clemenceau, hearing of Wilson's Fourteen Points, remarked that "The good Lord had only ten."

We went home in a huff in 1919, taking our hymns and our lemonade with us. In 1945, fear of the Soviet Union made everyone martially minded; under our leadership, the Concert of Europe played Sousa and there was at least as much marching as dancing. But now the martial mood is fading; the nations are beating their swords into punch bowls and their spears into chafing dishes.

A new party is beginning, and we shall have to rouge, to dance, and to flirt with the best of them. That will be harder today; our jewels are mortgaged and our gown is patched; we are not as young as we used to be and have put on a little weight. We can't afford to stay home and sulk this time, and since we can't afford to pay the piper, we can no longer expect to always call the tune.

It will not be impossible to shine at the ball. The Soviet Union is fatter and worse dressed than we will ever be, and its dance card is full. . . . There are plenty of partners willing to give us a whirl. The national interest is the key to our position in this strange new world of peace. Those interests have not changed much since colonial times: We want a world that is open to peaceful commerce, and one that is open to growth.

We can no longer impose these values on the rest of the world, but they remain persuasive. France, for instance, does not want an insular Europe if it means German domination. Korea feels the same way about Japan. Our interest in growth continues to be shared by developing nations.

There is nothing inevitable about the future. But to avoid a fate like that of Argentina, the United States will need to stop gloating about winning the Cold War and start to assess, soberly, its place in the global economy. . . .

# 28

---

# OIL AND POWER IN THE NINETIES

---

## James Schlesinger

**James Schlesinger argues in this essay that developments already in place ensure that global energy security will increasingly depend on oil imports from a small group of members of the Organization of Petroleum Exporting Countries (OPEC) and thus on political developments in the volatile Persian Gulf region. Although the essay was written before the Iraq-Kuwait crisis—which stimulated a sharp rise in the cost of oil and a military response by the United States and others—the forces in place before the crisis promise to remain relevant well into the future. Schlesinger served as U.S. Secretary of Defense during the administrations of Richard Nixon and Gerald Ford and as Secretary of Energy under President Jimmy Carter. He is author of *America at Century's End* (1989).**

It is my purpose in this article to examine certain trends in energy use and supply and their possible impact on geopolitics in the decades ahead. In energy, recent trends amount to the reemergence of older tendencies temporarily suppressed by the oil shocks of the 1970s. These will be related to prospective changes in military strength, in political attitudes, and geopolitical structures—which are also a reflection of forces discernible to the past, though less rigorously so than is the case for energy.

Used by permission of James Schlesinger.

302

. . . One cannot, of course, measure with any precision either the strength or the pace at which these trends may influence future developments. Moreover, one can have no assurance they will not be reversed. . . . Nonetheless, behind the trends that I shall specify, there is considerable momentum. They may be slowed, but it would take a supreme act of will to reverse them entirely.

As the seventeenth-century English political operative and savant, the Marquis of Halifax, stated: "The best qualification of a prophet is to have a good memory." Quite right, for the future is certain to be influenced by the reemergence of past tendencies which, for one reason or another, have been temporarily submerged. Among such tendencies is the intimate association between energy security and the strength of nations or, more broadly, the strength of alliance systems. That association—which in the past has led to military conflict to establish control over fields of coal or oil—has been partially obscured since World War II. The major power blocs have possessed sufficient energy resources—or sufficient political and military power to assure security of supply. But those halcyon days when energy security could be taken for granted came to an end in 1973. Since then the rise of nationalism, the rebirth of religious fundamentalism, and the weakened cohesion of the major power blocs have called renewed attention to the issue of energy security.

## THE ENERGY SCENE

Without doubt, the most significant, indeed the dominant, trend in energy is the rapidly growing dependency on OPEC and the producing nations of the Persian Gulf. In just four years [1986–1990] the demand of OPEC crude oil has risen by some 40 percent—thereby eliminating the atmosphere of desperation, instability, and cut-throat competition that marked OPEC in the middle of the decade. Of late, OPEC has had the comforting task of allocating shares of a *growing* pie. Moreover, the demand for OPEC's supply promises to continue to rise—steadily eliminating whatever surplus capacity presently (or prospectively) exists. This dramatic change in the market has in large measure been driven by developments in the United States. Others too have made their contributions, but in moving the world back toward a sellers' market in oil the United States has again demonstrated that it remains the leader of the Free World.

America's appetite for oil is growing. In four years consumption . . . increased some 15 percent, recovering from the comparatively low level of 15 million barrels per day (BPD) in 1985 to a level . . . approaching the peak reached before the second oil shock. . . . America's ability to satisfy this appetite from domestic resources has been shrinking. The result has been a growth in oil imports, a trend that has recently accelerated. By the end of 1990 imports will have grown by some 4.5 million BPD —roughly doubling in the five year period. Demand continues to rise. Production continues to fall—though the volume of this decline must diminish with time. Nonetheless, by the middle of the decade imports will again have increased by an amount similar to that of the last five years.

There is nothing that compels import growth to occur at this pace. Yet, despite the persistent political rhetoric, not to say hand-wringing, regarding national security, nothing has been done to arrest the growth of imports—and precious little is likely to be done in the foreseeable future. In this era the United States appears wedded to reliance upon "free market forces." Despite a deep-seated public myth or conceit regarding the robustness of America's energy industry (a conceit not significantly extending into the energy industry itself), America has in Ricardian terms virtually no comparative advantage in the production of crude oil. Indeed, it has an impressively high-cost oil industry, getting higher as depletion proceeds.

To be sure, there exist the usual possibilities of enhancing domestic oil production or achieving fuel substitution and limiting oil consumption through a variety of fiscal or regulatory measures. But fiscal options are drastically limited by . . . political constraints. . . . Discouraging oil consumption or directing usage to other fuels through regulatory devices is highly suspect at this time—save for motives of environmental protection. Thus, in brief, imports will continue to grow and to grow rapidly because the measures required to restrain such growth are not in accord with the prevailing national psyche.

Despite the continuing declamations regarding the villainy of the OPEC cartel—which curiously reached their peak at precisely the moment of the cartel's greatest weakness—the United States is now unquestionably the best ally OPEC has. The growth in U.S. import requirements (followed by a corresponding rise in OPEC production) has done more to remove excess slack from the market than has any other force. Though it will have much outside assistance, all by itself the U.S. will dissipate much of the remaining surplus capacity and make the market quite snug by the mid-1990s.

The United States has become the main engine for the restoration of OPEC power. From the perspective of the cartel, actions should speak louder than words. A friend in need is a friend indeed. The United States has been such a friend.

What is true for the United States is, to a lesser degree, true elsewhere. At least for the OECD (Organization for Economic Cooperation and Development) nations production has already peaked and will continue to decline. For non-OPEC producers, generally including the centrally-planned economies, it is likely to stabilize and then decline. World consumption continues to rise, perhaps most markedly among Third World nations.

As the market tightens, excess availability declines, and ultimately prices rise, other nations will pay increasing attention to the rapidly expanding role of the United States in the international oil trade. There will be renewed criticism for its propensity to squander energy. Such criticism flourished during the late 1970s, when the growing U.S. appetite for imports similarly pushed up the market. It will be the Return of the Energy Squanderer.

It should be also noted that by the mid-1990s the United States will be facing foreign exchange requirements of over $100 billion a year just to finance its oil imports. Particularly in light of the present health of the U.S. balance of trade, these additional payments for oil imports will detract both from the U.S. economy and from the strength of its geopolitical position.

It is not my primary purpose to speculate on the rate at which prices might be pushed up. If OPEC has learned a lesson from its overreaching at the end of the 1970s, it will exhibit restraint and allow the price to rise gradually enough that it attracts only minimal public attention. Nor is it my purpose to delve deeply into the financial repercussions of the growing oil trade for the balance of payments of importing nations. Suffice to say that the strong will survive and the weak will be hurt. The main point is to emphasize the steadily growing dependency on OPEC and upon the Persian Gulf, a region of the world not noted for its political stability.

As the outside world steadily becomes more dependent upon Gulf crude, the Middle East will become the focus of revived and ever increasing external interest. Even without such outside attention, internal passions and rivalries have turned that region into something like the world's cauldron. Add to those seething rivalries an ever-growing dependency and an ever-rising stake, and the Middle East becomes something akin to the Balkans before 1914—a potential tinder box. Any spark must draw the immediate attention of outside forces.

## THE GEOPOLITICAL SCENE

But, what is happening to those outside forces—those changes in military capabilities, political goals and attitudes, the cohesion of alliances, and the relative strength and weakness of economies which together provide the structure of geopolitics? Here the trends are less defined and less certain than they are in energy. Nevertheless, they are sufficiently well-defined that they can be delineated with some precision.

Perhaps the greatest uncertainty in determining what the geopolitics will be is the evolution of the Soviet Union, which is as yet unresolved. Under Mr. Gorbachev the Soviet Union, at least temporarily, has placed less stress on military intimidation. Starting with the Afghanistan adventure, but more spectacularly with the recent collapse in Eastern Europe and its own internal strains, the Soviet Union has visibly faded as a threat. But its future remains uncertain and, reflecting that uncertainty, questions persist regarding the perceptions of the military threat, superpower rivalry, and East-West tension. Right now one must judge that there will be, at a minimum, an extended armistice in the Cold War—with no return likely to the tensions of either the high point of the Cold War or the early 1980s. Nonetheless, in assessing the geopolitical future the Soviet Union does remain, as Churchill called it, an "enigma."

As the perception of the Soviet threat fades, the nations of the West will gradually (or perhaps precipitously) relax. U.S. military power will be substantially reduced—the changed appreciation of the threat environment reinforcing what had already become inevitable because of budgetary pressures.

The power of the West will decline, indeed *continue* to decline, as it has been doing in some sense since 1939 or 1945. The process of decolonization followed by the general withdrawal of the European colonial powers—perhaps most dramatically exemplified by the withdrawal of British power "east of Suez"—was for a long time masked by the preponderant power after World War II of the United States. It is quite clear, indeed it has become a cliché, that the era of *preponderant* American power is now ending. The United States will remain the single most powerful state on the world stage, but the period of *pax Americana* is now over. Western power, while it will remain formidable, will gradually be reduced—for demographic if for no other reasons. In the twenty-first century the population of the Western bloc will have fallen to less than 10 percent of the world's population—in contrast to the 30 percent that it was prior to World War II.

The spread of sophisticated military capabilities is likely to continue. The perceived decline of the Soviet threat and a less bipolar world means that the number of ready suppliers of military equipment is likely to rise. For similar reasons the inhibitions regarding sales will be weakened. The Middle East will continue to be a major and perhaps growing repository of such sophisticated military equipment. That would substantially reduce the ease and increase the military and political cost of outside intervention.

One should not be misled by the ease of U.S. intervention in the Gulf tanker war during the later 1980s to protect Kuwaiti tankers and generally to offset Iranian power (despite American protestations of neutrality in the war). Those conditions were unique. Iran, through its own follies and through the course of the war, had largely eliminated its own air and naval capabilities. The flow of events led it to a point of substantial exhaustion both militarily and economically. Given its weakness, particularly of its air and naval forces, it was remarkably, if not deceptively, easy for the U.S. to neutralize residual Iranian military power. Many in the West, however, are likely to trick themselves into believing somehow these unique conditions involving an exhausted Iran is the normal model.

Over time, Soviet capacity for military intervention in the Gulf region is likely to increase relative to the West—assuming that the Soviet Union can surmount its current "time of troubles." Western military forces will be reduced—along with the inclination, and perhaps the will, to become militarily engaged in the region. At the same time, Soviet conventional forces will remain immense. If logistics are improved, their capability for intervention will grow. The Soviet Union is near at hand; the United States is far distant. Thus, if there were a sudden introduction of outside forces—*and that remains a very big if*—it becomes increasingly plausible that the outsider would be the Soviet Union.* And the temptation to intervene may grow as the long-anticipated decline in Soviet oil production sets in.

What about the Gulf region itself? As the outside world becomes increasingly dependent upon the Gulf, the principal nations of the region will become far more influential. Their financial difficulties will rapidly or gradually come to an end. Their place in the sun will be restored—along with their self-esteem. They will become increasingly cocky. They will also become more tempting as a target.

The Middle East will likely continue to be marked by disunity. If so, as the oil market tightens, it will be subject to disruptions and supply interruptions due to indigenous conflicts. It is possible, of course, that the producing states may become more unified. Given the present conditions, and particularly the historic rivalry between the Persians and the Arabs, this appears implausible. Unity would likely be an imposed unity—an attempt at such imposed unity by the Ayatollah Khomeini has visibly failed. Nonetheless, if such unity could be achieved, it would further enhance the economic and political power of the region relative to the outside world.

Far more likely is a continuation of political disunity along with limited economic cooperation. The broader OPEC cartel will gradually be replaced by an "inner cartel" of the Gulf nations—those that have the reserves for additional production. The attitude and behavior of this "inner cartel" will come to be the chief, indeed the dominant, influence in oil markets.

Concern about the Soviet Union may at some point revive among the nations of the region—as the memory of the failed Afghan adventure recedes. Although the Soviet Union has proved to be a far weaker competitor in terms of military technology than generally was believed in the 1970s, its capacity for local intervention will not diminish significantly and could grow substantially. There are asymmetries in the ways in which the strength of the superpowers are reduced. Consequently, the nations of the region may ultimately choose to adopt the longtime Chinese injunction: Bring to one's aid the barbarian far-removed, thereby to neutralize the barbarian close at hand. In a sense that would represent a return to Persia's historic policy.

We can foresee a world that has grown increasingly and perhaps excessively dependent on the Gulf region for its energy resources and for the performance of

---

*At the time this article was written the author could not have foreseen the dramatic response of the United States and others to Iraq's invasion of Kuwait in August 1990; noteworthy is that both Iraq and Kuwait are Persian Gulf members of OPEC.—Eds.

its economies. The Middle East will thus become the cockpit of contending world forces—and a potential tinder box. If there is a major conflict, the Middle East is likely to be its vortex. "If there ever is a World War III," as one oil industry analyst has hyperbolically observed, "it will be fought over the Middle Eastern oil reserves."

The Middle Eastern nations themselves will be more influential, more self-confident, better armed, and, yet, probably still marked by disunity. Western capacity and inclination for intervention will likely diminish. The ability and the incentive for the Soviets to intervene may grow. Indeed, the latent threat of Soviet domination of the region (and of the world's oil valve)—with all that it implies—will not diminish for a long time. In their relations with the Soviet Union the nations of the Gulf will vary between fear and flirtation.

Let me close with two final observations. First, an early student of geopolitics, Karl Haushofer, reached his ultimate conclusion with the pithy declaration: "Who controls the Heartland, controls the world." That may have been academic or pseudo-academic melodrama—but it does provide food for thought. It might now be said that whichever great power may come to control the world's oil tap in the Gulf region, will to a large extent control the world.

Second, . . . recall the Beatitude: "The meek shall inherit the earth." Reportedly it was amended by the late J. Paul Getty to the effect that, the meek may inherit the earth, but not the subsoil rights. His judgment has been strongly reinforced by the actions of the Ayatollah Khomeini and by others. Whatever else, those crucial subsoil rights in the Middle East are not now, nor are they likely to be, controlled by the meek.

# 29

# THE MISLEADING METAPHOR OF DECLINE

## Joseph S. Nye, Jr.

**In this essay Joseph S. Nye, Jr., refutes the popular argument that the United States is a declining world power. He is especially concerned that the analogy with Britain's decline may be misleading, "for this directs attention away from the real problems arising out of long-term changes in world politics and suggests remedies that would weaken rather than strengthen America's standing." Nye is Clarence Dillon Professor of International Affairs at Harvard University. He is co-author of the influential book *Power and Interdependence* (1989).**

When the United States emerged from the Second World War with its armies victorious and its dollar impregnable, Arnold Toynbee argued that it had to succeed Britain as the leader of the world. Comparisons to Britain are still being made, but now they emphasize the negative rather than the positive. According to one recent poll, nearly half the American public believes that the United States, like post-imperial Britain, is in "decline."

Some scholars have suggested that America's decline follows a pattern that has recurred throughout history. A growing nation builds its military power to protect its expanding economic interests, but eventually the cost of sustaining

This article draws on material from Joseph S. Nye, Jr., *Bound to Lead: The Changing Nature of American Power* (New York: Basic Books, 1990). Some footnotes have been deleted and others have been renumbered to appear in consecutive order. Used by permission of Joseph S. Nye, Jr.

such power saps its strength and another rising economic power takes its place. The sociologist Immanuel Wallerstein sees such imperial overstretch as a regular happening, with Venice starting to decline around 1500, Holland around 1660, Britain around 1873, and America around 1967. Paul Kennedy, in the best-selling book *The Rise and Fall of the Great Powers,* . . . writes that "the difficulties experienced by contemporary societies which are militarily top-heavy merely repeat those which, in their time, affected Philip II's Spain, Nicholas II's Russia, and Hitler's Germany."

Such historical analogies suggest that major foreign-policy changes are in order, but if the analogies are misleading, the diagnosis may be wrong. Retrenchment could produce the very weakening of American power which it is supposed to avert. Withdrawal from international commitments might reduce American influence overseas without strengthening the domestic economy. In fact, the nations of the world have become so inextricably intertwined that efforts to draw back would surely be frustrated. . . .

Thus there is no virtue in either overstating or understating American strength. The former leads to a failure to adapt; the latter could lead to cures that do more harm than the disease.

## THE VICISSITUDES OF DECLINE

The idea of decline has haunted the western imagination since the fall of Rome, and a long history exists of premature and misleading predictions of decline. Many eighteenth-century British statesmen, for example, lamented Britain's decline as a result of losing the American colonies. Horace Walpole foresaw Britain's reduction "from a mighty empire . . . [to] as insignificant a country as Denmark or Sardinia!" Colored as they were by the eighteenth-century view of colonial commerce, such prophecies could not foresee the new industrial base of power in the Victorian period which would give Britain a second century at the top. Yet even then, at the height of Britain's ascendancy, Matthew Arnold worried of "an imminent danger of England losing immeasurably in all ways, declining into a sort of greater Holland."

Decline bundles together two quite different concepts: a decrease in external power, and internal deterioration or decay. A country, though, may experience decline in one sense but not in the other. For example, the Netherlands flourished internally in the seventeenth century but declined in power *relatively,* because other nations became stronger. Spain, in contrast, lost external power in part because it suffered an absolute economic decline from the 1620s to the 1680s.

Obviously, internal deterioration can contribute to a loss of external power. Even so, it is often difficult to identify which internal changes accounted for the loss of power and when they occurred. Scholars have advanced more than two hundred causes for the decline of Rome and still disagree on dates. The Romans themselves often saw their world in despairing terms; in fact, prophecies of decline were heard as early as 154 B.C., six centuries before the conventional date for the fall of Rome. In the prime years of decline—A.D. 300 to 450—the Roman economy remained healthy. . . .

Power is a relational concept. It depends partly on what is happening at home, but even more on what is happening outside. An empire may last for a long time after aspects of its civilization begin to decay at home, as long as outside challengers are weak. Although civic corruption and a loss of administrative and military efficiency may have allowed nomadic tribes to sack Rome, Rome's external challengers were weak. The "fall" in 476 came some two centuries after the onset of major corruption in the government and deterioration in the military.

A nation may also decline relative to others because it chooses not to use the resources of power at its disposal. For example, France in the early eighteenth century allowed its naval and fiscal resources to stagnate relative to Britain's; but, unlike Spain's decline in the previous century, the French one was not permanent. The stagnation in French war potential did not represent an absolute decline, as the subsequent military exuberance under Napoleon proved. Yet in terms of basic resources, the political scientist Charles Doran writes, "France's ability to expand militarily was greater in 1750 than it would be in 1805." To take a more modern example, the United States emerged from the First World War a potentially dominant global power. But it chose a policy of isolationism that made it a secondary player in world political events. American influence was less in 1928 than in 1918, but not because America had lost power.

## WHAT THE NUMBERS SAY

There is no question that the United States is less powerful at the end than it was in the middle of the twentieth century. Even by conservative estimates, the U.S. share of global production has declined from more than a third of the total after the Second World War to a little more than a fifth in the 1980s. The United States was strengthened by the war; the other great powers were devastated. In that sense American economic preponderance in the 1950s was anomalous, like being the boy on the block who dominates while others have the flu. American preponderance was bound to erode as other nations regained their economic health.

Paul Kennedy argues that the U.S. decline has been continuous: "The U.S. share of world GNP, which declined naturally since 1945, has declined much more quickly than it should have over the last few years." The political scientist David Calleo is even more alarmist: "Thanks to economic strain and mismanagement, relative decline has begun to turn absolute."

But the figures do not support the case for a continuous decline in America's share of world product. Charles Wolf, of the Rand Corporation, points out that "if a more appropriate and representative base year is used—say, the mid-1960s (or even a pre–World War II year such as 1938)—the remarkable fact is that the U.S. economy's share of the global product was about the same 'then' as it is 'now': about 22% to 24%."

Some estimates of the U.S. share of world product date the fading of what we might call the Second World War effect somewhat later than Wolf does, but the result is the same. For example, the economist Herbert Block estimates that the United States accounted for about a quarter of world product at the beginning of the twentieth century, and about a third in 1950. The postwar U.S. share declined until 1974 and then stabilized. The American Council on Competitiveness similarly finds that the U.S. share of world product has held constant at 23 percent since the mid-1970s. The U.S. share of the product of the major industrial democracies actually increased slightly in the 1980s. The Central Intelligence Agency, using numbers that reflect the purchasing power of different currencies, shows the American share of world product increasing, from 25 percent in 1975 to 26 percent in 1988.

Such numbers call into question the view that American decline has been either precipitous or continuous. They suggest instead that the Second World War effect lasted about a quarter century or so and that the American position thereafter stabilized. Most of the decline had worked its way through the system by the mid-1970s.

According to the overstretch theory, a great power is likely to find that it is spending much more on defense than it did two generations earlier, yet its world is less secure. But American numbers do not fit the theory. Even after the Reagan Administration buildup, the current U.S. defense outlay is about six percent of GNP; in the late 1950s it was about 10 percent.

Furthermore, the United States defense burden is not at all like those of Spain and France in their last days of grandeur. Philip II's Spain devoted three fourths of all government expenditure to war and war debt. The France of Louis XIV and the Russia of Peter the Great appear to have devoted 75 and 85 percent respectively of their revenues to war and the military establishment. In the United States today about 27 percent of the federal budget is spent on defense (including veterans' benefits). And unlike the historical examples, America's overseas commitments do not involve the permanent occupation and control of conquered territories.

The ratio of America's defense burden to its share of world product was actually lower in the 1980s than in the 1950s. Indeed, contrary to the theory of imperial overstretch, the U.S. defense burden today is lighter than it was in the 1950s, and the political burdens of U.S. commitment are lighter today than they were in the 1960s, during the Vietnam War.

This does not mean that the current defense budget is wisely constructed. On the contrary, the buildup of the 1980s was hasty and enormously wasteful, and the government has not made enough hard choices in cutting back the procurement of unnecessary weapons systems. Given the changes in world politics, a strong case can be made for allocating more resources to international institutions, communications, and assistance to critical countries. If such expenditures are necessary, the country can afford them. Unlike the historical examples—or the Soviet Union today, where defense expenditures constitute some 17 percent of GNP—the United States does not fit the theory of imperial overstretch.

## THE DECLINE OF BRITISH POWER

Some critics are skeptical of such aggregate measures and prefer historical analogy. The American situation, however, is different from the most frequently cited case, that of Britain. Explaining Britain's decline has become almost an industry in itself. A long list of domestic causes has been adduced, and has been in the making for a long time. As early as 1898 Henry Adams believed that "British industry is quite ruined." But he also believed that "Germany has become a mere province of Russia." In 1900 his brother Brooks Adams wrote that since 1890 "an impression has gained ground that England is relatively losing vitality, that the focus of energy and wealth is shifting, and that, therefore, a period of instability is pending." He blamed British lethargy and high living, in part, and pointed to the Boer War as an indication that Britain was no longer willing to accept casualties in war. Of course, that notion was soon disproved by the enormous British losses in the First World War.

In fact, the First World War showed Britain to be an impressive power. It had not only manpower but also industry capable of being mobilized for war, overseas investments that could finance the purchase of U.S. technology and war supplies, and a navy large enough to ensure control of the Atlantic. Britain could also call upon the resources of its empire. Of the 8.6 million members of the British forces in the First World War, nearly a third came from overseas (though four fifths of the expenditure was British). By 1918 Britain had the world's largest air force and navy, and the empire had reached its maximum size. In 1921 both popular and informed opinion in Britain agreed with General Jan Smuts, of South Africa, that the British empire had "emerged from the War quite the greatest power in the world."

Yet the war—or, more precisely, the thirty-year struggle with Germany—did more to hasten British decline than any other factor. Competing with Germany, rather than possessing an empire, is what drove up defense spending. It is perhaps too simple to say, along with Woody Allen in *Zelig,* that "Britain owned the world and Germany wanted it." But if Bismarck and his successors had not unified the German states into a single Continental force after 1870 (with a population larger than Britain's), the British era might have lasted longer. It was Germany, not the pre-1914 empire, that overstretched Britain.

Of course, the British era would not have lasted forever. Nothing does. Early in the nineteenth century Alexis de Tocqueville pointed out the enormous potential of the United States and Russia. In 1835 the English statesman Richard Cobden declared that "our only chance of national prosperity lies in the timely remodeling of our system, so as to put it as nearly as possible upon an equality with the improved management of the Americans." In 1883 the Cambridge historian Sir John Seeley argued that federation of the empire was the only way that Britain would be able to compete with Russia and the United States, which were "on an altogether different scale of magnitude." In 1878 the former (and future) Prime Minister William Gladstone worried that America "can, and probably will, wrest from us [our] commercial superiority."

In short, Britain's relative power was bound to decline, because of a number of external factors. The spread of industrialization raised new economic and military competitors. The growing strength of Germany meant that Britain would no longer have a free ride on the Continental balance of power. The spread of railways meant that Britain would no longer have as much time to raise interventionary forces and transport them to the Continent.

The distribution of power in the regional balances of the Atlantic and the Pacific was also shifting, because of the growing strength of both the United States and Japan. By the turn of the century British planners felt they could no longer afford a navy that dominated the Pacific and the Western Hemisphere as well as home waters. Thus Britain signed an alliance with Japan and appeased the United States with a number of conciliatory measures, including accession to the Panama Canal, which further enhanced American naval strength by allowing the United States to shift its fleet quickly between two oceans. Henceforth, as Aaron Friedberg, a political scientist at Princeton, has shown, Britain applied its traditional two-power naval standard—having a navy equal to those of the next two contenders—only to home waters.

A final external cause of the decline of British power was the rise of nationalism, which helped to transform the empire from an asset into a liability. In 1914 London declared war on Germany on behalf of the entire empire. But long before post–Second World War anti-colonial nationalism stripped away Britain's Asian and African colonies, the "white" dominions of Canada, Australia, and New Zealand were resisting rule from London. By the time of the Chanak crisis with Turkey, in 1922, London had discovered that it could not count on automatic support from the empire. After 1926 British military planners no longer considered the British Commonwealth to be a reliable basis for military plans. Commonwealth forces were at best a possible bonus. Yet, as the British historian Corelli Barnett points out, in wartime the continued existence of the empire "would pump away from England the military resources she needed for her own war in Europe." American Lend-Lease in 1941 provided those resources, but by 1945 "British power had quietly vanished amidst the stupendous events of the Second World War."

There were also important internal causes of the decline of British power. Among the most important were the failure to maintain the productivity of British industry, particularly in new sectors, and to improve the nature and level of education. The two factors were related. British governing-class education was really appropriate to a moment in history that had already vanished, according to the economist Andrew Tylecote. Britons hardly thought at all of British power in terms of industrial competitiveness, science, technology, or strategy. The nation found the imperial alternative "more attractive than the 'industrial' one, because its upper class was dominated by a landowning aristocracy which set the tone for the rest."

While Britain continued to produce entrepreneurs who responded to market incentives, they focused on the staples of textiles, shipbuilding, and light industry rather than the new science-based industries. Britain failed to invest in the latest technology in such critical new industries as chemicals, electricity, and precision engineering. As the British writer David Marquand has argued, "The most sophisticated sectors of the late-nineteenth and early-twentieth centuries depended far more on applied science. . . . It was in exports from these that Britain was most conspicuously outclassed." In 1913 Britain controlled two thirds of world exports of manufacturers in declining sectors (like textiles), but only one fifth of world exports in expanding sectors (like chemicals). Until 1902 Britain had no public secondary-school system, despite public awareness of German educational superiority. Britain had seven universities, to compare with twenty-two in Germany and nearly 700 colleges and technical schools in the United States.

The increasing economic importance of overseas investment was transforming Britain into a rentier society, in which financial interests maintained an overvalued currency detrimental to British industry. Overseas investment rose from 0.2 percent to 5.2 percent of GNP from 1870 to 1913. By 1900 eighty percent of the capital issues on the London market were for overseas investment. By 1914 Britain owned 43 percent of the world stock of investment overseas. As the Nobel laureate Sir W. Arthur Lewis put it, "She could not pioneer in developing new commodities because this now required a scientific base which did not accord with her humanistic snobbery. So instead she invested her savings abroad; the economy decelerated, the average level of unemployment increased, and her young people emigrated."

Finally, Britain's domestic political process did not allow the full transformation of Britain's potential resources of power into effective influence. Aaron Friedberg convincingly shows that the problem was not complacency; concern about decline was widespread. At the turn of the century the press expressed concern that England lagged in scientific organization, applied technology, and worker training. But the debate was confused, with little agreement about what measures would be useful or what responses appropriate. While a return to primacy was impossible after 1900, and Britain did seek out new allies after the

Boer War, the British elites could have done more to preserve Britain's position and to prepare for coming challenges.

British Conservatives, however, believed that Britain was financially stretched to its limit, and feared the economic effects of raising income taxes. They failed to invest in the forces needed to maintain global naval supremacy, and disguised that fact from the public by keeping the old slogans. Thus the empire became dependent on the good will of the new regional powers, the United States and Japan. Henceforth Britain had to avoid embroilment with more than one first-class power in more than one region of the world at a time. Furthermore, Britain did not implement conscription (as the other major European powers had done by 1872) or pay for an adequate army to help maintain the balance on the Continent in the new age of rail mobilization. The 1906 plan for 120,000 men to assist France proved woefully inadequate in 1914.

The British debate over trade was phrased in terms of the polar extremes of protectionism and free trade. Little attention was given to temporarily protecting critical sectors or forcing reciprocity on foreign markets. Colonial Secretary Joseph Chamberlain tried to rouse his Conservative colleagues to a more coherent response, but his protectionist scheme would have made things worse. Not surprisingly, it attracted the support of the least competitive elements of British industry. In any event, he wound up splitting his party. Prime Minister Arthur Balfour's moderate suggestion of selective retaliatory tariffs to force foreign markets open was lost in the ideological crossfire over free trade, and little attention was paid to the security implications of the British lag in the most modern sectors of industry.

Joseph Chamberlain was no more successful elsewhere in the security area. At a 1902 colonial conference he failed to persuade the colonies to share the burden of naval costs. His plaint that "the Weary Titan staggers under the too vast orb of its fate" did not pry forth new resources. Nor could he convince his colleagues that Britain's burdens were relatively light. In fact, the entire government budget was only 15 percent of GNP (in modern Britain it is nearly 45 percent). And although the Boer War created a deficit from 1899 to 1903, the budget was in surplus thereafter; the national debt in 1907 was not much higher than it had been in the 1880s. The historian A.J.P. Taylor estimates that Britain spent 3.4 percent of its national income on armaments in 1914, while Germany spent 4.6 percent, France 4.8 percent, and Russia 6.3 percent. Other estimates place Britain ahead of Germany but behind France in its military burden.

So why did Britain decide that it could not afford to maintain naval supremacy or an adequate Continental expeditionary force? In large part because the adherents of the prevailing economic orthodoxy believed in the negative effects of government spending, and they particularly opposed raising income taxes. The popular belief that Britain was suffering from imperial overstretch—despite the lightness of Britain's defense burden, at three percent of GNP—prevented

Britain from investing as well as it might have in the domestic and external resources of power which could have slowed decline.

Even if its leaders had played their domestic cards perfectly, however, Britain would have seen a significant decline in its power in the twentieth century. A.J.P. Taylor speculates that the impressive growth of German industry would have brought Germany to the mastery of Europe if it had not been for the First World War. The industrialization of America, Russia, and Japan was bound to shrink Britain's influence. Moreover, nationalism was soon to erode the empire. In a sense, Britain rose to its leading position because it was on the first wave of the Industrial Revolution in a pre-nationalist era. But it has always been remarkable that such a small country in Europe could control a quarter of the world's people in the largest Western empire since Roman times.

## HOW THE UNITED STATES IS DIFFERENT

There are at least four major differences in the positions of power held by Victorian Britain and modern America. The first is the degree of predominance. Britain's resources of power in the mid-nineteenth century were most impressive in naval force and manufacturing production. As the Harvard political scientist Robert Keohane has written, "Britain had never been as superior in productivity to the rest of the world as the United States was after 1945." Nor is the twentieth-century United States as dependent on foreign trade and investment as nineteenth-century Britain was. Even during its heyday, around 1875, Britain ranked third in military expenditure. Not only is the United States more powerful in more ways than Britain was but there are differences of scale that suggest that its power may persist longer. Today it requires a united Europe, not just a united Germany, to challenge the United States for global leadership. Britain, an island about the size of Oregon, ruled a quarter of the world. But, as we have seen, the empire quickly fell victim to nationalism and ceased to be a reliable basis for British military plans.

Second, at least since 1865 the United States has been a single, continental-scale economy immune to nationalist disintegration. Today American imports account for only 12 percent of GNP, in contrast to the British figure of 25 percent in 1914. At the peak of its power, in the 1870s, Britain's economy was only the third largest in the world, and it fell to fourth place in 1914. However, the American GNP today is much larger than those of the nearest competitor states. One should keep such differences of scale in mind when considering theories of overstretch.

Third, for all the loose talk (and looser definitions) of an American empire, there are important differences between Britain's territorial empire and America's areas of influence. Americans have more choice about types and levels of defense commitments than Britons had. There are more degrees of freedom for all parties. American trade is not drawn in the same degree to unsophisticated markets. By 1913 two thirds of British exports were going to semi-industrial and nonindustrial countries. Some modern historians argue that the territorial empire became a net drain on Britain. Whether one looks at NATO as a forward defense of American borders, in which Europeans provide most of the manpower, or as an act of American generosity, it is hard to see our alliances constituting a similar drain, particularly since the withdrawal of American troops to home bases would save money only if the units were also disbanded. Unlike Edwardian Britain, which had to leave its isolation and cast about for allies at the beginning of the century, the United States at the end of the century must transform and update the successful alliances with the great industrial democracies which have been critical to the global balance of power for the past forty years.

A fourth major difference lies in the geopolitical challenges that the two nations face. Most important, in 1900 Britain faced rising contenders in Germany, the United States, and Russia. The nearest of those contenders, Germany, had not only surpassed Britain in economic strength but also was becoming militarily dominant and a threat to Britain's supremacy on the Continent. America's external situation today is different. Its principal military adversary, the Soviet Union, is the power with a bad case of overstretch. Not only is the USSR confronted with an unstable Eastern European empire [no longer under direct Soviet control] but the Soviet economy has suffered a serious deceleration of the growth that previously allowed expansion. In addition, Soviet defense is often estimated to cost 15 percent of GNP, and some estimates place the costs of defense and empire at more than 20 percent of GNP—about three times as high as the relative burden on the U.S. economy. The British analogy would be apt if Kaiser Wilhelm II's Germany, rather than passing Britain in economic and military strength, had been declining and looking for the chance to take a breathing spell from its military buildup.

None of the other major world powers is now overtaking the United States in both military and economic strength. Although Western Europe has a skilled population, a robust GNP, and the improved Common Market coming in 1992, few observers think that European integration will progress soon to a single government or a single security policy. Similarly, China might be a potential rival of the United States' over a much longer term, but China's human and technological infrastructure is much less developed than that of the United States or even the Soviet Union. And while many Americans believe that Japanese economic strength is a greater challenge than Soviet military power, economic competition is not a zero-sum game, where one country's gain is its competitor's loss. Thus far Japan has chosen the strategy of a trading state rather than of a military power. There is no current analogue to the Kaiser's Germany. Even [the] reunited Germany [possesses] an economy only one-fifth the size of that of the United States.

The more interesting comparisons between Britain and America lie in the domestic realm. Here there are legitimate causes for concern. Productivity growth in the American economy has fallen to an annual rate of 1.4 percent from an average annual rate of 2.7 percent in the first two postwar decades. In the 1980s net national savings fell to an all-time low of 2.0 percent, and gross investment, at 17 percent of GNP, was at only about half the Japanese level of 30 percent. Civilian research and development accounted for 1.8 percent of GNP, while in Germany and Japan it accounted for 2.6 and 2.8 percent. Foreign inventors received almost half the U.S. patents granted in 1987, as compared with a third a decade earlier.

Even here one should be wary of too simple comparisons to Britain. Whereas Britain fell behind in the leading sectors of chemicals and electricity at the turn of the century, the United States remains one of the leaders in such critical new sectors as information processing and biotechnology. The United States attracts capital from the rest of the world; Britain exported it. Further, whereas emigration drained talented Britons from their homeland, immigration continually infuses the United States with new labor and energy.

Perhaps the most interesting domestic comparison, however, is political. Will the United States cope both with its international commitments as the nation that other nations look to for leadership and with its need for domestic reforms? The British experience suggests caution. The political processes of Victorian democracy tended to fragment the national debate. Conservative politicians failed to invest adequately in the future. There was a widespread reluctance to raise the level of taxation, which was low. Here the analogy with modern America becomes more apt: the United States is the world's richest country, but it acts poor. Although America is one of the most lightly taxed of the industrial countries, the American public seems unwilling to invest adequately in the future, and political leaders have done little to stem the flow of resources from investment to consumption in the 1980s. . . .

Americans are right to be concerned about the changing role of the United States in the world. However, seeing the problem as American decline and drawing analogies to Britain is misleading, for this directs attention away from the real problems arising out of long-term changes in world politics and suggests remedies that would weaken rather than strengthen America's standing. Withdrawal from international commitments would reduce U.S. influence without necessarily strengthening the domestic economy. Indeed, recent experience suggests that what the United States thereby saved in international expenditure might merely increase domestic consumption rather than investment.

Although the next decade will require Americans to cope with the debts of the 1980s, there is no reason why the world's wealthiest country cannot pay for its international commitments *and* its domestic investments. Americans can afford both social security and international security. The ultimate irony would be for Americans to perceive their country's short-term problems as indicators of long-term decline and respond in a way that cut them off from the sources of their international influence. As has happened many times before, the mix of resources that produces international power is changing. What is unprecedented is that the cycle of hegemonic conflict, with its attendant world wars, may not repeat itself. The United States at the end of the century retains more traditional resources of power than any other country has. It also has the ideological and institutional resources to retain its leadership in the new domains of transnational interdependence. In that sense the U.S. situation at the end of the twentieth century is totally different from that of Britain at the century's beginning. The problem for American power today is not new challengers for hegemony; it is the new challenge of transnational interdependence.

A post–Cold War strategy for managing the transition to complex interdependence over the next decades will require that the United States commit sufficient resources to sustain the geopolitical balance, maintain an open attitude toward the rest of the world, develop new international institutions, and restore the domestic sources of American strength through major reforms and large-scale investments. The twin dangers Americans face are complacency about the domestic agenda and an unwillingness to pay whatever is necessary to maintain their capacity for international leadership. Neither attitude is warranted.

PART **FOUR**

## ECOLOGY AND POLITICS

Some years ago T. S. Eliot lamented poetically that the world would end not with a bang but with a whimper. The nuclear sword of Damocles, which hangs by the slenderest of threads, continues to threaten a fiery and shattering apocalypse. The quest for security in an insecure world thus continues unabated. Still, there is a perceptible pause. For a generation, the *Bulletin of the Atomic Scientists* has used the hands of a clock—with the hour hand pointed toward midnight and the minute hand moving seemingly inexorably toward it—to symbolize how close humankind stands to the nuclear precipice. In 1988, for the first time in sixteen years, the minute hand was moved away from the witching hour, not toward it—from three to six minutes to midnight. In April 1990 the clock was again reset, this time at ten minutes to midnight. And the editors reasoned that "this is the greatest opportunity in four decades to create a safe, sustainable world. . . . People must work more vigorously to demilitarize their societies and effectively address fundamental issues of poverty, hunger, and environmental damage. . . . Additional concrete actions . . . are needed before the hands of the clock can be turned back further. Still, the termination of the Cold War has lifted a grim weight from the human psyche. It has returned to humanity its hope for a future, and the chance to create one."

Will humankind seize the chance? Even as the threat of a nuclear apocalypse recedes, numerous challenges broadly conceived as "ecological" threaten that the final cataclysm may still occur, though now more by accretion than by design or accident—but with results no less fatal. Whether nation-states and

321

other world political actors will prove able to cope effectively with these challenges is problematic.

Part Four of *The Global Agenda* examines various issues and perspectives comprising the politics of the ecological problematique. *Ecology* in this context refers to the relationship between humans and their physical and biological environments. The importance of ecological issues in world politics derives from the combination of world population growth and technological developments that has placed increasing strains on the earth's delicate life-support systems. Food and resource scarcities have dotted the ecopolitical landscape from time to time in recent years, but it is a series of other environmental challenges—including acid rain, depletion of the stratospheric ozone layer, and, perhaps most ominously, global warming through the greenhouse effect—that has captured worldwide attention and, together with the demise of Cold War competition, pushed the ecological problematique toward the top of the global agenda.

Environmental stresses result from human efforts to expand the global carrying capacity and to stretch the ability of the global habitat to sustain ever higher living standards for ever larger numbers of people. Technological innovations that propel modern industrialization permit new and more efficient use of environmental resources. They also result in pollution and other forms of environmental degradation of waterways, land masses, and the atmosphere that threaten the environment future generations will inherit. The global commons—resources such as the oceans, the seabed, the radio spectrum, and outer space—previously regarded as the common heritage of humankind, are now capable of exploitation by the technologically sophisticated, who may seek to deny them to others.

The range of global political issues encompassed by the ecological agenda is broad and, like issues of peace and security and economic interactions, complex. The critical importance of ecological issues is perhaps less well recognized, however. Unless we have learned of these dangers through some kind of consciousness-raising event, most of us have been socialized by parents, peers, educators, and policymakers to view international politics as concerned almost exclusively with issues of war and peace. And we tend to think of war and peace in terms of armies marching or diplomats conferring. Incorporating in this image a concern for the economic dimensions of human conflict is not difficult, for questions relating to the distribution of material wealth touch us all. For most, however, ecological issues are more remote. Unless we are touched directly by an issue, such as the disposal of toxic chemical waste or spent nuclear fuel, or atmospheric contamination in the form of acid rain, or soil erosion due to strip mining or deforestation, or life-threatening drought caused by excessive heat, ecological issues seem so future-oriented as to be of little immediate relevance or concern. And in the councils of government, the future generally has, at best, a weak constituency.

Compelling as our traditional views of world politics may be, an adequate understanding of the agenda of contemporary world politics must include consideration of ecological issues and the perspectives that seek to broaden our understanding of them. In part this is because such issues bear directly on issues of war and peace. A global environment characterized by transboundary pollutants and resource scarcities may invite the classic kinds of interstate conflict—and war—that once characterized competition over territory. Even comparatively abundant but unevenly distributed resources may create global conflicts if they lead to a level of dependence on foreign sources of supply that is perceived as a threat to national security, as happened with oil in the 1970s and early 1980s—and which, in the view of many, may happen again. If population growth and resource scarcities also portend, as some have argued, that there are "limits to growth," and that the consumption patterns of the past necessary to support the standards of living to which at least the Western world has become accustomed must be curtailed in the future, questions of equity and justice, already so prominent on the North–South axis of the global political agenda, will become magnified. And if resource scarcities and a drive to preserve present living standards compel those with the technological ability to "mine" the global commons also to claim sovereign jurisdiction over them, the stage will be set for the kinds of jurisdictional disputes around which so much of history has turned. Richard J. Barnet has pointed out the importance of these issues to people and to nations with the observation that "Whoever controls world resources controls the world in a way that mere occupation of territory cannot match." Finally, war, the traditional mechanism of settling interstate disputes, may itself bring about an ecological catastrophe.

War often precipitates desecration of the environment. Rome sowed salt on a defeated Carthage to prevent its resurgence; the Dutch breached their own dikes to allow ocean saltwater to flood fertile farmlands in an effort to stop the advancing Germans during World War II; the United States used defoliants on the dense jungles in Vietnam in a effort to expose enemy guerrillas; and, most recently, Iraq engaged in what the United States called an act of "environmental terrorism" without military purpose when it released millions of gallons of oil into the Persian Gulf during the 1991 war over Kuwait. In all of these cases the environmental damage was confined to a comparatively small locale or region. Nuclear war threatens an environmental calamity of global proportions.

The importance of ecological issues is indicated by the fact that the survival of the human species is contingent on the ability of the world's governing elites to summon the political will to devise policies that can preserve the earth's carrying capacity, on which life itself is dependent. The future of all people and nations is thus affected by how these issues are addressed, and the world that our children and their children will inherit will be profoundly affected by the choices made today. While some of these choices might appropriately be made by nation-states acting alone, others may not. Acid rain knows no boundaries. Nuclear contamination of the atmosphere threatens many nations. Climatological changes induced by fossil fuel consumption, and destruction of the protective ozone layer caused by other abuses, imperil all. Concerted international collaborative efforts are required to deal with these and the many other ecological issues on the global agenda.

Our first essay in Part Four of *The Global Agenda,* "The Ecological Perspective on International Politics" by Dennis Pirages, introduces the ecopolitical perspective, which is a way of thinking that stresses the interrelatedness in international politics of political communities with one another and with their environment. A key element of the perspective focuses on the demands human populations place on the carrying capacity of the physical environment. A second concerns natural resource constraints. Much of the history of international politics, Pirages explains, can be understood in terms of the domestic pressures for expansion abroad generated by the maldistribution of the supply and demand for natural resources in the global environment.

Technology is the third key element. On the one hand, technology, as noted above, can increase the efficiency of natural resource utilization. On the other hand, it can also lead to "by-products that can destroy important links in life-sustaining ecosystems." Thus, technology has enhanced the ability of nations to play the game of international politics, but it is also "altering dramatically the relations of human populations with each other as well as the ecosphere."

Implicit in the foregoing conclusion, and in the ecological perspective generally, is the belief that environmental problems cannot be managed by states independently—that they must act in concert to arrest the widespread environmental deterioration caused by population growth and technological advances. That theme is pursued by Michael G. Renner in our next essay, "Shared Problems, Common Security," in which the author urges a redefinition of what is typically thought of as "national security" to incorporate the realities of an environmentally interdependent world. "'Security' is commonly associated with safety against foreign attack," writes Renner. "But in an age of unparalleled environmental destruction, a reasonable definition of security needs to encompass breathable air and potable water, safety from toxic and radioactive hazards, and protection against the loss of the topsoil that assures us of our daily bread."

Environmental interdependence is evident in the threat posed by desertification and deforestation, in the imperative need to manage watersheds shared by many nations, and in transboundary air pollution, the depletion of the stratospheric ozone layer, and global warming. To attack these problems, Renner urges the formation of "environmental alliances" among different countries and at different levels of society in an effort to devise "imaginative new approaches" to "common ecological threats." He recognizes, however, that environmental concerns may fall victim to the conflicts of interests and rivalries that characterize international politics and to the inequalities in power and wealth that affect the capacity of different states to wield influence in world affairs.

Demographic changes occurring throughout the world in many ways reinforce the differing interests, rivalries, and inequalities already evident in the world. We live in a demographically divided world. Population growth in the industrialized countries of the North has slowed, but it continues its rapid pace in the developing nations of the South, where in the next 30 to 40 years 3 billion people will be added to the world's present population of 5.2 billion. Because of these differing rates of growth, demographic variables relate to sociopolitical phenomena in different ways, as the editors of *The Global Agenda,* Charles W. Kegley, Jr., and Eugene R. Wittkopf, explain in "Population and the Global Commons." "Generally the impact of population growth on economic development is the most immediate and important question facing developing countries," they write. "In contrast the main issues for developed nations tend to focus more on the impact of affluence on global resources and the global commons." But while the world may be divided demographically, because it is interdependent economically and environmentally, North and South alike will experience in multiple ways the consequences of the demographic trends already evident in the world. Patterns of emigration and immigration, often propelled by adverse ecological afflictions, are among them.

Another manifestation of the demographic linkage between North and South is found in the pressures exerted by population growth and rising affluence on world supplies of food. During the 1970s, when the phrase "limits to growth" was used to capture the widespread belief among policymakers and the informed public about the world's ecopolitical future, it was expected that the inability of national agricultural systems to meet rising demand for food would lead to widespread global food insecurity. A decade later, however, the phrase "a world awash in grain" was equally widespread, as both technological developments and shifts in the global marketplace undermined the neo-Malthusian gloom so evident only a short time earlier.

What can be expected during the decade of the 1990s? Lester R. Brown, an expert on global agricultural developments and environmental conditions, finds in his essay, "The Waning of Global Food Security," reasons to embrace once more the pessimism evident in the 1970s. Environmental degradation, population growth, and rising prices in the face of reduced production, he argues, will all erode the prospects for ensuring global and national food security. Ominously, as population pressures continue to rise, Brown also sees little on the technological horizon that will permit a return to the rapid increases in agricultural production enjoyed in earlier decades, and he warns that unless care is taken the very resource base on which rests the world's ability to feed its teeming billions could be destroyed.

Not everyone is as pessimistic about the role that technology might play in meeting future food needs, as we will note below. First, however, we should consider another environmental threat to agricultural productivity briefly discussed by Brown—global warming.

Global warming—captured in the popular phrase "the greenhouse" effect— has in recent years become a catchword for the truly global proportions of environmental problems, for it portends the ability of humankind to trigger irreversible changes in the world's climate. Unfortunately, global warming has also demonstrated our limited capacity to fully comprehend the processes at work in shaping the global habitat and to devise meaningful policy responses to planetary problems in the face of scientific uncertainty.

In our next essay, "Coping with the Uncertainties of the Greenhouse Effect," Jessica T. Mathews examines the theory of the greenhouse effect; how human activities contribute to what is widely expected to be a long-term rise in world temperatures during coming decades; and what the social, economic, and political consequences of significant temperature rises might be. She readily acknowledges that "to inquire about the impact of climate change on man and on the rest of the biosphere is to move from the realm of knowledge laced with uncertainty to that of ignorance threaded with a few traces of knowledge—and to pose an unanswerable question." Even faced with uncertainty, she urges that concerted action be undertaken now: "As I weigh probabilities and risks, the scale tips decisively in favor of action now, because by lucky chance, much of what we need to do to limit further commitment to global warming will benefit us as a nation and as a species even if our greenhouse predictions should turn out to be wrong." On the other hand, Mathews continues, "If our predictions should turn out to be right, steps taken now will be critical to the future of life on earth."

Technological developments associated with the burning of fossil fuels and the use of chlorofluorocarbons (CFCs) are the principal forces inducing climate change through global warming. Yet technology has also made possible widespread improvements in the standard of living of people throughout the world. It has enabled farmers worldwide to increase agricultural productivity at a rate that has surpassed even the rapid rate of population growth since World War II. Orville L. Freeman worries in "Agriculture and the Environment: Meeting the Food Needs of the Coming Decade" that concern for preserving the environment may inhibit the application of new (if still uncertain) technology to meet the enormous expansion in food production that the growth of world population during the remainder of this decade and into the next will require. What is needed, he argues, is a delicate balancing act designed "to bring the goals of feeding the world's population and protecting the world's environment into harmony. . . . Yes, we must protect our fragile environment and use our resources wisely. But there is a very serious danger that the voice of the world's hungry will not be heard if the environmental and food-related agenda is written to meet only the needs of well-intentioned but well-fed interests."

Realizing the delicate balance Freeman seeks may be possible if the world learns the maxim, not that there are "limits to growth," but, instead, "the growth of limits." This is the notion underlying the idea of *sustainable development,* which is the central concept in *Our Common Future,* the 1987 report of the World Commission on Environment and Development, popularly known as the

Brundtland Commission after the Norwegian Prime Minister who was its chair. Jim MacNeil, secretary-general of the Brundtland Commission and author of our next selection, "Sustainable Development: What Is It?" explains that *sustainability* requires "new paths of economic and social progress which 'meet the needs of the present without compromising the ability of future generations to meet their own needs.'" Thus sustainability means learning to live off the earth's interest, without encroaching on its capital.

The Brundtland Commission concluded that the world cannot sustain the growth that will be required to meet the needs and aspirations of the world's projected population unless it adopts radically different approaches to basic issues of economic expansion, equity, resource management, energy efficiency, and the like. Thus MacNeil explains that the agenda of sustainable development integrates "environmental and resource management issues . . . with the traditional issues of growth, employment, development, trade, peace and security." He also urges that the environment and sustainable development be treated as foreign policy issues of "paramount importance," as tensions over them may develop and the failure to address them may be seen "as a real threat to the security of neighbouring and other countries." If dealt with properly, on the other hand, the issues "could force a new spirit of international cooperation."

Can the world make the transition in attitudes and institutions to sustainable development so powerfully urged by the Brundtland Commission? The task is enormous, as the commission recognized and MacNeil's account demonstrates. It is all the more challenging given the structure of international politics, which is characterized by the absence of central institutions and the concentration of power in the hands of its constituent units, principally nation-states, for herein lie the conflicts of interest, the rivalries, and the inequalities in power and wealth that are the essence of international politics. These facts militate against the ability of states to devise effective transnational strategies for coping with threats to the planetary habitat, and in particular to common property resources.

When resources are held in common, individual actors have an incentive to exploit them to their maximum because the collectivity must bear the costs of exploitation, but they alone realize the benefits. The metaphor of the tragedy of the commons, a stock concept in environmental politics, helps to explain this typical national response to the global commons. Marvin S. Soroos examines the applicability of the metaphor in our next selection, "The Tragedy of the Commons in Global Perspective," and uses it as a springboard to probe several environmental issues and to explore strategies for avoiding environmental tragedies. Importantly, he relates these strategies to values (conservation, production, equity, and freedom), the realization of which necessarily often entails tough political choices as states seek to cope with ecological exigencies. Soroos concludes, surprisingly, perhaps, that states have undertaken at least in the area of atmospheric pollutants a greater degree of unilateral, voluntary actions to cope with environmental degradation than the tragedy of the commons would have predicted, and that the basic international infrastructure for avoiding disaster has also been put into place.

William Ophuls provides another viewpoint on this question in "The International State of Nature and the Politics of Scarcity." Clearly he is less than sanguine about the ability of humankind to manage its common problems given the anarchical "state of nature" of the international system. Some of the examples that Ophuls uses have become dated, but the overarching need for concern that he relates remains unabated. For Ophuls finds that the challenge of scarcity is more likely to precipitate conflict than it is to stimulate greater international cooperation. The absence in the international system of either higher law or higher authority and the persistence of the principle of sovereignty encourage struggle and pursuit of narrow self-interest, not collaboration. It may be a system crying out for recognition that under prevailing circumstances the future of each depends on the future of all, Ophuls observes, but it is nonetheless a system that in the short run rewards those who "help themselves" at the expense of others. The danger, Ophuls warns, is that all will likely suffer.

The final essay in *The Global Agenda* focuses on nuclear war as a potential route to ecological disaster. In "Nuclear Winter and the End of the Arms Race," Carl Sagan and Richard Turco, two preeminent scientists who contributed much to the development of the theory of nuclear winter, recount what is understood about the climatic catastrophe that a nuclear war and consequent nuclear winter would precipitate. The theory itself anticipates that nuclear war would spew so much dust, smoke, and poisonous gas into the atmosphere that it would transform the earth into a dark, frozen wasteland incapable of sustaining humankind's delicate life-support systems by precipitating a prolonged period of abnormal coldness, darkness, and ancillary atmospheric disturbances. It is a controversial theory, but it has been neither refuted nor repudiated by scholars or policymakers. Indeed, the catastrophic consequences of nuclear war have been officially recognized by the United Nations, symbolizing acknowledgment by the world community that a resort to force could spell the destruction of civilization and perhaps the extinction of the human species—regardless of who initiates a nuclear war and who its intended targets might be.

The theory of nuclear winter thus brings our concern in *The Global Agenda* for politics and ecology full circle to a concern for arms and influence and to the imperative for nations to collaborate, even in the face of discord between and among them, so that humankind might survive and the political, social, and material well-being of all be enhanced. Noteworthy in this respect is that Sagan and Turco are not pessimistic, but instead they see in the theory of nuclear winter the possibility that nations may at last appreciate their common fate: "Never before in human history has there been such a degree of shared vulnerability. . . . Nuclear winter has alerted us to our common peril and our mutual dependence." As the atomic clock retreats from midnight, the opportunities for lasting peace and addressing other pressing concerns multiply.

# 30

# THE ECOLOGICAL PERSPECTIVE ON INTERNATIONAL POLITICS

### Dennis Pirages

**Dennis Pirages describes the way human populations, natural resources, and technology intertwine to form the building blocks of an ecological perspective on international relations. The perspective focuses on the interaction of human relationships with the global ecosystem, humankind's sustaining environment, and on the social and political issues such interaction stimulates. Pirages is a professor in the Department of Government and Politics at the University of Maryland. He is the author of *Global Technopolitics: The International Politics of Technology and Resources* (1989), as well as a number of other works that focus on various dimensions of the ecological imperative.**

In 1971 Harold and Margaret Sprout introduced an important new perspective into the study of international relations with publication of *Toward a Politics of the Planet Earth.* Building a bridge between their earlier work on man–milieu relationships and the growing field of ecology, the Sprouts advanced visionary ideas now recognized as offering a new unifying paradigm for twenty-first-century social science. They suggested an 'ecological' approach to the study of international relations built around four related concepts: environment, envi-

Excerpt reprinted from "The Ecological Perspective and the Social Sciences," *International Studies Quarterly* 27 (September 1983), pp. 243–255, with the permission of the International Studies Association, Byrnes International Center, University of South Carolina, Columbia, SC 29208 USA. Bibliographic references not included in the excerpt have been deleted.

roned populations, environmental relationships and interrelated complexes (or communities) that compose, in the aggregate, an ecosystem coterminous with the earth's surface (Sprout and Sprout, 1971:30). . . .

The ecological approach pioneered by the Sprouts offers a potentially powerful organizing framework for two reasons. First, this approach is anchored in an evolutionary perspective which stresses changes in environment-society relationships over time. Although present global environmental pressures certainly call attention to this perspective, these man–environment relationships have been and will continue to be crucial factors in shaping relations among people and nations. . . . Second, the ecological perspective . . . gives theoretical priority to physical realities—man–environment relationships central in shaping social phenomena—and also recognizes tremendous variations in social responses to the same environmental pressures. The approach focuses on the interface between environmental ecosystems and human behavior. Human beings, social institutions and related value systems have shaped as well as been shaped by physical environments. But while the impact of changing natural environments on the physical evolution of human and other species has been carefully documented in the biological sciences, the related study of the environmental linkage to the evolution of social institutions, cultural values and relations among nations is still at the formative stage.

## ELEMENTS OF AN ECOLOGICAL APPROACH

. . . An ecological perspective applied to international relations begins with the observation that human beings share an ecosystem with many other species of flora and fauna. Seen in this manner, humans are 'a population of organisms and non-living matter (in) a biotic community, or ecosystem' (Sprout and Sprout, 1971:27). An ecosystem is composed of the total array of plant and animal species in an environment as well as the matter which cycles through the system (Watt, 1973:5). This perspective stresses the reciprocal functional relationships among organisms and between organisms and their physical environments (Ehrlich, 1977:128). The international ecosystem is the entire interrelated set of smaller systems nourishing life on this planet and is referred to as the biosphere, ecosphere, or global ecosystem. *Homo sapiens,* in this perspective, is a species governed by basic ecological principles applicable to other occupants of the ecosphere. Theories that attempt to explain how human beings, individually or collectively, behave in relation to nature or other human beings can be usefully anchored in the study of the evolution of the ecosystem–society interface.

Inquiry within an ecological framework profits from an understanding of at least three important concepts. The first concept is human populations and their related growth dynamics. In the most general sense, the human population of the world [now exceeds] five billion persons. But human beings live within and identify with smaller populations, closely knit groups that interact mainly with other members. Biologists and ecologists define a population of any species as a 'dynamic system of interacting individuals . . . that are potentially capable of interbreeding with each other' (Watt, 1973:1). While human populations could be defined in the same manner, it is more useful to define them by the relative frequency of communication among them. With minor exceptions, the clusters of most frequent verbal and mediated human communications are coincident with the boundaries of interbreeding human populations. Human populations can then be defined by the 'marked gaps in efficiency of communications,' a social scientific definition that is nearly identical with the biological equivalent (Deutsch, 1964:100). These communication gaps and inefficiencies both maintain and are maintained by differences in language, culture, values, beliefs, and levels of socioeconomic development.

Prior to the global spread of the industrial revolution, there were thousands of relatively isolated human groups that met either biological or communications tests as distinct populations. But the dynamics of modernization have pressed many of these disparate human groups into national populations. While the boundaries of states usually demarcate human populations, there are many subnational groups that have not been effectively integrated, thus complicating ecological analysis.

Human populations are subject to ecological and biological imperatives similar to those governing other species. These include a tendency to grow in numbers and demands until the limits of the carrying capacity of the relevant physical environment are reached, or even exceeded, in Malthusian dramas that have been repeated in all regions of the world throughout history. When food and other necessary resources have been abundant, human populations have expanded to utilize them, only to migrate or be trimmed back by pestilence and famine when factors such as weather or environmental despoilation have reduced the available resource base.

Natural resources are the second important concept in building a link between human populations and ecosystems. From an ecological perspective, a resource 'is anything needed by an organism, population or ecosystem which, by its increasing availability up to an optimal or sufficient level, allows an increasing rate of energy conversion' (Watt, 1973:20). Translating this into political terms, human populations, like populations of other species, have consumption potentials that are limited by the resource necessary for economic growth that is in shortest supply. Human populations have experienced tremendous increases in demand for added varieties and quantities of critical resources as a result of the industrial revolution, and most mature industrialized countries cannot now be sustained solely by the resources existing within national boundaries. The mix of available resources structures a population's potential for autonomous growth and development. However, the resources required for contemporary industrialization have not been distributed equally among states. In some cases countries have been generously endowed with resources, though decades of industrial activity have all but exhausted them. In other cases required resources have never been available. Whatever the reason, most highly industrialized countries (the USSR being a notable exception) now depend on resource bases outside of their domestic jurisdiction.

As national populations historically have run up against natural resource constraints on growth, domestic pressures have built up for accessing new supplies. This 'lateral pressure' has resulted in various types of expansionist activity that has had different impacts on external actors. As Choucri and North have put it, 'When demands are unmet and existing capabilities cannot be altered at a reasonable cost within national boundaries, they may be sought beyond' (1975:16).

The behavioral manifestations of lateral pressure and techniques used to channel it have assumed many different forms based upon the strength of perceived needs, types of domestic sociopolitical organization, culturally determined justifications, and the power of neighboring nations. Lateral pressure often resulted in initiatives that are harmful to those affected by them. In the historical development of many Western European countries a point was reached where external resources were perceived to be accessible and superior replacements for domestic supplies. Thus, it has been suggested that aggressive outward expansion of European influence in the fifteenth and sixteenth centuries resulted, at least in part, from twin domestic pressures of ecological scarcity and rising expectations (Wallerstein, 1974:39–48). The Portuguese, Dutch, British, Germans and eventually other European powers acquired territories in distant parts of the world that provided food, minerals, and even human resources. At the beginning of World War I, 84% of the world's land was or had been controlled by colonial powers (Fieldhouse, 1973:3).

From an ecological perspective these adventures by Western European nations could be seen as a response to enhanced technological capabilities combined with resource and growth dilemmas. From the perspectives of the inhabitants of conquered territories, they were experienced as exploitation and imperialism. In the colonizing nations, by contrast, such moves across borders were easily justified. The entrepreneurs responsible for colonization were supported by elaborate moral justifications for what, in retrospect, was the human variant of behavior typical of any species pushing against resource limits. In these cases, however, the human populations possessed technological capabilities to do something about the problem.

While colonialism and war represent malevolent aspects of lateral pressure, other solutions to resource limitations have had a somewhat more benevolent impact on global development. The creation of an integrated world economy and related division of labor based on comparative advantage is one such response. Benefits of these new economic arrangements, however, are not always perceived as being equitably shared by all populations involved, giving rise to charges that the old system of direct colonial resource exploitation has given way to a new one based upon economic inequities in market relationships (see Laszlo *et al.,* 1978: Chapter 2).

Technology is the third important concept in developing an ecological perspective. It is a force that has altered dramatically relationships of human populations with those of other species and with supporting ecosystems. Technological innovations have created both new demands for a wider variety of natural resources and increased efficiency of natural resource utilization. The bulk of technological innovation occurring during the industrial revolution took place under circumstances of relative resource abundance. The result was a series of innovations that met human needs largely by expanding the quantity of resources used. Over the last decade, however, in an environment characterized by perceived resource scarcity, technological innovation now focuses on qualitative improvements in resource utilization as well, more effectively using each consumed unit of natural resource. Technology is somewhat responsive to price signals and, in effect, 'creates' additional resources through new efficiencies under situations of perceived scarcity (Hueckel, 1976). It remains to be seen, however, if technology can survive its current diminishing returns and sustain a protracted efficiency revolution (see Giarini and Loubergé, 1978).

Technology also modifies human relationships with the environment by creating by-products that can destroy important links in life-sustaining ecosystems. 'With no exceptions, technological economic development has entailed increasing accumulations of residues, many of which cause damage to human and non-human populations, and continuing hazards of future damage' (Sprout and Sprout, 1978:24–25). The price paid for industrial economic growth has been an increased human impact on, and transformation of, ecosystems within which human evolution occurs. While technological progress has expanded the growth potential of human populations, its by-products threaten future long-term damage to the ecosystems sustaining human life if technology is not properly managed. Thus, the impact of technological development on relations among nations has been significant. Technology has enhanced national capabilities and the present international hierarchy, with its pronounced differences in wealth, power, and consumption, is in large measure a creation of uneven technological development. On a global scale, however, the waste products of industrial growth, such as acid rain and increased build-up of carbon dioxide, are altering dramatically the relations of human populations with each other as well as the ecosphere.

In summary, an ecological perspective on social behavior and institutions calls attention to human dependence upon the sustaining environment (ecosystems) within which life has evolved, for continued growth and well-being. The same ecological imperatives governing other species also shape relations among human beings both within and among countries. The problem of maintaining access to resources required for growth in human numbers and living standards plays an important role in motivating human behavior, shaping institutions and determining relations among nations. Technology is a key element facilitating transformation of resources into the artifacts that enhance individual, group, and national capabilities. . . .

. . . If human institutions, behavior and values are, to a significant extent, environmentally determined, it is better to understand these relationships than to pretend that they do not exist. But more important, many scholars have written about an impending 'post-industrial' revolution led by, among other things, a revolution in genetic engineering. . . . A post-industrial social scientific revolution could help avert an 'overshoot' of the global resource base by designing institutions based upon prescriptions deduced from a better understanding of environment-social evolution relationships.

## REFERENCES

Choucri, N. and R. North (1975) *Nations in Conflict.* San Francisco: W. H. Freeman.

Deutsch, K. (1964) *Nationalism and Social Communication.* Cambridge: MIT Press.

Ehrlich, P. (1977) *Ecoscience: Population, Resources, Environment.* San Francisco: W. H. Freeman.

Fieldhouse, D. (1973) *Economics and Empire, 1830–1914.* New York: Cornell University Press.

Giarini, O. and H. Loubergé (1978) *The Diminishing Returns of Technology.* New York: Pergamon.

Hueckel, G. (1976) 'A Historical Approach to Future Economic Growth', *Science,* March 14.

Laszlo, E. *et al.* (1978) *The Objectives of the New International Economic Order.* New York: Pergamon.

Sprout, H. and M. Sprout (1971) *Toward a Politics of the Planet Earth.* New York: Van Nostrand Reinhold.

Sprout, H. and M. Sprout (1978) *The Context of Environmental Politics: Unfinished Business for America's Third Century.* Lexington: University of Kentucky Press.

Wallerstein, I. (1974) *The Modern World System.* New York: Academic Press.

Watt, K. (1973) *Principles of Environmental Science.* New York: McGraw-Hill.

# 31

# SHARED PROBLEMS, COMMON SECURITY

## Michael G. Renner

**Nations commonly define their security in military terms, but the environmental problems many face today are inherently transnational, with the result that interdependence now characterizes environmental relations in the global community. States nonetheless still approach their shared problems through structures that militate against international cooperation. But, argues Michael G. Renner, global cooperation against common ecological threats is necessary if nations are to realize ecological security in an environmentally interdependent world. Renner is a senior researcher at the Worldwatch Institute, where he specializes in disarmament issues. He is a contributor to the well-known *State of the World* reports published annually by the Worldwatch Institute.**

Nations are no longer the sole masters of their destinies. Production, trade, investment, modern communications, transportation, and tourism are now global in scale, rapidly transforming our diverse planet into a well-connected unit. What happens in practically any part of the world resonates elsewhere. We have become accustomed to interdependence in economic affairs and we reluctantly acknowledge an uneasy mutual dependence for survival in the nuclear age, yet we are only beginning to comprehend that the same holds true for environmental relations as well.

This has not been a pleasant discovery. Acid rain from cars and power plants in Britain kills lakes and forests in Scandinavia. Ozone-depleting chemicals used in North America increase the danger of skin cancer in Australia. Residue from the pesticide DDT sprayed in Central America has been found in the Great Lakes region. In short, environmental degradation and pollution respect no human-drawn borders.

Interdependence in the military, economic and ecological realms is now a fact of life. It has already begun to erode traditional notions of security and even national sovereignty itself. "Security" is commonly associated with safety against foreign attack. But in an age of unparalleled environmental destruction, a reasonable definition of security needs to encompass breathable air and potable water, safety from toxic and radioactive hazards, and protection against the loss of the topsoil that assures us of our daily bread.

While interdependence in military or economic affairs always held out the possibility of unilateral action—at least as a last resort—environmental interdependence requires a new way of thinking. Air- or water-borne pollutants cannot be repelled by military means; neither can they, like foreign merchandise, be stopped at the border through protectionist measures. Soviet Foreign Minister Eduard Shevardnadze recognized this when he said that "the biosphere recognizes no division into blocs, alliances, or systems. All share the same climatic system and no one is in a position to build his own isolated and independent line of environmental defense."

There is a need for imaginative new approaches. Environmental alliances—formed by nations to act against common ecological threats—could tie together nations that share ecosystems; countries that are geographically distant but bear primary responsibility for global environmental problems; or political, ideological or military rivals that have little else in common other than an interest in avoiding environmental catastrophe.

### A WATERSHED ISSUE

According to the United Nations Environment Program, 35 percent of the earth's land surface is threatened by desertification. As a result, agricultural output and the economic well-being of about one-fifth of the world's population is either already adversely affected or soon to be. In Ethiopia, India and Mauritania, nations deeply in the grip of desertification, survival for some people is in question.

Human actions—plowing highly erodible land, overpumping water tables for irrigation, overgrazing rangelands, salinization of irrigated land, and deforestation—are the driving force behind desertification. In many countries, these practices result from population growth, unequal land distribution, and the lack of secure land tenure, which force peasants onto less fertile, more erodible land.

Particularly in Africa, desertification has sapped food-growing potential to the point where the livelihood of rural people and national food security—the ability to feed the domestic population—are compromised. The number of Africans who do not have enough food for normal health and physical activity totals more than 100 million, according to the World Bank.

Deforestation would seem an unlikely source of tension between nations, yet by aggravating soil erosion and silt accumulation in riverbeds, it can lead to devastating floods. Denuded watersheds in the Ethiopian highlands have exacerbated floods in neighboring Sudan, including one that ravaged Khartoum [in 1988]. India's flood-prone area has tripled since 1971. The frequency and magnitude of flooding in Bangladesh has increased markedly since mid-century. Last year's [1988] flood left 25 million Bangladeshis (a quarter of the population) temporarily homeless—a threat to national security on par with most wars.

Bangladeshis assign much of the blame for the floods to deforestation in the Himalayas, north of their border. This problem can be effectively counteracted only if Bangladesh, Bhutan, China, India and Nepal all agree to cooperate in reforestation efforts and flood-control measures. To study possible remedies and implement them, Bangladesh advocates establishing a regional water authority. China has expressed willingness to cooperate at least on a bilateral basis, but India remains opposed to a multilateral solution, fearing that a regional consultative body would interfere with its national water policy.

Because they play an important role in territorial demarcation, rivers and their associated watersheds frequently fall under the jurisdiction of several, possibly hostile states. An estimated 40 percent of the world's population depends for drinking water, irrigation, or hydropower on the 214 major river systems shared by two or more countries; 12 of these waterways are shared by five or more nations.

Conflicts over water use and quality simmer in virtually all parts of the world, but especially where water resources need to be shared equitably. About 80 countries are already suffering serious water shortages. Disputes center on water diversion, industrial and agrochemical pollution, salinization of streams through heavy irrigation, siltation of rivers, and flooding. . . .

In the Rhine River valley, for example, 20 million people in several countries, but particularly in the Netherlands, must have their drinking water filtered to remove heavy metals, hazardous chemicals, and salt deposited further upstream in France, Switzerland and West Germany. The situation was most extreme following an accident at Sandoz, Inc.'s chemical facilities near Basel, Switzerland, in November 1986. Large amounts of fungicides and mercury spilled into the river, forcing a three-week ban on the use of Rhine water for drinking.

The issue of who controls the waters of the Nile casts a shadow over relations between Egypt, the Sudan and Ethiopia. Egypt is using more water than it was allotted under a 1959 pact signed with Sudan, and its irrigation plans for the 1990s reveal that needs will continue to grow. Upstream, it seems that only a lack of funds is preventing Ethiopia from making good on its plan to divert more Nile water for its own use, which would directly affect Egypt's water supplies.

## AIRBORNE MENACE

As the long reach of acid precipitation illustrates, the impact of pollution is not confined to adjacent or proximate countries. The result of nitrogen and sulfur oxides emitted by cars and power plants, acid rain is taking a terrible toll on aquatic life and trees, especially in the Adirondack Mountains of New York and the Black Forest region of West Germany. It has led to a war of words between the United States and Canada, since more than half of Canada's acid deposition comes from its southern neighbor.

Across the Atlantic, all European countries are involved in an exchange of air pollutants that is as intensive as it is involuntary. Norway and Sweden are the only net importers of sulfur dioxide, which comes primarily from the United Kingdom. . . . Thorvald Stoltenberg, Norway's foreign minister, considers British reluctance to address the acid precipitation issue as important as any current mutual trade or defense issues.

Europeans have been confronted with another airborne menace. The powerful explosion at the Chernobyl nuclear reactor in 1986 hurled radioactive debris across large areas of the northern hemisphere. Initial recriminations against the Soviet Union for failing to provide adequate warning of the accident eventually gave way to concerns about the siting of nuclear reactors, enrichment and reprocessing facilities, and radioactive waste dumps closer to home.

In Europe, 119 nuclear power plants are located within 60 miles of a national border. Soon after the Chernobyl accident, the Danish parliament asked Sweden to close a plant located 19 miles from Copenhagen. As part of its decision to phase out nuclear power, the Swedish government pledged that the disputed unit would be the first to close. The French government received a plea from Luxembourg and local authorities in . . . Germany to cancel construction of four reactors at Cattenom, but it refused to do so. Similar issues have strained relations between Ireland and the United Kingdom, Austria and both . . . Germany and Czechoslovakia, Hong Kong and China, and Argentina and Chile.

Spurred by a stream of new scientific evidence, scientists' and policy-makers' attention is now shifting to the depletion of the ozone layer and the global warming trend. No nation can hope to escape the all-encompassing effects of these very real problems. The loss of stratospheric ozone, which shields life on earth from harmful ultraviolet radiation, implies grave threats to human health (through increased skin cancer rates and weakened immune systems), agricultural productivity, and marine fisheries. The security of nations is similarly compromised by global climate change brought on by the accumulation of carbon dioxide and other heat-trapping gases in the atmosphere. Rising sea levels, altered precipitation patterns, and shifting vegetation zones—likely effects of global warming—threaten to inundate densely populated low-lying coastal areas, disrupt harvests, and force untold numbers of species into extinction.

## A NEW DIPLOMACY

It would be delusory to underestimate the difficulties associated with shaping a global environmental agenda. The existence of broadly shared environmental problems does not automatically translate into common policies because national interests still might not necessarily converge. For example, only a handful of countries enjoy most of the economic benefits associated with the use of fossil fuels and chlorofluorocarbons (the chief ozone-depleting gas), but all nations will suffer from the ecological repercussions.

In addition, countries caught in the debt treadmill may view concerns for the environment as a luxury, even as more of their citizens suffer from this neglect. Indeed, numerous countries are driven to exploit their natural resources in a desperate effort to escape the debt trap. In Eastern Europe, too, dire economic straits have relegated the environment to second-class status.

Fearful of setting far-reaching precedents, governments are often reluctant to relinquish any of their hard-won sovereign rights for the sake of international cooperation. At a recent conference held to work out a cleanup program for the Rhine, environmental ministers from France, Switzerland and West Germany objected to a Dutch recommendation for international inspection of suspected pollution sites. They fell back on an old standby: the inspection would violate national sovereignty.

West Germany similarly rejected a proposal that would have entrusted the Secretariat of the Economic Commission for Europe with inspection of sources of sulfur dioxide pollution in Europe. Brazil, suddenly exposed last year [1988] to international pressure to halt the destruction of the Amazon rain forest, successfully resisted the formation of an international environmental agency it feared could intervene in strictly "internal affairs."

Despite the generally sorry history of international environmental cooperation, some advances have been made. As awareness of the transnational character of environmental degradation has grown and the need for remedies has become more urgent, an increasing number of bilateral agreements and international conventions have been concluded. The U.N. Environment Program has helped shepherd many of those efforts. Its most celebrated achievement to date is the 1987 Montreal Protocol that calls for a 50-percent cut in CFC production by 1998. But UNEP's mandate remains limited: like many other international organizations, it has no enforcement powers. And several of UNEP's attempts to draft rules on international responsibility for transboundary environmental damage have failed.

## LEADERS IN THE FIELD

The success of international environmental cooperation depends in large measure on bold and imaginative policies that strike a sound balance between conflicting national interests. In a departure from the format of formal international conferences and negotiations, one or more like-minded countries could commit themselves to reducing their fossil fuel consumption and phasing out CFC production and ocean dumping. They could then invite other nations to adopt similar restraints, which would eventually be codified in binding treaties. Nothing's come of it yet, but the Netherlands, Norway and Sweden are each considering policies that would either freeze or cut their carbon emissions.

Although they may not be classified as such, environmental alliances are becoming a reality. In 1984, at the initiative of the Scandinavian nations, nine European countries and Canada formed what is informally known as the "30-percent Club" in 1984. Aware that vast amounts of acid-rain-causing sulfur dioxide drifts across national borders, these nations pledged to reduce their emissions of this gas by at least 30 percent by 1993. A total of 19 countries have joined the club so far. A similar pledge to cut nitrogen oxides by 30 percent by 1998 was made [in 1988] by 12 European nations. . . .

Environmental alliances have also arisen around the North and Baltic seas. In 1987, the eight countries bordering the North Sea agreed to reduce their nutrient and toxic discharges by half by 1995. A similar accord has been signed by the seven Baltic nations. Cofunding schemes may play a role here, too, as Sweden is considering helping Poland finance pollution control measures.

A unique environmental alliance is shaping up in war-torn Central America. The region's governments agreed [in 1988] to establish a series of "peace parks" straddling the borders of Costa Rica, El Salvador, Guatemala, Honduras, Nicaragua and Panama. These parks are not only designed to preserve the region's fast-disappearing rain forests, but are also expected to transform what had hitherto been military staging grounds and battlefields into demilitarized zones.

## LAW OF THE AIR

Ultimately, national security depends on *all* countries becoming part of an environmental coalition to protect the atmosphere from ozone depletion and the buildup of greenhouse gases. In June 1988, the prime ministers of Norway and Canada, Gro Harlem Brundtland and Brian Mulroney, proposed to create a "Law of the Air" treaty analogous to the Law of the Sea. A world atmosphere fund, financed by a tax on fossil fuel consumption in the industrial countries, would provide the financial support for improving energy efficiency globally, switching to more benign fuels, developing acceptable substitutes for CFCs, and taking other remedial and preventive actions.

As the diplomatic history of the Law of the Sea has shown, making such a global accord become reality is a politically difficult endeavor. A Law of the Air treaty would require agreement about specific measures to reduce fossil fuel use and to apportion the cuts among the world's nations. Negotiations would have to settle the difficult issue of to what extent such cuts should be based on population size, economic performance, and past consumption. . . .

Regional and even economic differences have a better chance of being worked out if nations agree on the need to develop adequate institutions and mechanisms to guide the march toward a global environmental alliance. [Early 1989 witnessed] a barrage of dramatic-sounding but vague proposals from politicians around the world, including calls for 1) a global environmental charter, 2) an environmental security council to which members would cede certain of their sovereign rights, and 3) an international environmental "peacekeeping" force to enforce sanctions against countries that refuse to carry out agreed-upon measures.

These bold conceptual statements challenge the global community to establish a binding code of conduct for international environmental relations, just as it has done in diplomacy, war and trade. So far, the challenge goes unmet.

## PRESSURE FROM THE GRASS ROOTS

Grass-roots pressure plays an important role in pushing governments to give environmental concerns a higher priority. Environmental groups have sought not only to influence the policies of their own governments and corporations but, by linking up with their counterparts abroad, those of foreign governments and of the World Bank and International Monetary Fund. Greenpeace, for instance, has developed a truly globe-spanning network of activists mobilized on a wide range of issues. The Rainforest Action Network is pressuring development banks not to fund projects that destroy the remaining tropical forests. The Environmental Project on Central America is organizing American support for the Central American peace parks. Conservation International, the Nature Conservancy and World Wildlife Fund have pioneered innovative financial arrangements known as debt-for-nature swaps. Survival International is concerned with publicizing the links between environmental decline and threats to the livelihoods of indigenous peoples.

Environmental links across the East-West divide on the grass-roots level are still in their infancy. But Friends of the Earth and Greenpeace, among others, are busy building contacts with the nascent Eastern European and Soviet environmental movements.

## THE END OF NATIONALISM?

Nations have "outgrown" their borders, but the structures of nation-states remain firmly in place. While national decision-making is impaired in its effectiveness by the globalization of human activities, it remains a factor sufficiently strong to thwart international cooperation. Like membranes, national borders are at times porous, at times impermeable. They cannot stem the flow of goods, money or ideas, nor that of polluted air or water. Still, they often repel appeals for common approaches to shared problems.

Environmental threats seem to call for a global community of interests. But because interdependence has come about by default rather than by design, it does not automatically generate the political will needed for greater international cooperation. The world remains characterized by many conflicting interests and rivalries and plagued by enormous inequalities in power, wealth and capacity to influence global affairs. Environmental concern could either provide the glue that helps humanity overcome these divisions or it could simply compound them.

Greater security for all nations depends on creating a more stable and equitable basis for their relationships. Likely problems of implementation notwithstanding, "environmental security" offers a more fruitful basis for cooperation among nations than military security because it is both a positive and inclusive concept. While military security rests firmly with the competitive strength of individual countries or groups of countries at the direct expense of others, environmental security requires and nurtures more stable and cooperative relationships among nations.

Reflecting on the opportunities for increased U.S.-Soviet cooperation in environmental and other matters, former U.S. Ambassador George Kennan, now a scholar at the Institute for Advanced Study in Princeton, New Jersey, has argued that "in the very process of collaboration in a necessary and peaceful process, useful to all humanity, the neurotic impulses of military and political rivalry would be bound to be overshadowed; and the peoples might find, in the intermingling of their own creative efforts, a firmness of association which no other intergovernmental relationships could ever assure."

The perils of environmental degradation challenge the customary conduct of diplomacy and the established forms of governance. There is no easy panacea. Only the difficult process of global cooperation holds out hope that humanity will successfully meet this test.

# 32

# POPULATION AND THE GLOBAL COMMONS

## Charles W. Kegley, Jr., and Eugene R. Wittkopf

**The world is divided demographically, as the industrialized countries of the North approach zero population growth but the developing nations of the South continue to experience rapid increases in their numbers. Charles W. Kegley, Jr., and Eugene R. Wittkopf explore the domestic and transnational social, economic, environmental, and political problems that grow out of a demographically divided but economically and environmentally interdependent world. Kegley is Pearce Professor of International Relations at the University of South Carolina; Wittkopf is professor of political science at Louisiana State University. Together they have published *American Foreign Policy: Pattern and Process* (1991) and *World Politics: Trend and Transformation* (1989), from which this selection is taken.**

. . . How many people can the earth support? What is its ultimate carrying capacity? No one knows for sure, in part because human ingenuity and rapidly advancing technology keep stretching the boundaries. Thus the growth projected for today's more than five billion inhabitants into the next century will doubtlessly be accommodated. But at what cost—to human freedom, human welfare, and ultimately to the environment necessary to sustain humankind? . . .

From Charles W. Kegley, Jr. and Eugene R. Wittkopf, *World Politics: Trend and Transformation,* 3rd edition. Copyright © 1989. Reprinted with permission of St. Martin's Press, Inc. Explanatory notes have been deleted.

## TRENDS IN WORLD POPULATION GROWTH

Today's world population of more than five billion people constitutes a significant proportion of all the people who have ever lived, and it continues to grow. If present population trends are projected ahead eight centuries, ours will be a standing-room-only planet, with land surface of only one square foot per person. No one can seriously regard such a world as likely. Nor are the other images that have been conjured up to shock the public consciousness realistic portraits of the future. But what they do tell us is that the pressures of population growth pose a serious threat to the human condition, one unprecedented in scale. . . .

The explosive proportions of today's population growth are illustrated in Figure 1, which indicates that it took from the beginning of time until the early 1800s for world population to reach one billion people. Because of substantial declines in death rates, the world population reached two billion about 130 years later, around 1930. Since then, additional billions have been added even more rapidly: Three billion was reached by 1960, four billion in 1975, and 5 billion in 1987. As present trends unfold, the world will reach the six-billion figure before the turn of the twentieth century and ultimately stabilize at something over ten billion by the twenty-first century.

How rapidly the world adds billions to its number is predicted by its growth rate. Worldwide, the rate of population growth peaked at just over 2 percent in the late 1960s and then declined to 1.7 percent by the 1980s. Even this small slowing of the global rate of population growth is consequential, for it means that world population in the year 2000 will be 20 percent less than the 7.5 billion people that the birth and death rates of the 1950s would have produced had they continued uninterrupted.

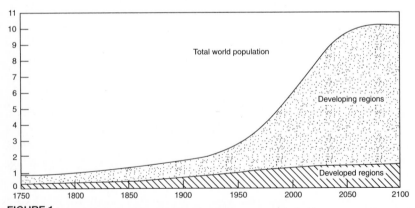

**FIGURE 1.**
World Population Growth, Global Regional Trends, 1750–2100
*Source*: Thomas W. Merrick, "World Population in Transition," *Population Bulletin,* Vol. 41, Number 2 (Washington, D.C.: Population Reference Bureau, Inc., January 1988 reprint), p. 4.

Whatever the ultimate rate of growth, the trends are apparent and the consequences inevitable; it is not a question of whether the world will become more crowded but of how crowded it will become. In 1986 the world grew by more than 83 million people, an amount equivalent to adding the entire population of France and Colombia to the world or populating New Zealand again every other week or the Bahamas each day. Even more will be added each year in the future [as] more people will be added to the globe's population in the last fifth of the twentieth century than at any other time in history—even though the world's population growth rate has slowed markedly and will continue downward in the years ahead. We can better understand why this result is inevitable if we go beyond the simple arithmetic of population growth and explore its dynamics.

### Factors Affecting National and Regional Variations in Population Growth

The rate of natural population increase in the United States in 1987 was 0.7 percent. This is an annual rate typical of industrialized nations today, where births and deaths have nearly stabilized. Hence, the difference between a typical industrialized nation and the world population growth rate of 1.7 percent is largely attributable to a population surge in the Third World, where sharply lower death rates since World War II have resulted from advances in medical science, agricultural productivity, public sanitation, and technology. The paradox posed by reduced death rates is that this favorable development has contributed to an accelerating rate of population growth in precisely those nations least able to support a burgeoning number of people.

Variations in national and regional population growth virtually ensure that today's demographic division of the world will persist into the future. In fact, it will widen. As shown in Figure 1, the 3.7 billion people who inhabited the Third World in 1985 will have grown to 4.8 billion by the year 2000, whereas the comparable increase among the developed nations will be only from 1.2 billion to 1.3 billion. . . .

The developing countries' high fertility rates (which measure the number of births by women in their prime reproductive years) derive from a variety of sources. Apart from the pleasures that children provide, entrenched religious norms often sanction and encourage parenting, prescribing the bearing of children (particularly male offspring in some cultures), as both a duty and a path to a rewarding afterlife. In addition, many societies' cultural traditions ascribe prestige and social status to women according to the number of children they bear. But most importantly perhaps, high fertility rates are affected by economic factors. Large families add more hands to a family's labor force today and may be a future source of social security for parents who live in societies that have no public programs to provide for the elderly. Under such conditions, parents usually try to have as many children as possible so that they can earn more today and be cared for in their old age. When the infant mortality rate is high, the incentives for creating many offspring are even greater—the more children that are produced, the higher the probability is that some will survive. . . .

### The Momentum Factor

Even more important to understanding the implications of today's population surge in the Third World (which is a result of high, but declining, birthrates and rapidly falling death rates) for tomorrow's world is the "momentum" factor. . . . The momentum factor helps explain why in the last quintile of the twentieth century more people will be added to the globe's population than at any other time in history.

Population momentum is especially great in societies with high proportions of young people. In these societies, families are formed and babies produced at a rate faster than older persons die. Even if these young people choose to have only two children, large numbers of young couples can still produce extremely large numbers of total births and hence a continuing momentum of growth. This process will continue until the age structures shift toward equal numbers of people in each age group. . . .

Slowing expanding population implies that the Third World must move toward a replacement-level rate of fertility—that is, two children to replace two parents—as many industrialized nations have already done. Even then, momentum will continue to fuel an expanding population. In general, population growth will continue for as many as fifty to seventy years after replacement-level fertility is achieved. This startling fact underscores the urgency of grappling with the population problem; for every decade of delay in achieving replacement-level fertility, the world's peak population will be some 15 percent greater. . . .

The obvious question, then, is how to achieve replacement-level fertility. Important insights can be found in the demographic transition theory, which is the most widely accepted explanation of population changes over time.

### The Demographic Transition Theory

The demographic transition theory seeks to explain the transition that Europe and later North America experienced between 1750 and 1930, when a condition of high birthrates combined with high death rates was replaced by a condition of low birthrates and low death rates. The transition started when death rates began to fall, presumably because of economic and social development and especially because of rising standards of living and improved control of disease. In such circumstances, the potential for substantial population growth was, of course, great. But then birthrates also began to decline, and during this phase population growth slowed. Such declines occur, according to the theory, because economic growth alters attitudes toward family size. In preindustrial societies, children are economic bonuses. As industrialization proceeds, children become economic burdens as they inhibit social mobility and capital accumulation. The transition from large to small families, with the associated decline in fertility, is therefore usually assumed to arise in industrial and urban settings. This fourth stage in the demographic transition was achieved when both the birth and death rates reached very low levels. With fertility levels near the replacement level, the result was a very low rate of population growth, if any at all. . . .

. . . The developing nations have not yet experienced the rapidly falling birthrates following the extraordinarily rapid increase in life expectancy that occurred after World War II. In fact, the precipitous decline in death rates has largely been the result of more effective "death-control" measures introduced by the outside world. The decline in the developing nations' death rates thus differs sharply from the long-term, slow declines that Europe and North America experienced. They have been the result of externally introduced and rapid environmental changes rather than the fundamental and evolutionary changes that affect a nation's policies, institutions, or ways of life. . . . In particular, the developing nations have failed to record the more or less automatic decline in fertility rates that follows the decline in the rate of mortality that, according to the demographic transition theory, is assumed to be associated with economic development. A population "explosion" is the inevitable result.

Although developing countries have yet to move toward replacement-level fertility, demographers generally expect that this will happen. This is the assumption underlying the projections . . . that the transition to low fertility and mortality will occur by the year 2025 and that fertility will decline to replacement level by 2040. Given the assumption, it is possible to foresee a stable global population of just over ten billion people early in the twenty-second century.

Projections so far into the future are inevitably subject to error for a number of reasons, not least of which is uncertainty about death rates. A large-scale conventional war or a limited nuclear war that could induce a climatic catastrophe through "nuclear winter" [see Selection 39 in this book], for example, could dramatically alter long-term population projections. A more populous world is also a more vulnerable one. Consider, for example, the difference in population density in Bangladesh and the state of Louisiana in the United States, two delta lands of similar size. Four and a half million people lived in Louisiana in 1986; 104 million populated Bangladesh. A natural disaster in Bangladesh—where typhoons are commonplace—carries a proportionately greater threat to life.

Death due to malnutrition and starvation may also affect the long-term growth of the world population. Twice in recent years, in the 1970s and again in the 1980s, broad stretches of the Sahel area in Africa experienced life-threatening drought and famine. Africa as a continent is also (for the time being) more threatened than others by AIDS (acquired immune deficiency syndrome), a mysterious, frightening, and fatal disease that threatens to become the plague of the twenty-first century, comparable to the Black Death of the Middle Ages. The World Health Organization estimates that fifty thousand Africans have symptoms of AIDS and that another two million or more are infected with the virus. . . . The threat posed by the fatal disease knows no national boundaries and has in fact spread epidemically to virtually every quarter of the world. . . .

Turning from deaths to births, the demographic transition theory, which is essentially based on the European experience prior to World War II, may be incomplete. It envisages four phases: (1) high birthrate, high death rate; (2) high birthrate, falling death rate; (3) declining birthrate, relatively low death rate; and (4) low birthrate, low death rate. The experience in Western Europe since the 1970s suggests a possible fifth phase: low death rate, declining birthrate. Some have called this Europe's "second" demographic transition (van de Kaa, 1987).

The total fertility rate in Europe during the past two decades has failed to stabilize at the replacement level (which is 2.1 births for every woman, roughly what is required for two children to replace two parents), as the demographic transition theory seems to predict. Instead, the total fertility rate for Western Europe as a whole stands at 1.8, with the highest rate in Ireland (2.6) and the lowest in West Germany (1.3) (in most of Africa, by comparison, it is over 6) (*Population in Perspective,* 1986: 7). As a result, a secular decline of Europe's population has been set in motion. Put differently, a West German population half its current size is now in view. We shall return later to some of the policy implications associated with this startling fact.

A second puzzle that the theory of demographic transition does not solve applies to developing nations: some seem to be stuck somewhere between the second and third stages of the transition. In such widely separated places as Costa Rica, Korea, Sri Lanka, and Tunisia, for example, death rates have fallen to very low levels, but fertility rates seem to have stabilized well above the replacement level (Merrick, 1986). Perhaps the reason lies in the absence of change in social attitudes toward family size of the sort Europe and North America have experienced.

Changes in cultural attitudes toward limitations on family size have been shown to be an important ingredient in environments where social and economic improvements are taking place. . . . Research also shows that the education and status of women in society combine to have a great influence on family size preferences.

> Women who have completed primary school have fewer children than those with no education. Having an education usually means that women delay marriage, seek wage-paying jobs, learn about and have more favorable attitudes toward family planning, and have better communication with their husbands when they marry. Educated women have fewer infant deaths; high infant mortality is associated with high fertility. Similarly, when women have wage-paying jobs, they tend to have fewer children (and conversely, women with few children find it easier to work). Unfortunately, as women

in developing countries attempt to move into the paid labor force, they will be competing with men for scarce jobs. (Population Reference Bureau, 1981: 5 . . .)

Despite the questions that the demographic transition theory leaves unanswered and the puzzles that remain to be solved, the theory underscores the critical linkages between demographic changes and changes in the larger socioeconomic environment within which they occur. Government policies often seek to change the former through the latter. . . .

## CORRELATES OF DEMOGRAPHIC CHANGES

The composition and distribution of societies' populations significantly affect how demographic variables relate to other sociopolitical phenomena. For example, the high proportion of young people in developing countries places strains on certain social institutions, whereas the higher proportion of older people in the developed countries creates other problems.

Generally the impact of population growth on economic development is the most immediate and important question facing developing countries. In contrast, the main issues for developed nations tend to focus more on the impact of affluence on global resources and the global commons. The growing imbalance of the world population between the have and the have-not nations as played out in global patterns of emigration and immigration bridges the two viewpoints.

### The Impact of Population Growth on Economic Development

Growth pessimists place considerable emphasis on the adverse effects of population growth on economic development. Clearly, population growth has contributed to the widening income gap between the world's rich nations and its poor. . . . At the individual level, population growth also contributes to lower standards of living, as poor people tend to have more children to support than do those who are relatively better off. "Also, by depressing wages relative to rents and returns to capital, rapid population growth devalues what poor households have to sell—their labor. Property owners gain relative to wage earners when the labor force grows quickly" (Repetto, 1987).

It is also true, however, that "politics and economic policies influence the distribution of income within countries far more than population growth rates do" (Repetto, 1987). This fact lies close to what is emerging as the conventional view among demographers and development economists of the effects of population growth on economic development. Contrary to the view of growth pessimists, the emerging consensus casts population "not as the sole cause of underdevelopment, but an accomplice aggravating other existing problems" (*The New Population Debate,* 1985 . . .).

**The Third World**   Consider, for example, the relationship between the age structures of developing societies and other socioeconomic variables. In developing countries, dependent children (those younger than fifteen years old) typically comprise 40 to 45 percent of the total population (compared with 25 percent in the developed world). This means there is only about one working-age adult for each child under fifteen in the Third World, compared with nearly three working-age adults in the developed countries. . . . Such a large proportion of dependent children places a heavy burden on public services, particularly the educational system, and encourages the immediate consumption of economic resources rather than their reinvestment to promote future economic growth.

As these same children reach working age, they also contribute to the enormous unemployment and underemployment problems that the developing nations typically face. Yet countries whose populations grow faster than their economies do cannot absorb increasingly large numbers of working-age people into the productive mainstream of their societies. According to the International Labor Organization, "the total labor force of the Third World Countries will be 600 million to 700 million larger in the year 2000 than it was in 1980. To employ all those additional workers, the developing countries would have to create more jobs than now exist in Western Europe, Japan, the United States, the Soviet Union, and the other industrialized nations combined" (Fallows, 1983: 45).

The impact of rapid population growth on subsequent unemployment is dramatized further by the situation in Latin America, whose combined population in the early 1950s stood at about 150 million. It is projected to soar to 845 million by the year 2025. Half of the population of Latin America in 1983 was eighteen years old or younger and about to enter the labor force (Fallows, 1983: 45). This presents Latin America with a labor problem that is, in the words of Robert Fox of the Inter-American Development Bank, "intractable." "[The problem] is based on a population already born. Latin American countries would have to create an average of 4 million new jobs each year until 2025 [to accommodate the growth]. The U.S., with an economy five times larger, averages 2 million new jobs per year" (cited in Fallows, 1983: 45–46).

Furthermore, the search for jobs contributes to the rapid growth of already massive urban areas.

> Living in Mexico City, they say, gives you the pollution equivalent of forty cigarettes a day—that's just one person's share of the six thousand tons of gas and soot that fall daily on the sprawling metropolis.
>
> Why would anyone want to live there? The straight answer is the chance of a job in one of the 300,000 factories that belch out the smoke in the first place. They might not comply with the anti-pollution legislation, but they do obey the laws of supply and demand: people want work and factories want workers. ("State of World Population '82," 1982: 79)

Globally, urbanization is proceeding at a rapid pace, but increasingly the world's largest cities will be in the Third World. Thirty-eight percent of the world's people were estimated to be living in cities in 1983, a figure projected to reach 52 percent by the end of the century. . . . Worldwide, by the year 2000 there will be fifty-eight cities of over five million people, compared with half that number in the early 1980s ("State of World Population '82," 1982: 79). More than half of these will be in the Third World, where a combination of natural growth and a desire to escape poverty in the countryside will fuel the expansion of the megalopolises. In many instances the estimated rates of growth and the numbers involved are astounding. Lagos, Nigeria, a city of 800,000 in 1960, will be a city of 9.4 million in 2000; Cairo, with 5.7 million inhabitants in 1970, will grow to more than 13 million by then; and Mexico City, with 10.9 million inhabitants in 1975, will become a massive urban center of some 31 million people.

Urbanization places added pressures on the need for expanded social services associated with rapid population growth, because urban development requires more investment in infrastructure than does rural development. It also increases the pressures on local agricultural systems, because there are fewer hands in the countryside to feed the growing number of mouths in the city. Urbanization thus contributes to the need to import food from abroad, thereby further straining already limited resources. And within the urban areas themselves, the often deplorable living conditions contain the seeds of social unrest and political turmoil. . . .

Ironically, as present trends unfold, Third World countries will bear not only the greatest burden of a burgeoning population of young people but also, eventually, of older people as the enormous number of today's youth grow to maturity and old age fifty years hence. Although the Third World today contains three-quarters of the world's people, it contains only half of those over sixty. By 2025 . . . the Third World will increase its share of the "gray generation" to three-quarters ("The Age of Aging," 1982: 82). It is a generation with which the advanced industrial societies of the West are beginning to grapple now.

**The First World**   For developed countries, the move toward zero-population growth has resulted in a gradually aging society, as comparatively fewer babies are born and life expectancy increases. Some gerontologists . . . have speculated that a gradually aging society will tend to be a more conservative one politically. Others have argued that the move toward zero-population growth will have untoward effects on the economic systems of advanced industrial societies, which seem to thrive on the growth in aggregate demand. There is evidence to refute both of these views. . . . But what is beyond dispute is that older people will increasingly comprise a social and potential political force worldwide. . . .

Already in developed nations, the proportionately larger number of older people has created a dependency problem that will be greatly magnified after the turn of the century. . . . By the year 2025 there will be a billion people over sixty—one person in seven, compared with only one in twelve in 1950, but there will be comparatively fewer people of working age to support them as a result of today's declining population growth rate. As we noted, Third World countries will experience the greatest increase in these numbers. North and South will thus face a common demographic problem: "Only by harnessing the skills of the elderly alongside the strength of the young can we prevent the aging [from] becoming an ever-increasing burden to us all" ("The Age of Aging," 1982).

Coping with a gradually aging population is a necessary consequence of the move toward zero-population growth. Providing for the increasing number of dependent elderly relative to the number of productive workers is already a matter of political concern in Europe, Japan, and North America, where fertility levels are already below replacement. In Western Europe in particular, two other concerns have joined with this one to form the basis of an intense political debate about the wisdom of pursuing pronatalist policies (designed to raise fertility) and the consequences of failing to do so. Much of the debate turns on questions of individual versus collective welfare. . . .

Proponents of pronatalist measures are concerned with the "continued vitality of national populations that do not replace themselves: no children, no future, is the key phrase" (van de Kaa, 1987). National pride, concern for the nation's place among the world powers, and sensitivity to the vitality of European culture in a world where non-European countries grow much faster are also at issue. . . .

On the other hand, opponents of pronatalist measures "dismiss as exaggerated the specter of Europe as a decrepit society of ruminating octogenarians." They "attach no special value to their own cultures" and tend to oppose stimulating population growth in a world where this is already a serious problem. They believe that "economic resources rather than military resources or population size determine a country's international standing" and that "economic integration is a much more effective way to maintain Europe's international position than stimulating the birth rate." Finally, they question whether it makes sense to stimulate births when Europe already suffers from high levels of unemployment. "With modern technology eliminating jobs, workers are encouraged to work shorter hours, part-time, or retire early and immigration is halted," the argument continues, "so why should we have more people?" (van de Kaa, 1987).

### The Impact of Population Growth on the Global Commons

The untoward effects of population growth on economic development often play themselves out through excessive pressures on natural resources and the desecration of the delicate life-support systems on which humankind depends. Worldwide, there is mounting evidence of rapid deforestation, desertification, and soil erosion. . . . It is most acute where population growth and poverty are most apparent.

> Growing populations without access to farmland push cultivation into hillsides and tropical forests, with destructive effects on the soil. The demand for firewood is a primary reason for massive deforestation. Twenty percent of household income is spent on firewood in Addis Ababa. In the Gambia and Tanzania, wood has become so scarce that each household spends more than two-thirds of worker days per year gathering needed wood. (Murray, 1985: 10)

In the case of the Sahel in Africa, growing populations of livestock as well as humans hastened the conversion of productive land into a desert that ultimately led to famine *(The New Population Debate,* 1985). Nowhere is the tragedy of the commons illustrated more graphically.

The process of desertification demonstrates how overshoot of the carrying capacity of biological systems multiplies.

> Once the demand for fuelwood exceeds the sustainable yield of local forests, it not only reduces tree cover but also leads to soil erosion and land degradation. When grasslands deteriorate to where they can no longer support cattle, livestock herders often take to lopping foliage from trees, thus putting even more pressure on remaining tree cover. Both contribute to a loss of protective vegetation, without which both wind and water erosion of soil accelerate, leading to desertification—a sustained decline in the biological productivity of land.
>
> A decline in the diversity of plant and animal communities marks the onset of desertification. This in turn leads to a reduction of soil organic matter, a decline in soil structure, and a loss of water retention capacity. It also lowers soil fertility, reduced further by increasing wind and water erosion. Typically the end result is a desert: a skeletal shell of soil consisting almost entirely of sand and lacking in the fine particles and organic matter that make soil productive. (Brown et al., 1987: 26)

According to Lester Brown and his associates at the Washington-based Worldwatch Institute,

> In countries where rates of population growth remain high, a three-stage "ecological transition" emerges that is almost the reverse of the demographic transition in that its end result is disastrous. In the first stage, expanding human demands are well within the sustainable yield of the biological support system. In the second, they are in excess of the sustainable yield but still expanding as the biological resource itself is being consumed. And in the final stage, human consumption is forcibly reduced as the biological system collapses. (Brown et al., 1987: 26–27)

Excessive population growth doubtlessly strains the environment and contributes to destruction of the global commons. But so does excessive consumption. In this respect it is not the poverty-stricken, growing masses of the South who place the greatest strains on the global habitat, but the affluent, consumption-oriented minority in the North, where one person consumes forty times what the average person in Somalia consumes. The United States heads the list;

comprising but 5 percent of the world's population, Americans consume 40 percent of world resources every year. . . .

The disproportionate impact of the world's rich is especially apparent in the demands they place on global supplies of food and energy. . . Here we . . . note only briefly some of the issues related to the global commons that are linked to the energy-intensive, consumption-oriented life-styles of those making up the First World.

One is deforestation. In the South it is occurring as expanding populations search for fuelwood. In West Germany and elsewhere in Europe it is occurring for reasons that remain uncertain, but the belief is that chemical changes in the atmosphere are responsible for killing the forests (see Postel, 1986).

*Acid rain* is a common atmospheric consequence of burning fossil fuels. The burning of coal in particular produces sulphur and nitrogen oxides in the atmosphere which, after traveling long distances, return to the earth in rain or snow, thus contributing to the acidification of lakes, the corrosion of materials and structures, and the impairment of ecosystems. Acid rain has fallen in measurable amounts in the Scandinavian countries, the United States, and Canada. In recent years Canada has alleged that it suffers adversely from the failure of the United States to curb atmospheric pollution, which causes the acid rain that kills aquatic life and damages crops and forests in Canada.

The burning of fossil fuels has produced another environmental condition known as the *greenhouse effect.* Combustion, especially the burning of coal, releases carbon dioxide into the atmosphere. As the concentration of carbon dioxide increases, it could cause the average temperature of the earth's surface to rise by several degrees, with an even greater increase in the now-frigid polar regions. . . . Eventually, shifts in the world's climatic patterns could have political, social, and economic consequences, as the world's traditional food-producing areas are affected, its rainfall patterns are altered, and its coastal waters rise. . . .

First World countries have also contributed disproportionately to the destruction of the ozone layer that protects the earth from dangerous, cancer-producing ultraviolet rays from the sun. The damage occurs when artificial chemicals known as chlorofluorocarbons are released into the atmosphere. The chemicals are widely used in refrigerators and air conditioners as refrigerants, in styrofoam cups, in cleansers for computer components, and as aerosol propellants for such things as deodorants. Currently, nearly a million tons of the destructive chemicals are released into the atmosphere every year, where they can remain active for more than a century. . . .

Other examples of environmental stress associated with affluence can be added to this brief list. They include soil erosion caused by the expansion of energy-intensive, mechanized agriculture to marginal lands; water shortages caused by the massive requirements of modern agriculture, industry, and residential living; and depletion of ocean fisheries caused by technology-intensive overfishing and pollution of spawning beds. Together they reinforce a fundamental point: The belief that there are "too many people" ultimately has meaning only in relation to something else, such as the availability of food and renewable and nonrenewable resources and pressures on the global commons. Measured against any of these yardsticks, it is not the world's less-developed nations of the South that exert the greatest demands and pressures on the global carrying capacity; it is the advanced industrialized societies of the North.

### Global Patterns of Emigration and Immigration

Fertility, mortality, and migration are the three basic demographic variables that determine all population alterations. Migration has been especially important, indeed, an increasing source of concern in Europe, the Middle East, and the United States, and promises to become even more so as population growth in the Third World over the next several decades creates pressures toward outward movement. Major cultural changes can be expected in the receiving countries of the North where fertility levels are already below the replacement level, with the result that a larger proportion of their populations in the future will be made up of recent immigrants from nations culturally different from their descendants.

Immigration is now the primary demographic variable in U.S. population growth. With fertility in the United States below the replacement level since the early 1970s, immigration accounted for more than a quarter of the nation's population growth between 1980 and 1985, and the proportion is growing. . . . Even more important is the dramatic shift in the origins of the immigrants over the past two decades.

> Europeans made up 90 percent of immigrants 100 years ago when the Statue of Liberty was dedicated and more than half still in 1965 when a new influx was prompted by the law change that lowered barriers that had been based largely on race. Only 11 percent of the 570,000 legal immigrants recorded in 1985 came from Europe. Asians accounted for 46 percent of the legal total and Latin Americans—mainly Mexicans and almost all Spanish-speaking—made up 37 percent. (Bouvier and Gardner, 1986: 4)

In addition to legal immigrants, the United States has absorbed large numbers of illegal immigrants, variously estimated to be somewhere between 200,000 and 500,000 per year, most of whom entered through Mexico.

Migrants are of two types: political refugees who move because of threats to their convictions or fear for their lives and those who move for economic reasons. The United Nations High Commission for Refugees keeps tabs on about eleven million refugees worldwide, a number that more than doubled in less than a decade. . . . More than half are concentrated in the Middle East, and about a third are in Africa. Refugees are often by-products of war. For example, many of the Asian immigrants to the United States in the early 1980s were victims of the Vietnam War. Political turmoil and civil strife in El Salvador, Nicaragua, Guatemala, and elsewhere in Central America and the Caribbean have caused an influx of migrants from these areas.

Other than refugees, migrants, both domestically and internationally, typically are in search of a better standard of living and way of life. Internationally, migrants are often willing to take jobs in faraway lands shunned by local people. Typically this means they earn less than the natives do but more than they would earn in their homelands, even doing the same thing. From the point of view of the host countries, migrants often are welcomed, not only because they are paid low wages for tasks that natives do not want to perform, but also because the country accepting migrants pays little if anything for their health, education, and welfare needs. The home countries for their part sometimes encourage people to emigrate as a way of reducing unemployment and because migrants can be counted on to return considerable portions of their income to their families at home.

Although the United States is a nation born of immigrants, public attitudes in recent years have clearly indicated a preference for limiting the number of legal immigrants and preventing the influx of illegal aliens into the country. Such attitudes reflect a growing concern about the impact of immigrants on traditional American values, not unlike that raised in Europe in the context of the debate over the wisdom of pursuing pronatalist government policies.

In Europe, immigrants came to be especially important after World War II when they provided much of the unskilled labor needed to assist in reconstruction. Others migrated from former colonies, notably the British Commonwealth, to settle in the "mother" country. The mid-1970s was the peak of the "guest worker" era, when one of every seven manual workers in Germany and Britain was a migrant, as were a quarter of those in France, Belgium, and Switzerland. . . . However, with unemployment now the primary economic problem in Europe, migrants are no longer as welcome. . . . Clashes between Germans and Turks, between Britons and Indians and Pakistanis, and between French people and migrants from North Africa are recurrent. . . .

The Middle East is also the scene of migrant-related tensions. Here oil money attracted foreigners, where in many of the receiving countries they now constitute two-thirds of the labor force. . . . Many came from other Arab countries, but large numbers also came from outside the region, mainly from India, Pakistan, Thailand, and South Korea. Echoing a now familiar theme, there is concern for the impact of non-natives on Arab culture and religion, but here the large majority of aliens who are not citizens can never hope to be. The question is whether foreigners will be able to stay in the oil-rich countries as revenues from oil recede. The question portends controversy among the nations and peoples concerned.

The foregoing demonstrates how critical international immigration has become to today's transforming global political economy. In many Northern nations in particular, migration, not population growth, is *the* population problem. Nevertheless, the two problems are linked and promise to become inseparably so as environmental degradation and lost economic opportunities in the South arising from a rapidly expanding population prompt the search for a better way of life in the North.

## REFERENCES

"The Age of Aging." (1982) *UN Chronicle* 19 (July): 82–84.

Bouvier, Leon F., and Robert W. Gardner. (1986) "Immigration to the U.S.: The Unfinished Story," *Population Bulletin.* Vol 41, no. 4. Washington, D.C.: Population Reference Bureau.

Brown, Lester R., Edward C. Wolf, Linda Starke, William U. Chandler, Christopher Flavin, Cynthia Pollock, Sandra Postel, and Jodi Jacobson. (1987) *State of the World 1987.* New York: Norton.

Fallows, James. (1983) "Immigration: How It's Affecting Us," *The Atlantic* 252 (November): 45–52.

Merrick, Thomas W. (1986) "World Population in Transition," *Population Bulletin.* Vol. 41, no. 2. Washington, D.C.: Population Reference Bureau.

Murray, Anne Firth. (1985) "Population: A Global Accounting," *Environment* 27 (July/August): 7–11, 33–34.

*The New Population Debate: Two Views on Population Growth and Economic Development.* (1985) Washington, D.C.: Population Reference Bureau.

*Population in Perspective.* (1986) Washington, D.C.: Population Reference Bureau.

Population Reference Bureau. (1981) *World Population: Toward the Next Century.* Washington, D.C.: Population Reference Bureau.

Postel, Sandra. (1986) *Altering the World's Chemistry: Assessing the Risks.* Worldwatch Paper 71. Washington, D.C.: Worldwatch Institute.

Repetto, Robert. (1987) "Population, Resources, Environment: An Uncertain Future," *Population Bulletin.* Vol. 42, no. 2. Washington, D.C.: Population Reference Bureau.

"State of World Population '82." (1982) *UN Chronicle* 19 (July): 77–82.

Van de Kaa, Dirk J. (1987) "Europe's Second Demographic Transition," *Population Bulletin.* Vol 42, no. 1. Washington, D.C.: Population Reference Bureau.

# 33

# THE WANING OF GLOBAL FOOD SECURITY

Lester R. Brown

**Prospects for ensuring national and global food security declined markedly as the world entered the 1990s, eroding the optimism of only a few years earlier. Lester R. Brown argues the future remains bleak as population growth, environmental degradation, rising food prices, and the threat of climate change undermine the ability of national agricultural systems to provide food sufficiency. Brown, president of the Worldwatch Institute and director of its annual *State of the World* reports, is renowned worldwide for his many provocative publications on global environmental conditions.**

The ranks of the hungry are expanding . . ., reversing the trend of recent decades. Uncertainties and stresses from a changing climate are now being overlaid upon an already tightening food situation. In the absence of a major commitment by governments to slow population growth and strengthen agriculture, food insecurity and the social instability associated with it will preoccupy the political leaders of many countries during the 1990s.

At the start of the 1987 harvest, world grain stocks totaled a record 459 million tons, enough to feed the world for 101 days. When the 1989 harvest [began] , the "carry-over" stocks [stood] at about 60 days of consumption. During a brief two years, world reserves of grain—which account for half of all human caloric intake when consumed directly and part of the remainder in the form of meat, milk, cheese, butter, and eggs—. . . plummeted from the highest level ever to the lowest since the crisis years of 1972–1975.

Grain stocks . . . declined precipitously because food demand . . . continued its population-driven rise while production [fell] at a record rate. In 1987, a monsoon failure in India contributed to an 85-million-ton drop in world output. In 1988, drought-reduced harvests in the United States, Canada, and China reduced world grain output a further 60 million tons. . . .

This reversal in humanity's agricultural fortunes . . . occurred rather abruptly. For those accustomed to reading as recently as early 1988 of a "world awash in grain," the latest downturn in grain output may come as a surprise. Although not widely recognized at the time, the impressive growth in world production following the doubling of world grain prices in 1973 was achieved in part by plowing highly erodible land and in part by drawing down water tables through overpumping for irrigation.

Farmers can overplow and overpump with impressive results in the short run, but for many the short run is drawing to a close. The result is a worldwide retrenchment in cultivated area and a dramatic slowdown in the spread of irrigation. As highly erodible cropland brought under the plow during the agricultural boom years of the 1970s is taken out of cultivation, and as falling water tables in key food-producing countries force a reduction in irrigated area, the growth in world food output is slowing.

## FOOD INSECURITY IN AFRICA AND LATIN AMERICA

Evidence that environmental degradation in some regions is altering the food prospect—and, in turn, the human prospect—is unmistakable. In Africa, a deteriorating agricultural resource base, record population growth, and economic mismanagement lowered grain output per person throughout the 1970s. During the 1980s, mounting external debt reduced capital available for investment in agriculture, exacerbating the decline.

The social effects of agricultural adversity are now becoming highly visible throughout the continent. In mid-1988, the World Bank reported that "both the proportion and the total number of Africans with deficient diets have climbed and will continue to rise unless special action is taken." The World Bank went on to say that "barely a quarter of Africans are living in countries where food consumption was increasing in the 1980s, down considerably from about two-thirds in the 1970s."

In Africa, the number of "food insecure" people, defined by the World Bank as those not having enough food for normal health and physical activity, now totals over 100 million. Some 14.7 million Ethiopians, one-third of the country, are undernourished. Nigeria is close behind, with 13.7 million undernourished people. The countries with 40% or more of their populations suffering from chronic food insecurity are Chad, Mozambique, Somalia, and Uganda. The

World Bank summarized its findings by noting that "Africa's food situation is not only serious, it is deteriorating."

The island of Madagascar, whose population of 11 million is expanding by 3% per year, reveals in some detail how population growth and environmental deterioration are affecting people. As with the rest of Africa, per capita grain production peaked in 1967 and declined gradually until 1983, when the fall accelerated. Since then, average grain consumption has fallen by nearly one-fifth, pushing food intake below the survival level for many. Infant mortality, the most sensitive indicator of nutritional stress, rose from 109 to 130 per thousand between 1980 and 1986. Short of a miracle, the future of this country, with a birth rate among the world's highest and a rate of topsoil loss greater even than that of Ethiopia, is not bright.

This deterioration is not limited to Africa. In Latin America, which exported more grain than North America did a half-century ago, per capita grain production has fallen 7% since reaching an all-time high in 1981. In its 1988 report "The Global State of Hunger and Malnutrition," the U.N.'s World Food Council reports that the share of malnourished preschoolers in Peru increased from 42% to 68% between 1980 and 1983. Infant deaths [rose] in Brazil during the 1980s. If recent trends in population growth, land degradation, and growth in external debt continue, Latin America's decline in food production per person will almost certainly continue into the 1990s, increasing the number of hungry, malnourished people. The Council summarized its worldwide findings by noting that "earlier progress in fighting hunger, malnutrition and poverty has come to a halt or is being reversed in many parts of the world."

## RISING GRAIN PRICES

When domestic food production is inadequate, the ability of countries to import becomes the key to food sufficiency. During the late 1980s, low-income grain-deficit countries [had to] contend not only with an increase in grain prices, but also in many cases with unmanageable external debt, which severely [limited] their expenditure on food imports. The World Bank nutrition survey of Africa just cited was based on data through 1986; since then, conditions have deteriorated further as world grain prices have climbed.

The effect of higher grain prices on consumers is much greater in developing countries than in industrial ones. In the United States, for example, a $1 loaf of bread contains roughly 5¢ worth of wheat. If the price of wheat doubles, the price of the loaf would increase only to $1.05. In developing countries, however, where wheat is purchased in the market and ground into flour at home, a doubling of world grain prices translates into a doubling of prices to consumers. For those who already spend most of their income on food, such a rise can drive consumption below the survival level.

For debt-ridden, food-deficit, low-income countries, higher world prices of wheat, rice, and corn mean lower consumption and more hunger. Higher corn prices will affect most directly corn-consuming countries in eastern Africa and Latin America. The rising price of rice will reduce caloric intake among the low-income populations of Asia, where 90% of the world's rice is consumed. . . .

### THE THREAT OF CLIMATE CHANGE

Already faced with a deteriorating food situation, the world is now confronted with climate change, an additional threat to food security. The drought-damaged U.S. grain harvest in 1988 illustrates how global warming may affect agriculture over the longer term in the United States and elsewhere.

Climate change will not affect all countries in the same way. The projected rise of 1.5°–4.5° C (3°–8° F) is a global average, but temperatures are expected to increase much more in the middle and higher latitudes and more over land than over the oceans. They are projected to change little near the equator, while gains in the higher latitudes could easily be twice the anticipated global average. This uneven distribution will affect world agriculture disproportionately, since most food is produced in the middle and higher latitudes of the northern hemisphere.

Though they remain sketchy, meteorological models suggest that two of the world's major food-producing regions—the North American agricultural heartland and a large area of central Asia—are likely to experience a decline in soil moisture during the summer growing season as a result of higher temperatures and increased evaporation. If the warming progresses as the models indicate, some of the land in the U.S. western Great Plains that now produces wheat would revert to rangeland. The western Corn Belt would become semiarid, with wheat or other drought-tolerant grains that yield 40 bushels per acre replacing corn that yields over 100 bushels.

On the plus side, as temperatures increase, the winter wheat belt might migrate northward, allowing winter strains that yield 40 bushels per acre to replace spring varieties yielding 30 bushels. A longer growing season would also permit a northward extension of spring wheat production into areas such as Canada's Alberta province, thus increasing that nation's cultivated area. On balance, though, higher temperatures and increased summer dryness will reduce the North American grain harvest, largely because of their negative impact on the all-important corn crop.

Judging by the historical record, the odds are against severe back-to-back droughts, but with the warming now apparently under way, hot, dry summers are likely to become more frequent. In the event of another disastrous drought, U.S. grain exports would drop dramatically. The world would face a food emergency for which there is no precedent in the decades since North America emerged as its breadbasket. There would be a desperate effort to corner available supplies as world grain prices soared to record levels. In such a situation, preventing starvation among the world's poor would require affluent countries to reduce the amount of grain fed to livestock.

Asian and African countries, in particular, would find it impossible to feed their people without North American grain. Many of the world's major cities— Leningrad, Cairo, Lagos, Caracas, and Tokyo, for example—depend largely on grain from the United States and Canada. In an integrated world food economy, all countries suffer the consequences of poor harvests.

## MEETING FUTURE FOOD NEEDS

In many ways, the 1990s will be unlike any decade that the world's farmers have ever faced. There will be little opportunity for expanding cultivated areas; irrigated land, while growing slowly worldwide, is declining in some key countries. For the world's more advanced farmers, there are few new technologies to draw upon. In many countries, returns on the use of additional fertilizer—which has been the driving force behind the worldwide expansion of food output over the past four decades—are diminishing. And, finally, the prospect of global warming now hangs over the future of agriculture.

On the demand side, the annual increment in world population is projected to climb to record highs in the years immediately ahead. The 86 million people added in 1988 are expected to be joined by at least 90 million annually during the early 1990s. Most of the added millions will live in countries where nutrition is already inadequate and, in many cases, deteriorating.

Restoring the rapid growth in world food output that existed from 1950 to 1984 will not be easy. Among the areas where massive increases in output are unlikely, because yields are already high and response to the use of additional fertilizer is low, are Japan, China, Western Europe, and North America. Some regions, such as the semiarid west African Sahel, have no technologies available that will sharply boost output. On the other hand, India, Argentina, Brazil, and the Soviet Union all have a large potential to raise yields.

For some countries, many of which are in Africa, local rainfall is too low and irrigation water too scarce to permit the extensive use of fertilizers. Fortunately, alternatives exist for many of these countries, which may never develop a fossil-fuel-based agriculture. While these will not lead to the dramatic gains in yield of the Green Revolution technologies, they can boost production markedly among subsistence farmers, where the need is greatest. In many tropical and subtropical regions, agroforestry (the incorporation of trees and field crops into a single farming system) is proving to be highly productive. The trees can provide food, forage, fuel, organic matter in the form of leaf drop, and, if they are nitrogen-fixing, nitrogen for the crops grown in the immediate vicinity.

Where labor is abundant relative to land, labor-intensive agricultural techniques such as multiple cropping (growing more than one crop per year) and intercropping (simultaneously planting more than one crop on a piece of land) can make a big difference. So can the composting of organic wastes, including straw, livestock manure, and leaves. In densely populated parts of Africa and Asia, the stall feeding of livestock, also labor-intensive, both helps control land degradation from random grazing and concentrates livestock manure, making composting easier.

As population pressures build, land can be farmed more intensively using such techniques as biointensive gardening. This has figured prominently in efforts to expand production of vegetables to supplement cereals and tubers on the Philippine island of Negros. The technique, involving hand-tillage of the seedbed to one foot or more in depth, relies on local materials to improve and maintain soil fertility. Among the local inputs used in these highly productive plots are compost manure, wood ash, bonemeal, leucaena leaves (from a fast-growing nitrogen-fixing tree), and crushed eggshells. Like the high-yielding rices that originated in the Philippines, this technology has a potentially broad application in other countries.

## PROTECTING THE RESOURCE BASE

One of the keys to raising output on a sustainable basis is protecting the resource base. With cropland becoming scarce, future food security depends on safeguarding it both from conversion to nonfarm uses and from the erosion that reduces its inherent productivity. Nearly a decade ago, U.S. Assistant Secretary of Agriculture Rupert Cutler observed that "asphalt is the land's last crop." Once productive cropland is lost to suburban development, shopping malls, or roads, it is difficult to restore it to food production.

A few countries, such as Japan, have carefully crafted programs designed to protect cropland. In 1968, Japan adopted a comprehensive zoning plan that put all land in one of three categories—industrial, agricultural, or other—and made it illegal to build on cropland. Faced with acute land pressures, Japan confronted the issue early and in doing so established an approach to cropland preservation that is simple, effective, and easily adapted to conditions in other countries.

. . . [Such] data as are available indicate that soil erosion is slowly reducing the inherent productivity of up to one-third of the world's cropland, though increased use of chemical fertilizers is temporarily masking this deterioration. Worldwide, an estimated 25 billion tons of topsoil is being lost from cropland each year, roughly the amount that covers Australia's wheat lands.

National success stories in the effort to conserve topsoil are few. Among the major food-producing countries, the United States is the only one systematically reducing excessive soil erosion. Its Conservation Reserve Program both encourages conversion of highly erodible cropland to grassland or woodland and penalizes farmers who do not manage their soil responsibly by denying them the benefits from farm programs. In 1987, the program's second year, U.S. soil losses were reduced by 460 million tons, the greatest year-to-year reduction on record for any country.

In a world where fresh water is becoming more scarce, future growth in irrigation may depend on greater investments in the efficiency of water use. Stopping leakage from irrigation canals and ditches and abandoning the use of wasteful irrigation technologies present obvious opportunities. Israel, with its underground drip system and other advanced irrigation technologies, has expanded its irrigated area by using available water supplies more carefully. In many countries, the key to such gains is the elimination of water subsidies, which actually encourage the inefficient use of irrigation water.

Early international agricultural research efforts concentrated heavily on raising yields of wheat and rice, the world's principal staple foods. In recent years, the Consultative Group on International Agricultural Research—a network of 13 ably staffed agricultural research centers, all but one in the Third World—has shifted its attention to raising output of such minor staples as millet, chickpeas, and cassava, crops produced by low-income, subsistence farmers. Although a far more demanding undertaking, this research effort is responsive to the needs of a large group of farmers, many of whom do not have access to fertilizer.

In a warmer world, where fresh water is becoming scarce, scientists can help push back the physical frontiers of cropping by developing varieties that are more drought resistant, salt tolerant, and early maturing. The payoff on the first two could be particularly high. It is in this area that biotechnology may be helpful in speeding up the plant-breeding process.

### GRAIN STOCKS AND LIVESTOCK

Ensuring an adequate level of grain stocks requires taking into account not only year-to-year variations in weather but the uncertain effects of rising temperatures as well. Global warming will deepen the uncertainty surrounding each year's crop and probably increase the frequency of reduced harvests. For example, the three drought-reduced U.S. harvests in the 1980s could increase to four or five in the 1990s and even more thereafter. With much of the 20 million hectares of cropland idled under U.S. supply-management programs scheduled to return to production in 1989, the need to establish a more formal set of guidelines for managing world grain reserves will become increasingly urgent.

If world food supplies tighten in the years ahead, the distribution of available supplies will become even more important than when the world was plagued with surpluses. High on the list of questions will be how much of the world's grain supply can be fed to livestock. At present, roughly 500 million tons of an annual harvest of usually 1.6 billion tons is consumed this way.

If the U.S. cropland now set aside under the supply-management programs were returned to production, the only remaining major food reserve to fall back on if carryover stocks of grain are depleted would be the grain consumed by livestock. When grain prices rise sharply, as they did in 1973, higher meat prices and the resulting drop in consumer demand force a reduction in the amount of grain fed to livestock. Tragically, by the time grain prices actually affect consumers' consumption of meat, milk, and eggs, the world's poorest may not be getting enough grain to survive.

The relative efficiency of converting grain to various types of animal protein also affects the world grain supply-and-demand balance. The least efficient livestock product is beef produced in feedlots, where it takes roughly seven pounds of grain to produce a pound of meat. The grain used in producing a quarter-pound hamburger could feed a person in a low-income country for two days. The production of broiler chickens, much more efficient than beef, requires two pounds of grain per pound of meat. Thus, shifts from beef to poultry, already under way in some societies for health reasons, help stretch the world supply of grain.

In the final analysis, future food security may lie more in the hands of family planners than farmers. Agricultural policy makers and farmers acting alone may not be able to ensure adequate food supplies in the years ahead. What is needed is a major assist of the sort that China's family-planning ministry has provided that country's farmers over the last two decades, a lift that, when combined with economic reforms in agriculture, helped raise food output per person by nearly half between 1976 and 1984.

# 34

# COPING WITH THE UNCERTAINTIES OF THE GREENHOUSE EFFECT

Jessica T. Mathews

**The theory underlying the natural greenhouse effect has been understood for more than a century, but now human activity has become the agent of large-scale changes in the global climate. Jessica T. Mathews examines what is known and what remains uncertain about the causes and consequences of global warming. Recognizing that uncertainties abound, she concludes that efforts undertaken now to mitigate global warming will pay environmental dividends "even if our greenhouse predictions should turn out to be wrong." Mathews is vice president of the World Resources Institute and served on the U.S. National Security Council as director of the Office of Global Issues from 1977 to 1979. She is editor of *Preserving the Global Environment: The Challenge of Shared Leadership* (1991).**

Based on past experience, we expect a fair amount of scientific certainty about environmental threats before we struggle with the societal change required to mitigate them. We know that as conflicting scientific views slowly converge, economists will sort out the costs and benefits of alternative responses, and as concrete evidence of a problem piles up, public concern will grow, building the foundation for a political solution. This process may take many years, even decades, but we can always go back and clean up the damage that accumulated

Adapted especially for this book from Jessica Mathews, "Coping with the Uncertainties of the Greenhouse Effect" in *Harvard International Review*. Used by permission of Jessica Mathews and *Harvard International Review*.

along the way. And if the cleanup turns out to be far costlier than prevention would have been, that is deemed an acceptable price to pay for certainty. We can at least console ourselves that waiting for theories to coalesce allowed us to avoid premature action that might have entailed worse consequences.

But the greenhouse effect overturns all that we think we have learned about science and policy and dealing with environmental threats. Scientists cannot produce all the needed answers, only a range of possibilities, so economists cannot proceed with the usual cost-benefit analyses. Citizens cannot wait for the usual evidence to trigger their entry into the fray, for the greenhouse fingerprint may not be perceptible until we are decades into irreversible climate change. The atmosphere defies cleanup efforts, since many greenhouse gases persist for a century or more. According to philosopher of science Jerry Ravetz, the forthcoming struggle to deal with global environmental change may "transform the image of science from that of a stately edifice to that of a can of worms." Now, he urges, we must all learn to "cope with the imperfections of science, with radical uncertainty, and even with ignorance, in forming policy decisions for the biosphere."

French mathematician Jean Fourier formulated the theory describing the natural greenhouse effect more than 150 years ago, and it has changed little since. Fourier theorized that earth's atmosphere was transparent to the sun's radiation, but it would absorb lower energy radiation re-emitted by the earth, thus warming the system. This theory has proved robust, and no respectable scientist doubts its validity. But it became a subject of more than theoretical interest when, with the advent of the industrial revolution, man began introducing unnaturally high concentrations of greenhouse gases into the earth's atmosphere.

At first, the human contribution was mostly carbon dioxide, a product of all carbon-based combustion. Today, human activity is contributing five principal greenhouse gases—carbon dioxide, methane (natural gas), nitrous oxide, ozone (a pollutant and health hazard in the lower atmosphere, though a protective screen against ultraviolet radiation in the stratosphere) and chlorofluorocarbons (CFCs), which have the dubious added distinction of destroying stratospheric ozone. We know exactly how fast and why concentrations of some of these gases are rising, but we are uncertain about such questions for others.

Since the onset of industrialization, the atmospheric concentration of carbon dioxide has increased by 25 percent (half of that during the past thirty years), and it is now growing by 0.5 percent a year. Fossil fuel combustion accounts for roughly 75 percent of excess carbon, and deforestation for up to 25 percent, for when forests are burned they release large quantities of carbon built up over decades or centuries. The concentration of methane, which has doubled in this century, is rising by one percent a year, but the causes are obscure. It may be that there are so many links between methane and human activity—from cattle ranching to rice paddies to leaky gas pipelines—that methane emissions are simply tracking population growth. The source of CFCs, rising by five percent each year, is no mystery, for these gases—used mainly in refrigeration, insulation, and (outside the United States) aerosol sprays—are entirely man-made. Ozone in the lower atmosphere, formed when the sun "cooks" byproducts of fossil fuel combustion, is rising by roughly one percent a year in the Northern Hemisphere. Finally, nitrous oxide is rising by 0.2 percent a year; its sources are uncertain, but the main suspects are fossil fuel combustion, certain soil bacteria and nitrogen fertilizers.

Alas, atmospheric chemistry is not quite so neat as this summary suggests. Pollutants interact with each other and with the air in an intricate maze of reactions. Carbon monoxide, for instance, though not itself a greenhouse gas, increases methane and ozone concentrations by chemically removing a molecule that would otherwise prevent the formation of methane or ozone.

In the slow motion of geologic time, the average global temperature has fluctuated within a relatively narrow band of about five degrees Centigrade during alternating glacial and interglacial periods over the 160,000 years for which we have an icecore record. When the last great ice age reached its coldest point about 18,000 years ago, average global temperature was about 4.5°C colder than it is today, and much of North America was buried under hundreds of meters of ice.

Whether large or small, past climate fluctuations occurred outside the scope of human intervention. But now, for the first time, human activity is the agent of large-scale change. The question among scientists is no longer whether the greenhouse gas buildup will change global climate, but how much and how quickly it will change.

In the past 140 years, the earth's average temperature has risen by more than 0.5°C. This does not sound like much, but it is merely a foretaste of a more serious future, for earth is at any given moment committed to far more climate change than is evident. Scientists believe that greenhouse gases already banked in the atmosphere have committed earth to a temperature rise of 1 to 2.5°C over the next half-century or so—even if we contribute not another molecule.

This delay results from the long (but as yet unknown) time it takes for heat absorbed by the atmosphere to spread throughout the system, principally the oceans. Reaching a new equilibrium—a steady state at which earth radiates as much energy to space as it absorbs from the sun—depends on a complex set of interactions among atmosphere, clouds, oceans, land, ice and the biosphere. The time lag before the full temperature rise resulting from any given concentration of greenhouse gases is actually realized could be anywhere from a few decades to a century. The longer this lag, the more difficult it will be to forge a policy response to global warming.

By 2030, if climate models are correct and current emission and deforestation trends continue, the earth would be committed to an eventual increase of 1.5 to 4.5°C. An increase of even 1.5 degrees would make the planet warmer than it has been for 160,000 years (some 120,000 years before modern man emerged);

4 degrees would usher in a climate more extreme than earth has seen for at least a million years. If our present understanding, derived from huge three-dimensional computer models, proves correct, this warming will alter most characteristics of the global climate and of our everyday weather.

Temperature increases in the high latitudes would be much greater than the global average. Omaha, Nebraska, for example, could expect to have 21 instead of only three 100°F or hotter days per year, and Dallas might sweat through 78 instead of its current 19. Today's booming Sunbelt could well become a wilting Swelterbelt. Shifting rainfall patterns may turn the centers of large continents, including the US grain belt, into dust bowls. The timing and pattern of the monsoons, to which tropical agriculture is delicately tuned, are also expected to change. Ocean currents may shift. Scientists do not yet understand ocean circulation well enough to predict changes, but one possibility is a diversion of the Gulf Stream that could make Western Europe's moderate climate far colder. By 2050, sea-level is expected to rise one to four feet, due to the thermal expansion of water and the melting of land-based ice. The Antarctic ice sheet is now growing, so sea-level rise may be closer to the low end of that range. If, however, over the much longer term the ice sheet should either melt or slide off into the ocean, sea-level would rise 20 feet, with catastrophic consequences.

Such broad global predictions are modestly reliable, but we cannot predict the climate of particular regions with anywhere near the same degree of confidence. Moreover, there is a great deal we do not understand about the global climate system. For example, a warmer earth means more evaporation and, most likely, more clouds. Depending on the height and type of clouds and the latitude where they occur, more clouds may either trap more heat, thereby reinforcing the warming, or reflect more sunlight back into space, thereby cooling the atmosphere. Though clouds are likely to have a major impact, it is impossible with today's knowledge to predict whether they will trigger a positive or negative feedback loop. The same can be said of feedback between the atmosphere and the biosphere. For example, global warming may increase the rate of respiration more than it does the rate of photosynthesis, increasing carbon dioxide concentrations and thereby ratcheting the temperature up further over time. Nor are these uncertainties the whole story. We may be due for some surprises because the greatest risks may well come from an entirely unexpected direction.

To inquire about the impact of climate change on man and on the rest of the biosphere is to move from the realm of knowledge laced with uncertainty to that of ignorance threaded with a few traces of knowledge—and to pose an unanswerable question. The climate's influence is so pervasive that it will never be possible to predict the whole impact of a postulated degree of global warming. The rising sea level alone, for instance, will erode beaches and barrier islands, destroy coastal wetlands and estuaries on which fisheries and wildlife depend and contaminate water supplies with saltwater—to say nothing of damage from flooding and storm surge. Since two-thirds of the world's population live within fifty miles of a coastline, accurately forecasting the aggregate cost of sea-level rise alone is extraordinarily difficult.

The prospects for the five to 30 million other species with which we share the planet are, if anything, even harder to predict. Most biologists are pessimistic about organisms' capacities to adapt to these rates of climate change that are an order of magnitude greater than any they have ever faced in nature. They foresee a spasm of species extinctions and the wholesale rearrangement of biological communities, since plants, animals and insects live together in a delicately balanced, co-evolved interdependence in which the loss of a single species can spell havoc for the rest. A quarter of earth's species could die out over the next half century if deforestation continues at today's rates in the absence of climate change; the probable synergy between climate change and habitat loss could well lead to an even higher extinction rate.

## INTERNATIONAL IMPLICATIONS

Although research on the impact of climate change is barely under way, studies are turning up potential problems nearly everywhere they look, from national security (How would the US-Soviet strategic balance be affected by an ice-free Arctic where their nuclear submarines now run under cover?) to public health (How far and how fast will tropical disease-bearing insects march North?). Buttressed by direct experience of such recent extremes as the 1986 Southeastern drought, the 1988 Midwestern drought and Hurricane Gilbert, the research harvest suggests that climate change will have an omnipresent impact, though the exact social, economic and biological costs remain to be discovered—or experienced.

Nonetheless, there will be some beneficial effects as well. Increased rainfall might turn arid areas into fertile cropland. Some plants, fertilized by added carbon dioxide, may grow faster and larger, though many of them will be weeds. Northern regions with adequate soils and water supplies could become major agricultural producers in the newly lengthened growing season. Icebound ports could become centers of commerce. But so great is the range of likely consequences that no country can count on being a net winner. Indeed, the claims being made only a few years ago that countries such as Canada and the Soviet Union would profit from global warming are now much muted, if not wholly retracted.

A climate-altered world would almost certainly not be divided into camps of winners and losers. While a certain amount of warming might be beneficial, further warming in the same country could be destructive or even catastrophic. Of necessity, analysts try to determine the results of discrete units of change—say, two, four or eight degrees of warming—but change will actually be a continuum with no resting points along the way for societies and ecosystems to adapt and regroup. Societies that might be coping successfully with two degrees of warming would already be committed to an additional several degrees, depending on the concentrations of greenhouse gases already banked in the atmosphere. Thus, policy options suggesting that climate change will come in neatly packaged units—such as "What will the United States have to do to adapt to a two-degree warming?"—miss the point. Arriving at any endpoint, a given amount of global warming and no more, is possible only some decades after the human community has taken steps to reduce greenhouse gas emissions.

Do such steps exist? Yes, unequivocally. And each of the four outlined below would confer other benefits besides holding down the heat.

• Banning production of CFCs—which account for 20 percent of global warming—is by far the easiest step, and it's already underway. In June 1990, 93 nations meeting in London under the auspices of the Montreal Protocol agreed to phase out CFC production (rather than the 50 percent cut agreed to earlier) and to commit $240 million to transferring ozone-friendly technology to developing countries over the next three years. By switching to available or foreseeable substitutes, it should be possible to eliminate CFC production, if not emissions, before the year 2000, with small political and economic cost. This stepped-up timetable is especially good news since CFCs are such bad news: molecule for molecule, they are 20,000 times more potent a greenhouse gas than carbon dioxide, and they last for 75–150 years in the stratosphere, all the while attacking the ozone layer that makes life on land possible.

• Reducing fossil fuel combustion—which accounts for 50 percent of global warming—essentially requires a technological revolution that reinvents energy use along environmentally safe lines. But for starters, we could double energy efficiency in the United States using existing technologies; Japan and West Germany use half as much energy as the United States per unit of GNP, so such a move would increase US competitiveness in the world market and reduce smog and acid rain as well. The move from carbon-rich to carbon-lean fuels and ultimately to non-fossil energy sources could be encouraged by eliminating subsidies that tilt the market toward fossil fuels and by instituting a carbon tax that would discourage waste and pollution.

• Halting tropical deforestation—which accounts for about 15 percent of global warming—will be monumentally difficult, but it will produce immediate benefits. At present, an acre and a half of tropical forest disappears every second, and four species die out each hour, most of them in the tropics. The consequences that flow from deforestation—drought, flooding, soil erosion, crop loss, siltation and shortage of fuel wood—impoverish nearly a billion people in the developing world. Preserving tropical forests (and ultimately regrowing some forest cover) could alleviate widespread poverty and hunger and reduce the rate of species extinction. The decisions made by tropical countries themselves will have the most impact on whether forests survive, but the industrialized North could help a good deal by relieving their crushing debt burden and making new funding available for sustainable forestry projects.

• Curbing population growth—most intense in developing countries, where the median age is around 15—would relieve pressure on the environment generally. Between 1950 and 1987, world population doubled to five billion. If current growth rates continue, population is expected to stabilize at 14 billion around 2120, with 95 percent of that growth in the developing countries. If imagining a workable solution to the greenhouse problem seems hard today, devising one that will provide for nearly triple today's population strains credulity. Aid programs focused on both environmentally sound economic development and increased access to family planning services could help developing countries lift their populations out of poverty and reduce stress on their over-exploited natural resources.

Taking such steps would require a societal transformation at many levels the world over. How should policymakers and citizens act in the face of scientific uncertainties? Should they demand traditional standards of proof before undertaking broad change? Or, given the irreversible nature of greenhouse warming and the fact that far more of it is in the pipeline than is perceptible, should they shoulder the burden of possible error by taking steps now to mitigate warming? For me, the choice is clear. As I weigh probabilities and risks, the scale tips decisively in favor of action now, because by lucky chance, much of what we need to do to limit further commitment to global warming will benefit us as a nation and as a species even if our greenhouse predictions should turn out to be wrong.

If our predictions should turn out to be right, steps taken now will be critical to the future of life on earth. The global action needed to mitigate warming—especially the enabling perception that all nations and peoples share a common destiny—will help future generations adapt to the temperature rise to which the earth is already committed. If we take these actions now, our descendants, however hard-pressed to adapt to an earth hotter than humankind has ever seen, will at least know that an endpoint is in sight.

# 35

# AGRICULTURE AND THE ENVIRONMENT: MEETING THE FOOD NEEDS OF THE COMING DECADE

## Orville L. Freeman

**Feeding the world's burgeoning population will require a massive increase in global food production. In this essay the author argues that a balance must be struck between concern for protecting the world's environment and the development and application of agricultural and food-related technology necessary to avoid mass starvation. Orville L. Freeman served as U.S. secretary of agriculture during the Kennedy and Johnson administrations and is president of the Agriculture Council of America.**

Estimated population growth for the next quarter century is so enormous that warning bells should be sounding in every quadrant of the globe. Feeding this population may well be the greatest challenge we have ever faced—one that will test the world's productive and technological capabilities to their very limits. . . . [It] will take total mobilization of all global productive resources, including land, infrastructure, people skills, and technology, to prevent massive famine in the decade of the 1990s and beyond.

Even conservative projections call for a population increase of over one billion people—bringing the world's population to 6.2 billion by the year 2000. These same projections predict a population of nearly 11 billion by the year

From *The Futurist,* published by the World Future Society, 4916 Saint Elmo Avenue, Bethesda, MD 20814. Used by permission.

373

2050. This increase will take place in a world where already over 75% of the population can barely feed themselves, almost 500 million people are severely malnourished, and 15 million children worldwide die each year from starvation and related illnesses—that is over 41,000 every day. In this regard, I think that many people—particularly those in the relatively well-fed industrialized world—simply cannot relate to the concept of subsistence, where securing enough food to sustain life is the focal point of each day's activities.

In the United States, for all but a relatively small segment of the population, the task of securing food means no more than a trip to the nearby supermarket, where we choose from more than 8,000 items to meet our needs. In fact, one of our major food-related concerns is how to eat less! For that reason, I sometimes think we are ill-prepared to wrestle with the realities of what it will take to feed the rising number of people in the world. In fact, there is no precedent in our history that even comes close to approximating the population and food-supply pressures we will experience in the next 10–20 years.

To give some definition to the magnitude of the challenge this presents, let me cite one statistic that drives this point home more clearly than any other I have encountered: In the next two to four generations, world agriculture will be called on to produce as much food as has been produced in the entire 12,000-year history of agriculture. This is a very sobering prospect and a challenge of unprecedented magnitude. To meet this challenge, difficult and delicate choices will have to be made, none of which will likely emerge without heated debate.

## A DIFFICULT BALANCING ACT

Choosing alternatives or making trade-offs is most difficult when each is desirable and the moral imperatives for each are both clear and compelling. Nowhere is this dilemma more apparent than in the current debate over protecting our planet's increasingly fragile environment and feeding its growing hungry population. Here we have goals that should be compatible. After all, the earth's resources were put in place to meet humanity's needs, the most basic of which is eating.

Unfortunately, the balancing act between producing food and preserving the environment appears cast in an increasingly hostile framework that in the end can only be counterproductive. We must exercise every caution to guard against the tyranny of a single issue dominating what must by definition be a very complex balancing act that frequently calls for difficult trade-offs.

In order of priority, then, the first challenge we must address is how to bring the goals of feeding the world's population and protecting the world's environment into harmony. They need not and must not be mutually exclusive. To maximize our productive capabilities and minimize the effect this production has on the environment, the vital connective tissue is technology. We must foster and harness the technological means through which both goals can be served—applying science to meet the objectives of both humanity and our environment.

Unfortunately, this does not seem to be the direction in which we are headed. From what I read and hear of late, technology is being cast in an increasingly dim light—a scapegoat for a host of environmental ills that humans have inflicted on their planet.

Application of technology, including agricultural application, has certainly not been without its missteps over the years. But fortunately, the industrial world is demonstrating a growing understanding that the price of environmental abuse is high and that the damage can be irreversible. We must strengthen this realization where agriculture is concerned.

At the same time, however, we must acknowledge that, without sophisticated food-production technology, we would not have the food supply we enjoy today and certainly could never meet the needs of the population realities nearly upon us.

## POPULATION GROWS, FOOD PRODUCTION FALLS

In the three decades following the early 1950s, the world—led by Europe and the United States, followed by many Third World countries—witnessed unprecedented advances in the development and application of agricultural and food-related technology. The resulting increases in production and delivery of food—the so-called Green Revolution, in which world grain output multiplied 2.6 times—has been truly phenomenal. Since the early 1980s, however, a gradual tightening of the world food situation on the production side is taking place with little corresponding response on the population side of the equation.

India, for example, more than tripled its wheat harvest between 1965 and 1983. Since that time, India has not increased its grain production at all, and its population—with 500 million people at the subsistence level—continues to climb rapidly. China boosted its grain production by nearly half between 1976 and 1984, but it has not reached the 1984 level since that record year—and population continues to grow. In Africa and South America, the two continents with the fastest-growing populations, food production has fallen far behind population growth. Since 1980, Africa's population has grown at an explosive 3% rate annually. But in that time period, its food production has grown only 1.8% annually—barely half as much as the rate of population growth. In most African countries, food production continues to fall progressively behind population growth.

If we are to avoid mass starvation among the exploding populations in Third World countries, we need to examine what caused the Green Revolution, because that type of production surge is exactly what has to be repeated in the decades ahead. We also need to look at the factors that caused the slowdown in productivity to see what can be done to return to previous growth levels.

## THE NEED FOR ANOTHER GREEN REVOLUTION

There seems to be general agreement on five major forces behind the Green Revolution:

1 The hybridization of corn.
2 The ninefold increase in fertilizer use between 1950 and 1984.
3 The near tripling of irrigated areas in that same period.
4 The rapid spread of new, high-yielding wheat and rice seeds in Third World countries.
5 The use of chemical insecticides, herbicides, rodenticides, and fungicides.

This latter category—crop-protection chemicals plus nitrogen fertilizer—currently is the popular whipping boy in the environmental debate. But we would do well to remember that these chemicals currently account for as much as 40%–50% of world agricultural production, particularly in light of the anticipated population–food pressures.

Regarding the causes of the slowdown in productivity growth, there is less solid agreement, but some of the problems we recognize are:

1 Shortage of land, with millions of acres withdrawn from production because of erosion.
2 Scarcity of water from drought and heavy irrigation, which has drawn down water tables rapidly in many places in the world.
3 The current absence of dramatic new technology that matches that which was so instrumental in stimulating productivity between 1960 and 1984, despite the predicted potential of future biotechnology.

Whatever the causes, it is clear that world grain carry-over has dropped to an alarmingly low level–a 16-year low with only a 17% reserve, which is less than two months' supply. To put this in perspective, this is very close to the 1973–1974 situation, when the United States became so concerned about tight supplies that it embargoed soybeans.

In the face of the reduced number of acres planted worldwide and a rising global demand, this trend will likely continue unless returning the world to a high rate of food productivity commands a top priority as we look to the future. To do this, there is no question that technology must play a major role. Any effective blueprint for increasing agricultural productivity worldwide must incorporate development and application of crop and food-related technology. To suggest that agricultural technology is the enemy of humanity or the environment is to ignore the realities of food production and population trends. Of course, there are potential risks in agricultural and food-related technology that should keep us ever vigilant. We must constantly strive for smart use and avoid misuse.

## REJECTING THE "GOOD OLD DAYS"

At the same time as we measure the impact of technology, we must take into account the effects of advances in scientific techniques that are taking place with breathtaking speed. . . . In seeking solutions to complex questions, we have to exercise an abundance of caution to avoid tossing out the baby with the bathwater. . . .

As attractive as some would make it sound, a return to the "good old days" and a pristine environment simply is not feasible. Many of us were around for some of those so-called "good old days." I, for one, am not interested in going back. I remember unpasteurized milk, no penicillin, wormy apples, and fresh fruit and vegetables only in the summer months. A return to that would represent a giant step backward and one that ignores the needs of our growing world population.

Technology that is intelligently conceived and carefully implemented, including the measured and careful application of fertilizer and crop-protection chemicals, represents the hope for the future and, as such, should be a cornerstone of food and agricultural policy for the coming decades. In this regard, the way must be paved for coming biotechnology and the fantastic possibilities this whole area of science opens up regarding both crop and livestock production and uses of agricultural products. Agricultural technology can be the tool that brings humanity and the environment into harmony and productive coexistence. For that reason, it should be embraced, not rejected, both in its conception and its application.

## SERVING HUMANITY AND THE ENVIRONMENT

I think we make a potentially dangerous mistake when we frame the question in an adversarial light: to serve humanity or the environment. The needs are not mutually exclusive. In fact, they are totally interdependent. My caution is this: In our haste to atone for environmental "sins" of the past, we must not delude ourselves about the realities of the future. What we have to do is measure and manage carefully how we apply technology today and how we oversee the evolution from one type of technological solution to another. We must guide the world to technology that meets the needs of both humanity and the environment. . . .

There is no question that meeting the food needs of the coming decades will exert increasing pressure on an already strained environment. However, no matter how compelling the case for reducing these environmental pressures is, we simply cannot turn our backs on the needs of the hungry.

The realities of food production in much of the Third World, where the population increases will be the greatest, are vastly different from what is experienced in the bountiful agricultural lands of the United States. Developing countries are striving for subsistence, while U.S. production currently is approximately 40% over domestic needs—and that is with millions of acres idled. The United States must keep its productivity high in order to provide food assistance to starving people and also to sustain and stimulate emerging agriculture in the developing world. Third World countries need the technological means through which their infant agriculture can achieve productive levels capable of feeding their growing populations and at the same time strengthening growth and expansion of their entire economy.

These are real needs and real solutions that cannot be ignored. Yet, there is danger that they will be obscured while the affluent 10% of the world looks for a broad brush and quick fix to environmental problems that have been decades in the making. Here I urge caution. Yes, we must protect our fragile environment and use our resources wisely. But there is a very serious danger that the voice of the world's hungry will not be heard if the environmental and food-related agenda is written to meet only the needs of well-intentioned but well-fed interests.

# 36

# SUSTAINABLE DEVELOPMENT: WHAT IS IT?

## Jim MacNeill

In 1987 the World Commission on Environment and Development, popularly known as the Brundtland Commission, published its report entitled *Our Common Future*. The central concept in the commission's work, explains Jim MacNeill, is *sustainability*. Thus the commission anticipated "a new era of growth," "not the type of growth that dominates today, but sustainable development based on forms and processes that do not undermine the integrity of the environment on which they depend." MacNeill served as secretary general of the World Commission on Environment and Development. Previously he had been director of environment for the Organization for Economic Cooperation and Development and is now director of sustainable development at Canada's Institute for Research on Public Policy.

. . . There is no doubt that if the nations of the Third World are to grow at the pace and scale needed to meet the needs and aspirations of their burgeoning populations, *sustainability* must become the overriding criterion of their economic, fiscal, trade, aid, energy, food and other sectoral policies. . . . The need to test national policies against the criterion of *sustainability* is just as great, if not greater, in the Second and First Worlds. With some 20 percent of the world's population, we consume nearly 80 percent of the world's goods. If we are to

Footnotes have been deleted. From a paper prepared for the Joint Economic Committee of the U.S. Congress. Hearings of the Subcommittee on Technology and National Security, June 13, 1989.

slow the rate at which we are crossing certain critical thresholds, such as those related to depletion of the ozone layer, global warming and acidification, the shift to sustainable forms of development must be led by the industrialized countries. . . .

Sustainable development embraces all of the issues that we have long thought of as environmental and resource management issues, and the power of the concept is that it integrates them with the traditional issues of growth, employment, development, trade, peace and security. These issues are compelling. They are moving rapidly to the top of political agendas all over the world. . . .

## THE WORLD COMMISSION ON ENVIRONMENT AND DEVELOPMENT

During the 4 years ending in December, 1987, I had opportunity to manage a global enquiry into the "state of the world." . . . It has become known as the "Brundtland" Commission, after our Chairman, Prime Minister Gro Harlem Brundtland of Norway. . . .

Our report, entitled "Our Common Future," was very timely, and it has already had a significant impact in many countries . . . and in several international organizations. . . .

## THE SUSTAINABILITY QUESTION

A lot of people today are wrestling with the concept of "sustainable development." Just what does it mean? . . .

. . . During its three years of work, the Commission returned constantly to what I called "the sustainability question"—Can growth on the orders of magnitude projected over the next 1–5 decades be managed on a basis that is sustainable, economically and ecologically?

The answer is not evident, since the obstacles to sustainability are mainly social, institutional and political. Economic and ecological sustainability are still dealt with as two separate questions in all governments and international organizations, where they are organized in separate compartments such as ministries of finance and departments of environment . . . But our economic and ecological systems are now interlocked. Global warming is a form of feedback from the Earth's ecological system to the World's economic system. So is the ozone hole, or acid rain in Europe and Eastern North America, or soil degradation in the prairies, deforestation and species loss in the Amazon, and many other phenomena.

The world's population has multiplied more than three times since 1900. Its economy has expanded 20 times. The use of fossil fuels has grown by a factor of 30, and industrial production by a factor of 50, four-fifths of this since 1950. The gains in human welfare have been breathtaking, and the potential for future gains is ever more awesome.

The processes that produced these gains have also produced trends that raise serious questions about their sustainability. Even so, the most critical imperative of the next few decades is further rapid growth. We estimated that a further five- to ten-fold increase in economic activity would be required over the next 50 years in order to meet the needs and aspirations of a world population projected to double in that period from 5 billion to 10 billion. And to begin to reduce mass poverty. If we don't reduce mass poverty, there really is no way to stop the accelerating decline in the planet's basic stocks of ecological capital, its forests, soils, species, fisheries, waters and atmosphere.

Mass poverty will not be reduced without significant economic growth. If we are to achieve sustainable development during the first part of the next century, we must aim at two things in the Commission's view: first, a minimum of 3 percent per capita national income growth and second, vigorous policies to achieve greater equity within developing countries. . . .

A five- to ten-fold increase in economic activity sounds enormous but, because of the magic of compound interest, it represents annual growth rates of only 3.2 and 4.7 percent. What government of any country, developed or developing, doesn't aspire at least to that! In fact, in developing countries, growth at these rates is hardly enough to keep up with projected population growth, let alone reduce current levels of poverty.

If we are already crossing a number of critical thresholds, is there any way to multiply economic activity a further 5 to 10 times, without it undermining itself and compromising the future completely? That is the sustainability question. . . .

It concerns the Industrialized World perhaps more than the Third, but it is especially poignant in Third World countries. They face debilitating domestic trends, not just economic, but also ecological and political, and a lot of evidence suggests that in many cases there is a clear connection between them. Population growth is outstripping economic growth in many of them, and two-thirds have suffered a fall in per capita income, in some as great as 25 percent. The . . . debt problem, especially in Africa and Latin America, and deteriorating terms of trade, including unstable commodity prices, growing protectionism in developed market economies, and stagnating flows of aid all combine to force attention on short term crisis, rather than longer term development.

Most Third World countries have resource-based economies. Their stocks of environmental resources—their soils, forests, fisheries, species, waters and parks—form their basic economic capital. Given population and other trends, their long-term economic development depends on maintaining, if not increasing, these stocks and enhancing their ability to support agriculture, forestry, fishing, mining, and tourism for local use and export.

During the past several decades, however, these basic capital accounts have been declining at an accelerating rate. . . . Every 10 seconds the world's population grows by 25 people; every 14 seconds, the planet's stock of arable land falls by one hectare. Many developing countries are today in deeper ecological debt than financial debt. The consequences include not only increased hunger and death, but also social instability and conflict, as environmental degradation and resource depletion and social conflict drives refugees in their millions across national borders.

## SUSTAINABLE DEVELOPMENT

. . . And after looking at the evidence, [the Bruntland Commission] concluded that growth on the scale needed cannot be sustained if it rests on a continuing draw-down of the Planet's basic ecological capital.

We did not get bogged down in prophecies of doom . . . We preferred instead to emphasize the possibility, as we saw it, of a "new era of growth," not the type of growth that dominates today, but sustainable growth, growth based on forms and processes of development that do not undermine the integrity of the environment on which they depend.

Sustainable development is the over-riding political concept of "Our Common Future." . . . We define sustainable development in ethical, social and economic terms. Most generally, we defined it as new paths of economic and social progress which "meet the needs of the present without compromising the ability of future generations to meet their own needs." . . . We also put forward a number of criteria, or conditions that have to be met in order for development to be sustainable. We referred to them as "strategic imperatives for sustainable development."

### Strategic Imperatives for Sustainable Development

1 Reviving growth to meet human needs and aspirations.

2 Ensuring a more equitable distribution of the proceeds of growth, within and between nations.

3 Ensuring a sustainable level of population.

4 Conserving and enhancing the resource base.

5 Reducing the energy and resource content of growth.

6 Re-orienting technology and managing risk.

7 Merging environment and economics in decision-making.

In addition, . . . the Commission stresses throughout that sustainable development depends on a political system that ensures effective citizen participation in decision-making, in other words, human rights and democracy; an economic system that is able to generate surpluses on a sustainable basis; and an administrative system that is flexible, with a built-in capacity for self-correction. . . .

## GROWTH AND EQUITY

I have already mentioned the first two imperatives for sustainability: (1) rapid growth to meet human needs and aspirations, and reduce poverty and (2) strong policy measures to achieve a more equitable distribution of the proceeds of growth, within and between nations. On both conditions, we are at the moment moving in the wrong direction.

. . . The most skewed distribution of income and power is to be found in the poorest nations, but the distribution of income between the rich nations and the poor nations is just as grotesque. And it is getting worse. The traditional net flow of capital from the industrial to developing countries was reversed in 1982. Over $43 billion annually is now transferred in the other direction. And that is only what the World Bank counts. In addition, today's trading patterns contain a massive transfer of the environmental costs of global GNP to the poorer resource-based economies of the Third World. A study conducted for the Commission estimated these costs at about $14 billion a year—more than one-third of the total amount of development assistance flowing annually in the other direction. And that $14 billion is a low estimate because it only includes the costs related to environmental pollution, not those related to resource depletion.

## ENSURING A SUSTAINABLE LEVEL OF POPULATION

The third imperative is strong measures to slow the rate of population growth and bring and hold them at sustainable levels. This is fundamental. . . .

First, the issue is not simply one of numbers. A child born in a rich industrialized country, where levels of energy and material use are high, places a much greater burden on the planet than one born in a poor country. The industrialized world found that development is the best means of population control. It has even proved capable of negative rates of population growth, when accompanied by urbanization, rising levels of income, improved education, and the empowerment of women.

Second, similar processes are at work in some developing countries. In addition, many are beginning to take strong direct measures to bolster social, cultural and economic motivations for couples to have small families and, through family planning programs, to provide all those who want them with the education, technological means and services required to control family size. But time is short and these efforts should be encouraged. They require much greater financial and research support, and especially political support, than they have been getting from industrialized countries. Here again, we seem to be moving in the other direction. . . .

## CONSERVING AND ENHANCING THE RESOURCE BASE

Another essential condition for sustainable development is that a community's or a nation's basic stock of natural capital should not decrease over time. A constant or increasing stock of natural capital is needed not only to meet the needs of present generations, but also to ensure a minimum degree of fairness and equity with future generations.

This condition can be applied to renewable resources, but what does it mean for non-renewable resources? By definition, use must reduce the capital available. With some major exceptions such as oil and gas, it seems unlikely that the use of most non-renewable resources will be limited by supply. Instead, their use will be limited by their impact on renewable resources. The extraction, use and disposal of non-renewable resources should take into account their impact on other resources, such as the atmosphere, and should foreclose as few options as possible. The rates of depletion of non-renewable resources should also take into account the criticality of the resource, the availability of technologies for minimizing depletion, and the likelihood of substitutes being available.

Can the world's expanding economies begin to live off the interest of the Earth's stock of renewable resources, without encroaching on its capital? At the moment, we are moving backwards at an accelerating pace, but the question is open. If the annual draw on the Earth's basic economic capital is to be brought within the capacity of natural systems to generate it, the industrialized world will need to increase by several orders of magnitude its support for strategies aimed at abating pollution, at protecting and preserving essential resource capital, and at restoring and rehabilitating those assets that [are] already depleted and exhausted. . . .

Much more important, however, we need to begin to reform the public policies that sometimes unintentionally, but actively, encourage *de*forestation, *de*sertification, *de*struction of habitat and species, *de*cline of air and water quality. These policies, and the often enormous budgets they command, are much more powerful than any conceivable measures to protect environments or to restore and rehabilitate those already damaged. Unless and until these policies are reformed, nations will not be able to keep up, let alone catch up, with the increasing rates of depletion of their natural capital. . . .

## REDUCING THE ENERGY AND RESOURCE CONTENT OF GROWTH

A rapid reduction in the energy and resource content of growth is another essential condition of sustainable development—and number 5 on our list. During the past couple decades, the link between GNP and energy growth has been broken, as has the link between GNP growth and growth in water, steel, aluminum, cement, some chemicals and many other materials. The link between growth and environmental emissions and resource depletion has consequently also been broken.

Nowhere has this been more marked than in energy. Following the first oil shock, between 1973 and 1983, OECD nations improved their energy productivity on average by 1.3 percent annually. Prior to the last oil shock, that is the sharp fall in prices, some countries, including Japan and Sweden, had reached productivity increases of more than 2.0 percent per annum.

Three points. First, meeting this condition is essential if the industrialized world is to play the leading role it must play in slowing the rate of global warming and addressing other threats to Third World development and global security. The Commission concluded that steady annual increases in energy productivity would be necessary in order to slow global warming, reduce acidification and urban air pollution. Again, we are moving in the other direction, with subsidy, tax and pricing policies that increase the use of fossil fuels and $CO_2$ and other emissions.

Second, improved macro-economic efficiency is another way to express this condition for sustainable development. Increasing energy and resource efficiency at the level of industrial plants or communities adds up to increasing the efficiency of the national economy. When industry, agriculture and local communities achieve higher levels of resource and environmental productivity, the national economy in which they operate becomes more competitive. The difference in energy intensity alone between the U.S. and Japanese economies, for example, creates a cost advantage of the order of 5 percent for the typical Japanese export. . . .

Third, countries that have already achieved considerable progress in this direction are at the top of the international list of economic performers. Between 1973 and 1984, the energy and raw material content of a unit of Japanese production dropped by 40 percent. Sweden, West Germany and some other countries did as well or better.

The non-market economies of Eastern Europe did not share in this efficiency revolution. Neither did many developing countries, including most of the OPEC nations. If governments of developing countries don't give a much higher priority to measures to encourage more efficient forms of energy and industrial development, it is hard to see how they will reverse the increasing pollution and depletion of the resource base they now confront. Moreover, their economies will be unable to compete in the international marketplace if they continue to attract industries that use high levels of energy and resources per unit of output, and that are inefficient and polluting. . . .

In most countries, existing subsidy and regulatory structures promote the very opposite of what is needed for a sustainable energy future. They ignore external costs, favor waste and inefficiency and underwrite traditional sources of power—coal, oil and nuclear—rather than renewables. In doing so, they impose enormous burdens on already tight budgets, and on often-scarce reserves of foreign currency. . . .

## MERGING ENVIRONMENT AND ECONOMICS IN DECISION-MAKING

The last but most important condition for sustainable development is merging environment and economics in decision-making. Our economic and ecological systems have become totally interlocked in the real world, but they remain almost totally divorced in our institutions and our policies.

During the '60s and '70s, governments in over 100 countries, developed and developing, established special environmental protection and/or resource management agencies. They invariably failed, however, to make their powerful central economic and sectoral agencies in any way responsible for the implications of their policies and expenditures on the environment. Yet, these are the agencies with the policy power and the budgets to determine the form and content of growth and, consequently, the options for the future.

The resulting balance of forces has been grotesquely unequal. Environmental agencies were added on to bureaucracies with limited mandates, limited budgets and little or no political clout. They must now be given more capacity and more power to cope with the effects of unsustainable development policies. The most urgent task, however, is to make our central economic, trade, and sectoral agencies directly responsible and accountable for ensuring that their policies—and the budgets they command—encourage development that is sustainable. Only in this way will the ecological dimensions of policy be considered at the same time as the economic, trade, energy, agricultural, and other dimensions—on the same agendas and in the same national and international institutions. . . .

## FINANCING SUSTAINABLE DEVELOPMENT

The Commission recommended substantial increases in multilateral and bilateral assistance for institutional development and for strengthening programs to enhance the resource base for development. Marshalling sufficient investment for these purposes will require further initiatives, and it suggests serious consideration of a special international conservation banking program or facility linked to the World Bank. Such a facility could provide loans and facilitate joint financing arrangements for the protection and sustainable development of critical habitats and ecosystems, including those of international significance. . . .

The Commission also considered several possible international sources of revenue for financing action in support of sustainable development. These included revenues from the use of the international commons and taxes on trade in certain commodities. Although they may seem politically unrealistic at present, global trends are such that the realities of politics will change. . . .

Military expenditures . . . represent an enormous pool of capital, human skills and resources, and much of it could be usefully shifted to more productive purposes. Nations spend nearly $1 trillion a year on military security, more than $2.7 billion a day. Developing countries have increased their arms budgets fivefold in 20 years, and some are spending more on their military than on education, health, welfare and the environment combined.

Some see hope for such a shift in the growing awareness of some major political leaders that environmental destruction on the present scale presents as great a threat to the security of many countries and of the planet as do hostile armies. The Commission argued that the world community needs a new and broader concept of security, one that includes environmental as well as economic and political security. With a broader approach to security and security assessment, nations would begin to find many instances in which their security could be enhanced more effectively through expenditures to protect, preserve and restore basic environmental capital assets than through expenditures for arms.

The Commission argued that environment and sustainable development must be treated as a foreign policy issue of paramount importance. There is potential for real tension over these issues, especially if the failure of certain countries to address them were seen as a real threat to the security of neighbouring and other countries. On the other hand, if properly approached, they could force a new spirit of international cooperation—and fresh thinking about multilateral approaches to other issues.

# 37

# THE TRAGEDY OF THE COMMONS IN GLOBAL PERSPECTIVE

Marvin S. Soroos

The "tragedy of the commons" is a key concept in ecological analysis. Marvin S. Soroos describes the metaphor, relates it to many of the specific issues on the global agenda of environmental issues, and suggests strategies for averting environmental tragedies. Noteworthy is his observation that "remarkable progress has been made in establishing the international infrastructure needed to preserve the natural environment," which manifests itself in a variety of voluntary, regulatory, restrictive, and community ownership approaches to the global commons. Soroos is professor of political science at North Carolina State University and is author of *Beyond Sovereignty: The Challenge of Global Policy* (1986).

## THE ENVIRONMENT ON THE GLOBAL AGENDA

In recent years, the deteriorating condition of the natural environment has risen dramatically in prominence on the agendas of both national governments and international institutions such as the United Nations and the European Community. The environment is a relatively new issue, having begun to receive substantial attention from policy makers and publics only a little more than two decades ago. While specific ecological problems received attention considerably earlier, they were not viewed as part of a much larger crisis in the relationship between a rapidly growing and industrializing world population and the natural order upon which it depends for its survival.

This essay was written especially for this book. Used by permission of Marvin S. Soroos.

Two events took place in 1972 which were especially important in the emergence of the environment as a global issue. One was the publication of the Club of Rome's influential and controversial report entitled *The Limits to Growth* (Meadows et al., 1972). It warned of an uncontrollable collapse of modern civilization within a century if bold steps were not taken to control exponential growth trends in population and industrial production that would otherwise overshoot the availability of food, deplete the planet's one-time endowment of nonrenewable reserves of fossil fuels and minerals, and seriously degrade the environment with pollutants. The other event was the convening of the United Nations Conference on the Human Environment in Stockholm, which focused world attention on a wide range of interrelated environmental problems and led to the creation of the United Nations Environment Programme (UNEP), which has done much to stimulate national and international efforts to preserve the natural environment.

Numerous problems appear on the global environmental agenda, each of which has serious consequences in its own right. On the land areas, tropical forests are being burned or logged at an alarming rate with little concern for the resulting extinction of untold numbers of species of plants and animals, many of which remain to be recorded. Deserts are expanding in many parts of Africa and Asia, in large part due to human activities—in particular the stripping of wood areas for firewood, the overgrazing of livestock, and improper irrigation. Overuse and misuse of land has reduced its fertility and led to substantial erosion of topsoil; aquifers are rapidly drawn down to irrigate expanding agricultural operations. A legacy of toxic waste dumps threatens the health of millions of people.

The marine environment has been badly contaminated by pollutants, especially in largely self-contained areas such as the Mediterranean Sea, the Baltic Sea, the Caribbean Sea, the Red Sea, and the Persian Gulf. The most spectacular sources of pollutants into the oceans have been accidents involving supertankers, the best known being the groundings of the *Torrey Canyon* in 1967, the *Amoco Cadiz* in 1978, and the *Exxon Valdez* in 1989. Larger quantities of pollutants enter oceans and seas from land-based sources, such as river systems laden with sewage, industrial effluents, and runoff from agricultural areas containing fertilizers and pesticides. The oceans have also been a repository for toxic substances ranging from chemical weapons and radioactive wastes to sludge from sewage treatment plants.

Atmospheric pollutants became the leading environmental concern during the 1980s. In the heavily industrialized regions of Europe and North America, the severe consequences of the transboundary flow of pollutants, in particular sulfur and nitrogen oxides responsible for acid precipitation, became all too apparent as aquatic life disappeared in numerous freshwater lakes and a phenomenon known as "forest death syndrome"—widely referred to by the German term *walsterben*—spread rapidly and intensified in forested areas. The 1986 disaster at the Chernobyl nuclear power plant in the Soviet Union exposed hundreds of millions of Europeans to potentially health-damaging levels of radioactive iodine 131 and cesium 137.

Even more alarming are the warnings of the scientific community about the depletion of the stratospheric ozone layer and the apparent trend toward a general warming of the atmosphere. These two problems are central to what has become known in recent years as the "global change" problematique, which refers to a number of complex and interrelated alterations of the natural environment resulting from the growing scale of human activities.

Concern over ozone depletion has been heightened in recent years by the discovery of a large "ozone hole" over Antarctica during the spring season and a general thinning elsewhere. Scientists have linked the destruction of ozone to chemical compounds known as CFCs, which are widely used in aerosol sprays, refrigerants, foam packaging and insulation, and cleaning solutions, as well as halons used primarily in fire extinguishers. A reduction of the ozone layer, which shields the earth from the sun's intense ultraviolet radiation, would have significant consequences for human health, in particular the incidence of the deadly melanoma form of skin cancer. More importantly, increased exposure to ultraviolet radiation would likely disrupt aquatic and terrestrial ecosystems.

Forecasts of a general warming of the atmosphere take into account the increased concentrations of "greenhouse gases" such as carbon dioxide, methane, and CFCs. A $1.5°$ to $4.5°C$ increase in average temperatures is a distinct possibility by the mid-21st century if current trends continue in the buildup of greenhouse gases. Many scientific questions remain to be answered on the consequences of a warming of this magnitude. Coastal cities and low lying agricultural areas may be inundated as ocean levels rise by an anticipated .5 to 1.5 meters, farming elsewhere may be disrupted by changing temperatures and rainfall patterns, and numerous ecosystems such as forests may be unable to adapt to rapidly changing climatic conditions.

The international community has been very active over the past two decades in its efforts to address many of these environmental problems. The Stockholm conference of 1972 was the first of a series of major world conferences sponsored by the United Nations, sometimes referred to as "global town meetings," that keyed on specific global problems, several of which are environmentally related. Among these were world conferences on population (1974 and 1984), food (1974), human settlements (1976), water (1977), desertification (1977), new and renewable sources of energy (1981), and outer space (1982). The Third United Nations Law of the Sea Conference (UNCLOS III), which was convened twelve times between 1973 and 1982, took up several environmental problems, most notably the depletion of marine fisheries and pollution of the oceans. The World Meteorological Organization (WMO) co-sponsored with the Canadian government a conference on "The Changing Atmosphere" in Toronto in 1988 in addition to World Climate Conferences in 1979 and 1989. A major

United Nations Conference on Environment and Development is planned for Brazil in 1992 on the twentieth anniversary of the landmark Stockholm conference.

A more significant development, however, has been the establishment of a network of international institutions that address environmental issues. The United Nations Environment Programme (UNEP), which is headquartered in Nairobi, Kenya, plays a central role in stimulating and coordinating action on environmental problems both by other international agencies and by nations. The organization has taken a leading role in identifying and investigating ecological problems and in monitoring the state of many aspects of the environment through its Global Environmental Monitoring System (GEMS). Several specialized agencies affiliated with the United Nations have a longer history of concern with environmentally related problems, including the International Maritime Organization (IMO) on pollution from oceangoing vessels, the WMO on the effects of atmospheric pollutants on the weather, the World Health Organization (WHO) on the impact of pollutants on human health, the International Atomic Energy Agency (IAEA) on the dangers of radioactive substances, the Food and Agricultural Organization (FAO) on the condition of ocean fisheries and the effect of environmental degradation on food production, and the International Labor Organization (ILO) on environmental hazards in the workplace. Environmental problems have also had a prominent place on the agendas of numerous regional organizations, most notably those of the European Community.

Nongovernmental organizations (NGOs) have been active participants in efforts to address global environmental problems at both national and international levels. The Stockholm conference drew participation from 237 NGOs, and more than 6000 are registered with the Environmental Liaison Center in Nairobi. The International Union for the Conservation of Nature and Natural Resources (IUCN) and the World Wildlife Fund (WWF) have been collaborating with UNEP on the World Conservation Strategy that was launched in 1980. The International Council of Scientific Unions (ICSU) has been called upon for much of the scientific information that has guided the formulation of international policies and regulations on environmental matters. ICSU recently launched the International Geosphere-Biosphere Program, an international scientific project that will mobilize the world's scientists to conduct research on the relationships between atmospheric, marine, and terrestrial ecosystems and the impact of human activities on them. Public interest groups such as Greenpeace, Friends of the Earth, European Environmental Bureau, and the Sierra Club International publicize environmental problems and prod national governments and international bodies to take action on them.

Despite the relative newness of the environment as a global policy problem, remarkable progress has been made in establishing the international institutional infrastructure needed to preserve the natural environment. There is certainly reason to wonder, however, whether 160 sovereign states will achieve the level of international cooperation that will be needed to effectively address problems of the magnitude and complexity of climate change.

## GLOBAL TRAGEDIES OF THE COMMONS

Garrett Hardin's (1968) well-known allegory of the "tragedy of the commons" is a useful model for analyzing the human sources of many environmental problems and the strategies by which they might be addressed. The allegory has applicability to all levels of political organization ranging from the smallest village to the global community of states. Let us first review Hardin's story and then consider how it applies to several of the global environmental problems mentioned in the previous section. Potential strategies for averting a "tragedy" are taken up in the next section.

We are asked to imagine an old English village that has a community pasture on which the resident herdsmen are freely permitted to graze their individually owned cattle for their own profit. Such an arrangement, known as a "commons," works well as long as the number of cattle is small relative to the size of the pasture. But once the combined herd of the villagers reaches and exceeds the "carrying capacity" of the pasture, the grasses are gradually depleted and the undernourished cattle produce less milk for their owners. If more and more cattle are added to an already overcrowded pasture, the result is its total destruction as a resource and the villagers can no longer derive a profit from grazing cattle on it. Such an unfortunate eventuality is what Hardin refers to as the "tragedy."

Hardin contends that such a tragedy is virtually inevitable when there are no legal limits on the number of cattle the villagers may graze on the pasture. Each villager can be expected to calculate that the profits derived from adding a cow to the pasture will accrue to himself exclusively. Alternatively, whatever costs arise due to what this cow contributes to an overgrazing of the pasture will be divided among all the herdsmen of the village. Therefore, the individual villager figures that he has more to gain personally from adding a cow to the pasture than to lose from the resulting damage from overgrazing. Moreover, the logic that leads the villager to add a single cow to an already overused pasture also holds for even further additions by him. And what is rational behavior for one villager is equally rational for others. Thus, if the villagers pursue their individual self-interest, the pasture will be destroyed by the ever-increasing herd.

Why do the village herdsmen, upon seeing the earlier signs of the unfolding tragedy, fail to exercise restraint in adding cattle, realizing that they will all pay a heavy price if the pasture becomes badly overgrazed? The answer lies in the possibility that at least one among them will not act responsibly, but rather will continue to add cattle to the pasture. This so-called "free rider" not only takes advantage of the restraint of the other villagers for his own financial benefit but also may bring about the very tragedy they were attempting to avert. Thus, unless the villagers are confident that all will limit their herds, they become resigned to the inevitability of a tragedy and continue adding cattle to the over-crowded pasture in order to maximize their personal share of what the pasture has to offer before it is rendered useless.

Global environmental problems are obviously much more complex than the story of destruction of the common pasture in the English village. Nevertheless, distinct parallels exist between the causes of some global problems and the reasons for the tragedy in Hardin's parable. The similarity is especially notable in the case of the living resources of the ocean. Coastal populations have harvested fish in the oceans for millennia, but until recently the catch was well below the carrying capacity of the fisheries. The situation has changed dramatically in recent decades, both because of a rapidly growing world population that is looking more to the oceans for a source of protein and because technological advancements have made it possible to sharply increase the catch. Schools of fish can now be located more efficiently using helicopters, radar, and sonar, while strong synthetic fibers and mechanical hauling devices allow for the use of larger nets that will hold much greater quantities of fish. Drift nets up to 30 miles in length have been widely used with a devastating impact on marine life. Perhaps the biggest change in the modern fishing industry has been the use of gigantic stern ramped trawlers and factory ships with the capacity for on-board processing of the catch, which are often accompanied by numerous specialized support vessels. Such a "fishing Armada" can stay away from its home port for many months while intensively harvesting fisheries in distant reaches of the oceans.

Traditionally, international law has treated the oceans as a commons, the only exception being a 3-mile zone of territorial waters that was conventionally placed under the jurisdiction of coastal states. Fishermen from all lands could help themselves to the ocean's bounty for their private gain because fish became their property upon being caught. Under these rules the total world catch has quintupled since 1950. The 1988 catch of 97.4 million metric tons of fish is close to the Food and Agriculture Association's estimate of a sustainable yield from the oceans of 100 million metric tons annually (World Resources Institute, 1990, p. 180). A "tragedy" has already occurred for species such as cod, halibut, herring, anchovy, swordfish, haddock, and the California sardine as evidenced by a dramatic drop in catches because not enough fish were left to regenerate the stock for the future.

Depletion of these fisheries came about for essentially the same reasons that the herdsmen added cattle to an already overgrazed pasture in Hardin's English village. Operators of fishing fleets receive all of the profits from the sale of their catch while dividing the costs associated with overfishing with all others harvesting the same fishery. Furthermore, fugitives that they are, fish passed up by one fleet in the interests of conservation are likely to turn up in the nets of others, who as free riders continue to deplete the fishery.

Pollution of the oceans and atmosphere also fits the pattern of Hardin's "tragedy of the commons." But rather than taking something out of an area that is beyond the jurisdiction of nations, pollution involves its use for the disposal of unwanted substances. Few problems arose as long as the amount of pollution generated by human activities was small relative to the vastness of the mediums into which they were introduced. But as with other resources, there are limits to the amount of pollutants that can be absorbed and dispersed by the oceans and atmosphere before serious problems begin to emerge, as is now apparent in the case of the ozone-depleting and greenhouse pollutants. The task of determining harmful levels of pollution is complicated by the delay between the time substances are introduced into the environment and the time at which the consequences become apparent.

As sinks for pollutants, the oceans and the atmosphere have also traditionally been treated as international commons. All countries have been free to make use of them for getting rid of wastes whose disposal would otherwise be expensive or inconvenient. Introducing pollution into these mediums can have considerable offsetting costs, but from the perspective of the polluters, these costs are shared very widely while the benefits of having a cheap way of discarding wastes accrue to them exclusively. Thus, strong financial incentives are present for continuing the polluting activity. Moreover, any restraint that is exercised out of concern for the quality of the environment is likely to be futile and self-defeating if other polluters, including one's competitors, do not exercise similar responsibility.

Population can also be looked upon as a "tragedy of the commons" type of problem, as Hardin does in his original essay and his later theory of "lifeboat ethics" (Hardin, 1974). In this formulation, food and other resources correspond to the pasture of the English village, births to the herdsmen. Parents, it could be argued, derive significant private benefits from children, such as companionship and affection, a source of labor, and security in old age. The environmental costs associated with what their children contribute to the overpopulating of their country or the world as a whole are shared with the rest of the population. Couples may also calculate that any restraint they exercise in limiting the size of their families will have little or no beneficial impact, because others who are less ecologically responsible will continue to have large numbers of offspring. The parallel is strained by the fact that most people do not have free access to the food and resources they need for their children but must pay for them. Hardin's suggestion is that free access to necessities, as through welfare payments or international food assistance, in effect creates a commons and the subsequent behavior that brings about its destruction.

## AVERTING ENVIRONMENTAL TRAGEDIES

Several strategies hold some promise for avoiding the "tragedy" that Hardin forecasts will occur if all villagers have open access to the community pasture. One is to encourage *voluntary restraint,* possibly through education about the ecological consequences of irresponsible actions and by bringing social pressures to bear on members of the community who have not moderated their actions. Hardin has little faith in voluntary restraints because of the prospect that free riders will take advantage of the situation. A second option is to adopt *regulations* that limit the number of cattle each villager can graze on the pasture. Such rules, which can take the form of limits, prohibitions, and standards, should be restrictive enough to keep the total use of a resource from exceeding its carrying capacity. For regulations to be effective, however, there must be sufficiently strong inducements for compliance, such as stiff penalties for violators.

The last two possibilities for averting a tragedy would discard the commons arrangement. The pasture could be *partitioned* into fenced-in plots, each of which would be assigned to an individual villager. Under this setup, each herdsman would not only receive all the profits from grazing cattle on his section, but would also absorb all the costs if he allowed it to become overgrazed. Thus, a built-in incentive exists for him to conserve his plot, or what Hardin refers to as "intrinsic responsibility." *Community ownership* of the herd is the final alternative. Rather than allowing privately owned cattle to graze the pasture, as under the other arrangements, access would be limited to a publicly owned herd, with the profits being distributed among the villagers. Under such an arrangement, the community as a whole would not only receive all the profits, but also absorb all the costs of overgrazing. Thus, the managers of the community herd would have little incentive for allowing the pasture to become overgrazed.

Examples of all four of these strategies can be observed in the efforts of the international community to address environmental problems. Because nations are reluctant to sacrifice any part of their sovereignty to a higher authority, it is sometimes impossible to do more than encourage them to act responsibly to minimize damage to the environment beyond their borders. In this regard, one of the most commonly cited articles of the Stockholm Declaration of 1972 sets forth the principle that "States have . . . the responsibility to ensure that activities within their jurisdiction or control do not cause damage to the environment of other States or of areas beyond the limits of national jurisdiction."

Appeals to states to act voluntarily in an ecologically responsible manner have generally not been auspicious successes. However, there has been an encouraging tendency in recent years for a number of European countries to act unilaterally in setting target years for ambitious reductions of emissions of air pollutants, such as the sulphur and nitrogen oxides responsible for acid precipitation and the CFCs that are causing ozone depletion. At least nine countries pledge to reduce $SO_2$ by half by 1995, four of which are aiming at a two-thirds reduction. Twelve states are committed to cutting nitrogen oxide emissions by 30 percent by 1998 (French 1990, pp. 115–16). These national goals, which go significantly beyond internationally agreed upon limits, are ostensibly a response to political pressures from environmentally concerned publics and an effort to set an example that other states will hopefully follow.

More is accomplished to ameliorate environmental problems when specific obligations are written into regulations that are negotiated and adopted in international institutions. Approximately twenty international fishery commissions, the equivalents of the village government in Hardin's story, have been created by fishing nations to conserve the fisheries that they harvest in common. Some of these commissions established rules that limit the annual catch below what is known as the "maximum sustainable yield" (MSY) of the fishery. One strategy is to limit fishing to a prescribed season, which is abruptly closed when the combined efforts of the fishing operators approach the MSY. Other commissions assigned a share of the MSY to countries based on their historical share of the catch from a fishery.

International restrictions have also been adopted to reduce pollution of the marine environment. The landmark Convention for the Prevention of Pollution by Oil was adopted in 1954 and amended several times in the International Maritime Organization (IMO). Among the provisions of the treaty is a prohibition on discharges of crude and heavy fuel oils in the seas within 50 miles of coastlines. In 1973, the IMO adopted another convention, known as MARPOL '73, that covered a broader range of pollutants and extended the prohibition to the discharge of oily substances to areas deemed especially vulnerable to damage from pollution. The disposal of toxic substances in the seas is the subject of other international treaties, the most important one being the London Convention of 1972. It establishes a "black list" of highly toxic chemicals such as mercury, DDT, PCBs, persistent plastics, high level radioactive wastes, and agents of chemical or biological warfare that may not be disposed of in the oceans, and a "gray list" of less harmful wastes that may be dumped under controlled conditions.

Compared to the oceans, the atmosphere is still a relatively underdeveloped subject of international law. The Economic Commission for Europe (ECE), which includes eastern and western European countries in addition to the United States and Canada, adopted a protocol in 1985 that commits ratifiers to a 30 percent reduction in $SO_2$ emissions by 1993 (based on 1980 levels) and an additional protocol in 1988 that freezes nitrous oxide emissions at 1987 levels by 1994. Similarly, the 1987 Montreal protocol mandated a 30 percent reduction in the production of CFCs by 1993 and a 50 percent cutback by 1998. Alarming reports on the Antarctic ozone hole prompted 93 countries to agree in London in June 1990 to a complete phaseout of ozone destroying chemicals by 2000, with the exception of less developed countries, who will have a ten-year grace period.

For international regulations to be effective, mechanisms may be needed both for detecting violations and for sanctioning the violators. Few international agencies are well equipped to perform these tasks. Certain international fishery commissions have had programs for monitoring compliance with their rules through on-board inspections of fishing vessels. Likewise, the ECE sponsors a network of stations that monitors the transboundary flow of air pollutants between its members. Sanctions are generally left to other states that have an interest in seeing to it that international rules are being followed. For example, a United States law provides that countries which violate international agreements on the protection of marine mammals will lose 50 percent of the quota of fish they would otherwise be permitted to harvest in the 200-mile coastal fishery zone of the United States.

The partitioning of resources used by numbers of states is a feasible strategy for avoiding some but not all environmental problems. Pollutants introduced into the atmosphere cannot be confined within the boundaries of states because air circulates with prevailing wind currents. Likewise, ocean currents widely disperse many of the pollutants introduced into the marine environment.

Ocean fisheries, most of which are located near coastlines, are more susceptible to partitioning. The Convention on the Law of the Sea, which was adopted in 1982, but still lacks the 60 ratifications needed to come into effect, would grant coastal states jurisdiction over the resources of the oceans and seabed out to a distance of 200 nautical miles off shorelines, in what is called an "exclusive economic zone" (EEZ). Coastal states are empowered to determine the maximum catch within their EEZs and to decide who will be allowed to harvest fish up to this limit. They may reserve the fisheries for their own nationals or allow foreign operators to take part of the catch, possibly for a negotiated fee.

Such an arrangement can be an effective way of conserving fisheries consisting of localized or sedentary species provided the coastal state is diligent in managing them and has the means of enforcing the limits that it has set. Highly migratory species, such as the skipjack tuna and some species of whales, which move through the EEZs of two or more countries and the high seas as well, pose a more complicated problem because cooperation among several states is needed to prevent overharvesting. A similar problem occurs with andromous species, most notably salmon, which live most of their life spans in the high seas, where they can be legally harvested by any country, but migrate to freshwater streams to spawn. Coastal states are reluctant to invest heavily to conserve spawning habitats if the stock is likely to be overfished by other countries on the high seas. Here again, cooperative arrangements among several states are necessary if the fishery is to be conserved.

Community ownership of the means of using a resource is rare at the international level. The primary stumbling block to an international consensus on the Law of the Sea Convention is the provision for a commercial arm of an International Seabed Authority, which would be known as the Enterprise. In competition with private seabed-mining firms, this international public corporation would mine the mineral-rich nodules lying on the floor of the deep seas. The private firms would be required to assist the Enterprise both by sharing the fruits of their prospecting efforts and by making mining technologies available at reasonable commercial rates. The objective behind the creation of the Enterprise would not, however, be to conserve the nodules, which are in bounteous supply. Rather it is designed to ensure that less technologically advanced countries will have an opportunity to participate in the development of a resource declared to be the "common heritage of mankind" by the General Assembly in 1970.

Of the four principal types of strategies that can be adopted to avert a tragedy, regulations appear to have the broadest applicability and the greatest potential for success. Appeals for voluntary restraint too often go unheeded and some of the most critical natural resources cannot physically be divided into self-contained sections. Moreover, a community in which sovereign states are the predominant actors is simply not ready for international public enterprises to play a major role in exploitation of natural resources. The governments of most nations, however, recognize the need for rules to preserve those aspects of the global environment that are beyond the jurisdiction of any state. This is not to say, however, that they don't often balk at agreeing to specific regulations and complying with them.

## RECONCILING ALTERNATIVE VALUES

Each of the four strategies for averting an environmental "tragedy" that were outlined in the previous section has certain advantages and disadvantages. Which is the most appropriate in a specific context depends in part on the relative priority that is given to values such as conservation, production, equity, and freedom.

*Conservation* implies that the resource is neither overused nor misused, so that its future value is not substantially diminished. In the analogy of the English village, conservation means that the pasture is not overgrazed to the point that there is a noticeable decline in the grass cover, which reduces the number of cattle that can be sustained. In the case of ocean fisheries, conservation implies that enough of the stock of the fish remains after the harvest to allow for a regeneration of the fishery up to its optimal levels. In regard to pollution, conservation can be interpreted to mean not allowing pollutants to reach a level at which serious harm to the environment begins to take place. For example, acid-forming precipitants would not be allowed to reach the concentration at which forests and freshwater aquatic life show signs of dying.

*Maximizing production* is often a strong competing priority. The herdsmen in the village depended upon their cattle for a livelihood and, therefore, could not accept sharp cutbacks on their herds. Their interests would be best served by an arrangement that allows them to graze as many cattle as possible without bringing about an environmentally destructive overshoot. International fishery commissions have sought to calculate a maximum sustainable yield on the basis of the best available scientific evidence on the number of fish that can be caught annually without jeopardizing their regeneration. This figure is then used to set limits on the annual catch. Requiring costly equipment for preventing pollution can have a substantial effect on industrial production, especially if a total cleanup is the objective. It should be noted that the dictates of short-term production and profit may be at odds with the same values over the longer run. Short-term gain may be achieved by ravaging the resource until it is totally destroyed, while long-term profitability depends upon careful stewardship of the resource to preserve its future value.

*Equity* implies fairness in the strategy that is adopted. What is fair is subject to divergent interpretations. For example, in the village setting, does the principle of equity dictate that all the herdsmen be allowed to graze the same number of cattle on the pasture regardless of size of family or the number of cattle they owned before limits were imposed? Likewise, if the pasture is partitioned, would it be necessary for all to have equally sized plots? If the pasture is to be used by a community-owned herd, should all households receive an equal share of the profits? Similar issues of equity have complicated the task faced by fishery commissions in dividing up the total allowable catch among member countries. To what extent should the national shares be based on factors such as geographical proximity, population size, investment in fishing fleets, and distribution of the catch historically? The fairness of the provisions for EEZs under the new ocean law has been criticized on grounds that most of the productive fisheries will come under the control of a handful of states.

In the case of measures to control pollution, the fairness question arises over whether the percentage reductions in emissions should be required of all countries. Less developed countries, which historically are responsible for a small share of the pollutants causing problems such as ozone depletion and global warming, may contend that it is their "turn to pollute" to achieve their aspirations for economic development and a higher standard of living for their populations.

From one perspective, equity is a matter of all being equally free to exploit a resource even though some, by virtue of their capital and advanced technologies, may be better able to take advantage of available opportunities. From another perspective, equity is an outcome that is at least equally favorable to the poorer, less advantaged members of the community. At UNCLOS III a sharp dispute arose over rules for developing the seabed between a small group of advanced states that possessed technologies for mining the mineral-rich nodules and the large majority of countries that would be left out of the potential mineral bonanza unless they could participate in an international enterprise.

*Freedom* suggests flexibility in the types of activity that are permitted. Most actors—be they states, corporations, or individuals—value freedom and are reluctant to submit to limitations on their behavior. Freedom for states is embodied in the principle of sovereignty; for corporations, in the doctrine of free enterprise; and for individuals, in the principle of human rights, as expressed in documents such as the Universal Declaration of Rights of 1948. In a frontier situation, where population is sparse, a greater amount of freedom of action can be tolerated without the prospect of severe environmental degradation. As population becomes more dense and puts heavier demands on the environment, as it has done globally in recent decades, maintaining the quality of the environment becomes a more pressing problem.

Reliance on voluntary restraints is an attractive possibility from the standpoint of maintaining maximum freedom of action, but stronger measures are usually needed to preserve the environment. Thus, fishing fleets have had to accept limits on their catch or confine their efforts to prescribed seasons. Some have had to negotiate for the right to fish in waters that fall within the newly created EEZs of coastal states, whereas before they had open access under the "freedom on the seas" doctrine. Operators of supertankers must submit to many rules that pertain to the structure of their vessels, how they are equipped, and where they may dispose of oily substances. Chinese couples, because of their country's one-child policy, have lost the right to determine the size of their families.

No strategy can be expected to maximize all four of these values. While conservation is often compatible with the achievement of equity, it is likely that sacrifices will have to be made in production, at least for the short run, and especially in freedom of action. Conservation measures may, however, work in favor of maximizing the long-term production of renewable resources. In regard to freedom, it should be kept in mind that the freedom of one party to act often impinges on the freedom of others. For example, the freedom to use CFCs indiscriminately may negate the freedom of others to enjoy being in the sunshine without fear of excessive exposure to ultraviolet radiation.

## CONCLUSIONS

Having taken note of the emergence of the environment as a major global issue and the initiation of an international response, this essay demonstrates some ways the story of the overgrazing of the pasture of the English village parallels several of the most serious environmental problems appearing on the agendas of international institutions. Hardin's story is helpful for understanding the motivation behind a variety of environmentally destructive behaviors, even by those who are well aware of the consequences of their actions. It is also useful for identifying courses of action that have potential for averting an environmental "tragedy" and the problems inherent in reconciling the objective of conservation with other values, such as maximizing production, achieving equity, and allowing freedom of action.

The allegory fits some situations much better than others. It is especially applicable to the exploitation of limited resources in international commons, such as the oceans, atmosphere, radio waves, and outer space. It is of less value in analyzing the exploitation of resources that lie entirely within the boundaries of states, notably fossil fuels, minerals, forests, and agricultural land, which have not been freely accessible to users from other countries. Proposals have been made, however, that some of these latter resources be considered the "common heritage of mankind." For example, the millions of species of plants and animals that exist on the planet have been described as the "genetic heritage of mankind," even though the specimens of many are geographically concentrated within the borders of a single state (Myers, 1984). Likewise, unique human artifacts from ancient civilizations, such as temples, sculptures, and paintings, have been designated by UNESCO as the "cultural heritage of mankind." Identifying them as such confers a responsibility on the states in which they are located to preserve them for present and future generations of the world's population.

## REFERENCES

French, Hilary R. (1990) "Clearing the Air," pp. 98–118 in Lester R. Brown et al., *State of the World 1990*. New York: Norton.

Hardin, Garrett. (1968) "The Tragedy of the Commons." *Science,* Vol. 162, pp. 1241–1248.

Hardin, Garrett. (1974) "Living on a Lifeboat." *Bioscience,* Vol. 24, pp. 561–568.

Meadows, Donnella H., Meadows, Dennis L., Randers, Jørgen, and Behrens, William H. (1972) *The Limits to Growth.* New York: Signet.

Myers, Norman. (1984) *The Primary Resource: Tropical Forests and Our Future.* New York: Norton.

World Resources Institute. (1990) *World Resources 1990–91.* New York: Oxford.

# 38

# THE INTERNATIONAL STATE OF NATURE AND THE POLITICS OF SCARCITY

William Ophuls

Is international conflict more or less probable in a world of scarcity? William Ophuls argues the former. Noting the absence of higher law or authority in the international system, implied in the principle of sovereignty to which all nation-states subscribe, he concludes that while ecological scarcity may cry out for international cooperation, "the clear danger is that, instead of promoting world cooperation, ecological scarcity will simply intensify the Hobbesian war of all against all." Ophuls has served as a commissioned officer in the United States Coast Guard and as a foreign service officer in the United States Department of State.

## THE INTERNATIONAL MACROCOSM

If in the various national microcosms constituting the world political community the basic dynamics of ecological scarcity apply virtually across the board, in the macrocosm of international politics they operate even more strongly. Just as within each individual nation, the tragic logic of the commons brings about the overexploitation of common property resources like the oceans and the atmosphere. Also, the pressures toward inequality, oppression, and conflict are even more intense within the world political community, for it is a community in name only, and the already marked cleavage between rich and poor threatens to

Reprinted from William Ophuls, *Ecology and the Politics of Scarcity* (San Francisco: W. H. Freeman and Company, 1977), pp. 208–219. Copyright 1977 by William Ophuls. All rights reserved. Footnotes have been deleted. Used by permission of William Ophuls.

become even greater. Without even the semblance of a world government, such problems depend for their solution on the good will and purely voluntary cooperation of nearly [170] sovereign states—a prospect that does not inspire optimism. . . .

## THE GLOBAL TRAGEDY OF THE COMMONS

The tragic logic of the commons operates universally, and its effects are readily visible internationally—in the growing pollution of international rivers, seas, and now even the oceans; in the overfishing that has caused a marked decline in the fish catch, as well as the near extinction of the great whales; and in the impending scramble for seabed resources by maritime miners or other exploiters. There is no way to confine environmental insults or the effects of ecological degradation within national borders; river basins, airsheds, and oceans are intrinsically international. Even seemingly local environmental disruption inevitably has some impact on the quality of regional and, eventually, global ecosystems. Just as within each nation, the aggregation of individual desires and actions overloads the international commons. But, like individuals, states tend to turn a blind eye to this, for they profit by the increased production while others bear most or all of the cost, or they lose by self-restraint while others receive most or all of the benefit. Thus, Britain gets the factory output, while Scandinavia suffers the ecological effects of "acid rain"; the French and Germans use the Rhine for waste disposal even though this leaves the river little more than a reeking sewer by the time it reaches fellow European Economic Community member Holland downstream.

However, if the problems are basically the same everywhere, the political implications of the tragedy of the commons are much more serious in the international arena. It has long been recognized that international politics is the epitome of the Hobbesian state of nature: despite all the progress over the centuries toward the rule of international law, sovereign states, unlike the citizens within each state, acknowledge no law or authority higher than their own self-interest; they are therefore free to do as they please, subject only to gross prudential restraints, no matter what the cost to the world community. Brazil, for example, has made it plain that it will brook no outside interference with its development of the Amazon, and well-meaning ecological advice is castigated as "scientific colonialism" (Castro 1972). Also, despite strong pressures from the international community, the U.S.S.R. and Japan have openly frustrated the effort to conserve whale stocks—both at the negotiating table and at sea. In international relations, therefore, the dynamic of the tragedy of the commons is even stronger than within any given nation state, which, being a real political community, has at least the theoretical capacity to make binding, authoritative decisions on resource conservation and ecological protection. By contrast, international agreements are reached and enforced by the purely voluntary cooperation of sovereign nation states existing in a state of nature. . . . The likelihood of forestalling by such means the operation of the tragedy of the commons is extremely remote. Worse, just as any individual is nearly helpless to alter the outcome by his own actions (and even risks serious loss if he refuses to participate in the exploitation of the commons), so too, in the absence of international authority or enforceable agreement, nations have little choice but to contribute to the tragedy by their own actions. This would be true even if each individual state was striving to achieve a domestic ready-state economy, for unless one assumes agreement on a largely autarkic world, states would still compete with each other internationally to maximize the resources available to them. Ecological scarcity thus intensifies the fundamental problem of international politics—the achievement of world order—by adding further to the preexisting difficulties of a state of nature. Without some kind of international governmental machinery with authority and coercive power over sovereign states sufficient to oblige them to keep within the bounds of the ecological common interest of all on the planet, the world must suffer the ever greater environmental ills ordained by the global tragedy of the commons.

## THE STRUGGLE BETWEEN RICH AND POOR

Ecological scarcity also aggravates very seriously the already intense struggle between rich and poor. As is well known, the world today . . . is sharply polarized between the developed, industrialized "haves," all affluent in a greater or lesser degree and all getting more affluent all the time, and the underdeveloped or developing "have nots," all relatively and absolutely impoverished and with few exceptions tending to fall relatively ever farther behind despite their often feverish efforts to grow. The degree of the inequality is also well known: the United States, with only 6 percent of the world's population, consumes about 30 percent of the total energy production of the world and comparable amounts of other resources, and the rest of the "haves," although only about half as prodigal as the United States, still consume resources far out of proportion to their population; conversely, per capita consumption of resources in the Third World ranges from one-tenth to one-hundredth that in the "have" countries. To make matters worse, the resources that the "haves" enjoy in inordinate amounts are largely and increasingly imported from the Third World; thus economic inequality and what might be called ecological colonialism have become intertwined. In view of this extreme and long-standing inequality (which moreover has its roots in an imperialist past), it is hardly surprising that the Third World thirsts avidly for development or that it has become increasingly intolerant of those features of the current world order it perceives as obstacles to becoming as rich and powerful as the developed world.

Alas, the emergence of ecological scarcity appears to have sounded the death knell for the aspirations of the LDCs. Even assuming, contrary to fact, that there were sufficient mineral and energy resources to make it possible, universal industrialization would impose intolerable stress on world ecosystems. In short, the current model of development, which assumes that all countries will eventually become heavily industrialized mass-consumption societies, is doomed to failure. Naturally, this conclusion is totally unacceptable to the modernizing elites of the Third World; their political power is generally founded on the promise of development. Even more important, simply halting growth would freeze the current pattern of inequality, leaving the "have nots" as the peasants of the world community in perpetuity. Thus an end to growth and development would be acceptable to the Third World only in combination with a radical redistribution of the world's wealth and a total restructuring of the world's economy to guarantee the maintenance of economic justice. Yet it seems absolutely clear that the rich have not the slightest intention of alleviating the plight of the poor if it entails the sacrifice of their own living standards. Ecological scarcity thus greatly increases the probability of naked confrontation between rich and poor.

## WHO ARE NOW THE "HAVES" AND "HAVE NOTS"?

An important new element has been injected into this struggle. The great resource hunger of the developed and even some parts of the developing world has begun to transfer power and wealth to those who have resources to sell, especially critical resources like petroleum. As a result, the geopolitics of the world has already been decisively altered.

This process can be expected to continue. The power and wealth of the major oil producers is bound to increase over the next two decades, despite North Sea and Alaskan oil and regardless of whether the Organization of Petroleum Exporting Countries (OPEC) manages to maintain . . . unity.

Some believe that oil is a special case and that the prospect of OPEC-type cartels for other resources is dim (Banks 1974; Mikesell 1974). While these assessments may be correct, it seems inevitable that in the long run an era of "commodity power" must emerge. The hunger of the industrialized nations for resources is likely to increase, even if there is no substantial growth in output to generate increased demand for raw materials, because the domestic mineral and energy resources of the developed countries have begun to be exhausted. Even the United States, for example, already imports 100 percent of its platinum, mica, chromium, and strontium; over 90 percent of its manganese, aluminum, tantalum, and cobalt; and 50 percent or more of twelve additional key minerals (Wade 1974). However, the developed countries seem determined to keep growing, and assuming even modest further growth in industrial output, their dependence on Third World supplies is bound to increase markedly in the next few decades. Thus, whatever the short-term prospects for the success of budding cartels in copper, phosphates, and other minerals, the clear overall long-term trend is toward a seller's market in basic resources and therefore toward "commodity power," even if this power grows more slowly and is manifested in a less extreme form than that of OPEC.

Thus, the basic long-standing division of the world into rich and poor in terms of GNP per capita is about to be overlaid with another rich-poor polarization, in terms of resources, that will both moderate and intensify the basic split. Although there are many complex interdependencies in world trade—for example, U.S. food exports are just as critical to many countries as their mineral exports are to us—it is already clear that the resource-rich Third World nations stand to gain greater wealth and power at the expense of the "haves." . . .

Other problems abound. For example, international financial and monetary institutions, established for a simpler world of indefinite growth and a clear demarcation between "haves" and "have nots," are creaking under the unprecedented strain of the rapid shift in economic and geopolitical realities. In addition, poor countries without major resources of their own will suffer—indeed, already have suffered—major setbacks to their prospects for development. This is true not only of the hopelessly poor Fourth World, but also of countries whose development programs have already acquired some momentum. . . .

In sum, world geopolitics and economics are in for a radical reordering. Western economic development has involved a net transfer of resources, wealth, and power from the current "have nots" to the "haves," creating the cleavage between the two that now divides the world. In particular, the enormous postwar growth in output and consumption experienced by the industrialized nation was largely fueled by the bonanza of cheap oil that they were able to extract from relatively powerless client states in the Middle East. The success of the oil cartel is a signal that, from now on, wealth and power will begin to flow in the opposite direction. But only the relatively few "have nots" who possess significant amounts of resources will gain; the plight of the rest of the poor is more abject than before. Thus the old polarization between rich and poor seems likely to be replaced by a threefold division into the rich, the hopelessly poor, and the nouveaux riches—and such a major change in the international order is bound to create tension.

## CONFLICT OR COOPERATION?

The overall effect of ecological scarcity in the international arena is to intensify the competitive dynamics of the preexisting international tragedy of the commons, so that increased commercial, diplomatic, and, ultimately, military confrontation over dwindling resources is more likely. At the same time the poor, having had their revolutionary hopes and rising aspirations crushed, will have little to lose but their chains. Also, to many of the declining "haves," ill-equipped to adapt to an era of "commodity power" and economic warfare, the grip of the nouveaux riches on essential resources will seem an intolerable stranglehold to be broken at all costs. Thus the disappearance of ecological abundance seems bound to make international politics even more tension ridden and potentially violent than it already is. Indeed, the pressures of ecological scarcity may embroil the world in hopeless strife, so that long before ecological collapse occurs by virtue of the physical limitations of the earth, the current world order will have been destroyed by turmoil and war—a truly horrible prospect, given the profoundly anti-ecological character of modern warfare. . . .

Some, on the other hand, hope or believe that ecological scarcity will have just the opposite effect—because the problems will become so overwhelming and so evidently insoluble without total international cooperation, nation states will discard their outmoded national sovereignty and place themselves under some form of planetary government that will regulate the global commons for the benefit of all humankind and begin the essential process of gradual economic redistribution. In effect, states will be driven by their own vital national interests—seen to include ecological as well as traditional economic, political, and military factors—to embrace the ultimate interdependence needed to solve ecological problems (Shields and Ott 1974). According to this hypothesis, the very direness of the outcome if cooperation does not prevail may ensure that it will.

Unfortunately, the accumulating evidence tends to support the conflictual rather than the cooperative hypothesis. Faced with the new power of the oil barons the first impulse of the United States was to try to go it alone in "Project Independence," while Japan, France, and others maneuvered individually to ensure their own future supplies, torpedoing the solidarity of the consuming countries confronting OPEC. Canada has served notice on the United States that it intends to end America's ecological colonialism; henceforth, the resources of Canada will be saved for its own use. Thus, the rich seem readier to follow "beggar thy neighbor" policies than to cooperate among themselves. Sympathy for the plight of the poor is even less evident. Some talk about expanding still further the scale of ecological colonialism; a West German research group has even put forward a scheme for the diversion of West Africa's Niger River to supply Europe with heat for energy (Anon. 1974). For others, continued interdependence of any kind with the poor is seen as so problematic and so full of threats to the sovereign independence and high living standards of the rich that the only sensible course is autarkic self-sufficiency.

Naturally, there has been considerable talk about cooperative international action to deal with the problems of ecological scarcity, but little or no momentum toward greater cooperation has developed. In fact, all the talk may have served chiefly to heighten further the tensions within the world community.

## AN UPSURGE OF CONFERENCE DIPLOMACY

By the late 1960's some of the alarming global implications of pollution and general ecological degradation had become widely apparent, and preparations began for a major international conference at Stockholm in 1972. Depending on one's point of view, the Stockholm Conference—to give it its proper title, the United Nations Conference on the Human Environment—was either a major diplomatic success or an abysmal failure. On the positive side, the elaborate preparations for the conference (each country had to make a detailed inventory of its environmental problems), the intense publicity given the over two years of preliminary negotiations, and the conference itself fostered a very high level of environmental awareness around the globe. Virtually ignored by diplomats in 1969, the environmental crisis had by 1972 rocketed right up alongside nuclear weapons and economic development as one of the big issues of international politics. The second major achievement of the Stockholm Conference was the establishment of the United Nations Environment Program (UNEP) to monitor the state of the world environment and to provide liaison and coordination between nation states and among the multitude of governmental and non-governmental organizations concerned with environmental matters. Finally, a few preliminary agreements covering certain less controversial and less critical ecological problems, like setting aside land for national parks and suppressing trade in endangered species, were reached either at the conference or immediately thereafter.

Despite these acknowledged achievements, environmentalists were by and large rather unhappy with the conduct and outcome of the conference. They were especially disillusioned, for example, by the way in which the original ecological purity of the conference's agenda was rapidly watered down by pressures from Third World countries, who made it plain that they would have nothing to do with the conference unless, in effect, underdevelopment was converted into a form of pollution. Moreover, a great part of the proceedings was devoted not to the problems of the agenda, but to the kind of "have" versus "have not" debate discussed above, and routine ideological posturing on political issues like "colonialism" consumed additional time. Also, cold-war politics refused to take a vacation; for example, the U.S.S.R. boycotted the conference because East Germany was not given full voting status. Thus the perhaps naively idealistic hope of many that the ecological issue would at last force quarrelsome and self-seeking sovereign nation states to put aside stale old grudges, recognize their common predicament, and act in concert to improve the human condition was completely dashed.

Worse, some of the features of the current world order most objectionable from an ecological point of view were actually reaffirmed at Stockholm—namely, the absolute right of sovereign countries to develop their own domestic resources without regard to the potential external ecological costs to the world community, and the unrestricted freedom to breed guaranteed by the Universal Declaration of Human Rights. In addition, established international institutions, like the World Health Organization and the Food and Agriculture Organization, extended distinctly lukewarm cooperation to the organizers of the conference, both because of bureaucratic jealousy and because of fear that environmental concerns would force them to alter or abandon programs, like all-out support for the Green Revolution and the eradication of malaria with DDT, that are a large part of their raison d'être. As a result, the Secretariat of UNEP was given little real power and only a minimum of resources to perform its coordinating and monitoring functions. Also, the headquarters of UNEP were eventually established in Nairobi, and although this has had the very positive effect of keeping the Third World interested in UNEP and its programs, it has definitely hampered the expansion and effectiveness of the global environmental monitoring and liaison that was to be UNEP's prime responsibility.

Since 1972, there have been more environmentally oriented conferences—principally the U.N. World Population Conference in 1974, the U.N. World Food Conference in 1974, and a series of U.N. Law of the Sea Conferences from 1974 to the present. However, there has been little progress since Stockholm. The World Population Conference somehow managed to end "without producing explicit agreement that there was a world population problem" (Walsh 1974). The World Food Conference produced few concrete achievements and left crucial problems on its agenda unsolved. The Law of the Sea Conferences have promoted progress toward a global consensus that seems likely to become the basis of an international treaty once future negotiating meetings dispose of some of the still unsettled issues.* Unfortunately, the basis of this emerging consensus is an agreement to carve the oceans into national zones of exploitation, instead of making them into the common heritage of mankind; thus, as at Stockholm, the principle of national sovereignty has been ever further entrenched.

The forces that prevented Stockholm from fulfilling its promise were even more strongly in evidence at these and other post-Stockholm international meetings directly or indirectly concerned with environmental issues. First, the spirit of militant nationalism that has animated so much of the history of the postwar world has not abated. Thus states insist on the absolute and sovereign right of self-determination in use of resources, population policy, and development in general, regardless of the wider consequences. Second, the demand by Third World countries for economic development has, if anything, increased in intensity, and whatever seems to stand in the way, like ecological considerations, gets rather short shrift. Third, largely because their prospects for development are so dim, Third World countries have begun to press even harder for fundamental reform of the world system (a "new international economic order"); thus every discussion of environmental issues like food and population is inevitably converted by Third World spokesmen into a discussion of international economic

*The Law of the Sea Treaty was concluded in 1982.—*Eds.*

justice as well, which enormously complicates the process of negotiation. In short, environmental issues have become pawns in the larger diplomatic and political struggle between the nations.

In addition, diplomats, like national leaders, have attempted to handle the issues of ecological scarcity not as part of a larger problematique, but piecemeal, so that their interaction with other problems is all but ignored. For example, the World Food Conference was solely concerned with the problem of feeding the hungry and gave virtually no attention to the eventual ecological consequences of growing more food or subsidizing further overpopulation with radically increased food aid. To some extent, therefore, the successes of international conferences that simply try to solve one small piece of the larger problem are as much to be feared as their failures.

If one wished to be optimistic, one could conclude that the world community has taken the first halting attitudinal and institutional steps toward meeting the challenges of ecological scarcity. A more realistic assessment would be that little has been accomplished so far and that major impediments to further progress loom large. One might even be forced to conclude, more pessimistically, that the world political community as presently constituted is simply incapable of coping with the challenges of ecological scarcity, at least within any reasonable time.

## PLANETARY GOVERNMENT OR THE WAR OF ALL AGAINST ALL

. . . Even before the emergence of ecological scarcity, the world's difficulties and their starkly Hobbesian implications were grave enough. Some saw the "revolution of rising expectations" pushing the world toward a situation in which wants greatly exceeded the capacity to meet them, provoking Hobbesian turmoil and violence (Spengler 1969). Also, ever since Hiroshima the world has lived in a state of highly armed peace with a nuclear Sword of Damocles dangling over its head. We have all learned to live with the bomb, and the hair suspending the nuclear Sword has indeed held, although for how much longer no one can say. Now the world must live under the blade of another Sword of Damocles, slower to fall but equally deadly. Unfortunately, the hair holding this environmental Sword has come loose; pollution and other environmental problems will not obligingly postpone their impact while diplomats haggle, so the Sword is already slicing down toward our unprotected heads. There is thus no way for the world community to put the environmental issue out of mind and go on about its business, as it has done with the bomb. The crisis of ecological scarcity is a Sword that must be parried, squarely and soon.

Thus the already strong rationale for a world government with enough coercive power over fractious nation states to achieve what reasonable men would regard as the planetary common interest has become overwhelming. Yet we must recognize that the very ecological scarcity that makes a world government ever more necessary has also made it much more difficult of achievement. The clear danger is that, instead of promoting world cooperation, ecological scarcity will simply intensify the Hobbesian war of all against all and cause armed peace to be replaced by overt international strife.

## REFERENCES

Anon. 1974. "Take Water and Heat from Third World," *New Scientist* 62:549.

Banks, Fred. 1974. "Copper Is Not Oil," *New Scientist* 63:255–257.

Castro, Joao A. de A. 1972. "Environment and Development: The Case of the Developing Countries," *International Organization* (26):401–416.

Mikesell, Raymond F. 1974. "More Third World Cartels Ahead?" *Challenge* 17(5):24–31.

Shields, Linda P., and Marvin C. Ott. 1974. "Environmental Decay and International Politics: The Uses of Sovereignty," *Environmental Affairs* 3:743–767.

Spengler, Joseph J. 1969. "Return to Thomas Hobbes?" *South Atlantic Quarterly* 68:443–453.

Wade, Nicholas. 1974. "Raw Materials: U.S. Grows More Vulnerable to Third World Cartels," *Science* 183:185–186.

Walsh, John. 1974. "UN Conferences: Topping Any Agenda Is the Question of Development," *Science* 185:1143–1144, 1192–1193.

# 39

# NUCLEAR WINTER AND THE END OF THE ARMS RACE

Carl Sagan and Richard Turco

**Although it has long been asserted that a nuclear war could result in the destruction of civilization and the possible extinction of the human species, during the 1980s insights from diverse branches of science converged behind the theory of "nuclear winter" to describe how the impending apocalypse could occur. Carl Sagan and Richard Turco review the theory and its projected consequences and find in it hope, not despair, as the shared vulnerability nuclear winter portends "has alerted us to our common peril and our mutual dependence." Sagan is David Duncan Professor of Astronomy and Space Sciences and director of the Laboratory for Planetary Studies at Cornell University. He has been awarded the Pulitzer Prize and many other awards of distinction. Turco is professor of atmosphere sciences at the University of California at Los Angeles. He is an associate editor of the American Geophysical Union's *Journal of Geophysical Research* and co-author of *Environmental Consequences of Nuclear War* (1989).**

This is a [chapter] about a disquieting scientific discovery. It is also about the prospects of life and death for everyone on Earth. . . . The prospect of what we have called "nuclear winter" challenges political, economic, social, and religious

Copyright © 1990 Carl Sagan and Richard Turco. All rights reserved. Used by permission of the authors.

412

ideologies. . . . Nuclear winter seems to leave some people despairing, some rejecting the prospect out of hand, and others fired up to make political change. Few who consider the matter are left indifferent.

. . . At a time of swiftly moving U.S./Soviet relations and of an emerging consciousness of the need to protect the global environment, we propose that nuclear winter has much to teach us.

. . . [Arms] control and the elimination of at least some nuclear weapons systems are being not only seriously discussed, but actually implemented. The present comparative warmth in the relations between the United States and the Soviet Union stands in sharp contrast to the chill of the Cold War. Understandably, there is now a tendency to think of the problem of nuclear war as solved, or at least as in the process of being solved, so we can at last ignore it and turn our attention to the vast array of other pressing problems. This opinion is surprisingly widespread. It blossoms especially when superpower summit meetings are cordial. It is, we believe, a dangerous illusion.

For all the genuine goodwill in the present attitudes of the superpowers and the profound changes in their relationship, the simple fact is that, at this moment, over 10,000 nuclear weapons on each side are, with fine premeditation, aimed at specific targets on the other. Some of those targets have millions of people in them. In the nosecones of missiles and in the bombracks of aircraft the weapons wait—faithful, obedient servants holding themselves in quiet readiness. When they are activated, they will fly away, halfway around the planet it may be, sent on their one-way missions by the merest word. These are the strategic weapons, designed to travel from one homeland to another. Then there are nearly 35,000 tactical nuclear weapons, with more modest objectives. The bombs that destroyed Hiroshima and Nagasaki were on such a scale. Altogether there are nearly 60,000 nuclear weapons in the world. Behind the welcome improvements in rhetoric and relations, the machinery of mass murder still waits, purring and attentive. It is no exaggeration, no hyperbole to say that billions of people are at risk. It is a little early for complacency.

Of all the perils facing the human species, nuclear war and nuclear winter . . . pose the greatest dangers. As long as such a multiply redundant, hair-trigger capability for mutual annihilation exists, all assurances of safety will ring hollow. *Challenger* and Chernobyl remind us that high-technology systems into which enormous amounts of national prestige are invested can go disastrously wrong. The politics of the United States and the Soviet Union are unpredictable—as recent events have richly demonstrated. We do not know who will accede to power in the coming years and decades. Nuclear weapons, like diseases, proliferate. The longer the major nuclear powers dally about substantial mutual arms reductions, the less moral authority and political credibility they bring to preventing proliferation of these weapons to other nations, and the broader becomes the set of issues and national interests that could ignite a nuclear war. Safely reversing the nuclear arms race should have, in Andrei Sakharov's words, "absolute priority over all other problems of our times."

An era of improved relations between the United States and the Soviet Union is the optimum time to work to reassess military doctrine and policy, to reconsider weapons systems on order, to reverse the arms race. No significant reversal is possible, however, without far-reaching changes in the attitudes that each nation bears toward the other. But such changes are, by the beginning of the last decade of the twentieth century, clearly under way. . . .

## THE IDEA OF NUCLEAR WINTER

World War II had ended with the explosion of the fission or atomic bomb, the most devastating weapon until then invented by the human species. Seven years later a weapon a thousand times more powerful was devised—the fusion or hydrogen bomb, so potent that it employed the fission bomb only as a trigger, as a match to set it off. In the decades since Hiroshima and Nagasaki the number, variety, and power of nuclear weapons increased. Many nations felt it essential to acquire them. They became entrées to international respectability; the admission fee to big power status; means of intimidating other nations, of unleashing patriotic pride, of manufacturing domestic political success. They worked wonders. Means were devised to carry them in long-range aircraft; to launch them atop rockets from hardened concrete holes in the ground or from submarines sitting at the ocean depths; or to convey them in pilotless air-breathing vehicles that fly close to the ground under the radar, following every geographic contour. Brilliant, dedicated scientists and engineers labored to squeeze as many as a dozen of them—each directed to a different target—into the nosecone of a single missile; and to learn how to pack so many such missiles into a single submarine that one boat could destroy 200 cities of some faraway nation. The accuracy of these "delivery systems" improved. Some nuclear weapons could hit a football field halfway across the planet. Each could obliterate an area far larger than a football field, and burn hundreds or thousands of square kilometers.

The world accumulated tens of thousands of nuclear weapons—always in the name of peace. Our side—whichever side we happened to be on—was always stable, cautious, peace-loving. The other side was always unpredictable, dangerous, warlike. Each side needed its vast arsenal, or so those in power told their citizens, only to deter the other side from using *its* vast arsenal. Their hands were tied. It was all the fault of the adversary. Trillions of dollars were spent.

The military establishments of the various nuclear-armed nations had, of course, an obligation to assure that at least their national leaders—if not their citizens, in whose name all this was being done—understood the consequences of nuclear war. Hundreds of nuclear weapons were exploded above and below ground and their effects monitored: blast, fire, radiation. There were some surprises, some ways in which nuclear explosions were *unexpectedly* dangerous. In many cases the new facts were discovered accidentally; and they were often classified as state secrets, so as not to erode public support for the nuclear arms race. . . . Radioactive fallout was worse than had been guessed. High-altitude nuclear explosions were discovered to attack the protective ozone layer. The electromagnetic pulse from an explosion in space caused surprising malfunctions in electronic equipment in distant satellites and on the ground below. These unanticipated side effects should have been a warning that there might be other, still more serious, still undiscovered consequences of nuclear war. But for nearly four decades no military scientist, no defense intellectual, no policy analyst ever seriously thought of anything like nuclear winter.

With our colleagues Brian Toon, Tom Ackerman, and Jim Pollack, it was our fate to be the first to calculate what the climatic consequences of nuclear war might be. From our last names (ref. 2.2), others gave our little research group the acronym "TTAPS"—appropriate, perhaps, given the nature of our findings. All of us had studied the atmospheres and environments both of the Earth and of other worlds. We were used to thinking globally, trying to understand the big planetary picture. . . .

In a nuclear war, powerful nuclear explosions at the ground would propel fine particles high into the stratosphere. Much of the dust would be carried up by the fireball itself. Some would be sucked up the stem of the mushroom cloud. Even much more modest explosions on or above cities would produce massive fires, as occurred in Hiroshima and Nagasaki. The resulting smoke is much more dangerous to the climate than the dust. These fires consume wood, petroleum, plastics, roofing tar, natural gas, and a wide variety of other combustibles. Two kinds of smoke are generated. Smoldering combustion is a low-temperature, flameless burning in which fine oily, bluish-white organic particles are produced. Cigarette smoke is an example. By contrast, in flaming combustion— when there's an adequate supply of oxygen—the burning organic material is converted in significant part to elemental carbon, and the sooty smoke is very dark. Soot is one of the blackest materials nature is able to manufacture. As in an oil refinery fire, or a burning pile of auto tires, or a conflagration in a modern skyscraper—more generally, in any big city fire—great clouds of roiling, ugly, dark, sooty smoke would rise high above the cities in a nuclear war, and spread first in longitude, then in latitude.

The high-altitude dust particles reflect additional sunlight back to space and cool the Earth a little. More important are the dense palls of black smoke high in the atmosphere; they block the sunlight from reaching the lower atmosphere, where the greenhouse gases mainly reside. These gases are thereby deprived of their leverage on the global climate. The greenhouse effect is turned down and the Earth's surface is cooled some more.

Because cities and petroleum repositories are so rich in combustible materials, it doesn't require very many nuclear explosions over them to make so much smoke as to obscure the entire Northern Hemisphere and more. If the dark, sooty clouds are nearly opaque and cover an extensive area, then the greenhouse effect can be almost entirely turned off. In the more likely case that some sunlight trickles through, the temperatures nevertheless may drop 10 or 20°C or more, depending on season and geographical locale. In many places, it may at midday get as dark as it used to be on a moonlit night before the nuclear war began. The resulting environmental changes may last for months or years.

If the greenhouse effect is a blanket in which we wrap ourselves to keep warm, nuclear winter kicks off the blanket. This darkening and cooling of the Earth following nuclear war—along with other ancillary consequences—is what we mean by nuclear winter. . . .

A typical temperature for a point on the *land* surface of the Earth, averaged over latitude, season, and time of day, is roughly 15°C (59°F). If there were no greenhouse effect whatever, the corresponding temperature would be about −20°C (−4°F). The difference between the planetary environment with the greenhouse effect and without it is the difference between clement conditions and deep freeze. Tampering with the greenhouse effect—especially in ways that reduce it—can be very risky.

. . . If we were to double the present concentration of the greenhouse gas carbon dioxide in the Earth's atmosphere—as will happen in a few decades if present trends continue—the surface temperature will likely increase by a few degrees. . . . Following a major volcanic explosion the temperature can *de*crease by as much as a few degrees. During an Ice Age, the global temperatures are a few degrees colder yet, approaching the freezing point of water. And in a nuclear winter, depending on severity, the temperatures can become still colder, ranging well below freezing. Just how cold it gets depends on many variables, including how the nuclear war is "fought." . . . But even the middle range of these nuclear winter effects . . . represents the severest climatic catastrophe ever to have occurred during the tenure of humans on this planet. Even in the range of temperature overlap, a mild nuclear winter is harsher than a severe Ice Age, because of its rapid onset (weeks rather than centuries or millennia)—although its duration is much briefer.

The prediction of nuclear winter is drawn not, of course, from any direct experience with the consequences of global nuclear war, but rather from an investigation of the governing physics. (The problem does not lend itself to full experimental verification—at least not more than once.) The models derived are calibrated and tested by studies of the ambient climate of the Earth and other planets, and by observed climatic perturbations caused by volcanic explosions, massive forest fires, and great dust storms. . . .

Conventional wisdom, no matter how deeply felt, may not be a reliable guide in an age of apocalyptic weapons. A number of studies have addressed the strategic and policy implications of nuclear winter. If the climatic consequences of nuclear war are serious, many have concluded that major changes in strategy, policy and doctrine may be required. . . . This broad impact stems from two basic facts about nuclear winter: (a) its occurrence would present an unacceptable peril for the global civilization and for at least most of the human species; and (b) it puts at risk in the devastating aftermath of nuclear war not only survivors in the combatant nations, but also enormous numbers in noncombatant and far distant nations—people, most of them, wholly uninvolved with whatever quarrel or fear precipitated the war.

Since we have not yet had a global nuclear war, our conclusions must remain inferential and therefore necessarily incomplete. Some counsel that policy should not be decided on the basis of incomplete information. But policy is *always* decided on incomplete information. Nuclear winter has now attained standards of completeness and accuracy at least comparable to those on which many vital real world policy decisions are made. . . .

## CURRENT SCIENTIFIC KNOWLEDGE OF NUCLEAR WINTER

The theory of nuclear winter, first introduced in 1982, has been a subject of controversy. . . . Debate is common when new scientific ideas are introduced, and healthy. However, much of the controversy over nuclear winter has been artificially generated at the borderline where science and policy intersect. Some has been fueled by confusion among nonspecialists over certain technical findings, and by comparisons of various computer models without sufficient care having been taken to resolve, or even to note, differences in initial assumptions. Among the troubling issues, laden with ideological connotations, raised by the nuclear winter theory are the possibilities that a major consequence of nuclear war eluded the American and Soviet nuclear arms establishments for thirty-seven years . . .; that a "small" nuclear war might have widespread, perhaps even global, catastrophic climatic consequences; that distant nations would be in jeopardy, even if not a single nuclear weapon were detonated on their soil; that massive retaliation, and equally, attempts at a disarming first strike, in a variety of policy frameworks, would be disastrous for the nation employing such policies (and for its allies)—independent of its adversary's response; and that the size and nature of the present nuclear arsenals as well as the central role of nuclear weapons in the strategic relations of the United States and the Soviet Union may be not merely imprudent, but a policy mistake unprecedented in human history. . . .

In the years since the original TTAPS (ref. 2.2) study, the scientific basis of the nuclear winter theory has been extended, refined, and strengthened. . . . The basic climate changes predicted by the original nuclear winter theory have been upheld by the bulk of later research, including research with significantly more sophisticated models. . . . Recent analyses of chills, freezes, obscuration of the Sun, and crop failures caused by wildfire smoke . . . and volcanic aerosols . . . support the theory. . . . Expert summaries of the field have now been published by the Scientific Committee on Problems of the Environment (SCOPE) of the International Council of Scientific Unions, . . . by the World Meteorological Organization, . . . and by the United Nations. . . .

One way of calibrating the seriousness of the average global coolings predicted for nuclear winter is to compare them with the slow global warming attributed to the increasing greenhouse effect. The decade of the 1980s . . . witnessed, on global average, the five hottest years of the preceding 130. . . . A few investigators have proposed that these years, and especially the sweltering summer of 1988, provide the first clear climatic signature of the increasing greenhouse effect. By the beginning of the decade of the 1990s, the entire global temperature increase since the industrial revolution is estimated at about 0.5°C. This is a planetary average, over latitudes, seasons, and time of day. It seems small, but it can have profound local consequences. It constitutes the highest average global temperatures in the last 120,000 years. . . . This is one way of calibrating the meaning of the 10 to 25°C temperature declines predicted for the baseline nuclear winter: Nuclear winter constitutes 20 to 50 times the maximum temperature changes attributed to the increasing greenhouse effect, about which there is— and properly so—grave concern. . . . And the nuclear winter climatic changes would occur thousands of times faster.

. . . [We] do not claim that a given sort of nuclear war will inevitably produce a given severity of nuclear winter; the irreducible uncertainties are too large for that. What we do claim is that the most likely consequences of many kinds of nuclear war constitute climatic and environmental catastrophes much worse than the worst our species has ever encountered—and that prudent policy should treat nuclear winter as a probable outcome of nuclear war. . . .

### THE WITCHES' BREW: POISON GAS, RADIOACTIVE FALLOUT, ULTRAVIOLET LIGHT

The principal and most widely discussed aspects of nuclear winter are the cold and the dark. But when we introduced the term, we intended it to encompass other serious long-term consequences of nuclear war, of which we identified three: the production of heavy, ground-hugging clouds of toxic gases from the burning of modern cities; the worldwide distribution of radioactive fallout, attached to some of the same fine particles that block the sunlight; and the assault on the protective ozone layer that ordinarily blocks deadly ultraviolet sunlight from reaching the surface of the Earth. The physics of each of these ancillary catastrophes is related to the machinery of nuclear winter. For example, recent studies show that the heating by sunlight of high-altitude clouds of soot and dust work to deplete the ozone layer; the main consequences transpire after the obscuring particles have fallen out of the atmosphere, but before the ozone layer has had time to heal itself. . . .

**EXTINCTION?**

. . . There is so much life on Earth, with so many diverse adaptations, that we cannot destroy it all. Cold comfort for us—because it is well within our powers to destroy the global civilization, other species, and perhaps ourselves. We are already, every day, rendering species of life on Earth extinct without nuclear war. Extinction of many more species may be possible in the wake of a nuclear war. But for us, understandably, an important question is whether we can make *humans* extinct. . . .

People concentrate themselves in large cities, so killing them there has become easy in the nuclear age. . . . But people also live in towns and country-side. This is why killing a quarter of the population of a nation through the direct (or "prompt") effects of nuclear weapons is much easier than killing, say, half or three-quarters. That's where nuclear winter comes in. Nuclear winter is a way for nuclear weapons to find and kill those who live far from cities.

Certainly, the casualty estimates from prompt effects in a nuclear war are appalling: The U.S. nuclear war protocol (Single Integrated Operational Plan, SIOP) of 1960 vintage would have destroyed every city in the Soviet Union and China, with estimated direct fatalities around 400 million. . . . Presidential Review Memorandum 10 (February 18, 1977) estimated some 250 million fatal-ities in a U.S./U.S.S.R. central exchange. . . . Since then, estimates of the dan-gers of radioactive fallout have had to be revised—to take account of the tenfold underestimate of intermediate timescale fallout radiation doses in official publi-cations, and the consequences of attacks on military and commercial nuclear fuel facilities; global casualties from radioactivity alone are now estimated at 80 to 290 million . . . with the higher numbers, in our opinion, more likely. Thus, several hundred million prompt fatalities may occur in a full-scale nuclear exchange, with up to a billion more fatalities if urban centers and nuclear fuel facilities worldwide are heavily targeted; . . . separate, longer-term fatalities—especially from nuclear winter-related crop failures and resulting malnutrition and starvation—might amount to several billion. . . . Many others would die from the collapse of the society (unavailability of physicians, hospitals, and medicines, for example), the spread of disease, and (later) the increased ultravio-let radiation. Under these, perhaps pessimistic, estimates, the sum of prompt and long-term fatalities approaches the total human population of over 5 billion. A key issue, addressed below, is survival in the midlatitudes of the Southern Hemisphere.

With the technological base in ruins, and accessible key resources depleted, recovery of the global civilization after nuclear war is in doubt. There would also be, in the words of Andrei Sakharov, "the rise of a savage and uncontrol-lable hatred of scientists and 'intellectuals' . . . , rampant superstition, fero-cious nationalism, and the destruction of the material and informational basis of civilization"; it would introduce a new "age of barbarism." . . .

Destruction of the global civilization is very different, though, from extinction of the human species. However, the multiple stresses on biological systems, and likely interactions (synergisms) among these stresses, could fundamentally alter ecological relationships on which humans now depend. Considering a nuclear winter scenario at the severe end of the spectrum of possibilities, a distinguished group of ecologists and biologists argue that massive species extinctions—especially but not exclusively at tropical and subtropical latitudes where there are few adaptations to cold—would ensue (ref. 5.13). They conclude:

> It seems unlikely, however, that even in these circumstances *Homo sapiens* would be forced to extinction immediately. Whether any people would be able to persist for long in the face of highly modified biological communities; novel climates; high levels of radiation; shattered agricultural, social, and economic systems; extraordinary psychological stresses; and a host of other difficulties, is open to question.

The SCOPE report (ref. 3.11), the most comprehensive analysis of the biological implications of nuclear winter, does not explicitly address human extinction, but it does indicate that the deaths of several billion people, mainly from starvation, is possible in the climatic aftermath of a large-scale nuclear war. That would be added to the estimated prompt casualties of many hundreds of millions, severe post-traumatic stress on the survivors, . . . and a range of as yet undiscovered synergisms among the individually adverse environmental consequences. Small groups of survivors would be particularly vulnerable to accidental unfavorable fluctuations in the physical or biological environment. . . . The conclusion remains: Human extinction is by no means excluded. . . .

## RISK

Compared with other potential catastrophes—and there are getting to be a fair number of them—how big a risk of nuclear war are we running today? How much effort should we put into trying to prevent it—given all the other crises clamoring for our attention?

There is a range of possible outcomes of nuclear war, each with an associated risk. The risk, in the simplest terms, can be estimated as the probability that the event occurs multiplied by its cost—cost in lives, in misery, in lost knowledge, in the destroyed artifacts of our cultures and the sensibility of our civilization, cost measured by any standard we like. Even remote contingencies must be taken seriously if their consequences are sufficiently apocalyptic—a view traditionally embraced by military planners and nuclear strategists. . . . War is too serious a matter, they have been telling us for generations, to base our plans merely on the most probable actions of a potential enemy. We must plan on capability, not intention. We must prepare, we are told, for the worst case. The stakes are too high to do anything else. It would be tellingly inconsistent if this ancient military doctrine were to be abandoned at the very moment we confront the ultimate worst case. . . .

The probability of a nuclear war within the next decades is unknown. But because of the enormous numbers of nuclear weapons and their delivery systems, and the intrinsic imperfections of machines and people, nuclear war is not only possible, but if we wait long enough, it may be inevitable. . . .

## WHAT IT TAKES TO GENERATE NUCLEAR WINTER

. . . The following general trends in the climatic consequences of nuclear war have been clear for some time:

**(1)** The severity of climatic impacts would, over an important range, tend to increase with the quantity of smoke . . . injected into the atmosphere;

**(2)** Inland continental regions would suffer more severe effects than coastlines and islands;

**(3)** The absolute temperature drops would be largest in summer and smallest in winter, although a springtime war might result in the most serious agricultural (and therefore human) consequences; and

**(4)** Superimposed on the average temperature changes predicted by current models would be natural extremes of weather adding significantly to the potential severity. . . .

A single night below freezing is enough to destroy the Asian rice crop. A 2 to 3°C average local temperature drop is sufficient to destroy all wheat production in Canada, and 3 to 4° all grain production. Crops in the Ukraine and the American Midwest would also be severely injured by a 3 to 4°C temperature drop. . . . A 5°C regional drop would bring us back to Ice Age global temperatures. . . . A 10°C temperature decline with the accompanying darkening of the Sun . . . would devastate grassland ecosystems throughout the Northern Hemisphere (despite their much larger temperature resiliency than our pampered crops); here something like a step-function *biological* threshold seems to apply. . . . A 10°C temperature drop from contemporary conditions also represents the coldest global climate at the peak of the Wisconsin Ice Age. But land temperature declines of 5 to 10°C are calculated even for mild nuclear winters . . ., and much larger temperature declines may well occur. . . .

This gives us a sense of where the threshold might be—the injection into the atmosphere of enough smoke to produce a few-degree (perhaps 1 to 4°C) temperature drop on land. . . .

## CONSEQUENCES OF EXECUTION

. . . The combatant nations in a nuclear war can expect—apart from the cold and dark of nuclear winter—to be devastated by blast, fire, prompt radiation, pyrotoxins, radioactive fallout, and high ultraviolet intensities. Even in the most restricted counterforce scenarios, where urban targets are meticulously avoided, early radioactive fallout would exact an enormous toll. . . . A more general strike on the hundred largest cities would promptly kill tens of millions . . . and destroy the economic infrastructure of the nation under attack. Even in the worst such scenarios, however, many tens of millions would initially survive, although under extraordinary physical and mental stress. Enormous numbers of lingering deaths would be expected. . . . These are some of the consequences of execution.

The warring nations would be among the richest in the world, generally with ample stores of grain and other raw and processed foods. Many would enjoy self-sufficiency in mechanized agriculture. But given low temperatures and light levels; large areas of agricultural land contaminated by radioactivity and toxic gases, and later irradiated by ultraviolet light; the interruption or destruction of critical subsidies of fuel, fertilizer, seed, irrigation, herbicides, pesticides, and the facilities to harvest, store, process, and deliver foods; and with plagues of insects—agricultural yields should plummet sharply for long periods or disappear altogether. . . . In the combatant nations, most of the survivors of the first few days of the war would die, chiefly from starvation. This also is among the consequences of execution.

Birds and mammals are more vulnerable to the cold, dark, and radiation than are the insects they prey upon, and plagues of insects, perhaps of biblical proportions, may ensue. Insects are carriers of disease microorganisms which would be spreading just when hospitals are destroyed, physicians killed in large numbers, medicines rendered unavailable, and the immune systems of the survivors weakened by unprecedented physical and emotional stresses. This is an example of "synergism," the adverse multiplicative interaction of the consequences of execution.

Despite these grim prospects, some optimistic forecasters have projected the recovery of the gross national product and quality of life in America within a few decades. . . . Presumably, they imagine such notions of national recovery to apply, in varying degrees, to other parts of the world as well. It has also been suggested officially that residual agriculture could almost immediately support the survivors of a nuclear attack on the U.S. and that recovery would be swift. . . . We are deeply skeptical. Nuclear winter casts a long shadow on predictions of recovery for the combatant nations. Even the mild end of the spectrum of climatic anomalies predicted by current nuclear winter models implies widespread crop failures in the year or two following a nuclear war . . . —as occurs on a smaller scale in "volcanic winter" after a major volcanic explosion. Little, if any, agriculture in the Northern mid-latitude target zone is likely to succeed in the first year, and production for at least several more years would probably be frustrated by unpredictable and anomalous weather. . . . The prognosis for a population afflicted with widespread and profound injuries; unprecedented exposure to radioactivity and pyrotoxins; severe problems of sanitation and disease;

societal and psychological trauma; lack of food, potable water, medicine, and medical care; bizarre and extreme weather variations—including intervals of deep cold, violent storms, drought, and eventually, increases in the intensity of searing solar ultraviolet radiation—would seem to be unfavorable.

Civil defense preparations in nations at risk have focused on the temporary protection of citizens from blast and fallout, or their resettlement in areas unaffected by the war. However, the U.S. and many other countries have realized that the construction and maintenance of effective shelters for the entire threatened population would be far too costly to undertake seriously. . . . Soviet planners have pursued shelters for other than the civilian and military leadership mainly as a means of reassurance of the potential victims—i.e., for political reasons. . . . Moreover, even the most sophisticated mass shelters would be designed only for short-term occupancy (perhaps several weeks). There are no civil defense plans for the bulk of the surviving population in a severely degraded environment—nor could there be. To avoid the awkward admission that large-scale civilian shelters are worthless, given the probable postwar environment, American civil defense planners have chosen to ignore nuclear winter altogether; there is no hint even of the possibility of nuclear winter in the planning documents of the government entity with the sunniest disposition, the Federal Emergency Management Agency. . . .

Ironically, a nationwide shelter system designed without regard for long-term effects might increase the post-shelter demands on agricultural and medical systems (the latter, because many of the shelter survivors would have received debilitating but sublethal radiation doses, acquired diminished immune system capacity and/or developed serious illnesses while in confinement). In the light of nuclear winter, standard civil defense shelters can be seen as briefly postponing, but hardly preventing, the deaths of large numbers of those obtaining shelter after a central exchange. And nuclear winter makes "crisis relocation" of urban refugees to a supportive and nurturing countryside a forlorn hope.

To summarize, in combatant nations, nuclear winter profoundly threatens the surviving population and poses severe challenges to societal and economic recovery after nuclear war. . . .

## NUCLEAR WINTER IN NATIONS MINDING THEIR OWN BUSINESS

. . . In a massive nuclear conflict, noncombatant nations outside the two primary alliances might expect:

**(a)** potential nuclear detonations at key military or economic facilities within or near their borders, including airfields, ports (especially those equipped for submarines), communications and manufacturing sites, petroleum facilities, and other economic targets;

(b) cessation of trade with combatants and other supplier nations, particularly in food, medicine, fuels, fertilizer, seeds, and manufactured goods;

(c) influx of refugees, many suffering from serious malnutrition, injuries, and illnesses; and desperate pleas for aid from neighboring nations; and

(d) long-term environmental disturbances, perhaps of unprecedented severity.

Most of the nonaligned or weakly aligned nations of Africa, South America, and Asia apparently do not anticipate such nuclear ministrations at the hands of the superpowers. Others, like New Zealand, have sought to minimize the risk of direct nuclear attack by reducing the number of potential targets within their borders. . . .

The SCOPE biological analysis (ref. 3.11) treats the effects of worldwide disruptions in agricultural trade. Hundreds of millions of people are found to be in jeopardy of starvation, even without major climatic perturbations. The projected 1990s food import/export deficits for many of the developing nations is already in the 10 to 50% range without nuclear war or nuclear winter. Moreover, refugees from war zones would swell local populations, increase demands on food and other supplies, and hasten the spread of disease. Political relations among surviving nations might degenerate rapidly, and local warfare could erupt, compounding the misery. Distant nations therefore are wholly justified, it seems to us, in pressing the superpowers for massive nuclear arms reductions.

The noncombatants would be faced with food shortages and starvation for years, accompanied by global pandemics, especially lethal because many human immune systems will be radiation-damaged. . . . Radioactive fallout, chemical toxins from burning cities, and ultraviolet radiation could be delivered in dangerous doses; and the predictability of weather and climate, upon which societies and civilizations depend, could be transformed into a prolonged and chaotic nightmare of cold, drought, and storms. According to the SCOPE Report, noncombatant nations might ultimately suffer more casualties than combatant nations. . . .

Consider Japan, for example. It has the strongest economy and by some standards is the most powerful nation on Earth. Imagine—we think this highly unlikely—that in a global nuclear war not a single nuclear weapon explodes on or over Japan. Nevertheless, clouds of nuclear winter smoke and radioactive fallout would be rapidly carried by the prevailing westerlies to Japan from targets in China, Mongolia, Siberia, and the Koreas. Comparatively small declines in temperature (including a single night below freezing) are sufficient to destroy the Japanese rice crop. Japan imports over 50% of its food and over 90% of its fuel. World trade would be nearly eliminated in a major nuclear war even apart from nuclear winter. If chronic nuclear winter effects last for several years, followed by severe increases in the intensity of solar ultraviolet light at the surface (from ozone layer depletion), it is not hard to see that the Japanese economy would be destroyed and most Japanese citizens might be killed. Were Japan targeted, the consequences would be even more serious. Many developing nations with less stable food supplies and more fragile economies—even those at much more southerly latitudes—might be still more thoroughly destroyed. Populous nations such as Nigeria, or India, or Indonesia might collapse without a single nuclear weapon falling on their soil.

The prompt and a number of the long-term consequences of nuclear war—many recognized for years—have apparently not moved the superpowers, their allies, or the nonaligned potential victim states to more than feeble action, except to accelerate the arms race. Nuclear winter, however, in which billions of noncombatants may starve to death, has helped many nations, combatant and noncombatant alike, to change policies on the issue of nuclear war. . . . Nuclear winter seems to have reawakened concerns about potential global apocalypse, even in distant and Southern Hemisphere nations that once thought themselves immune to—or even the potential beneficiaries of—a U.S./Soviet nuclear war.

More than 85% of all the humans on Earth live in the Northern Hemisphere. A nuclear war and nuclear winter that was wholly restricted to the Northern Hemisphere could therefore destroy most humans. If significant amounts of fine particles were carried from the Northern Hemisphere to the Southern Hemisphere (or were produced in the Southern Hemisphere), or if the enormous nuclear winter-generated hole in the ozone layer eventually moved across the Equator, or if global pandemics were sufficiently serious, then the environmental effects of nuclear war could threaten the remainder of the human species. . . .

## MINIMUM SUFFICIENT DETERRENCE (MSD)

Major cuts in the world nuclear arsenals are in the interest of everyone on earth. They give no special advantage to the Americans or the Russians or anybody else. They are not driven by politics or ideology or national allegiance—only by our interest in staying alive. If we like, we can accept the posture of nuclear deterrence. We can even consider it a good idea to threaten some other country's largest cities. But don't we want to make sure that no conceivable circumstance, no computer malfunction, no mad leader, no intelligence or communications failure, *nothing* could destroy our civilization and endanger our species? This isn't an argument about who's right in the quarrels between the big powers; it isn't even a question of nationalism versus world order. It's only a question of everyone—including the billions of people with no part in whatever quarrel would lead to nuclear war—having a right to a future. . . .

Clearly there are safe and unsafe, stabilizing and destabilizing, ways to reduce the nuclear arsenals. There are steps that seem prudent in the short term, but which are roadblocks to long-term progress. As in the arms race itself, there are political impediments to change—including the common-sense prenuclear age perception that reducing a nation's arsenal makes it weaker. Nevertheless, some steps seem clear. For example, it would be safest to destroy the most destabilizing weapon systems first—especially "MIRVed" missiles, those with many warheads.

We propose several approaches to be taken (together, in appropriate proportions). . . .

**(1)** Multilateral destruction of the most vulnerable and destabilizing strategic systems (e.g., silo-based MIRVed missiles) and comprehensive deMIRVing of what is left—back to one nuclear warhead per missile;

**(2)** Phasing-out of short-flight-time intermediate range delivery systems in Europe and Asia, as has already been partially accomplished under the terms of the INF (Intermediate-Range Nuclear Forces) Treaty;

**(3)** Gradual elimination of all forward-based tactical nuclear forces, including short-range missiles, that are in danger of being overrun in a conventional invasion (and therefore vulnerable to the "Use 'em or lose 'em" temptation);

**(4)** Reduction, balancing, and substantial pull-back and demobilization of . . . conventional forces in Europe (as are now underway) . . .;

**(5)** Abandonment of the Strategic Defense Initiative (SDI) as presently constituted, and any comparable Soviet programs, and maintenance of the military role in space exclusively for communications, weather forecasting, surveillance, launch warning, and treaty compliance missions . . .;

**(6)** Reduction, and the earliest possible phasing out, of all nuclear weapons testing as the minimum sufficiency regime begins to be established; and

**(7)** Strategic force levels reduced to around 100–300 warheads each for the U.S. and U.S.S.R., with substantial reductions for other nations.

While these proposals are broad, they have now all been offered at the highest levels in discussions and negotiations between the United States and the Soviet Union; they have all been discussed (and to varying degrees endorsed) by specialists; and they are all, in our opinion, technically and politically achievable. Justifications for all of these measures . . . have been made and widely discussed without explicit reference to nuclear winter. We believe that the spectrum of possible climatic outcomes of nuclear war greatly increases the cogency and urgency of taking these steps, but that they make sense even without nuclear winter. . . .

## ABOLITION

. . . In the draft address which turned out to be his last written words, . . . Albert Einstein professed his belief that, should the quarrel among the nuclear-armed nation states degenerate into war, "mankind is doomed." He then made clear why he thought change would be so difficult:

> Despite this knowledge [of the consequences of nuclear war], statesmen in responsible positions on both sides continue to employ the well-known technique of seeking to intimidate and demoralize the opponent by marshaling superior military strength.

They do so even though such a policy entails the risk of war and doom. Not one statesman in a position of responsibility has dared to pursue the only course that holds out any promise of peace, the course of supranational security, since for a statesman to follow such a course would be tantamount to political suicide. Political passions, once they have been fanned into flame, exact their victims. . . .

But such a course may no longer be tantamount to political suicide. Global economic interdependence, the unexpected opening up of the Soviet Union and Eastern Europe to the rest of the world, the emerging European Union, the improving effectiveness and acceptability of the United Nations and the World Court, and the growing political success of environmental agendas—as well as the linking-up of the world through telephone, television, facsimile machines, and computer networking—are all working in the same direction. . . . Suddenly there has emerged a potent set of positive and negative incentives— carrots and sticks—drawing and driving the nation-states together.

Because it threatens the largest number of people and because its dangers have global venue, the prospect of nuclear winter is not least among these influences. Never before in human history has there been such a degree of shared vulnerability. Every nation now has an urgent stake in the activities of its fellow nations. This is most true—because here the danger is greatest—on the question of nuclear weapons. Nuclear winter has alerted us to our common peril and our mutual dependence. It reaffirms an ancient truth: When we kill our brother, we kill ourselves.

We have entered a most promising time—not just because the walls are tumbling down, not just because money and scientists long devoted to the military will now become available for urgent civilian concerns, but also because we finally are becoming aware of our unsuspected—indeed, awesome—powers over the environment that sustains us. Like the assault on the protective ozone layer and global greenhouse warming, nuclear winter is a looming planetwide catastrophe that is within our power to avert. It teaches us the need for foresight and wisdom as we haltingly negotiate our way through our technological adolescence.

From the halls of high Olympus where strange dooms are stored for humans, there is reason to hope that, in our own time also, there is a way out—a path where no man thought.

# REFERENCES

**2.2:** R. P. Turco, O. B. Toon, T. P. Ackerman, J. B. Pollack, and C. Sagan, "Nuclear Winter: Global Consequences of Multiple Nuclear Explosions," *Science 222,* 1983, 1283–1297. TTAPS is an acronym constructed from the surnames of the authors.

**3.11:** SCOPE (Scientific Committee on Problems of the Environment of the International Council of Scientific Unions) Report 28, *Environmental Effects of*

*Nuclear War,* Volume I, *Physical and Atmospheric Effects,* A. Pittock, T. Ackerman, P. Crutzen, M. MacCracken, C. Shapiro, and R. Turco (1986), and Volume II, *Ecological and Agricultural Effects,* M. Harwell and T. Hutchinson (Chichester: John Wiley, 1985).

**5.13:** P. R. Ehrlich, J. Harte, M. A. Harwell, P. H. Raven, C. Sagan, G. M. Woodwell, J. Berry, E. S. Ayensu, A. H. Ehrlich, T. Eisner, S. J. Gould, H. D. Grover, R. Herrera, R. M. May, E. Mayr, C. P. McKay, H. A. Mooney, N. Myers, D. Pimentel, and J. M. Teal, "Long-Term Biological Consequences of Nuclear War," *Science 222,* 1983, 1293–1300.